DEANE BEMAN

GOLF'S DRIVING FORCE

The Inside Story of The Man Who Transformed Professional Golf Into a Billion-Dollar Business

by Adam Schupak

EAST COTTAGE PRESS

East Cottage Press
100 South Eola Dr., Suite #604
Orlando, FL 32801
www.eastcottagepress.com

Distributed by The Booklegger.

Printed in the United States of America.

www.golfsdrivingforce.com

First Edition: April 2011

Library of Congress Cataloguing-in-Publication Data

Schupak, Adam.

Deane Beman: Golf's Driving Force / by Adam Schupak.

ISBN 978-0-615-45879-3
I. Golf. 2. PGA Tour – History. 3. Beman, Deane R. (Deane
Randolph), 1938- . I. Title

DEDICATION

This book is dedicated to the thousands of tournament volunteers who spend countless hours each week making PGA Tour events successful for their communities.

On December 5, 2005, a dinner was held at the Breakers Hotel in Palm Beach, Fla., to celebrate the milestone of raising $1 billion for local charities from the proceeds of events on the PGA Tour, the Champions Tour, and the Nationwide Tour. The following is the address I was privileged to give on that occasion:

"The drive to a billion will go down as one of the best public relations campaigns ever – in sports or in business. That's ironic because the charity connection with golf wasn't conjured up by some P.R. guru to paper over some image problem with the game of golf or our players.

The PGA Tour, in 1979, made charity a requirement for PGA Tour tournament organizations' to keep faith with and honor the thousands of volunteers who make tournament golf, the Tour and our players successful. Without the volunteers there would still be tournaments; but the Tour would look like a nine-hole muni compared to the PGA Tour of today.

When I became commissioner in March of 1974, I told the Tournament Policy Board I saw the Tour as not just a sports league, but a public trust; and I intended to balance the interests of the players, the community tournaments and the game of golf. By 1979, we had begun to make good financial progress for the players. Much of this progress came by the community sponsors putting up more of their hard earned money into purses. By then we began to fully understand and focus on the vital role of charity in the overall success of the Tour.

I was already familiar with the charities connected with Tour events like the Evans Scholarship in Chicago, the St. Jude Hospital in Memphis and Eisenhower Medical Center in Palm Springs, Calif. But one visit to a tournament charity really hit home. My wife Judy and I went to east Texas to visit the boys' camp funded by the Salesmanship Club through their running of the HP Byron Nelson Championship in Dallas.

That visit, more than any other, made me realize that the volunteers weren't doing all of this work just to make a bunch of golf pros rich. The tournament was a means to their end – their charity and their community.

In late 1979, the Tournament Policy Board passed a landmark policy in the world of sports. From here forward all PGA Tour tournaments must be run for charity and preferably be a 501-c3 organization. We wanted the leading money winner on the PGA Tour to be charity. Most tournaments had some charitable element. But that policy decision in 1979 etched into stone that charity must be a core element of all future PGA Tour events.

I'm proud to be able to honor not just the volunteers but to honor our corporate sponsors whose investment in tournament golf makes the events so much more rewarding for each community in which we play.

I'm proud to honor our players who fully support sharing the rewards of tournament golf with hundreds of local charities and do their own charity golf events in their hometowns.

I'm proud to have been part of the team that helped put charity at the heart of the PGA Tour."

Deane R. Beman

TABLE OF CONTENTS

A NOTE ON THE WRITING

The information in this book was largely obtained from more than 200 of my interviews. Thanks to the participation of so many former Tour staff members, Tour players, broadcasting executives, business partners, journalists, golf industry observers, and even Deane Beman's childhood friends, I was able to reconstruct dialogue to bring scenes to life. With the exception of a few living sources who figure in this story and limited their involvement, the main characters were uncommonly generous with their time and recollections. By necessity, the reader should understand that this involves calling on sometimes selective memories, especially when the events, in many cases, happened so long ago.

As such, I have tried to be faithful to the actual conversations that took place, all of which were obtained from one or both of the people engaged in them or by someone who was a firsthand witness to them. In many instances, I interviewed every person in the room at the time. Every living independent director, player director and PGA president who served on the Tour's board during Beman's tenure shared his recollections and observations of events.

The magazines *Golfweek, Golf World, Golf Digest,* and *Sports Illustrated* were invaluable for this project. Their reporting and analysis were the starting point for a book trying to cover Beman's 20-year tenure and the Tour's history from its formation in 1968. I was given unprecedented access to Beman's files, which provided a timeline and record of how and when critical decisions were made. In reconstructing pivotal moments, I relied often on the minutes from Tour policy board meetings dating back to the very formation of the Tour in 1968, and materials prepared for those meetings. PGA Tour Productions made all of their video resources available to me. With few exceptions, all anecdotes in this book had at least two sources (or best attempts were made to do so). Writer Ken Auletta may have explained the reporting challenges best: "A reporter tries to guard against inaccuracies by checking with a variety of sources, but it is useful for a reader – and an author – to be humbled by this journalistic limitation."

DEFINING MOMENT

J ack Nicklaus was first to arrive for the meeting at Bay Hill
Club and Lodge. He checked his watch. He was early. It
was March 9, 1983, pro-am day at the Bay Hill Classic in
Orlando, and Nicklaus had requested to see his longtime golf
rival, Arnold Palmer.

This wasn't a social visit. Nicklaus' agent, Chuck Perry,
urged him to discuss with Palmer their mutual discontent with
the direction the PGA Tour was headed under its commissioner,
Deane Beman. Even with the pros playing for more money than
ever before, the Tour's elite grumbled about its leadership. So
The Golden Bear decided to take The King on a hunt.

Nicklaus was escorted to Palmer's office, a former storage
unit in a corner of the Bay Hill golf shop of the resort he owned.
Standing in the doorway, Nicklaus glanced around and with a
look of disbelief turned to the pro shop attendants and asked,
"This is Arnold's office?" They assured him he was in the right
place. Nicklaus looked around, sized up the motley collection
of art, family photos and books, shook his head, then said with
a gasp of astonishment, "He comes in here everyday?"

Moments later Palmer approached Nicklaus and welcomed
him into his quaint and cluttered office. Alastair Johnston, the
high-powered IMG executive who attended to Palmer's business
affairs, and IMG's founder, Mark McCormack, were there too.

Once seated, Nicklaus quickly took the lead. He outlined
his concerns, berating Beman for breaking with precedent. The
Tour's purpose, Nicklaus said, should be limited to assembling
the schedule, marking the golf course, and setting the hole

locations. Tournament operations should be the bailiwick of sponsors, volunteers and tournament directors. In short, Nicklaus was at odds with the Tour's growing role as a marketing engine and proclaimed its marketing initiatives had crossed the line.

Just three years earlier in 1980, the Tour established a marketing department, which was renamed PGA-PGA Tour Properties, Inc. in 1982, after it entered a partnership with the PGA of America. The Tour had already signed deals for an official credit card, airline and cruise line. Nicklaus complained that the growth of such initiatives represented unwanted competition for his and Palmer's own branding opportunities. Every shirt sold with the Tour's golf man logo meant one less shirt sold with either Nicklaus' Golden Bear logo or the multicolored umbrella that Palmer trademarked.

It was with a twist of irony that Nicklaus mentioned logoed shirts. In the book, "Arnie: Inside the Legend," author Larry Guest recounted how during the height of their spirited rivalry, Palmer made it a habit to ridicule a friend or club member who arrived at the first tee in his presence wearing a golf shirt emblazoned with Nicklaus' Golden Bear.

"What'cha doin' wearin' that pig on your shirt?" Palmer often chided, pinching the emblem along with several layers of skin beneath it and twisting hard.

Indeed, some say it is more than happenstance that once the Nicklaus camp learned of Palmer's demeaning exploits, they redesigned the logo, giving the bear a slimmer silhouette.

This rivalry of sorts off the course worked both ways. When Palmer ducked out of the meeting for a bathroom break, Nicklaus queried Johnston if this was truly Palmer's office or had he chosen to meet here to avoid drawing any attention? When Palmer later was informed of Nicklaus' flabbergasted reaction, he seethed. Within a week, Palmer ordered renovations to modernize and expand his office. "That meeting with Jack cost a couple million dollars," Johnston said.

When the meeting resumed, Nicklaus expressed his other concerns. He believed the Tour should limit its role in negotiating and packaging television rights. Nicklaus and Palmer operated their own Tour events and preferred to sell the TV rights individually rather than have them grouped with the Tour's other tournaments. Of greater concern, they wanted permission to conduct other television specials and relax non-compete restrictions during the off-season. Nicklaus concluded: "I'll do everything in my power to stop that man," he said of Beman.

Nicklaus beseeched Palmer to put their business interests before any lingering animosity for each other. It was time to orchestrate a palace coup.

"Well?" Nicklaus muttered.

Palmer nodded in agreement, delivering a verdict of damnation. The two shook hands setting in motion a power struggle that raged behind the scenes for several months.

To understand how the Tour became the success it is today, one must examine this oft-overlooked moment. During this period, Beman, then 44, faced the biggest threat of his tenure.

"It wasn't a power struggle," Beman said. "It was a total revolution."

A few months later, the men he worked for would call Beman to the carpet. In a packed ballroom at Westchester Country Club's turn-of-the-century clubhouse in Harrison, N.Y., players stood in tense, solemn expectation for what some were calling a public hanging. It was this climactic moment that defined, and then catapulted, the Tour to an era of dynamic growth.

*   *   *

Six weeks after Nicklaus and Palmer's rendezvous, a fairly routine meeting of the PGA Tour tournament policy board was set to adjourn on May 17 in Atlanta, Ga., site of the Atlanta Classic. Beman led a lively discussion. Much had been accomplished, including the approval of Bay Hill's status as an invitational and the creation of the TPC Greens Committee to evaluate changes to the TPC Sawgrass course. No one wanted to see the meeting drag on. But then Jim Colbert, one of the four player directors on the 10-member board, interrupted with a final question that struck everyone by surprise. He asked the independent board of directors' to assess the Tour's performance.

Seated at one end of a long rectangular table, Colbert sensed that his fellow board members took offense at the innocent question. From all corners, puzzled looks confronted him. To the men in the room, the answer seemed self-evident. E.M. (Del) de Windt, chief executive officer of the Eaton Corp. of Cleveland and the Tour's chairman of the board, spoke rapidly, with an eagerness for one of his favorite subjects. Beman, indeed, had done much more than just continue in the role formerly held by Joe Dey. De Windt reminded Colbert that when Beman became commissioner in 1974, he inherited a Tour playing for $8.2 million in total prize money, with $400,000 in the bank, rented office space in New York, and its largest capital asset was an IBM Selectric typewriter.

De Windt noted that in 1979, Beman assessed some brutal facts. Professional tournament golf experienced a period of relatively flat growth and uncertain prospects for several years in the 1970s. Television ratings declined and research indicated a shrinking demographic for the game. Many felt that golf had not kept pace with other professional sports in terms of marketing, promotion or spectator innovations; nor had the Tour developed any significant revenue sources besides television rights fees, which, in 1980, accounted for nearly 80 percent of all Tour cash receipts.

Against this sobering background, Beman developed his vision for the Tour: promoting the game aggressively, increasing revenue by competing more effectively in the sports marketplace and broadening the base of support for tournament golf and the game. In the nine years that had passed since Beman had assumed leadership of the Tour, de Windt crowed, Beman found a 415-acre piece of swampland in Ponte Vedra Beach, Fla., and persuaded the developer to sell the land to the Tour for $1. He moved the Tour's headquarters there and built the TPC Sawgrass Stadium Course, marking the launch of a network of spectator-friendly courses.

Beman ushered in the creation of the Senior PGA Tour just in time to showcase the magnetism of Palmer as he entered the twilight of his career. Tournament purses were on the rise, de Windt bragged. Charitable contributions had reached record levels. New revenue streams from TPCs to marketing partners were beginning to pay handsomely. The Tour's financial picture had never been better. All of this was irrefutable. When de Windt finished speaking in near reverent tones of Beman's record, Colbert said, "That's what I thought. But we're fixin' to get hammered."

It was a jolt no one in the room could've anticipated. There was a collective stunned silence. Colbert slumped forward, his forearms on the table, and broke the silence with an explanation. It was a few weeks ago, he said, while competing in the 1983 Byron Nelson Classic in Irving, Texas, that he entered the locker room to find Nicklaus holding court in front of an audience of 20 other pros. This gave Colbert an uneasy feeling. Nicklaus was friendly and respected by his peers, but he wasn't the type to linger around the clubhouse. So Colbert leaned against a locker behind Nicklaus – yet well within earshot – and listened to the Golden Bear disparage the way Beman ran the Tour like a feudal lord. Colbert stood there, arms folded, and watched in dismay as heads bobbed in agreement. Colbert summed up the grievance session with this assessment: "Jack thought the Tour was all but running a used car lot."

At this point, Colbert didn't know that Nicklaus and Palmer had already formed an alliance to overthrow Beman. Everyone in the board meeting recognized Nicklaus as among golf's foremost powerbrokers. He carried clout as one of the few players of his day who moved the needle and was at the top of the sports marketing pyramid. What was Nicklaus up to?

From across the table Colbert's eyes met Beman's. There was such a vast understanding in Beman's eyes. His brow, pleated with worry, was a summation of all the things he didn't have to say: trouble loomed.

The locker room meeting Colbert had witnessed fore-shadowed what was soon to come. Before long, Beman would stand accused of being a power-hungry dictator, who was steering the Tour in the wrong direction. His list of detractors included a roll call of future Hall of Famers. They unleashed their frustrations, signing their names to a letter that demanded Beman's dismissal.

"They wanted a new commissioner," Colbert said with his clipped, assured conviction. "That's all there was to it. They wanted Deane out. He was getting into their business."

Back in the boardroom, Beman, preparing his own defense,

scribbled down nine points on the cover of his board book. In the minds of the independent directors, this was emblematic of a proxy fight with stockholders. They all were successful businessmen, the type who had risen to their positions of power by quelling an uprising or two, and they advised Beman how to proceed. Perhaps the most influential was de Windt. His eyes bounced from Colbert to Beman and he suggested the Tour produce an annual report. Information had been periodically provided to the membership through the year at various player meetings. Players also could discuss individual concerns with the Tour's player relations representative, Mike Crosthwaite. But the Tour never produced a formal report to the membership.

"Any legitimate business should provide an annual report to its stockholders," de Windt opined. The rest of the Tour's independent directors – Bob Kirby, chairman and CEO of Westinghouse, and Card Walker, chairman and CEO of Disney – echoed de Windt's suggestion. Beman agreed the Tour would begin producing one immediately.

Colbert's warning proved the equivalent of Paul Revere's midnight ride through Boston when he shouted, "The British are coming!" Having a head start helped Beman's staff prepare for the player uprising – and they needed all the good fortune they could get, considering the rebellion's ringleader was such a worthy opponent.

For much of their lives, Beman and Nicklaus rejoiced in each other's triumphs. They first met at the 1953 USGA Junior Amateur Championship in Tulsa, Okla., when Beman was just 15, Nicklaus a towheaded teen of 13. They became competitors, frequent practice-round partners, and Walker Cup teammates, too. Neither has forgotten the time they were partners in an afternoon alternate-shot match during the Americas Cup in Ottawa in 1960. Having layed up on the par-5, fifth hole, Beman's third shot required a short iron. After evaluating their options, Nicklaus asked, "What do you think?" Beman reached into his bag and said, "Should I hit my sand wedge or Charlie Coe's?"

Their fellow American teammate's club had been wedged into Beman's bag, most likely when the clubs were cleaned between rounds. The penalty was automatic loss of hole, making them 5 down. "We ended up losing 1 down," Nicklaus said.

Nicklaus learned to chart courses from Beman, who assembled a rudimentary yardage book in the mid 1950s and scribbled more sophisticated notes after witnessing top amateur Gene Andrews use one at the 1958 U.S. Amateur. Nicklaus scoffed at Beman's meticulous nature at first. "Try it one time," Beman urged. Nicklaus did so the week of the 1961 U.S. Amateur at Pebble Beach, broke par every round he played and won. When Nicklaus showed up as a professional at the 1962 L.A. Open, he was surprised to find he was the only one who walked off yardages, and jotted notes on index cards. Soon others adopted the practice, and before long a yardage book became an indispensable part of a pro's equipment.

Nicklaus affectionately called Beman "his swing doctor," and even has credited Beman for playing pivotal roles in two of his record 18 major victories. On the first memorable occasion, Beman suggested Nicklaus try his spare center-shafted Bull's Eye putter prior to the 1967 U.S. Open at Baltusrol. Smitten with the putter, Nicklaus nicknamed it "White Fang" (the brass head was painted white to prevent sun glare) and rolled to victory.

The other in February before the 1971 PGA Championship (at the original PGA National now known as Ballen Isles) when Nicklaus and his wife Barbara had invited the Bemans over to their North Palm Beach, Fla., home for a game of cards. During the game, Beman mentioned that he noticed during a practice round that Nicklaus wasn't completing his backstroke when putting. After the Bemans won the card game, Nicklaus dashed to his pool deck, where he practiced on an Astroturf green. Thanks, in part, to Beman's timely tip, Nicklaus one-putted 29 times on the grainy greens that week – "the best putting in a tournament in my life," he said – and rode a confident stroke to a two-shot victory. His second PGA Championship title made him the first professional to twice capture the modern career Grand Slam.

If Nickaus won more titles, Palmer won the most fans. Professional golf's original superstar was Palmer, who with his matinee idol looks and go-for-broke style emerged as golf's first celebrity pitchman in the early 1960s. His one-time collegiate opponent, Mark McCormack, recognized Palmer's potential as a global brand. Their deal formalized with nothing more than a handshake, gave birth to sports management goliath IMG. During Palmer's first two years with McCormack, his endorsement earnings reportedly grew from $6,000 to $500,000, the kind of success never seen in golf before. But it proved to be just a harbinger of the hundreds of millions of dollars Palmer would earn even after he ceased to be a competitive golfer.

At Palmer's urging, Nicklaus, when he turned professional in 1962, also signed with McCormack. But in 1970, Nicklaus fired IMG because he was reportedly frustrated at playing "second fiddle" to Palmer at the management firm. "To have held on to Nicklaus, I couldn't have expanded the company," McCormack later explained to *Sports Illustrated.* "I'd have had to personally watch over him. Instead, I was creating IMG. I'd have won the battle and lost the war."

In 1975, Nicklaus hired a former college president and magazine publisher, Chuck Perry, to manage his business affairs. As president and CEO of Golden Bear International, Perry set about expanding Nicklaus' marketing effort. According to a March 1977 article in the *Ocala (Fla.) Star-Banner*, Golden Bear employed 178 people and Nicklaus's vast empire stretched from golf clubs, bags and balls to car dealerships, a travel agency, a radio station, cattle ranches, real estate developments, a natural gas company, and of course, a golf course architectural shop.

In 1983, Nicklaus, Palmer and Tom Watson were the top corporate endorsers in golf. Perry, along with Watson's agent, Chuck Rubin (at the time he was also Watson's brother-in-law) persuaded Nicklaus and Watson that the marketing and growth of the Tour would undercut their entrepreneurial opportunities. Beman visited with Watson in his hometown of Kansas City to address some of his concerns. They met for five hours. Watson's perception was summed up neatly in a 1992 quote to *Golf Digest* in which he expressed his reservations about the Tour's direction: "I think the basic problem is that the Tour is competing with its own players. It's marketing the Tour for the players, but at the disadvantage of the successful players who could go out and market their own image."

Beman and others believe that Rubin and Perry planted the seed with their clients to overthrow the commissioner. "Rubin was the guy who stirred the pot," de Windt alleged.

In short, the agents argued that if the Tour entered into a relationship with a *Fortune 500* company, it undermined the players' abilities to sign their own deals. On the surface, Perry's argument had merit, and it appealed to Nicklaus, who shared his "zero-sum" outlook in which there could only be winners and losers. Beman's distance from the sport since his retirement as a player in 1974 provided him with a different perspective, but he still understood the mindset of the professional athlete.

"Nicklaus looked at business the same way as he did a golf competition; for every dollar one side made, the other side had to suffer a loss," Beman said. "That there could be more than one winner in the same contest was as foreign to professional golfers as conceding a 5-foot putt."

The agents preyed on their clients' underlying fear that the Tour would snatch lucrative deals from them. One of their chief complaints: By getting into real estate through the development of Tournament Players Clubs, the Tour was directly competing with certain players who had their own design and development business.

This particularly disturbed Palmer and Nicklaus, who already were earning lucrative contracts for their design work. It was just as alarming for Watson, who had begun collaborating with former USGA president Sandy Tatum and architect Robert Trent Jones Jr., on Watson's first golf course project – the design of the Links at Spanish Bay in Pebble Beach, Calif.

Beman scoffed at the notion that the Tour was stunting its players' business ventures. He said they failed to grasp that by marketing the Tour and growing the game, everybody could win.

"If the pie grew bigger they would still be the top chefs," Beman explained, referring to the trio of Nicklaus, Palmer and Watson. "They would still have their pick of the plums."

Beman ticked off examples such as when the Tour negotiated an agreement making National Car Rental the official rental car of the PGA Tour. That scenario, he insisted, didn't harm Palmer's long-standing relationship with Hertz. In fact, it motivated Hertz to become more active in golf, and Palmer's value to the company increased. But Nicklaus and Palmer rejected this line of reasoning and maintained that the Tour had overstepped its boundaries.

At that time, the Tour owned one golf course, the TPC Sawgrass, which had opened in 1980. Already it showed a positive cash flow. Another TPC course was under construction near Denver, and a third was about to break ground in Coral Springs, Fla. The Tour's latest hire was Kay Slayden, the former president of Fuqua Industries, to head the Tour's marketing and properties division, and the ink was barely dry on lucrative licensing agreements with R.J. Reynolds and Seiko. Nicklaus and Palmer's objections called for the dismantling of those relationships. In short, they proposed climbing into a time machine and teleporting right back to the era of Dey, Beman's predecessor.

"This positive energy we had was almost 10 years in the making," Beman said, "and the freight train was gaining momentum."

Yet, Nicklaus and Palmer didn't buy into Beman's grand vision for the Tour and stood ready to derail it. Oddly, Palmer hardly consulted with McCormack during this time. McCormack had been present for the Bay Hill meeting but he was in Europe enjoying tennis' French Open, when the effort to oust Beman took flight. Beman viewed IMG as a major rival, considering its rapidly growing influence in golf, and regarded McCormack a clever strategist. He often said that if McCormack had been more actively involved in the rebellion, he "might've been a dead duck."

Johnston, for one, is convinced McCormack wouldn't have stood in his client's way. "Deflating 'the Czar' would not have been a bad thing for IMG," Johnston said.

Beman had been tagged "the Czar of golf," a derisive nickname that evoked players' hostility toward his rising authority in the golf community. It also reflected a larger disdain for the way they felt he acted as prosecutor, judge and jury. Having played a key role in the breakaway of the Tour with Nicklaus, Palmer said he felt a sense of responsibility to ensure the next generation of players was afforded the same opportunities he enjoyed. When a letter to the Tour's policy board chairman called for Beman's head, Palmer just signed.

*   *   *

What started in Orlando at Palmer's tournament in March and gathered steam during Byron Nelson's tournament in April, came to a head at Nicklaus' tournament, The Memorial, in late May.

Held near his hometown of Columbus, Ohio, the Tour stop that Nicklaus founded and hosted since 1976, is famous for being at the mercy of Ohio's unpredictable springtime weather. On May 26, 1983, rain and thunderstorms delayed the first round of the tournament. While they waited for the raindrops to stop, Nicklaus called a closed-door player meeting with a dozen of the biggest names on Tour and a handful of their agents. It had a one-item agenda: "Do you like the way Beman is running our Tour?" The question, when not framed in a derogatory tone, could have resulted in glowing testimonies. But on this occasion, there was only grumbling and a unanimous, "No."

Beman had a complicated relationship with the game's superstars. As a former player, Beman was blessed with the understanding of someone who had played inside the ropes. He won four times in five years on Tour, but he also lost his share of tournaments to Palmer and Nicklaus. As commissioner, the diminutive Beman had grown in stature and in importance. His friendship with Nicklaus had cooled considerably under the circumstances.

"To understand Beman, you have to grasp that he was the one golfer of the Nicklaus generation who had so much heart, so much ambition and so much brains that, when golf history is written, he will not have to stand in Nicklaus's shadow," wrote Thomas Boswell in *The Washington Post*. "They will be separate, unequal, but both enormous figures."

It was understandable that Nicklaus and Palmer didn't appreciate Beman bossing them around. What those two competitors saw in Beman was a future that didn't necessarily benefit them.

"Deane worked as hard as he could to have a socialist state," Nicklaus said in *"Arnie & Jack,"* the definitive book examining the complicated relationship of Palmer and Nicklaus by author Ian O'Connor. "The stars were knocked down. He created a Tour in his own image."

Beman was shocked that Palmer and Nicklaus failed

to understand the Tour's direction. Beman's authority was established in the Tour's original charter and granted, in part, by Nicklaus and Palmer. They spearheaded the Tour's separation from the PGA in 1968. Nicklaus took part in hiring the lawyers that drew up the papers to form the corporation. So why were golf's two biggest names so up in arms? In fact, Nicklaus' agent had already drafted a letter to the board chairman. IMG's Johnston brought a copy of it to the meeting and jotted the names of all the players that were in attendance upon it. As rain showers pelted the course, Nicklaus canvassed the room asking, "Who's with me?"

On the morning of May 27, 1983, while a handful of player agents met to discuss the events of the night before over breakfast, Nicklaus and Palmer signed off on a letter addressed to the chairman of the tournament policy board. Watson's name joined 11 other prominent golfers of the day – Johnny Miller, Lee Trevino, Raymond Floyd, Lanny Wadkins, and Tom Weiskopf among them – who supported the uprising. If Beman was guilty of anything, it was ignoring the sage advice of former New York Yankees manager Casey Stengel who once said, "The secret of successful managing is to keep the five guys who hate you away from the four guys who haven't made up their minds." In retrospect, Tim Smith, Beman's deputy commissioner, blamed an unkind weather pattern for stirring the rebellion.

"We used to laugh about how all the trouble happens in rain delays," Smith said. "The players sit around, they are miserable, and when the talk turns to headquarters it's not about how good a job they've done."

Beman and the leading players had quarreled before, but this conflict was different. The three-page, single-spaced letter was a referendum rejecting all that Beman had envisioned for the Tour. It read as follows:

Dear Mr. de Windt:

For the past several years we have become concerned about the direction of the PGA Tour and the role of the Commissioner. As players, we believe that we have a responsibility, not only to ourselves but to the future generation of Tour players, to our

Tournament Sponsors and to all the fans and communities who support professional golf in this country and around the world.

We strongly believe that the role of the PGA Tour should be limited to organizing and managing a schedule of professional golf tournaments for the benefit of Tour members. This was the sole reason that our organization was formed and it is still the only justification for its existence.

It is our opinion that the Tour's efforts in course development, marketing, club management, rules of golf and other ventures divert the energies of the Commissioner's office and substantially increase the operating overhead and unnecessarily expands the bureaucracy of the organization. In addition, we believe that these activities create a major conflict of interest with the individual members of the Tour.

The players of the PGA Tour (both past and present) have delegated the organization and management of our tournament schedule to the Tour. However, we never intended to create a "monster" which is competing against the individual interests of Tour players in commercial areas outside of tournament golf. Our concerns are shared by a significant number of Tour players. The specific areas include the following:

(1) GOLF COURSE DEVELOPMENT: The Tour should not own, manage, operate or endorse golf courses. The concept of spectator golf is valid, but having the Tour involved in it on a commercial basis is not a wise course of action. The Tour's responsibility should be limited to support and advice for others to develop such projects. The Tour should not be an equity participant, with ongoing management responsibilities, in future golf course projects.

(2) MARKETING: The PGA Tour should not market its logo or provide its endorsement in any area which conflicts with individual player's rights. The entire marketing program of the Tour should be suspended, although we realize that existing contracts will have to be honored to the contract's conclusion, but not renewed.

(3) TV PACKAGE: In the formulation of the TV Package, all Sponsors must be given equitable treatment by the Tour in the distribution of TV pool funds. The TPC should not be exempted from the formula.

(4) PLAYER TELEVISION RIGHTS: We recognize that the Tour must be entrusted with our rights in order to negotiate the television package with respect to our participation in PGA Tour events. With regard to non-Tour televised events, or other opportunities available to individual players that do not affect the Tour's events, we feel individual players should retain their rights to negotiate independent of the Tour.

(5) THE ROLE OF THE TOUR: The mandate of the PGA Tour is to create and organize Tour events. This responsibility includes maintaining excellent sponsor relationships and providing highly professional and responsive Tour field staff and operations which result in the best possible Tour events. We do not intend to stand silently by while the Tour continues to exceed its mandate by progressively encroaching upon the basic rights of all the Tour players. Nor, do we intend to watch the Tour Commissioner become the "Czar of Golf" at the expense of other important organizations within the golfing community.

So, we urge you to shift the PGA Tour's emphasis away from what we consider to be an unauthorized and ill conceived course of action which will be detrimental to all concerned. We will work with you on re-charting the Tour's course if you are agreeable. If not, we will have no other choice but to take whatever action is required to protect our individual and collective rights.

The issues outlined in this letter have been fully discussed with the players whose names appear on the enclosed sheet. These players fully subscribe to the content of this letter.

In the upper right hand corner, simply the signatures of golf's two cultural icons: Palmer and Nicklaus.

To the left, a list of concurring tour pros was attached; it named Andy Bean, Ben Crenshaw, Raymond Floyd, Hale Irwin, Tom Kite, Johnny Miller, Gary Player, Craig Stadler, Lee Trevino, Lanny Wadkins, Tom Watson and Tom Weiskopf. All of the above had attended the previous day's meeting with the exception of Player, who they forgot to invite and later apologized to for the oversight.

Carbon copies of the letter were sent to the nine other members of the Tour policy board, but not Beman. When the faxed letter arrived at de Windt's office in Cleveland, the Tour's chairman of the board barely could conceal his alarm. His first reaction: "We have to squash this thing before it becomes a full-fledged uprising." Word spread. Beman and his staff had heard the news even before the letter arrived on de Windt's desk. Nicklaus had exited the closed-door meeting at The Memorial and told Jim Simons, a player director on the Tour policy board, that the players had agreed to take action. Then Nicklaus called Colbert, who was home in Las Vegas resting his brittle back, so he too would be aware of the players' decision. Colbert alerted Beman a letter had been sent. Beman first read the contents of the letter after de Windt's secretary dictated it to Beman's assistant. Beman felt a sinking feeling in his gut as he studied the charges. His lips curled in disgust when he noticed that Floyd, Irwin and Kite, three former policy board members, had signed the letter.

"The Tour was moving into turf that had been left to the players, specifically the design of courses," Irwin explained. "It was a real concern. I think of all the things that we had to face on the Tour that (issue) was probably the most explosive among the players. If there was a breaking point in his tenure, that was it."

Beman was furious, feeling betrayed, and demoralized when his eyes reviewed one sentence that stopped him in his tracks: The letter alleged that he and the board had "exceeded its mandate" and further charged that these activities were "un-authorized." These words were designed to galvanize their co-conspirators but Beman wondered if its authors' had inadvertently provided the ammunition for a possible counterattack.

* * *

Deane Beman walked straight across the room and sat down at his desk. Digesting the news, he began to plot his defense. If Nicklaus and Palmer were successful in rallying more of the players to their side, then all that he and his staff had worked nearly a decade to build could crumble down. Golf, Beman feared, would return to being on par with professional bowling and rodeo. The Tour's carefully constructed brand identity would be jeopardized, and corporate partnerships would be dissolved. The superstars would grab the largest share of the pie and the rest of the players would be nibbling around the crust.

Smith, who came to the Tour after serving in President Jimmy Carter's administration and who was the Tour's first full-time attorney, was among a small cadre of business dynamos and legal minds that Beman recruited to the Tour. Now Smith wondered if he made a mistake leaving his well-paying Washington law firm to join Beman in Florida. Others fretted that they might lose their jobs if the leadership team was tossed out of office. Their worries were justified. Beman actually advised Pete Davison, the TPC's director of golf, that if he was thinking of building a house or buying one, he ought to postpone such a decision. Beman wrestled with whether he ought to fight at all. Gone was the brave front erected for the staff.

"I sat in the cool of my own bedroom, bathroom, and office thinking, 'They don't want you. They don't want this. So why bother?' " Beman said.

"It was the only time I ever saw Deane shattered," said IMG's Johnston. "When I met with him he had lost weight. His complexion was gone and he looked stressed out. It was the only time that I thought he was going to cut bait, if you will."

Surrender simply wasn't in his nature. But a more pressing concern had to be resolved: The players questioned the overall role of the Tour. To Beman, the Tour was a highly undervalued brand on the verge of taking off. He was determined to preserve what he believed was his duty – to grow the Tour. Otherwise, Beman knew the commissioner would be diminished to nothing more than a glorified tournament organizer, coordinating schedules and marking hole locations.

"To many of the pros, the commissioner was merely the guy who kept the rules book on his desk and had Bob Hope's unlisted phone number," wrote the *Houston Post's* Mickey Herskowitz in *Golf Digest*.

Beman also was motivated to fight on because he knew some of his initiatives were beginning to resonate with the players. A retirement plan for them certainly had appeal as did higher purses. And they bought into his push for charity fundraising. But without the power to deliver such benefits, Beman understood his job would be pointless. Beman told Smith that if the players won and insisted on withdrawing from golf course ownership, he intended to negotiate a deal for TPC Sawgrass as part of his buy-out; the TPC would generate a lot more revenue than any compensation the Tour would ever pay him. Even though Beman knew he would come out better financially in defeat, he felt obligated to pursue victory for the good of the Tour.

To be sure, Beman wasn't the type to crumple like a tissue. He rolled up the sleeves of his white shirt above the elbows and went to work. He recruited Colbert, the feisty Kansan of pithy expression and considerable charm who always wore his collar turned up and a bucket cap when he played, to act as an intermediary with Nicklaus.

Colbert was scheduled to be in Ponte Vedra Beach, Fla., to attend the first architectural advisory committee meeting with Pete Dye to discuss concerns with the TPC Stadium Course on Monday, May 30. So were Nicklaus, Crenshaw, Irwin, and Ed Sneed. Beman asked Colbert to fly in early so he could present his plan of containment. Using Colbert as a messenger was Beman's best option to avoid a direct confrontation.

"Jim's not a shrinking violet," Beman said. "He's a real tenacious competitor and I needed somebody, particularly a player, so there was a level of mutual respect as well as someone who had the courage to go toe-to-toe with Nicklaus."

In his bulldog style, Colbert acted as crusader on the Tour's behalf. Nicklaus wasn't in the field for that week's Kemper Open but he was attending a business trip in the D.C. area. At the conclusion of the TPC Sawgrass meeting, he offered a seat on his personal plane to Colbert, who jumped at the chance to "talk to" Nicklaus about the letter.

Colbert boarded "Air Bear" armed with a copy of the Tour's original Delaware corporation charter from Beman. The commissioner had rummaged through his files and found the agreement between the Tour and the PGA of America setting forth the Tour's independence. The bylaws said specifically that the Tour could run tournaments, build and own golf courses, and participate in the selling of licensed products. Among the architects of the Tour's declaration of independence: Nicklaus who was on the original board of directors. (Palmer attended those early meetings but was never a board member.)

Digging up this document was pivotal to Beman's cause. And he could thank his meticulous nature for remembering it. After Beman was chosen to replace Dey, the Tour's original commissioner, Beman spent two months prepping for the post. During that time, Beman commuted to the Tour's New York City headquarters and buried his nose in the Tour's books. He researched its history, reading board minutes and corporate documents in chronological order. That was the first time he examined the Tour's original charter. Later that year, Beman reviewed the corporate charter again when he changed the Tour from a for-profit Delaware corporation to a 501-c6 association.

Privately, Beman cautioned Colbert to avoid an argument on the merits of the five points in the letter. Trying to convince Nicklaus that Beman's initiatives were beginning to work and starting to produce income just would confirm in Nicklaus' own mind that he was right; marketing and licensing programs were taking money out of his pocket. Focus on the ramification of the charges that the CEO's of Eaton Corp., Westinghouse and Disney were being charged with exceeding their authority, he suggested. "Because if the players simply said on reflection, 'We do not think these activities are in the best interests of the players,' it's match over – shake hands and go home," Beman reiterated.

Back on "Air Bear," Colbert waited until the plane reached cruising altitude before opening his briefcase and addressing Nicklaus. Colbert pulled out the Tour's incorporation documents and read from its original corporate charter. It granted the board and its commissioner far-reaching powers.

Recounting this seminal moment de Windt noted, "Jack and Arnold were hell-bent on tossing Deane out. But everything (the Tour) was doing was agreed upon when the Tour was established as a separate entity."

Nicklaus was rendered speechless. Finally, with an edge of suspicion creeping into his voice, he asked, "Who granted those privileges?" Colbert first pointed at the Tour's player directors, who voted for the charter, circled the name Nicklaus and said, "You did."

That was the extent of Nicklaus's cross-examination. His eyes grew wide. He squirmed in his seat and slouched despondently. Colbert then underlined Nicklaus' name on the letter to the Tour chairman, handed it to Nicklaus and didn't sugarcoat the severity of the situation. Colbert scolded Nicklaus, telling him he had impugned the integrity of the Tour, the commissioner, and the independent directors: "If you don't withdraw your letter, the Tour will spend every nickel it's got to hurt your name."

"It couldn't be a mediation," Beman said in a moment of reflection. He cracked a wide grin. "It had to be a conceded putt by a formidable competitor and sportsman. Jack saw that he was dead wrong. He was trapped by his own words in the letter and his previous actions as a board member. He realized he potentially had a serious PR problem. He had something to lose."

It wasn't often in Nicklaus's competitive career that in a 30-second span he went from a commanding lead to a sure loser. Colbert and Nicklaus spent the rest of the short flight discussing damage control. In particular, Colbert feared that one of the agents who spearheaded the uprising might leak the letter. When the plane landed, they resumed discussions in a hotel room; this time Nicklaus' agent, Chuck Perry, joined them. "Show him what you showed me," Nicklaus demanded.

Perry quickly realized that efforts to unseat Beman had been thwarted. Then Nicklaus acted swiftly to prevent any problems from Rubin. "To Jack's credit, he picked up the phone and called Rubin and threatened him to an inch of his life," Colbert said.

The revolt had been quelled, thanks mostly to a messenger.

"I believe Jim Colbert saved Deane's job," said Mark Kizziar, a past PGA president and a member of the Tour's board at the time. "I've never said it to Deane and I've never said it to Jim, but I believe it."

* * *

Having grown up in suburban Washington, D.C., the fundamentals of a political fight came naturally to Beman, even if many of his critics accused him of having a political tin ear. On the belief that an ounce of prevention is worth a pound of cure, Beman's staff and some of the players in his corner launched their own campaign to rally support while Colbert was straightening out Nicklaus at 35,000 feet. Time was precious to turn the polls. Before the first round of the Kemper Open at Congressional Country Club, Smith, who was dispatched there, and Beman noted each player in the field as either for, against or undecided. First, Smith attempted to shore up those in Beman's corner before turning his attention to players he believed he could "flip."

Under Beman's directive, Smith worked the locker room and putting green at Congressional that week. Having headed the 1976 Virginia campaign for President Carter and then quarterbacked the White House scheduling team, Smith was more than qualified to deliver the Tour's message, but by his own admission, he committed some clumsy miscues. In one instance, Smith buttonholed Tom Kite. Beman was miffed that Kite had endorsed the initiatives questioned in the letter during his term on the board and then turned around and signed the letter. In conversing with Kite, Smith portrayed the clash as a choice between what's good for a few superstars versus what's good for the Tour overall. Kite, a future Hall of Famer, didn't appreciate the implication: "You mean this is between the superstars and the 'other players,' and you're calling me an other player," he said. Kite's usual warm smile was replaced by a cold stare. Always a smooth talker, the unflappable Smith laid it on thick, pronouncing Kite "a different kind of superstar."

Player directors Colbert, Larry Nelson and Peter Jacobsen fanned out on the range and in the locker room, lobbying on the Tour's behalf. Colbert, for one, wasn't above playing dirty. He fully absorbed the consequences and didn't stand for player indifference when so much was at stake. As part of his tactics, Colbert bluffed that Nicklaus, Palmer, and Watson were planning to launch their own tour in which only 30-40 players would participate and share in the bounty. The implication was obvious: The livelihood of the rank and file could be threatened. With the painting of such a scenario, many players agreed to protect the status quo.

"That wasn't (Nicklaus, Palmer and Watson's) intent but you do get your ducks in a row just in case, right?" Colbert reasoned. "We had them lined up."

Support for Beman came from several corners. Veteran CBS Sports executive producer of golf Frank Chirkinian didn't mince words, telling the rebellion-minded that they were making a monumental mistake. Chirkinian pulled former U.S. Open champion Jerry Pate into the CBS trailer and claimed credit for straightening him out. Another ally, John Miller, a leader in the Phoenix Thunderbirds and the head of the American Golf Sponsors, made calls on the Tour's behalf. He told *Golf Digest*, "We're solidly behind (Beman). He's done a lot of good for the Tour – players and sponsors alike – in the last nine years, and he's got good people working for him."

Although Nicklaus and Palmer had secured the support of the game's elite players, it was becoming clear that a vast majority of the membership could go either way and tournament sponsors weren't fully on their side.

Amid all the lobbying, de Windt sent a four-page reply to the players' letter noting, "several of the key factual premises of your letter should be corrected, or at least further discussed." His response made one thing clear: The board backed Beman. de Windt concluded: "Reasonable people can differ on the best way to arrive at worthwhile goals. If we all have the best interests of the Tour and its members, along with the sponsors and their charities and the public in mind, then surely an exchange of facts and information about the best way to achieve those goals is in order, rather than confrontation and ultimatums."

On June 5, de Windt defended Beman publicly after an Associated Press story implied that Beman's position was in jeopardy, or would be determined at the upcoming players meeting. "It is completely inaccurate," he said. "The great progress made in recent years...is a tribute to his leadership."

Nicklaus and Palmer agreed to meet with Beman on June 9 for a tete-a-tete hours before that evening's special players' meeting in Harrison, N.Y. Neither player was in the field at the Manufacturers Hanover Westchester Classic. Nicklaus traveled from Pittsburgh, where he played nine holes at Oakmont Country Club in preparation for the following week's U.S. Open. Palmer was scheduled to compete in the Senior Players Championship at Canterbury Golf Club in Cleveland. On

June 7, he and Johnston, his IMG business manager, met at Canterbury with Beman, who ordered a rush print job so he could show them an advanced copy of the Tour's annual report.

When Palmer's plane was approximately 50 miles from the airport in N.Y., Palmer waved for Johnston to approach the cockpit, handed him a headset and told him to listen.

"He turned on the channel and whose voice was coming through but Jack Nicklaus," Johnston recalled. "We were on the same wave length or something and I could hear his conversation with his office."

When N1AP landed early that afternoon at Westchester County Airport, Nicklaus waited to greet Palmer. So did Mike Crosthwaite, the Tour's director of sponsor-player relations, who was assigned to lead golf's two giants in a separate car to a meeting at the home of Lew Lapham, the Tour's former policy board chairman. First, Nicklaus and Palmer conferred on the tarmac. Nicklaus recounted the episode to *The Washington Post's* Thomas Boswell: "When I got off the plane, Arnie said to me, 'About 90 percent of the answers we wanted are in this report and they're satisfactory.' " Nicklaus hadn't seen the annual report, which was distributed to the membership shortly before that evening's players' meeting.

Palmer and Nicklaus climbed into one vehicle and briefed each other on recent developments. Bob Goalby, who was traveling with Palmer to the senior event, wisely hopped in the front seat with Crosthwaite. Goalby didn't want to be in the middle of those two. Crosthwaite could see Palmer and Nicklaus arguing in the rear-view mirror. "Fingers were flying," he remembered.

"Jack was playing a little foxy with Arnold and saying he didn't know this or that, when Arnold had heard him speak of it with his office," Johnston said. "Arnold was sort of chuckling on the inside."

From the Westchester County Airport, the ride took 15-minutes or so to Lapham's summer home in Greenwich, Conn.

"Lapham was having his house painted," Crosthwaite remembered. "We get out of the car and these painters see Arnold and Jack and they jumped off the scaffolding. 'Sorry, no autographs now,' I said."

The meeting began at 4 p.m. Beman, de Windt and Smith arrived first and had already settled in for the meeting. Lapham, who had been vice chairman of Bankers Trust, had finished serving on the Tour's board, but he remained a trusted confidant with a genuine affection for the game. Lapham, 74, had deep roots in golf. His father had been one of the founders of Cypress Point Golf Club in Pebble Beach, Calif. Indeed, when famed designer Alister MacKenzie laid out the course, he called on a young Lapham to hit balls to determine the placement of bunkers off the tee and routing of the holes.

It was potentially an uncomfortable moment but by the time the two parties met at Lapham's house any rancor seemed to have vanished. Nicklaus and Palmer were hoping to avoid public ridicule. "They were looking for a way out and we were trying to help them," Beman remembered. "It was a far different meeting than it might've been."

After a few short cordials, the meeting started and de Windt spoke first. In his phlegmatic form he said, "Before we go too far I want you to review this," and handed the golfers a copy of the Tour's first annual report.

Opening up the report, they couldn't miss de Windt's letter to the membership on page 1, addressing its concerns. In his "Message from the Chairman," de Windt wrote:

> *With the current growth and relative prosperity of the Tour, it is sometimes hard to remember that, as recently as three or four years ago, the Tour's economic future was thought to be in considerable doubt. The first meeting of the Tournament Policy Board that I attended was called in December 1979 by my predecessor, Bob Oelman, CEO of National Cash Register, to review the following trends:*
>
> - *Television ratings for PGA Tour golf were down for the fourth consecutive year (off 12 percent in 1979 alone)*
>
> - *Junior participation in the previous year had declined*
>
> - *A survey of Tour galleries had shown the overwhelming majority to be active golfers; the Tour was not effectively competing for the general sports fans interest*

- *The growth rate and demographics of golf indicated that the problem was getting worse, not better.*

It was against that backdrop that, in 1980, the Board made a fundamental commitment to its current strategy. Specifically, the Board approved a number of new programs, all with two main goals in mind.

(First) to promote greater public interest in the PGA Tour and golf; and (secondly) to produce increased income for players and local charities by developing additional sources of revenue beyond television.

These new programs included a variety of projects now familiar to most members: the Tour's statistics program; the Vantage electronic scoreboards and the promotion of "Stadium Golf."

The new strategy and programs appear to have had a positive impact. For example:

- *Television ratings and sales substantially increased, resulting in new multi-year contracts at significantly higher rights fees;*

- *Both total prize money and charitable contributions by Tour sponsors increased to record highs;*

- *The first Players Championship at a stadium golf facility produced considerable public interest and new income for the Tour;*

- *The first two $1,000,000 Tour events were announced (Las Vegas and the Seiko Tucson Match Play events);*

- *The number of events paying prize money of $400,000 or more increased from three in 1980 to 21 in 1983;*

- *The goal of materially supplementing television revenue from other sources is beginning to be achieved; marketing and Tournament Players Clubs, for example, will begin to make a solid contribution to the net revenue of the Tour.*

Any organization – and perhaps especially one like the Tour – needs to re-examine and reaffirm its basic goals and policies from time to time. Certainly, such an organization needs to communicate continuously its plans and programs to those most affected – in this case its members.

The first annual report by the Board to the Membership is

intended as a first step towards improving the vital process of defining goals and communications, purposes and problems in both directions.

(signed)
*E.M. de Windt
Chairman, PGA Tour
Tournament Policy Board
June 1, 1983*

In the annual report, Beman and his staff concentrated on the task at hand: an emphatic defense of his tenure as commissioner. "It read like a legal brief," said Smith, its author.

In years past, Tour information had been distributed periodically to the membership in piecemeal fashion. This new annual report represented the first comprehensive document framing all of the Tour's accomplishments in perspective. It contained 36-pages printed on glossy stock and featured four-color charts, graphs, photos and statistics. The report highlighted a handsome profit statement. Tour revenue had soared from $4 million in 1974 when Beman became commissioner to over $20 million in 1983. Prize money climbed from $8.2 million to $22.6 million with another $1 million placed in the newly-established player retirement fund. Charitable contributions jumped from $2 million to $7 million during his tenure. Tour assets increased 20-fold compared with 1974 levels.

"The idea was total transparency," Smith said. "Don't take it from us, take it from a 'Big 6' accounting firm."

Nicklaus and Palmer skimmed it again and found their concerns were covered in the report. Nevertheless, de Windt and Beman explained the report point-by-point with the certainty of a sommelier. With a cigarette between his knuckles, Nicklaus chain-smoked throughout the meeting, something he rarely did anymore. Nicklaus and Palmer realized that continuing their challenge would be frowned upon by corporate America, which was becoming increasingly intimate with the Tour. When de Windt finished, Palmer spoke in resignation.

"We didn't need to send that letter," Palmer said.

The two quickly withdrew their objections. To break the mood, Palmer joked that Nicklaus got him into this mess. Beman struck a conciliatory tone and agreed to concede that the Tour communicated poorly with the members. He promised the problem would be rectified. To Beman, this strategic ploy of taking a personal public relations hit allowed golf's superstars a way to save face. Everyone rose and exchanged firm handshakes. Palmer and Nicklaus departed the meeting in one car, a ride that must have been as silent and depressing for them as rolling down Magnolia Lane after missing the cut at the Masters.

"It was the equivalent of a secret meeting between the Soviets and the Americans during the Cold War," said Larry Nelson, a player director on the Tour's board at the time. "One side could've pressed the red button to launch an atomic bomb, but they came to their senses. To those people who were aware of it, we were nervous and extremely relieved at the outcome."

Beman, his staff, and members of the board drove separately to attend the players meeting on the eve of the Manufacturers Hanover Westchester Classic. It didn't slip their notice that the confrontations denouement would occur at a tournament, which had witnessed its purse grow from $250,000 in 1974, when Beman became commissioner, to $450,000 that week.

With Smith having courted players in Washington, Colbert having set Nicklaus straight, and now Palmer having admitted his folly, Beman felt invigorated. He knew his chances of prevailing had improved dramatically over the past month. But this case hadn't been dismissed; the jury was still out. "No one knew whether enough water had been poured on the fire or whether it would rekindle," Beman said.

Just to complicate matters further, the final round of the Kemper Open presented another calamity. The last threesome of the tournament, Fred Couples, Scott Simpson and T.C. Chen played in an interminable clip, taking more than five hours to complete their rounds on Sunday. Under the rules, the field staff had no choice but to fine each of the players, along with six others who clocked in at over five hours, $200 each for slow play. That didn't sit well with some players. Beman supported the full enforcement of the rule, but the timing of the disciplinary action couldn't have been worse.

That was the backdrop to the most highly anticipated meeting in Tour history. Players wondered would Beman survive? Would the Tour in its current format survive? The conflict had been boiling for weeks.

"There was an expectation on the players part that they were going to tell the guy who worked for them that this was how it was going to be," said Dale Antram, Beman's executive assistant at the time and a Tour employee for 22 years.

Fireworks were expected, but nobody struck a match. What the players didn't realize was that Nicklaus and Palmer had already waved the white flag at their pre-meeting.

Back in the ballroom, the hall was packed with faces and bodies. Nearly every contestant in the 156-player field that week was there. As the men grumbled, Smith heard one voice pipe up that a public hanging always drew a big turnout. David Graham, with a wolfish grin and in his distinctive Aussie-Texan accent, snickered that the intrigue was better than Watergate. Bed sheets covered the windows. Bob Greene, The Associated Press golf writer, paced the hall wondering what was going on in there.

"Oh nothing, Bob," Crosthwaite told him, as he resumed his post at the closed-door meeting.

Inside, there was no hint of the truce that had occurred earlier that day. Beman and the members of the board stood in the front of the room outfitted in coats and ties. An irritated Palmer had washed his hands of the situation, driven to the airport, boarded his Cessna Citation and returned to Cleveland for the Senior Players Championship. Of the secondary signees of the letter, only Watson was absent. Nicklaus stayed behind to handle the situation. Policy board chairman de Windt opened the meeting at 7 p.m. by reading a prepared statement from Nicklaus and Palmer.

"Two weeks ago we privately met and communicated to the board some concerns and questions about the current policies and future directions of the PGA Tour," the duo wrote. "It has never been our intent, however, to create any public controversy about the Tour or its current leadership, both of which we support...Our main purpose – to get more information and to involve more leading players in helping to shape the future of the Tour – has been accomplished. The board has been very responsive..."

The Nicklaus-Palmer statement said they "still have some questions about certain types of marketing activities and certain type of golf course ventures involving the Tour," but that "based on the new understanding we have gained of the board's policies and purposes, we pledge our assistance and cooperation."

The floor was turned over to Nicklaus, who asked to address the standing-room-only crowd. He stared out towards his fellow competitors, commanding silence without saying a word.

"Thank you, everyone for being here," Nicklaus said, simply and solemnly.

Nicklaus spoke for 10 minutes, the players listened as if at a church congregation. Holding the annual report in his hand, Nicklaus said that all the players could see for themselves how well the Tour leadership had performed.

"Under the circumstances, we think it best to formally withdraw our previous communication to the board and (Arnold and I) now consider the matter closed," Nicklaus said.

When one player raised his hand and asked, "Where's the letter? What's in the letter?" Nicklaus dodged the question saying it wouldn't do anyone any good to read it. He grinned as if in pain, a player said. Nicklaus reiterated that they had withdrawn the letter. It was a stunning turn of events. Kite, for one, nearly fell out of his chair.

Beman appreciated Nicklaus looking his fellow players in the eye and the clarity of the verdict. "It was one of the classiest moves I've ever witnessed," Beman said.

The entire meeting would last four hours, but Nicklaus hightailed out of there after doing his part. As he made his way to the hotel's lobby, he told *The Washington Post's* Thomas Boswell that the player turnout "probably was the largest response ever...the fellows are just dying to have some information.

"This has in no way been an affront to Deane Beman," Nicklaus continued, "(but) if Deane has one fault, it's that he keeps a lot of things to himself."

Slipping into a car waiting to whisk him to the airport,

Nicklaus concluded, "I'm going to stick to playing golf for a while."

* * *

In the aftermath, Beman knew that the days ahead would be difficult. They demanded not only determination but also diplomacy, flexibility, patience and judiciousness. There would be greater scrutiny and pressure to succeed. The evolution from "Ma and Pa" operation to the marketing machine it is today had received a green light to proceed.

"He didn't let a few arrows shot his way deter him from doing what he believed needed to be done," said Tour veteran and former policy board member Dave Stockton.

Beman's contract was renewed one year later, extending it five more years. As time rolled by, the independent contractors he worked for agreed Beman was skilled at his work, and accepted that a commissioner is necessary for their business. Yet he felt underappreciated, even resented, by the people who depended upon him.

"I was not a commissioner that was loved," Beman said. "I do believe I was respected. But I wasn't trying to run a popularity contest. I was trying to break new ground."

While Beman reconciled with Palmer and Nicklaus long ago, in all of their future encounters neither Palmer nor Nicklaus ever have offered an admission of error to Beman. Even now, Beman contends that Nicklaus – based on ample evidence from material he's written – still wouldn't acknowledge he might have been wrong despite the way the Tour flourished. "Nicklaus and self-doubt have never met," Beman said.

In 1986 Nicklaus told *Golf Digest*, "Where I have a conflict is in the real estate area. The biggest competition I have in building golf courses is the Tour. I find myself marketing against an organization I'm part of...and that can be troubling. Deane has tried to solve that by having the players design some of the courses. That has helped."

When the letter of protest was broached for a 1987 *Forbes* article, Nicklaus said, "We got defeated and I've kept my mouth shut ever since."

Watson countered that, in his case, his concerns came to bear. He contended the Tour's marketing pact with Coca-Cola (signed in 1991) compromised his own long-standing relationship with the company, which dropped him as an endorser soon thereafter. "I stand by my remarks," Watson said.

Palmer has expressed little remorse for his role in the attempted coup, too. When asked if he still opposed the Tour's marketing and licensing programs, he said, "I think they have intruded on the player's rights to a degree. I still disagree on some of the aspects and the personal rights of the players, but overall (Deane) has done a wonderful job."

The TPC network of courses turned out to be the best investment the Tour ever made and directly funded the retirement plans of the letter signers. They benefited by millions of dollars.

As time rolled on, even Beman and his staff could reflect back on this period and make light of it.

"Oh yeah, we called it 'The Troubles,' " Smith said in his best imitation of an Irish brogue. "In reference to Michael Collins and the Irish Revolution and all that."

Beman contends that if the letter hadn't used such highly-charged language the players' revolt would have prevailed. If their protest had simply said they disagreed with the ownership of TPC's, marketing and the pursuit of corporate licensing agreements, Beman told his staff "we will not win this battle."

Accusing the Board of unauthorized activities and exceeding its mandate was a serious charge that in the corporate world is a label that can irreparably damage a CEO's reputation and goes to the fundamental trust that any executive must possess to be able to represent their shareholders. In the sports world any commissioner who loses this trust is "down the road," as the players say when they miss the cut. What a difference four words – "exceeds its mandate" and "unauthorized" – make, Beman later pondered. "The PGA Tour could be a far different organization than it is today if the players had won."

Almost 12 years later, Palmer and Nicklaus shared a podium as co-chairmen in a bash to honor and poke some good-natured fun at Beman, who had recently retired. Held at the old Jacksonville railroad terminal now converted into a convention center, 1,500 guests attended the gala. On March 21, 1995, Jay Haas, representing the tournament policy board, presented Beman with a vintage motorcycle, a 1947 Indian Chief. Apart from golf, bikes were his consuming passion. The event raised $150,000 for area charities that Beman supported. To punctuate the evening, both Palmer and Nicklaus offered a salute to the former commissioner.

"Some people will object," Palmer said, "but those of us in the game will give Deane a nod for a job well done."

"He's responsible for a lot of what happened with the Tour today," Nicklaus chimed in.

Furman Bisher, the longtime *Atlanta Journal-Constitution* columnist, said the admiration was the first time they had said anything kind about Beman in years. But it wasn't a complete love fest. Bisher noted that seating for 10 at the tables sold for $5,000. When Golden Bear, Nicklaus' company, was solicited, it passed.

FIRST COMMISSIONER

J oe Dey broke the news at the 1969 United States Golf Association Annual Meeting in New York City. After 35 years as the USGA's executive director, Dey was accepting a job with the newly formed Tournament Players Division of the PGA of America.

Jaws dropped in shock. A collective groan echoed in the room. Dey's decision even surprised his staff. He reigned as a stern guardian of American amateur golf and an arch-enemy of commercialism. At the time, his joining the pro ranks was the equivalent of Richard Nixon suddenly running for political office as a Democrat.

Pundits expressed doubt, too. "This is like putting one of the Bobbsey twins in charge of the Cosa Nostra," a hard-bitten golf writer said. "He'll need a pistol and a bullet-proof vest instead of a rulebook."

But Dey, during an impassioned speech, explained his decision, saying that he was 61, that the USGA was in good shape and likely to remain so with or without him, and that he had a unique opportunity to create something beneficial to golf.

What Dey didn't say when he announced his move was that the pros needed him. But others were less bashful. Jack Nicklaus, speaking to *Golf Digest*, summed it up best: "Joe Dey is the only man for the job."

It was an invitation Dey couldn't resist. A dispute between the players and the PGA was virtually boiling over when Deane Beman turned pro at the age of 29 in 1967. Players sought full autonomy to run the tour as they saw fit or else they threatened to establish a rival tour. The furor consumed the better part of the next two years. Just when it seemed that the two parties were on the verge of splitting over irreconcilable differences, they reached a truce forming a new organization for touring pros within the PGA. The players desperately needed a proven leader, but Dey dismissed the notion that he would be the "czar" of pro golf.

"Czar isn't the right word," he explained to the *Sporting News*. "The more appropriate word is commissioner."

That's the title Dey was given on Jan. 22, 1969. He signed a 5-year contract worth a reported $65,000-$75,000 annually, according to *Golf World*.

"Besides," Dey added, "the last (Russian) czar, Nicholas, contracted hemophilia, then was assassinated and burned.

"I don't want that happening to me."

* * *

In his blue blazer, Joe Dey Jr. (pronounced die) carried two pocket-sized books: the New Testament, which he quoted from daily, and the Rules of Golf, a book he helped author. They governed his life.

Twice along the way Dey almost "took the cloth." He would have been a natural clergyman, for he was a devout Christian and devoted churchgoer. Instead, through golf he performed a special ministry. His pulpit became the first tee. Known to all as "Mr. Golf," Dey devoted his career, spanning nearly four decades, to the game. He preached that amateurism is the heart of the game.

"He runs the game of golf the way Charlemagne ran France – firmly but with love," wrote *The Los Angeles Times* columnist Jim Murray.

A native of Norfolk, Va., Dey joined the USGA after stints as a sportswriter for two Philadelphia newspapers, including the *Philadelphia Evening Bulletin*, for which he covered Bob Jones' grand slam finale at Merion Cricket Club in 1930. Dey's job that week – to describe every shot Jones hit.

"I had a pad of paper and a relay of caddies," Dey recalled years later in a *Met Golfer* profile. "I'd write the text for each hole then give it to the kid who legged it to the press room, where a telegrapher sent it into the office."

Dey became acquainted with USGA Executive Committee members living in the Philadelphia area, and when the association pursued a new executive secretary to replace Thomas McMahon, it recommended Dey. On Dec. 10, 1934, at the age of 27, he became executive secretary of the USGA and its 700 member clubs. He served his first year under then-association president Prescott Bush, father of George H. and grandfather of George H.W. (who both achieved a higher calling).

The USGA staff, closeted in two tiny offices above a bank on East 42nd Street in New York, consisted of Dey and his secretary when he joined. Dey handled tournaments and shuffled paperwork for its many volunteer committeemen. Frank Hannigan, who went to work for Dey in 1961 as public information manager, recalled how Dey loved to tell the tale of being reprimanded by USGA treasurer Harold Pierce of The Country Club in Brookline, Mass. Dey had sent two separate letters to Pierce on the same day when both could have been enclosed in the same envelope. Pierce, known as "fierce Pierce" in golf circles, insisted Dey could have saved three cents, the price of a first-class stamp.

"Dey was singularly successful in bringing to fruition his novel idea that the USGA's role should be educational and ecumenical," Hannigan wrote of his former boss upon his selection as the 1992 Memorial Tournament honoree. "I thought I was working on a mission when I was at the USGA. It came from Joe."

At any U.S. Open, Dey seemed omnipresent, keeping a magisterial eye on the proceedings. He walked the final 18 holes of the 1951 U.S. Open with Ben Hogan when he shot 67 at Oakland Hills to slay "the monster," and marched stride for stride with a weary, heat-sapped Ken Venturi during his 1964 Open triumph at Congressional Country Club. Dey even enjoyed rising at 5 a.m. to supervise the placing and cutting of the cups for the day's round. *Sports Illustrated* dubbed him "the man who makes the grass grow," a nod to the U.S. Open's trademark thick rough that distinguishes it from all other major tournaments. Even during the hottest of U.S. Opens, he always wore a coat; favored a long-sleeved white, buttoned-down Brooks Brothers dress shirt; a conservative, striped necktie and an armband marked either "USGA" or "Rules Committee." He often was stationed at the first tee of the association's major events to call out "Play away."

It was on such an occasion that a teenaged Jack Nicklaus met Dey for the first time at the 1953 U.S. Junior Amateur in Tulsa, Okla. With the earliest morning tee time at 7 o'clock sharp, the crew-cut kid arrived on the first tee just in time to face his opponent, Stanley Ziobrowski.

"Joe Dey gave me a good lacing down," Nicklaus recalled. "'Young man, 30 seconds later and you'd be starting at the second tee 1 down,' and so on. That was my introduction to Joe Dey. I was a 13-year-old kid mind you, and that made me remember him pretty well."

Nicklaus never missed a starting time due to that lesson. In the proceeding years, Nicklaus was hailed as the greatest amateur since Bobby Jones. Despite all his achievements, Nicklaus maintained his intention to spurn the professional game and follow the example of Jones, his boyhood idol. However, the pressure to turn pro intensified after his second U.S. Amateur win in 1961.

Nicklaus was then a young married man with a six-week-old son. He'd become a homeowner. He still was working toward a degree at Ohio State University, and earning $24,000 from insurance sales and promotional work for a slacks company. "That was a lot of money back then," Nicklaus recalled in *The Palm Beach Post*.

United Press International writer Oscar Fraley had floated the rumor that Nicklaus, intending to turn pro, had met with Mark McCormack, Arnold Palmer's agent, to explore his potential as a play-for-pay athlete. At the time, Nicklaus was competing in the Americas Cup matches in 1961. Associated Press golf writer Will Grimsley was at Monterrey Country Club in Mexico and badgered him for the story. "In those days, if you said you were going to turn pro, you were a pro," Nicklaus noted.

He told Grimsley he had no intention of doing so. But in his book, "Jack Nicklaus: My Story," he admitted he contacted McCormack, who predicted Nicklaus in his first year could make at least $100,000 through endorsements and other promotional work – in addition to his earnings on the course. The conversation never escalated beyond the hypothetical. At the time, Nicklaus had decided to maintain his amateur status. However, when he arrived back home, he talked to his father, Charlie, about his future.

"I realized I couldn't achieve my goals unless I played against the best," Nicklaus determined.

On Nov. 7, 1961, Nicklaus changed his mind and decided to turn pro. But first he wrote a lengthy letter to Dey on his father's Nicklaus Prescription Center letterhead explaining his decision, and posted it by airmail. Then he called Kaye Kessler of the *Columbus Citizen-Journal* and Paul Hornung of the *Columbus Dispatch* and, without explanation, requested that they come the next morning to the modest Nicklaus home on Elmwood Avenue in Upper Arlington.

Kessler arrived at 10 a.m. the following day. Nicklaus informed the two scribes that he would join the pro tour in 1962 and that McCormack "probably" would handle his business affairs. Nicklaus wanted the two writers to break the news since they had followed his exploits from the beginning. But Nicklaus embargoed this front-page story until he made certain his letter had reached Dey.

"I won't have him reading it in the papers or hearing it on the radio," Nicklaus said, according to Hornung's account in an article he wrote for the 1992 Memorial Tournament program. "He's going to hear it from me first."

Nicklaus then placed a call to Dey's USGA office in New York, but was told that he was away on business in Florida. Hornung suspected that Nicklaus might have a change of heart about turning pro. He had his story written, but told his editors to wait for his permission before rolling the presses. Deadline for his paper's home edition was 11 a.m. and fast approaching.

While the scribes waited, a *Dispatch* photographer snapped a shot of Nicklaus feeding his infant son, Jackie; the photo appeared with Hornung's column the next day. Next, Nicklaus dialed Dey in Florida, but didn't reach him. Meanwhile, Hornung fretted. Finally, at about 10:45 a.m., Nicklaus connected with Dey, explained the purpose of his call, and read passages from a carbon copy of the letter he sent. After hanging up, Nicklaus reported, "Joe gave me about as nice an answer as I could have gotten. He said, 'Whatever decision you made, I knew it would be the right one. It doesn't change anything between you and the USGA, or between you and me.' "

Hornung's story made the home edition. Years later, he recounted to Dey the circumstances of that morning. "I must say I'm flattered that Jack would show that kind of consideration for my feelings, but I'm not that surprised," Dey told Hornung.

Nicklaus' decision proved the model of amateur golf championed by Dey had become a quaint relic of the past. It wouldn't be long before Dey would accept that the influence exerted by the tour professionals was considerable. Nevertheless, Nicklaus and Dey's friendship grew stronger.

"Joe was in many ways like a second or third father to me," Nicklaus said. "From the moment I met him, I could tell he was in charge of the game of golf. Every time I had a question or a problem about what was right, I always picked up the phone and placed a call to Joe. I knew I would always get the right answer, whether it was what I wanted to hear or not."

So when the time came for the players to hire their first commissioner, Nicklaus was among the players who influenced Dey's decision.

Esteemed golf writer Charles Price recounted the story of the time he and Dey were paired at the Golf Writers Association of America's annual championship in Myrtle Beach, S.C. Sponsors supplied tee gifts – the usual fare such as a sleeve of balls and a towel. Dey declined everything, even a pack of tees. When it was his turn to tee off, he reached into his pocket and found he didn't have a tee. He borrowed one from Price.

"That's the last thing in golf Joe owed anybody," Price wrote.

Under Dey's watch, the roster of member clubs nearly quadrupled. Dey, presiding over a staff of 27, moved the USGA in 1951 into 'Golf House,' a stately five-story Stanford White town house that the elder J.P. Morgan built on East 38th Street, just off Park Avenue. By the time he left the USGA in 1969 his impact was undeniable.

"He is an anomaly of the modern world: a man of great

influence who labors gladly in obscurity, and by moving judiciously and firmly he has become the most powerful individual in American golf," Alfred Wright kindly wrote in *Sports Illustrated*. "The public knows of him only as a shadowy figure whose name occasionally gets into the papers along with one of his pronouncements on some sticky problem. Rarely is his picture seen. In golf, however, his voice is from Mount Olympus."

Throughout their squabbles with the PGA, players such as Palmer echoed Nicklaus in suggesting that they should try to hire a man like Dey, or even Dey himself, to run their affairs. Such a thought was presumed to be outlandish. Indeed, when a few players met with Dey, it was to ask his advice on what a new commissioner should do. Dey, ever helpful, provided his expertise, along with a list of names the players should consider for the job. Somebody asked, "How about you, Joe?" The answer startled everyone: He didn't say no. Maybe, eventually, became yes. "It took some persuading," Palmer recalled.

Nicklaus and Palmer, more than anyone else, recruited Dey. For a week, Dey contemplated his move. Only then did the man who ruled the amateur game with almost religious zeal decide to answer a higher calling to the game. The New Testament began on March 1, 1969.

*   *   *

Professional golf initially operated under one umbrella, the PGA of America. Founded in 1916, the PGA represented two groups of people pursuing completely different lines of work. It served as the establishment that administers the livelihood of the country club professional, driving-range pro, and public course operator. It also ran a series of golf tournaments in which the best of these teachers and golf-shop operators were able to compete for purse money. During the winter months, pros came south and resorts offered modest prize money to encourage them to play tournaments to publicize the resorts. Those "tours" ended when spring arrived. This model worked well until tournament golf evolved into big business. The players who competed began complaining about some of the organization's policies, and by the late 1960s, the disenchantment threatened to split the PGA.

The players resented restrictions such as a rule barring a tour rookie from accepting prize money for the first six months of his career. Another mandated a five-year waiting period before a player was eligible to participate in the Ryder Cup.

"The players thought they would be better off and have more direct control of their own destiny if they had their own organization," said Beman, who was a rising tour pro at the time.

For the pros, an era of bigger money had begun. In 1958, the total purse for the tour had been $1 million. A decade later, it had increased to $5 million. Tensions simmered. After all, the players felt they – not the administration – were responsible for the growth in purses. The PGA, on the other hand, considered itself a trustee for what it called the various owners of the tour. Max Elbin, the PGA's 15th president from 1965-1968, argued that the players should play and the PGA should administer, as it had for years.

"A philosophical difference of long standing between the men elected to guide your Association and the few privileged to enjoy the benefits of its tournament program has reached a flash point," Elbin reported to the PGA membership in 1968.

Elbin, the longtime pro at Burning Tree Golf Club in Bethesda, Md., called it a "thirst for power resulting possibly from too much prosperity." Elbin's perspective reflected purses for touring pros growing at a higher rate than salaries for club pros. But Beman and his fellow pros weren't interested in club pro wages. They looked at the salaries earned by athletes in other sports, and realized they were way behind.

"Relative to tennis, football, basketball, and baseball, we were in the dark ages," Beman explained. "Jack and Arnie were doing okay, but most of us were driving cars from city to city, struggling for a living."

The players began making demands, including insisting upon having their own commissioner to replace the PGA's Tournament Committee, which managed television contracts and tournament scheduling. They wanted a looser affiliation with the parent organization. Palmer in his memoir, "A Golfer's

Life," provided commentary of the player unrest, conceding "as crass as it sounds, the issue was really money – more precisely television money."

Palmer's agent, Mark McCormack, once wrote, "the PGA has two problems. It thinks small, and it thinks 'Me.' " For some players, the last straw occurred when the Tournament Committee, comprising four players and three PGA executives at the time, voted 4-3 to grant Frank Sinatra dates for an event at Palm Springs, Calif., within two weeks of the Bob Hope Desert Classic. The PGA cautioned the players that the community could not support – in volunteer workers and possibly at the gate – two events in such close proximity. The PGA also worried whether Hope and former President Eisenhower, who supported Hope's tournament as it aided his charities, would perceive the addition as an intrusion. The PGA requested the players contact Hope, and if he agreed to the scheduling, proceed with the tournament – with its blessing.

Instead, the Sinatra event was announced as a fait accompli, and Hope and Eisenhower were none too pleased. In response, the PGA's 17-man Executive Committee, consisting of 16 club pros and one touring pro, exercised its veto for the first time in history and cancelled the Sinatra event. Shortly thereafter, a $300,000 Miami event was scheduled in close proximity to the Doral Open. The new event's sponsor eventually withdrew, but players noted the inconsistency of the board's use of its veto power. Control and the PGA's ability to overrule the players was at the center of this debate.

The touring pros resolved to take action after they learned that the PGA had negotiated contracts without consulting them for the television rights to the World Series of Golf and Shell's Wonderful World of Golf. Furthermore, they were incensed that the PGA decided to put all the proceeds into its general fund, not the tour fund. More than 100 players assembled in Akron, Ohio, during the American Golf Classic and voted unanimously to secede from the PGA. Julius Boros, Billy Casper, Bob Goalby, Lee Trevino and Nicklaus were among the most vocal supporters.

On Aug. 14, 1968, at a press conference in New York City, the fight between America's touring pros and the PGA administration broke out into a full-fledged civil war. The players announced that beginning with the 1969 season, they would form their own tour, the Association of Professional Golfers (APG).

Tournament director Jack Tuthill recounted in "The History of the PGA Tour" its humble beginnings: "The (nominal) headquarters was in the Bronx (a New York City borough) because that's where Doug Ford's lawyer had his office. His name was Sam Gates (of Debevoise, Plimpton, Lyons and Gates). He was the acting commissioner. I had a little office in the Del Monico Hotel, in New York City, and didn't know if I was going to get paid. The players were funding the thing out of their own pockets."

Gates declared he had 205 clients. They planned a rookie school for Doral Resort in Miami. He also said a commissioner, reporting to a board of directors, would be employed to run it like a big corporation. According to an article in the Aug. 23, 1968, issue of *Golf World*, they opened a search for a commissioner, tossing out names such as Oklahoma University football coach Bud Wilkinson and the USGA's Joe Dey as potential candidates. Gates rolled out a 13-man steering committee composed of some of the brightest stars: Nicklaus, Casper, Ford, Goalby, Jerry Barber, Frank Beard, Dave Eichelberger, Lionel Hebert, Dave Marr, Bob Rosburg, Dan Sikes, and Kermit Zarley. Gardner Dickinson Jr., was named the APG's president.

"What we want is the right to cast the deciding vote over such matters as where, how, and under what conditions we will play," Dickinson told *Golf World*.

At least one player sided with his brethren, but felt that the action was hasty. "I was one of the players who signed a petition. But I think that the pros and PGA need each other, and that there should be further negotiations," said Palmer, the son of a PGA pro.

Hopes that Palmer could play peacemaker evaporated when he flew to Washington D.C., to address the executive committee of the PGA and offer his solution to the dispute. The PGA rejected Palmer's proposed one-year trial of allowing the players to run the tour themselves with a governing board composed of seven player members, four businessmen, and three members of the PGA Executive Committee.

The proposed board's composition gave the PGA no power to address the tour if it moved in a direction the PGA didn't approve. Its officers felt this was the equivalent of Macy's employees telling management they will take control of the store, but allow management to retain the Macy's name on the building.

With his plan spurned, Palmer joined the APG and was rumored to be willing to serve as interim commissioner. Some PGA officials and supporters derisively said that APG stood for the "Arnold Palmer Golfers." After wrestling with his decision, Palmer rolled to victory at the inaugural Kemper Open (played at Pleasant Valley in Sutton, Mass.), worth a $30,000 payout. He became the first tour player to eclipse the million-dollar mark in career earnings.

For months Gates, negotiating for the players, and PGA attorney William Rogers sought an amicable solution. Gates told *Golf World* he and Rogers had agreed on certain amendments to the PGA Constitution, which would have established the touring players as a separate section. But before the ink had dried, the PGA officers voted as a block against submitting the amendments before the PGA membership. "We cannot sell our birthright," Elbin reiterated.

He countered that the players rejected an eight-point plan that gave numerous concessions. Gates, however, called the plan "unacceptable." The split seemed inevitable. "We worked hard at it for two years," Goalby told *Golf World*. "I'm sorry, but I'm with the players."

Following the player break, the PGA held its own news conference in New York City. It announced it would continue to schedule a tour; any pros aligning with the fledgling circuit would be banned from competition on the PGA.

"Some of those who precipitated the difficulties may be surprised to find out how little time will be required to develop a new crop of capable players," Elbin said.

Roone Arledge, vice president of ABC Sports, attended the PGA press conference. He had just signed a two-year TV pact with the PGA, but he left open the door for a change of plans. "We'll televise where the players are," he said at the time.

With hope for détente dead, the PGA Executive Committee

met in Florida and abolished the Tournament Committee and named former tour supervisor Joe Black as new tour director. In September, a temporary restraining order was issued on behalf of the PGA by U.S. District Court in Wilmington, Del. It halted the dissident APG from entering into any agreements for events or staging a qualifying school until a hearing could be held.

By that time, both organizations had already begun negotiating with sponsors for 1969 dates. The Royal Canadian Golf Association deplored the stalemate as a "blow to golf everywhere," and said the Canadian Open would be conducted as an independent tournament rather than joining either circuit. Players from both factions would be invited. On the whole, the APG was scoring a decisive victory in the battle for current local sponsors. The American Golf Sponsors Association met in Houston and listened to presentations by both organizations. According to Black's book "A Few Good Stories," they held a press conference after their closed-door meeting and revealed their support of the APG thusly: "We have decided to go with the dancing girls." Soon, Dickinson announced that 19 existing tournaments already had signed on the dotted line and another 14 had requested contracts.

When the PGA met in Palm Beach, Fla., in November for its 52nd annual meeting, prominent tour players were conspicuously absent. For the first time, a Player of the Year award was not given. "We did not want to embarrass ourselves or the player who would have to come from the current crop of players," Elbin said. "Undoubtedly, the choice would have been one of those now a member of the APG, and we would have put him on the spot."

But feathers already had been ruffled. In early September of 1968, Leo Fraser, secretary of the PGA, added to the friction between the organizations by saying Nicklaus disseminated "false information designed to mislead the public" and "mouthed clichés that have distorted the truth." Nicklaus, who served as APG vice president, responded with a first-person rebuttal in the Sept. 16, 1968, issue of *Sports Illustrated*. It began, "The verbal attack recently unleashed on me by Leo Fraser... was, on the whole, inaccurate. Fraser did spell my name correctly – Jack Nicklaus. He even had my age right – 28. And .

he signed his own name properly – Leo Fraser. The rest of the cutting statement, though, was a personal assault."

The strongest rebuke of the players didn't come from PGA officials, but from two of the most distinguished champion golfers of all time. Rarely did the great amateur and 13-time major winner Bobby Jones publicly express his position on controversial matters in golf. But he made an exception when he addressed the players' dinner for the USGA Senior Amateur Championship in Atlanta in October 1968.

"There seems to be little appreciation today that golf is an amateur game, developed and supported by those who love to play it," Jones began in a speech reprinted in the Nov. 19, 1968, issue of *Golf World*.

"The tournament players apparently are choosing to regard themselves only as performers whose skills are to be sold to the highest bidder. They have great box office appeal in person and on television, and so earn magnificent incomes in these days of free spending and fat advertising budgets. Even so, they obviously could get more money under a different setup.

"This is certainly within the rights of the players, but it would seem that they are risking two things; first, that they may price themselves out of the market, and second, that they may disrupt the Professional Golfers' Association, which appears to be the best hope for a permanent ruling body of the professional game. Just now, it is difficult to see that anyone is suffering under the present arrangement.

"It may be that the tournament players can go their way and leave the teaching professionals to go theirs, but I very much doubt it. It would be so much better if they could all find shelter under one roof."

Walter Hagen, considered to be the first full-time touring professional and one of the stars who helped the tour flourish in the 1920s and '30s, echoed Jones with equal fervor: "Hasty action, by splitting the club pro and players can only hurt the game of golf. It is a game that has made possible an extremely pleasurable way of earning a living for so many. It is like a shot from which there is no recovery."

In late November 1968, during its annual meeting in Palm Beach Gardens, the PGA elected Fraser president. As Elbin's successor, Fraser, 58, brought 40 years of experience as a teacher and administrator in golf to his new position. At 17, he became head pro at a club in Saginaw, Mich. In 1946, he headed a group that purchased Atlantic City CC, where Fraser had been president ever since. He was elected the PGA's national treasurer in 1964. Fraser said he would "take every step to find an honorable peace."

Less than a month after Fraser assumed office, a truce was called. On Dec. 13, 1968, the PGA and APG hammered out an agreement entitled the "Statement of Principles," which has been modified through the years, but remains the basis for the PGA and Tour's operating agreement, even today. It kept professional golf competition under one umbrella. The touring pros were given a say in the policy-making decisions of the tour. A new entity, the Tournament Players Division of the PGA, was born under the governance of a 10-member board consisting of four players, three independent directors and three officers of the PGA. The development of an impartial party on the Tournament Policy Board was key to the agreement. Appointment of three businessmen or "independent directors" – J. Paul Austin, president of Coca-Cola; George Love, chairman of Consolidation Coal Co.; and John Murchison, a Texas financier – assured that the tour could avoid factional stalemates.

In dividing properties, the players took a popular exhibition called the World Series of Golf, while the PGA kept a biennial competition that at the time was sparsely attended – the Ryder Cup. (It would blossom into one of the most popular and profitable events in golf.) The certificate of incorporation for the PGA Tournament Players Division Corp. as a Delaware-based, for-profit company was recorded March 14, 1969. What was left unsaid was who owned the corporation – the players or the PGA? The players thought they got what they wanted. Little did they know, their independence would come, but at a higher price.

*   *   *

In the aftermath, the image of the players was badly tarnished. They were perceived as overpaid, spoiled and power-hungry. Television advertisers questioned the wisdom of their investments in the sport. Such was the environment when the newly formed TPD searched for its first commissioner and sought Dey.

"He was really, really needed," Jim Colbert told *Golf World* in a 2002 article. "His reputation, his character, his integrity – he was just so straightforward and trustworthy. The only question was whether he would do it."

In the final analysis, Dey declared during the USGA's Annual Meeting in January 1969, that he was accepting the position with the newly-formed TPD because there was something deeper at stake. "I could have taken into account many things," he told constituents of the USGA's then-3,700 member clubs, "but I confined myself to one criterion: Was the change worthwhile to golf?"

Dey took the better part of a week to make up his mind. In the March 1969 issue of *Golf Journal*, Dey penned an article titled, "It's really just a transfer," and wrote: "This transfer is just that – a transfer, not a departure, within the wonderful family of golf. Although the field of activity will be mainly in a commercial side of the game, I'll try to bear in mind the USGA criterion – What's best for golf?"

Fraser, the PGA president, dashed off a letter to USGA president Hord Hardin and its Executive Committee, expressing a similar sentiment: "You know, you people aren't really losing Joe, but we're gaining him."

Goalby noted that several players didn't like Dey at first. After all, many players were involuntarily "turned pro" by the USGA under Dey's watch. He had stripped them of their amateur status for taking golf clubs or receiving travel expenses. But it didn't take long for Dey to earn their respect. When the decision was announced, *Sports Illustrated* called Dey one of the few men who could bring order to the tour and described his personality as combining "the autocratic inclinations of (baseball's) Judge Landis with the practicality of (the NFL's) Pete Rozelle."

On the eve of his departure from the USGA, Dey noted that the game was at a crossroads, but he wasn't afraid of change. "We sit here in Golf House and the walls in this room are hung with clubs made 100 or 200 years ago. Over there are feather balls," Dey told *Sports Illustrated*. "To say the game is not going to change is flying in the face of history. What we are seeing today is not what we are going to be seeing a decade from now."

Such was the scene as Dey, at 62, crossed the street, almost literally, to the professional game. When he left the USGA, he established the Tour's headquarters only four blocks north of his former office in a grim 42nd Street building. *Detroit News* golf writer Jack Berry, contrasting the TPD's new digs with that of the USGA, dubbed it "Austerity House." During his five-year reign, Dey healed a relationship riddled with tension and distrust.

"Everybody knew he loved the game and would never do anything to hurt it," Goalby said.

Almost single-handedly, Dey, through the force of his reputation, changed the public's perception of tour players from "spoiled people to reasonable ones." Even Bobby Jones wrote a letter to the PGA's Elbin on Jan. 29, 1969, expressing his optimism about "the pro situation."

"I am beginning to feel hopeful," Jones wrote in private correspondence preserved in the USGA's Bobby Jones collection. "If all the boys will get behind Joe and give him a real chance, I am sure he will be able to work everything out."

Dey said he would welcome change, but achieving it proved far more difficult. That's not to say the tour didn't grow under Dey. During his tenure, purses increased from $5 million in 1968 to $8.5 million in 1974. Of the 14 percent annual increase, Dey wryly said it is "a little bit better rise than the cost of living index."

The tour upgraded some of its courses and improved their conditions, too. Dey also dreamed up the ideas of a minor-league circuit and a Players Championship – initially in the summer as a fitting climax to the championship season – which Beman eventually made into successes. After five years of steering the tour, Dey resigned his post, ending one of the most influential careers in golf.

"I retired because I was 66 last Saturday," said Dey of his birthday on Nov. 17, 1973. "It was silly to postpone the inevitable, and it is time for a new, fresh man to move in."

Next came the honors. In 1975, he was named the second

American captain – Francis Ouimet was the first – and 205th overall of the Royal & Ancient Golf Club of St. Andrews, Scotland. The position is considered the game's highest honorary position. It's unlikely anyone else ever will be the USGA's executive director, commissioner of the PGA Tour and captain of the R&A. Dey was inducted into the World Golf Hall of Fame in 1975. In 1991, he died at 83, at his home in Locust Valley, N.Y., after a five-year battle with cancer.

"Outside of my father and (instructor) Jack Grout, Joe Dey was the most influential person in my life," Nicklaus said in eulogizing him.

Since 1996, the USGA has given out the Joe Dey Award in recognition of meritorious service to the game of golf as a volunteer.

"Joe could have been whatever he set out to be – from secretary of state on down, or up," wrote William C. Campbell, the USGA's president in 1982-83. "How fortunate we are that he chose to direct his talents, energies and standards to the governance of golf, and that over the years he became such a weight-bearing pillar for it worldwide."

BECOMING COMMISSIONER

Deane Beman slid into the back seat of a courtesy car. It was early Tuesday morning on May 15 before the 1973 Danny Thomas Memphis Classic, and the car was shuttling him to a board meeting scheduled for 8:30 at Colonial Country Club. The tour's policy chair, Paul Austin, asked Beman to ride there with him and Joe Dey. As the car picked up speed, Austin, sitting next to Beman, turned to him and said, "It's not often that you get to be kingmaker."

Beman's eyebrows darted up in wonder. "What do you mean?" he asked. Austin told Beman in confidence that Dey, seated in front of him in the passenger seat, intended to announce his resignation soon. "Joe and I have talked about it, and we'd like you to be his successor," Austin said.

Beman was floored. That was the first he had heard that Dey was stepping down, not to mention that he was being considered as the next commissioner.

"Don't say anything to anyone," Austin implored. "Give me a call next week after you've had a chance to think it over."

In a few months time, Dey would deliver his surprise message. He intended to retire on Feb. 28, 1974, when his five-year contract with the tour expired.

After the tournament, Beman went home and thought about the offer. He thought back to the spring of 1951 when he was 13 years old and his father came home with six new sets of golf clubs from Sears Roebuck – one each for himself, his wife, his daughter and three sons (of which Deane was the youngest) – and told the family he had joined Bethesda Country Club and signed them up for group lessons.

Beman joined the junior golf program administered by Frank Emmett, who Beman long has lauded as one of the pioneers in the field. Later that year, Beman shot 113 in his first tournament at famed Congressional in Bethesda, Md. He became obsessed with the game and channeled all his energy into realizing his talent. Beman rose at 5 a.m. and hit balls for three hours before class. Then, when school let out at 1 p.m., he played past sundown.

At Columbia Country Club, where he often practiced, Beman stroked putts on the putting green long after dark; he would work under the light spilling over from street lamps on Connecticut Avenue. Whenever he parked in the lower lot, he flipped on the headlights of his car. Beman was a scratch golfer within two years and developed a tidy short game.

"We spent so much time honing our putting there that after a while the club's members probably assumed our parents were members, too," said Bill Dudley, his high school and college golf teammate.

Beman's parents were of modest means, but they sacrificed so he could play, practice, and learn how to compete. Others pitched in, too. Beman played regularly with Byron Moe, a 30-something airline pilot for Allegheny Airlines. Tired of fetching Beman at school, Moe bought him a green, 1948 Pontiac for $150 so he could skip classes and meet Moe at the course.

Beman's body of work as an amateur could've merited a spot in the World Golf Hall of Fame. At 15, his hair cut fashionably short, but not yet shaped in the buzz cut he later favored, Beman was the medalist at local qualifying for the 1953 U.S. Junior Amateur. Members of his home club chipped in so he could compete at the event. There, he and Jack Nicklaus met for the first time. Beman can remember clear as day his reward for earning medalist honors: an invite to be Ben Hogan's partner on Aug. 8, 1953, in an exhibition for the grand opening of Goose Creek Golf Club in Leesburg, Va. A reported crowd of 1,800 followed Hogan's every move in his first golf outing since returning home from winning the third leg of his slam consisting of the Masters, U.S. Open, and the British Open. He had fashioned one of golf's greatest seasons.

"It was the first time I'd ever met Hogan," Beman said. "He double bogeyed the first hole, and he didn't like it one bit. I don't think he cracked a smile the rest of the way."

Befitting his champion's status, Hogan rebounded, and he and Beman were 3 up with four holes to play when the match was halted due to a hail and lightning storm.

The experience confirmed Beman's desire to become a champion golfer. He scanned a list of amateur tournaments in *Golf World* magazine and selected the 1955 South Florida Amateur Championship in West Palm Beach, Fla., because it coincided with his high school spring break. He addressed a handwritten letter to its tournament director, Bessie Finn, at The Breakers Hotel, who issued Beman and his brother, Del, an invitation to play. (Beman knew his chances of acceptance would improve if he had his older brother, an accomplished golfer in his own right, join him as a chaperone.) When he showed the tournament invite to his parents, Beman conveniently omitted the fact that he had requested the spot, and begged for their permission. From an early age, Beman dreamed big.

"I engineered this trip to Florida in 1955 because I didn't want to just be a junior golfer. I wanted to win amateur tournaments," he said. "I thought going to Florida and getting a jump on the season was important."

At 16, Beman not only competed in Palm Beach, but won the event. Later that year, he burst on to the national scene by qualifying for the 1955 U.S. Open as a 17-year-old. Again, members of Bethesda CC, his high school teammates and friends helped fund his trip. Beman convinced his teachers to let him skip final exams so he could arrive a week early and practice. (The shop teacher, who doubled as the golf coach, was the easiest mark.)

"I was out there in California at Olympic Club by myself, a junior in high school, first time I'd traveled that far, and I met a man who was going to maybe win the U.S. Open that week," Beman recalled. "He and his wife took the time to see this youngster and put him under his wing, and fed him dinner a couple of nights. I missed the cut, but I made a friend for a lifetime in Jackie Burke."

Burke Jr. subsequently won the 1956 Masters and PGA Championship. Soon Beman, too, accomplished an equally rare feat – winning the U.S. and British Amateurs.

In May 1959, at Royal St. George's in Sandwich, England, Beman, at 21, became the youngest American to win the British Amateur. Earlier that year, he was playing a mid-morning round with three of his University of Maryland teammates when he reached the ninth hole. Dudley ran down the fairway with news that the USGA had named Beman to the Walker Cup team that would compete at Muirfield in Scotland. (On the trip overseas, Harvie Ward issued nicknames for all the teammates, including "Snow White" for Nicklaus and "B-B Eyes" for Beman.) For eight straight years, Beman performed admirably in international matches and represented 11 U.S. amateur teams: four Walker Cups, four World Amateur Teams and three Americas' Cups.

The dates for the British Amateur were scheduled in proximity to the Walker Cup so competitors could travel to southern England and play at Royal St. George's on the Kent coast. But Beman was responsible for paying his caddie fees, which he couldn't afford. He was a college student, married with an infant daughter, and had rent to pay.

How much did Beman pinch his pennies? Tired of helping a young, struggling local golf icon start his "rattle trap of a car," the man who collected the money from the coin-operated washing machine in the basement of Beman's apartment told him to paint red nail polish on the quarters and dimes he used. That's how the coin collector, who happened to be an avid golf fan, distinguished Beman's coins and kindly returned the money back to him in his mail slot.

"That's how tight things were back then," Beman said.

To raise his British Amateur caddie fees, Beman bet on his game. He only had $30 to his name; his friend Dudley, $20. They pooled their money, arrived at the 9-hole course at D.C.'s National Naval Medical Center and challenged the pro and a local hotshot, whom they frequently played, to a match. Typically, the wager was $2. This time they raised the stakes. Beman laid all the money on the table.

"We made three trips around there and tripled our money. I raised $150 and stayed for the British Amateur," Beman recalled.

Beman cruised into the finals and beat his teammate,

43-year-old Philadelphia insurance broker Bill Hyndman III, 3 and 2. Beman was greeted with a hero's welcome at Washington National airport. His friends lifted him on their shoulders, his father handed him keys to a new car, and he was presented with a key to the city.

In 1960, Beman won the U.S. Amateur 6 and 4 over Robert Gardner in the final. In the afterglow of a hard-fought victory, Beman perfectly painted a champion's emotions. He told the USGA's *Golf Journal*, "I feel very much like that old flag flying from the pole over there – limp, tired, tattered but proud and flying high."

Beman won his second U.S. Amateur in 1963, defeating Dick Sikes, 2 and 1. Beman would have claimed a third U.S. Amateur in 1966, but he double bogeyed the 72nd hole at Merion Golf Club and lost an 18-hole playoff by a stroke to Canadian Gary Cowan. (The Amateur switched to stroke play from 1965 to 1972.) He also earned a spot in the U.S. Open in 17 out of 18 years beginning in 1955.

"Deane was always an over-achiever," Nicklaus said. "Deane had great self-confidence. He believed he could play and he could. Deane beat a lot of people who might not have taken him as seriously as they should. He just whipped them, because he was a great competitor and he loved to play."

As a 1958 U.S. Amateur quarterfinalist and member of the 1959 Walker Cup team, Beman earned his debut performance in the Masters. On that first occasion, Augusta National co-founder Clifford Roberts introduced Beman to Bobby Jones, who was having lunch. Beman thanked him for the warm welcome, but added he had been at Augusta the year before. Jones, a bit perplexed, replied, "I didn't see you here last year."

Beman said, "I know and neither did any of your security."

Beman confessed to Jones about his adventure at the 1958 Masters. Then a sophomore at the University of Maryland, Beman had just finishing competing in a college tournament in Miami. He and five teammates drove through the night to attend the Masters.

"We had $6 between us and a university credit card," he recalled. "We used the credit card for gas, Cokes and crackers, and saved the cash."

They arrived in Augusta at 5 a.m. and jumped the fence by the fifth tee, which at the time was no more than 10 yards from the boundary fence. A road passes beyond it. They hid until daylight and dodged Pinkertons all day.

"Tickets would've cost $7.50," remembered Carl Lohren, one of Beman's teammates and co-conspirators. "We walked over to No. 10 and caught Hogan there, and I saw the greatest shot I'd ever seen in golf on his approach."

They watched the tournament all day and witnessed Arnold Palmer earn his first green jacket. When Beman concluded how much better it was this time to be welcomed at Augusta's gates, Jones chuckled.

Beman qualified for the Masters 14 times. In April 1961 at Augusta, Beman fell into a practice round with Hogan the week before the Masters. Five decades later, Beman can still describe in perfect detail how he partnered with Dow Finsterwald against Hogan and Fred Hawkins for a $10 nassau. Beman's game had rusted over the winter, and he hit the ball all over the lot that day. But he scrambled out of trouble and rapped in the winning putt on 18. Hogan didn't like the look of Beman's game. After they finished, Beman overheard Hogan say, "We'll play at the same time tomorrow," and then with a glance toward Beman, "but not with him again."

Beman's face smiled as he always did when he delivered this kicker. If his playing days were numbered, no one could ever take that memory from him.

*   *   *

As Beman weighed his options – to play or administer – he couldn't help but think of the injuries that curtailed his playing career. He fractured his right wrist, practicing on the frozen ground at his home course in preparation for the 1963 Masters. (The setback forced him to decline the tournament invitation.)

Unfortunately, the injury persisted, and by the 1966 U.S. Amateur at Merion the wrist became so inflamed that he wore a cast around it, except when he played golf. Unable to pick the club up quickly, he couldn't hit a proper bunker shot. That wasn't a problem because he avoided the bunkers until the 71st and 72nd holes. But when he did, his limitations proved disastrous. He bladed shots on each and frittered away a 4-shot lead. He lost the next day in an 18-hole playoff.

"I've only thought about that tournament at least once a day ever since," he wrote in "The U.S. Amateur: The History and Personal Recollections of its Champions."

At his next tournament in Mexico City, Beman was leading the Mexico Amateur on the final day when the pain became unbearable. Still in the lead, he picked up on the 12th hole. Hand surgery in November 1966 led to worrying about whether he would ever play again. He determined if he could, he would see if his game matched up with the best at the top level. When he recovered sufficiently, he relinquished a spot on his fifth Walker Cup team, ending a distinguished amateur career to turn pro. He was married, raising four young children, and owned a sizable mortgage.

"I don't want to be one of those people who sit back in later years and tell their kids how great they could have been," Beman said at the time. "If I don't do it now, I'm afraid I never will."

Beman joined the Tour after graduating from the 1967 Qualifying School at the ripe old age of 29, leaving a cozy lifestyle that he earned working at his insurance firm. While still in college in 1958, Beman started as a life insurance sales agent. In 1960, he formed a successful insurance brokerage with his amateur golf partner, Bill Buppert; the firm, Beman & Buppert Associates conducted business in over 20 states. When he abandoned his role as arguably the world's premier amateur golfer, plenty of naysayers second-guessed his decision. "He's too small," they said of the 5-foot-7, 150-pound Beman. "He'll give up so much distance off the tees to people like Palmer and Nicklaus that he'll never cut it in the pros."

Beman had succeeded at everything he tried, but even his college teammate, Lohren, wondered if Beman could prosper against the pros.

"And Deane goes right out and gets his card, and in his third tournament he loses to Palmer in a playoff," Lohren said.

A popcorn hitter by today's standards, Beman compiled his record off accuracy, especially with fairway woods, and a deft putter. Indeed, in his rookie year, when he lost to Palmer in a playoff at the 1968 Bob Hope Desert Classic, Beman misfired with a 4-wood approach to the green while Palmer got home with a 5-iron. But that errant shot was a rare miss. At the 1967 U.S. Open at Baltusrol, his first as a pro, Beman dominated the 465-yard par-4, first hole with his trusty MacGregor 4-wood. On the morning of the first round, Beman holed his second shot from 220 yards for an eagle 2. (Former USGA executive director David Fay, a high school student at the time, witnessed the shot as a spectator and later obtained the club from Beman for the USGA Museum.) The next two days, playing the 4-wood again, Beman made a pair of birdies. On Sunday, he settled for a par.

"He could carve your holiday turkey with his 4-wood," *Golf Digest's* Nick Seitz wrote. "He also could make wedge shots sing the national anthem."

Of Beman's renowned short game, former secretary of the Royal & Ancient Golf Club of St. Andrews, Sir Michael Bonallack, recounted the time Nicklaus said to him during the 1961 Walker Cup, "It's just not fair the way Deane does it. If I could chip and putt like he could, I could beat anybody."

Widely considered one of the best putters on tour, Beman "could read a green the way an Indian could read a track in the snow," wrote Jim Murray of *The Los Angeles Times*.

But Beman bristled when critics dismissed his abilities. He detested being typecast as a "fringe player" and recoiled when called a "journeyman pro." Many players were more obviously gifted than he, but Beman made up for his physical limitations by being one of the most tenacious competitors on tour. He won five titles (four official and one unofficial).

"Deane had an expression on his face that I'd never seen on a golfer," said Tour veteran Ed Sneed. "By that I mean there was an intense focus on the shot at hand. I don't recall seeing anyone more bent on succeeding than him."

In an abbreviated six-year career, Beman collected more than his share of memorable moments. He called Lohren, his former University of Maryland teammate and noted instructor, from The Thunderbird Motel in Jacksonville in 1968 and asked, "Are you ready to do some basket weaving? Because I'm a basket case." The following season Beman won the Texas Open, his first title. He endured a 100-degree fever on the final day in cool, damp conditions to win the 1971 Quad Cities Classic, and bested a young, hotshot rookie named Tom Watson to defend his title the following year.

Beman led for two rounds and nearly won the 1969 U.S. Open at Champions Golf Club in Houston. He roomed with Lohren that week. On the ride back to their hotel from a casual Friday night dinner at Arby's, Beman remarked, "I'm going to win this one and about six more (titles this year)."

He might have won, except in the final round his putter let him down. Beman hit a 5-iron to 15 feet and finally canned a birdie putt on the last hole to close within a shot of Orville Moody, the surprise leader. Beman, Al Geiberger and Bob Rosburg at 282 shared the clubhouse lead and stood behind the scorer's tent, waiting for what they expected would be the first four-way playoff in U.S. Open history. Moody hit his 8-iron approach to 12 feet and lagged his putt two feet short. In later years, Moody would become a proficient putter on the Senior PGA Tour with a long putter, but at this stage in his career he used a cross-handed grip with unpredictable results.

"Nobody thought Moody would make that putt, not even he did," Beman chuckled. "We were all thinking playoff."

Moody "shook it off his blade," as Beman put it, and wiggled it in the right half of the cup for an improbable first and only victory. Murray, the colorful columnist of *The Los Angeles Times*, compared Moody's triumph to "unhitching a horse from a plow and having it win the Kentucky Derby."

Duke Butler, who was executive director of the Houston Golf Association for 14 years and later one of Beman's top lieutenants, claims, "The most important shot of 1969 was Orville Moody's 2-foot putt." It changed Beman's fate as well as the Tour's.

Back then, the PGA and U.S. Open champion earned a lifetime exemption on Tour. Had Beman won, Butler insists Beman never would have been interested in becoming Dey's successor. Beman, competitor that he was, likely would have played straight through until he was eligible for the Senior Tour at age 50.

"If Moody hadn't made that putt," Butler contends, "the world of golf would've been significantly different."

As a pro, Beman was hampered by physical ailments, too.

He cracked two ribs when he collided with Jim Colbert trying to catch a pop-up in a friendly softball game in Akron, Ohio in 1968. (Beman was pitching; Colbert was playing shortstop.) A litany of other injuries followed: a hernia operation in 1970; a severely cut right hand, from the middle of the thumb to his wrist, before the 1971 U.S. Open at Merion; and wrist surgery on his left hand in November 1972.

That same year, Beman was elected to the TPD policy board. Almost from the outset of his pro career, his fellow pros asked him to be a voice on tour operations. As a measure of their respect for Beman, they named him to the Young Players Advisory Council, even though he wasn't a voting member of the tour yet. (He was elected to the tour policy board in 1972.)

Nevertheless, Beman couldn't believe he was being tabbed Dey's successor. After a week's deliberation, Beman arranged a call with Austin and Dey, and politely declined. Beman didn't agonize over the decision. Though many would have been seduced by the position's power and fame, Beman felt he had fallen short of his goals as a professional. He still had unfinished business as a player.

"I was very flattered, but I'd never been a failure at anything," Beman said. "To that point, it (1973) was my worst year of competition, and I felt like I was failing. I didn't want to walk away."

While Austin and Dey considered the possibilities of launching a national search for a replacement, Beman's game took flight again. His hand healed, his touch around the green resurfaced. He won another tournament, the Shrine-Robinson Open Golf Classic in July. The victory earned him exempt status for two years and vaulted him well inside the Top 60 of the tour's money list. He no longer felt like a failure. The next week, he began reconsidering the possibilities of being responsible for shaping the future of professional golf. The 35-year-old Beman posed two soul-searching questions to himself: "What am I going to do with my life? And how can I contribute most – as a player or a commissioner?"

In Napa, Calif., for the Kaiser International Open in October 1973, Beman scribbled his career objectives on paper. For starters, he wanted to win $20,000 in his last four events, which was the equivalent of notching a win or multiple top-5 finishes in today's era. In 1974, he envisioned a victory before the Masters, winning one major, and three other tournaments that year. In 1975, he set a goal of two titles before the Masters, two majors and five tournaments that year. When he reviewed the list, he came to an important conclusion.

"I said to myself, 'That won't do,' " Beman recalled. "I was 35, and I had endured all these operations. Even at the pace I outlined, I didn't have enough time left. I could never be what I wanted to be, which is one of the greatest players that ever lived."

His decision pivoted on this realization: He could contribute more to the sport as a commissioner than he ever could as a player. Beman called Austin and asked to be considered for the position. Lohren still marvels at Beman's decision. "Not too many people retire when they're No. 26 on the money list," he said.

Colbert never forgot Beman's excitement once he made up his mind. Colbert just had competed in Australia. He'd flown direct to Los Angeles then connected to Atlanta, caught a puddle jumper to Charlotte and driven the rest of the way to Pinehurst, N.C. Colbert had traveled for 45 consecutive hours when he arrived on Sunday, Nov. 4, for the tour's policy board meeting ahead of the World Open Golf Championship.

"I just wanted to check into the Pinehurst Inn and get to bed," Colbert recalled. "Hell, Deane met me at the parking lot."

They stood face to face and Beman said, "I'm on the list for the job now."

Confidence swelled in Beman's voice. Colbert looked him dead in the eye and replied, "You'd be good at it. I'll support you."

After a fitful sleep, Colbert showed up at 11 a.m., more than 2 hours late for the policy board meeting. But he arrived just in time to hear Dey publicly announce his intentions to step down and for Beman's candidacy to take flight. A special committee was formed comprising Austin, Dey, players Charles Coody and Lionel Hebert, and PGA president Bill Clarke to review candidates and recommend a successor to the board.

During that same meeting, one of Dey's most significant contributions to the Tour passed: He conceived staging its own stand-alone competition, the Tournament Players Championship, which today is one of the organization's most valuable assets. It debuted the following year in Atlanta. In the early years of the TPC, the winner was awarded a plaque called the Joseph C. Dey, Jr. Trophy. Among the board members who voted in favor of the concept was Beman. Scarcely eight weeks later he was named Dey's successor.

* * *

It's been said that two professional golfers can't even agree if it was raining if they were standing under the same umbrella. But when conversation shifted to Dey's replacement, tour members were almost unanimous in the belief that the selection of a player or former player as their leader would be difficult. They worried that such an individual would struggle to command the respect and authority of the other players, who had just been his peers. For more than two months, they discussed replacing Dey with a businessman who could tell them what to do and make them like it. The five-man board, however, interviewed: Beman, Dan Sikes and Jay Hebert, all players; Jack Tuthill, the tour's tournament director since 1964; James DeLeone, an Ohio-based lawyer who represented players, including Tom Weiskopf; and Nelson Harris, a banking executive from Philadelphia, who was affiliated with the tour as sponsor of the IVB-Philadelphia Classic. Based on his experience, Tuthill, a former FBI agent and no-nonsense guy, seemed a logical choice, but it was Harris who emerged as a worthy opponent to Beman. Of the candidates, only DeLeone is still alive. He interviewed in Hilton Head Island, S.C., during the Heritage Classic (which was played in September in 1973), and said he never gave the job serious consideration.

"I was just a stalking horse," DeLeone said. "Deane was their handpicked guy. Anyone close to the tour knew that."

The finalists were interviewed by the full board in Atlanta on December 18,1973. Beman prepared with great labor and zeal. It was late morning when he stepped inside Coca-Cola's board room. Beman began by presenting a 20-page, bound black book that included letters of recommendation and his views on the game and the job. He was the only candidate to present a written plan. All these years later, Beman still treasures his original copy. On the opening page, he outlined what would become the blueprint for his 20-year tenure under the headline, "How I View The Position of Commissioner."

His key points:
- To Carry Out the Policies Set Forth By the Tournament Policy Board.
- To Maintain the Proper Relationship Between the TPD and the PGA So That the TPD Always Is Representative of the PGA.
- To Keep Abreast of all Information Relative to the Game, the Running and Promotion of Professional Golf So That the Policy Board Will Have Adequate Information on Which to Base Its Decision.
- To Preserve the Interests of the Tournament Player and Balance Those Interests With Those of the Tournament Sponsors.
- To Preserve and Protect the Integrity of the Game of Golf.

Beman captivated the group. He laid out his feelings for the game, the position, and even touched on the uncertainty caused by the energy crisis then rocking the nation. He explained that he understood the players' problems because they had been his problems, too. He told the board he viewed the tour as a public trust. He preached discipline, accountability and a more business-like approach. The more he talked, the more he revealed his uncommon business acumen. No one under consideration had learned to negotiate the world of business and shared his intimate knowledge of professional golf. The meeting lasted an hour. When they excused Beman to hold a caucus, the men in the room shot knowing glances at each other.

"He had a notebook there with where we are today, and where we want to be so many years later. It was a roadmap," Coody remembered. "That's how things grow and become successful. It was impressive."

Even Lionel Hebert – whose brother, Jay, was a candidate – was convinced. "He said, 'Deane's our man,' " Coody added.

By the time he returned home that same day to Bethesda, Md., Beman was offered the job. Beman dissolved his interest in his insurance practice and his ownership stake in Con-Sole Golf Corp., a golf club manufacturing company, upon taking the commissioner post, and was elected on Dec. 28 in Atlanta. A press release was issued the following day at 3 p.m. Beman was hired for a three-year term for a salary of $75,000 annually, with the TPD holding an option to renew for at least three more years. Never before (and likely never again) had a player of such repute shortened his playing career to become his sport's principal administrator.

During his playing days, Beman gained Dey as an admirer. As his successor Dey continued his support: "He is highly qualified, knows the tour inside out and is bright and forward looking." Dey added he "couldn't think of anyone more qualified than Deane."

"The second most important thing Dey did as commissioner was to urge us to hire Deane Beman as his successor," wrote Bob Goalby in a 2009 article in *Sports Illustrated*. "At first none of us could see the wisdom of this move."

Indeed, the decision to hire Beman wasn't greeted warmly. From the beginning, there were rumblings of resentment. None of it, however, bothered Beman.

"Look," Beman told reporters in February 1974, "I'm sure some of the guys are disappointed, and it was hard for me to give up playing. I think I know what's good for the game and what's good for the tour. I'm going to be fair and go by the rules. I hope to earn the respect of the players, if I don't have it now."

Dey officially stepped down at the end of the month, but worked with Beman in the interest of an orderly transfer. It didn't take long for some players, who thought Beman was cast in a role beyond his experience and capacity, to establish who they thought was boss. Shortly after Beman started, he received a memorandum from former Masters and PGA champion Doug Ford: "We the following players would like the following: job description of each employee, salary of each position, and estimated budget for first year of operation."

It was signed by players Goalby, Lou Graham, Jerry McGee,

Andy North, Eddie Pearce, Bob Rosburg, J.C. Snead, Leonard Thompson, Art Wall, and Bob Wynn.

"That was the first thing that basically said, 'You're not doing anything unless we know about it, boy,' " Beman recalled.

Not everyone, however, was sorry to see Dey go.

"He's not one of us," a tour pro groused to *Golf Magazine* shortly before he resigned. "You talk to him and you feel like you're at a Billy Graham Crusade."

"He struck fear in me, kind of like my first sergeant in the Army," said Larry Nelson, a Tour rookie when Dey stepped down. "Deane understood the game and what it meant to be a player."

When Beman succeeded Dey on March 1, 1974, he presided over 27 employees – 12 in the field and 15 working out of its N.Y. headquarters. In one of his earliest moves, Beman re-located the tour's base to a one-bedroom apartment – until its leased, converted dentist's suite at the Kenwood Apartments on River Road in Bethesda, Md., became available. From this unassuming nerve center, Beman began building the tour into the organization it is today. When he stepped down June 1, 1994, the Tour owned its Ponte Vedra Beach, Fla., headquarters, employed more than 2,000 people, and total revenues soared from $3.9 million to $229 million. In time, Goalby and an overwhelming majority of the membership would be indebted to Beman's leadership.

Lohren believes such gratitude – and more is deserved: "All the money these guys are making, they ought to bow down and kiss his feet – every last one of them."

LEARNING ON THE JOB

W hen Deane Beman took over as commissioner on March 1, 1974, he inherited a fledgling tour that still in many ways was a loosely knit association of tournaments. He faced pressing demands, including having to make a tournament schedule and negotiate a television contract for the 1975 season. Not to mention the unexpected.

Shortly after he started, Beman was surprised to learn that the Tournament Players Division of the PGA was organized as a for-profit corporation. On his desk sat a series of checks for New York City taxes, New York State taxes and federal taxes that awaited his signature. They totaled $96,000. He read the documents, shook his head and wondered, "What are we doing paying taxes?"

He was also asked to sign a check for nearly $90,000 to the PGA of America for something notated as "royalties." Though the tour barely had $400,000 in total assets, Beman thought he was spending nearly half of that sum for unnecessary reasons.

Beman pored over the TPD's incorporation papers during a long flight. As a former insurance broker, Beman understood the ins and outs of nonprofit associations. He represented the National Third Class mail users and got IRS approval for the first deferred compensation plan without a forfeiture clause.

Beman thought the TPD could qualify as a nonprofit association, too. When he returned from the trip he went to the TPD's attorney, Sam Gates, a principal at the prominent law firm of Debevoise, Plimpton, Lyons and Gates and asked for an explanation. Beman wasn't satisfied with the perfunctory answers from his legal counsel.

"He conveyed to me, 'Hey kid, we know what we're doing. Why don't you just go back and run golf tournaments?' " Beman said.

At the time, Beman was moving the tour's headquarters to office space outside of Washington, D.C. It happened to be along the route to work driven by his friend, tax attorney Bob Schnabel, who in the years to come often made a detour there for a cup of coffee. But on this occasion, Beman phoned him looking for a second opinion and asked him to visit on an urgent matter. "Can we as an association of players be just like these other nonprofits?"

Schnabel answered, "Yes," but cautioned it would be difficult to gain such status because the TPD had five years of history of paying taxes as a for-profit organization.

"Do you mean to tell me if we were starting five years ago, fresh, we would have had no problem?" Beman asked.

Again, Schnabel replied, "Yes." Beman pictured endless rounds of petitions and appeals, and potentially years in court fighting with the Internal Revenue Service, which never takes kindly to losing a taxpaying customer.

"Let me tell you what we are going to do," Beman said. "Get your secretary, your wife, and put together a board of directors."

They formed a new organization, starting from scratch as if it was creating a rival tour. On May 3, 1974, Beman held a conference call with the board, who approved submitting an application to the IRS. The board filed a charter in Maryland to be a brand-new tour called the Tournament Golfers' Association of America. That was its corporate name; to the public it still was known as the TPD. Schnabel made sure to include the word association in the name.

"That's what we were claiming to be and that's what it is really," he said. "As the saying goes, it had the added side benefit of being true."

The PGA insisted the TPD not cite it as an example of a comparable tax-exempt organization in its application. The three PGA officers on the board were concerned the TPD's request could jeopardize the PGA's tax-exempt status.

"I was out on my own here and was looking for a little help but that help wasn't going to come from the PGA of America," Beman said.

While the tour was waiting for an answer, it faced an unexpected issue. On Aug. 13, 1974, Beman received an anti-trust inquiry from the U.S. Justice Department regarding the TPD's "conflicting event and television release rules." This rule served as the backbone of the TPD's ability to negotiate with tournament sponsors for events and television networks for broadcasting those events. The rights fees collected from the networks made up 80 percent of the TPD's total income, which supported its operation and helped local community tournament sponsors fund purses. Without this rule the TPD couldn't negotiate with others for the collective benefit of the players. In Beman's mind, this was a not too subtle shot over the bow at a "green" and untested commissioner by players' agents who coveted recovering some of the media rights for the professional golfers they represented.

At the Aug. 23 tour policy board meeting, Beman updated members on their filing as well as received permission to replace Gates' law firm with Rogers & Wells. The change caused some dismay for tour veterans who valued Gates' role in the tour's breakaway from the PGA. But Beman sought a savvy, Washington law firm to handle the Justice Department inquiry and found one in Rogers & Wells. The firm's namesake was none other than the honorable William P. Rogers, former attorney general of the United States under President Eisenhower.

Less than a month later, on Sept. 17, 1974, the IRS approved the TGA's application by return mail without requiring a hearing. Then, Beman received approval from the tour policy board during the Oct. 29 meeting to transfer its board of directors and all the administrative staff to the new corporation. He notified the IRS that it was disbanding the old organization. The move was done tax-free. The cost? A mere $2,700 in attorneys' fees. Said Beman: "I did that without the cooperation and support of our highly-paid former counsel."

That's how the tour became a 501-c6 organization that in IRS tax code parlance falls under the tax heading of a trade association or a business league. As a nonprofit, the TPD is permitted to retain income that might otherwise be taxable by Federal or state governments. It's one of several moves Beman orchestrated that would transform the tour's financial landscape.

Next Beman asked Schnabel if the 501-c6 status applied to The Tournament Players Championship too. Beman knew that the PGA ran the PGA Championship as part of its for-profit company. Instead of settling for the status quo, Beman again pursued a different approach. He believed that running a tournament was part and parcel of a tour's operation, and therefore, was "substantially related" to its exempt purposes, according to IRS regulations.

"What we wanted was to get a determination from the IRS stating that we could conduct the tournament and it wouldn't be considered unrelated business," Beman explained.

The tour won on this front, too. The move from a profit to nonprofit has been worth a lot of money over the years to the Tour, its players, and its community-based tournaments, Beman said. The Tour's financial department estimates that the figure exceeds $500 million.

"It gave us the ability to pass along these hundreds of millions of dollars to our players in prize money and retirement benefits and to local charities through tournament organizations," Beman said.

In the estimation of Mickey Powell, a past president of the PGA and former member of the Tour policy board, "If you want to get into dollars, that's the most significant thing he did by far. And nobody knows about it."

Beman shared his success with the PGA, showing the association how some of its for-profit ventures – the PGA Championship, Ryder Cup, and PGA Merchandise Show – could benefit by changing their status. Beman believed these projects were also substantially related to the PGA's exempt purposes, and suggested the PGA use the TPD as Exhibit A to support its case.

Another success that went unnoticed was Rogers & Wells' handling of the Justice Department inquiry. The case was closed after the Justice Department accepted that the conflicting event rule was essential to the viability of professional golf as a sport. Thus began the tour's long association with a law firm that helped the tour in so many ways.

If rectifying the TPD's tax status took smarts, then fixing its television contracts took guts. Beman may not have been schooled in the intricacies of television negotiating, but he was shrewd enough to perceive a flawed model.

When Beman took the reigns as commissioner on March 1, 1974, the TPD existed on one-year TV agreements. ABC televised the bulk of the tour's coverage, including most of the early-season events. These tournaments scored the highest television ratings, but ABC didn't pay appreciably more for them. At the time, the network also held the rights to three of the four majors – the U.S. Open, British Open and PGA Championship – none of which the TPD operated or received a rights fee for its players' participation. Then ABC required advertisers who bought time on the majors also to support the network's TPD events.

The balance of the TPD events received some network coverage. NBC broadcast the Dean Martin Tucson Open and the Bob Hope Desert Classic. CBS also provided coverage at two tournaments – the Glen Campbell L.A. Open and the Jackie Gleason Inverrary Classic – and had a long-running relationship with the Masters as well as the CBS Golf Classic. Hughes Television Network did a handful of events, but its partnership with the tour was a syndicated deal producing marginal income.

As Beman prepared to negotiate next year's deal with ABC, he discovered the network's contract guaranteed first right of negotiation and first right of refusal. That meant even if Beman received a more attractive offer from another network, ABC still received, as he put it, "a second bite at the apple." In short, it robbed the tour of much of its bargaining power.

"We paid dearly for that," he said.

The short-term nature of the tour's TV contracts didn't help matters, either. Negotiations, which usually began 9 months before the new season, didn't leave much time to work out an alternative deal if the networks rebuffed their offer.

To Joe Dey, dealing with the networks was easy. Dey had a longstanding relationship with ABC, stemming from his days negotiating rights fees for the U.S. Open, which even then was the USGA's most profitable venture. Before retiring,

Dey "educated" Beman on the television renewal process and bragged that the rights fee he asked for had never been rejected. Beman thought to himself: "Maybe you never asked for enough."

Indeed, Dey conceded that the pursuit of financial gains for his players was a foreign endeavor. "It was the first time I had to negotiate for anything," Dey said in *Golf World* upon his retirement."At the USGA it was a take-it-or-leave-it basis, in the pure air of amateurism. We were geared for what's best for the game. With the pros it was what's best for the players at the same time."

As a result of ABC's sweetheart deal, Beman learned that even if the other networks were interested, none of them would bother to enter into a bidding war. The bottom line: The tour's TV situation left Beman handcuffed.

"Here we are in the second quarter of 1974 without a television contract for '75 and our backs are up against the wall with no time to negotiate on our terms," Beman said.

He extended all three contracts for the 1975 season, settling for the same "business as usual," token increase Dey had been accepting. But Beman immediately began mapping out a different strategy for the future. For starters, the NY-based television consultant employed by Dey to market the TPD's rights decided to retire. Beman realized he needed help.

So in late 1974, Beman asked Steve Reid, one of his bridge partners from his tour days and closest friends, to retire from playing and become the tour's in-house television coordinator. Not only did Reid learn that NBC was interested in doing some more golf, he discovered that CBS – particularly its producer, Frank Chirkinian – sought a higher profile in the game, too.

CBS lacked interest in more live TPD coverage for one simple reason: the success of the CBS Golf Classic. The 13-week series, which pitted most of the best tour players in a match-play event, was filmed over less than two weeks at Firestone Country Club in Akron, Ohio. With one set up at one golf course, CBS essentially had devised its own sanctioned version of tour golf on the cheap. The players pocketed a share of a purse that grew as high as $225,000. The only loser in this equation was the tour, which collected a negligible rights fee of $15,000. That sum covered the travel expense of its rules officials, and not much more.

"That's all we got," Beman said. "It was foolish on our part to allow this giveaway to CBS."

Beman understood that the telecast was popular and promoted golf, but knew it prevented CBS from becoming a rival to ABC. So Beman hinted to CBS that the CBS Golf Classic might not be renewed for the 1976 season. The network responded by picking up two more live events on the 1975 schedule and raising its investment to a total of $500,000 in 1975.

"CBS probably thought that if it bought some live golf it would be able to keep the profitable CBS Golf Classic intact," Beman mused.

Beman, however, canceled the 13-week CBS series. The decision angered CBS and the players, who liked cashing the network's check. Based on Reid's key insights, Beman gambled that CBS, which already had established a golf audience, would need golf programming and have little choice except to negotiate for TPD's live events. He guessed right. In mid-'75, Beman asked the board to approve negotiating a multi-year deal.

"It wasn't a fair fight with the networks doing a year-to-year deal," Beman said. "The short-term deal was all to their advantage at the negotiation table."

For the first time, CBS emerged as a factor and agreed to a three-year contract worth $2.3 million annually for 12 tournaments. It was the TPD's first substantial rights fee increase. By eliminating the CBS Golf Classic, the tour netted eight more live events on CBS and an additional $1.83 million annually.

The tour then negotiated a three-year agreement with ABC for 1976-78, and removed the first right of negotiation and first right of refusal clause from the contract, according to the May 27 Atlanta board meeting. By the fall of '75, Beman had secured three-year agreements through 1978 with CBS for 12 tournaments annually and with ABC and NBC for 7 events each.

This set the stage for negotiations on a far more even-playing field. For rights covering 1979-81, CBS made a major play. The network submitted a preemptive bid for 18 events, including many of ABC's longtime staples. ABC didn't respond well to the news. By renouncing its allegiance to the network, the tour had committed the equivalent of high treason. ABC issued a press release that it had dropped the tour, and the story was splashed on the back pages of *The Daily News*. ABC continued to broadcast the majors, but it abandoned the tour beginning in 1979 for a number of years.

"They'll be back," Beman told Jim Colbert, who served three separate stints as a player director on the tour policy board.

"He knew we'd still do better with the other two networks, even with ABC not bidding," Colbert recalled. "And you know what? He was right."

Beman also braced for a fight over distribution of television revenues. Several tournaments were permitted to negotiate their own television deals. This undermined Beman's effort to pool the rights and hammer out the best collective deal. Dey also had recognized this problem and already had begun conversations with tournament hosts such as Bing Crosby and Bob Hope, with ambitions of bringing their events into the tour's fold. But Dey ultimately caved, accepting minimal monetary concessions that were Band-Aid measures at best.

When Beman surveyed the situation, he didn't like what he found. In 1974, the Andy Williams San Diego Open, the Westchester Open and Tournament of Champions had 70/30 deals, which allowed the tournament to keep 70 percent of the TV rights fee and the tour settled for 30 percent. The Bing Crosby Pebble Beach National Pro-Am was even less favorable to the tour: an 85/15 split. The Bob Hope Desert Classic received $222,500 of its $250,000 rights fee from NBC, and the Kemper Open paid a flat fee of $25,000 annually to the tour.

The special TV deals confounded Beman. None of the tour's most valuable rights fees went into the television fund to help support other events. Never one to mince words, Beman painted this conundrum as a classic case of "How do I make chicken salad out of this chicken shit I've been dealt?"

The TPD, he determined, had to control all the television rights so that the television money benefited all of the tournaments. At his first board meeting as commissioner on May 9, Beman gained approval to establish a timetable requiring the renegade tournaments to join the television pool fund.

"We're going to have the same deal for everybody," Beman declared.

He proposed a 3-year phase out for the tournaments in question. In 1975, they would keep 70 percent of the television revenue and the TPD would receive 30 percent. The following year, the tournaments got 50 percent, the TPD netted 30 percent, and 20 percent was earmarked for the television fund. By 1977, all of the rights-fee money would be administered through the TPD's collective TV fund. The Tournament of Champions was the first to cooperate. Many tournament organizers didn't like the change, Beman pointed out, but they agreed it should be done. But not everyone fell in step.

Crosby, the crooner, and Hope, the comedian, two revered personalities, weren't happy. They were the kings of the winter tour and they knew it. Besides the Masters and U.S. Open their tournaments fetched the highest ratings.

"Crosby was an icon. He and Hope had their friends and allies," Beman recalled. "They played hard ball, trying to get the players on their side. My administration took a lot of heat."

In a show of defiance, Crosby presented his case to the press. He expressed outrage that Beman would deprive his tournament's ability to generate revenue for charitable causes. But Beman stood his ground to the celebrity hosts, and bluffed that the players supported the new TV strategy and wouldn't attend their tournaments unless the hosts agreed to the new terms. He couldn't be sure how the players would respond. What he did know was that all of the events supported local causes. "I'm not going to sit back and try to decide whose charity is most worthy," Beman said.

He insisted success needed to be shared across the board to ensure financial stability for all the tournaments rather than a select few. Beman believed pooling television rights revenue was the fastest way to increase prize money and protect charitable donations.

"One of the best things about Deane as a leader was he didn't care about whether feathers would be ruffled," said Tim Smith, his former deputy commissioner. "He knew where the Tour needed to go and he wasn't going to be discouraged."

Other achievements laid the foundation for what was to come. On May 27, 1975, the board approved Beman's request to change the public name of the association from Tournament Players Division to the PGA Tour. "This was our first real step in setting the framework for branding in the future," Beman said.

Of course, not everything worked out, or went exactly as planned. But in order to move forward, Beman sometimes had to backtrack. For example, he discovered the independence the players thought they had achieved with the signing of the Statement of Principles in 1968 had required another negotiation. When Dey attended the joint board meeting of the PGA Executive Committee and the TPD's board of directors during his second week on the job in March 1969, PGA president Leo Fraser explained that the TPD was "to be only an informal arrangement under which the tournament players could have identity and that policy matters would rest in the tournament policy board." In short, the PGA's Executive Committee could disband the TPD's board and assume control of its contracts any time it wanted. The tour was "a division" of the PGA, and the PGA had legal control of it. These terms were unacceptable to Dey.

"It turned out the PGA had 'out-lawyered' the players," Beman said.

The minutes from the meeting held March 10-12, 1969, at the PGA's headquarters in Palm Beach Gardens, Fla., indicate Dey was shocked and dismayed that such matters hadn't been resolved prior to his employment. He asked to be excused from the discussions.

Reflecting upon what transpired that day, Beman recreates the scene in which the PGA angled for what he describes as "the big steal." Billy Casper, Gardner Dickinson, Jack Nicklaus and Dan Sikes Jr., were the player directors in attendance to represent the touring pro's interests.

"From the minutes of the meeting, it's clear that the PGA officers told Dey and the players, 'We understand what you want. We'll give you the right to form your own legal entity, but that's going to cost you,' " Beman said.

Final independence came with a staggering price in terms of today's tour. Fraser raised the topic of the tour paying a royalty at the Dec. 18, 1968, meeting in New York. Nicklaus attended that meeting. So did Beman, representing the Young Players Advisory Council. Initially, the PGA demanded 15 percent of all TPD revenues in exchange for approving a separate corporation to protect the players interest. The Tour's lawyer, Sam Gates, who negotiated the annual payment, sliced the figure in half to 7.5 percent of TPD revenues. In exchange for the reduction, the tour offered the World Series of Golf rights fee to the PGA. Before the PGA agreed to the terms, it also extracted the television negotiation rights to the PGA Championship from the tour. Its rights fee already was allocated to the PGA so the tour relented.

"Joe Dey was right. The tour must have its separate and independent legal status, but he never should have let Gates handle the negotiations. He was the one who agreed to this foolish arrangement in the first place," Beman said.

Beman decided the 7.5 percent licensing fee of the TPD's revenues needed to be rectified and fast. His vision of the Tour was to stand alongside other major sports in finances. The licensing fee had the potential to be huge in the future.

"I thought it would be untenable for that kind of money to pass through to the PGA as a result of this agreement," he said. "So I decided I had to clean up that mess."

On May 21, 1974, Beman met privately with the PGA's president Henry Poe and executive director Mark Cox before the tour's board meeting. He told them that most players had no knowledge about the royalty. But if they found out, Beman cautioned, another feud between the two organizations likely would erupt.

"If I had been on the board I would've raised all hell about it," said Don January, a player director for several terms including during the breakaway. "I remember when I heard it I thought, 'What are we doing that for?' "

To this day, the reasons why the Tour never really gained its independence in the original Statement of Principles remains shrouded in mystery. "I could never get to the bottom of this," he said. "But what difference did it make. I solved the problem."

This much everyone agrees upon. To buy itself out of a potentially expensive arrangement with the PGA, Beman crafted an ingenious deal. He recast the World Series of Golf from its longtime format as a four-man, 36-hole exhibition of that season's major winners into an end-of-the-year event after the PGA Championship. At the time, interest in the exhibition had waned. Ratings were down and NBC hinted that it would lower the next rights fee. Technically, neither the TPD nor the PGA owned the World Series of Golf. Cox Broadcasting did. It paid the PGA a sanctioning fee comparable to what the TPD received for the CBS Golf Classic.

"This property was diminishing in value," Beman explained. "It was something the PGA couldn't advance, but I could."

Beman envisioned the tournament schedule leading to a climax with the World Series of Golf held in September just as the NFL season kicked off. He would invite foreign winners to create a true World Series of Golf. It was Beman's first recognition that competitive golf would evolve into a global game.

Beman pitched the plan to CBS, which bit at the opportunity. Beman proposed sharing revenue from a new and expanded World Series of Golf with the PGA in exchange for terminating the royalty payment. He guaranteed the PGA the first $125,000 received, which exceeded the current royalty payment; revenue above and beyond that amount would be split evenly. The PGA's Cox liked the concept and simply planned to take Beman's idea and run with it. After all, the exhibition was a revenue generator for the PGA, not the Tour.

Beman countered, "Like hell. I'm not going to let you. You've got a four-man exhibition. If you want to do any more than that, you'll have to get our approval and we're not going to give it to you."

Eventually they formed a partnership and Beman acquired the World Series of Golf from Cox Broadcasting (no relation to the PGA's Mark Cox) for $160,000. The royalty payment to the PGA was no more.

"That's one of the things that always rankled the PGA," Beman said. "We bought ourselves out of the royalty payment with their own property."

On March 4, 1975, Beman received board approval to stage three seasonal championships – winter, summer and fall. In a letter to tour members, he expressed his enthusiasm: "What once was a series of events with highlights here and there is now becoming a complete Tour of championship tournaments." He constructed the fall package around the new World Series of Golf, a special limited field event.

"We were trying to make it be what is now the Tour Championship," Beman said.

It appeared to be a windfall for all parties involved. Beman reached a handshake agreement in February 1975 with media mogul Walter Annenberg to have TV Guide sponsor the seasonal championships and World Series of Golf. Beman was introduced by his attorney William Rogers to Annenberg. When Rogers was secretary of state under President Nixon, Rogers recommended appointing Annenberg as U.S. ambassador to the Court of St. James (U.K.). A noted golf enthusiast, Annenberg played frequently at his 9-hole course on his Palm Springs, Calif., estate. As part of a sponsorship deal totaling $500,000, the winner of each season would earn a prize of $100,000, and the overall champion of the World Series of Golf would bank $200,000.

"That was a lot of money back then," Beman said.

Another benefit: the Tour would get valuable promotion – a page each week touting that week's tournament and telecast – in *TV Guide*, a "bible" to more than 10 million subscribers.

More importantly, for players and fans, Beman wanted the World Series of Golf to be played at Shinnecock Hills Golf Club, a links-style course located in the town of Southampton on Long Island, and acknowledged to be the oldest formally organized golf club in the U.S. The Tour could've been at the site of the 1896 U.S. Open a decade before the USGA hosted the national championship there again. (The Walker Cup was held there in 1977.) Beman had a handshake agreement with Virgil Sherrill, the club's president known as "Mr. Shinnecock," and an old friend of Beman's from playing together at Seminole Golf Club, Sherrill's Florida winter retreat.

"I thought the World Series of Golf should be in the New York market," Beman said. "I thought Shinnecock was a throwback, walk-into-history type place."

Beman coveted the site. He knew landing such a prestigious host course at the tournament's outset would give it instant credibility. The Tour's board approved the new PGA agreement to replace the 7.5 percent royalty as well as the three-year deal with Annenberg. Because the sponsorship of the World Series of Golf fell under their partnership, the agreement required the PGA's Executive Committee to vote in favor of it, too. It passed. But PGA president Henry Poe made a public announcement before the deal was consummated, a move Beman suspects Poe made to give the PGA a public relations boost and credit for striking the new deal. Poe, however, clumsily spoiled Annenberg's planned press conference. An enraged Annenberg had second thoughts about entering a relationship with what he called a "rinky dink" organization like the PGA and scotched the deal.

"That was a terrible day," Beman said, putting it bluntly.

Without *TV Guide* footing the bill, going to Shinnecock proved financially risky. Beman tried in vain to secure another sponsor. He still wanted to proceed with Shinnecock, but the PGA balked. The World Series of Golf returned to Firestone, which that year hosted the American Golf Classic on the North Course and World Series of Golf on the South Course in back to back weeks. Beman never landed another sponsor for the seasonal championships and the concept fizzled.

"It's a real shame," he said. "Shinnecock would've been fantastic. It was a great event anyway, but it could've been spectacular."

At the time, few appreciated Beman's coup in eliminating the royalty payment to the PGA and the savings it portended for the Tour. In late 2010, Beman asked the Tour's financial department to review the Tour's annual reports and estimate how much money the Tour would've paid to the PGA over the years under the original agreement approved by the first Tour policy board, which included player directors Casper, Dickinson, Nicklaus, and Sikes. The amount is staggering. The Tour estimates payments of between $600 million and $900 million would have passed to the PGA through 2010 – monies that go into prize money, the player retirement plan, and local tournament charities – if not for Beman's wisdom in striking a better deal for the players. Of his many accomplishments big and small, this may be Beman's least known and most overlooked in his story.

*   *   *

Beman faced other tournament issues too. In May 1975, he canceled the popular Tournament of Champions at La Costa Resort & Spa in Carlsbad, Calif., saying its format conflicted with the new World Series of Golf. But in reality, Beman took such severe action after *Penthouse* magazine wrote a revealing story linking La Costa's owners to a mob-connected gambling ring. He believed it was paramount to protect the tour's charter, which included strong anti-gambling provisions. But tour pros, upset about the lost playing opportunity, voiced their discontent. "Why not just cancel Christmas, too?" protested player Jerry McGee.

Led by La Costa club pro Tommy Jacobs, who used to play the Tour, players organized a petition to save the event. On May 27, players requested a meeting with Beman at the Atlanta tour stop. "We aren't questioning his authority," one pro told *Golf World*, "but we are questioning the way he handled the whole affair."

Beman absorbed the criticism and conceded to the players' demands by reinstating the winners-only affair. He referred to this open revolt as an early battle lost in which he learned that policy and popularity of a decision many times were not in harmony.

"But I felt if you stand for something, then you really have to stand for it when push comes to shove," he said. "I did not prevail on that one and got my nose bloodied a little bit."

It was his first public rebuke and a lesson learned.

"To the outside world you may be the commissioner of golf," Beman said, "but to the players you are the man that works for them."

He encountered similar resistance when he tried to advance one of Joe Dey's most controversial concepts: designated tournaments. Dey hatched the idea as a way to ensure strong fields for tournament sponsors. Tour players are independent contractors, and they treasure their freedom to make their schedule as much as their trophies. Dey campaigned hard for the players to relinquish some of this inalienable right. At first, Dey proposed 15 such events, promising purses of at least $200,000. The players opposed it. "To designate certain tournaments is to downgrade others," Gary Player said in *Sports Illustrated*.

When he announced his retirement in 1973, Dey acknowledged his failure to push through designated tournaments as one of his major disappointments.

"Our members are independent contractors, but they must understand, and I hope this doesn't come to them the hard way, that they must oblige the sponsor and it is not one-sided," he told *Golf World*.

Beman supported Dey's idea during his stint as a player director on the policy board. As commissioner, Beman scaled back expectations and settled for three tournaments – The Colonial National Invitational, Kemper Open and World Golf Hall of Fame Open – the first year. When the experiment debuted in May 1974 at Colonial, it summoned a command performance. Nicklaus played in Fort Worth for the first time in four years. Ticket sales skyrocketed. "The whole week added up to a designated triumph," *Sports Illustrated's* Dan Jenkins wrote.

But soon it became apparent that its history would be brief, inconsequential and considered a failure. In short, Dey's philosophy was based on a faulty assumption that if more of the better players showed up, the rest would fall into place. The faulty part of it was he assigned the designation to the best tournaments.

"They already had the best players," Beman argued. "They didn't have a problem. They didn't need help anyway."

"The burden fell on the top 5 to 10 players," said Hale Irwin, a three-time U.S. Open champion. "Deane looked at what other opportunities the Tour had to grow the business. Maybe they wouldn't be just in the playing side."

The number of designated tournaments was reduced to two the following year and subsequently used to ensure top Tour members returned immediately to the U.S. following the British Open. By the end of the 1977 season, designated tournaments were a thing of the past.

"It didn't do anything to make the tournaments better," Beman said. "It only gave the sponsors' more players but it didn't do anything on the ground to better organize, better promote, better market the tournament."

In retrospect, Beman is quick to point out his own naïveté of the problems and challenges of occupying the Tour's top post.

"I had just won my fourth tournament on Tour and had a fully-exempt, two-year status and I traded it for the job of commissioner," he said with a smile. "Looking back on it, you just wonder what I was thinking about."

Indeed, Beman had to face a number of unsettling realities. Bowling attracted higher ratings and a more lucrative TV rights fee than golf. Tennis, behind charismatic Americans Jimmy Connors and John McEnroe, surged in popularity. Golf had its superstars too, but something was lacking.

"We had to attract the sports fan and raise the profile from just 'Jack and Arnie' to establish the Tour as an important brand in sports…and put golf in the same stratosphere as baseball and football – both of which had stars, but an organizational identity that transcended its stars. That was a tall order," Beman said. "It wasn't a perception problem, it was a reality problem. Until I became commissioner, there was no strategic plan to build the product to compete. Everyone just assumed that if Nicklaus and Trevino could make enough birdies and win enough tournaments everything else would take care of itself."

These were formidable obstacles. In those early years, Beman felt ill-equipped to tackle the tasks that lay before him. How big was the learning curve? Beman put it in golf terms.

"I would like to be able to say we were amateurs in a professional world," he said. "But upon reflection, we were no better than a bunch of juniors trying to play on Tour. That's how far removed we were from having the knowledge and tools we needed to compete with other sports and forms of entertainment."

Before Beman took over, the Tour's singular focus was conducting tournaments. Beman knew he had to perform more than what he derisively termed a "ropes and stakes" job. He set out to redefine the Tour as a modern and progressive enterprise. But even some members of Beman's inner circle, such as his first deputy commissioner, Clyde Mangum, a holdover from the Joe Dey days, resisted Beman's departure from the status quo. Against this backdrop, Beman persisted. "I couldn't do my job and find the future of the Tour unless I changed the culture," he said.

That change would come, but not without that epic clash between Beman and the titans of the game, Nicklaus and Palmer.

Ironically, one of Beman's earliest moves dealt with ropes and stakes. He assigned Mangum to create a tournament staff procedures manual.

"Make no mistake about it," Beman said, "our tournament staff was and is the best in the world." But he added, "We spent too much time on simple operational matters such as course conditions and why practice tees hadn't been cut. There was never enough time for business progress."

The process of running tournaments had never been codified. It cried for a system, Beman said. Touring pro Dave Hill put it more bluntly. "The field staff has always been about as well organized as a Fourth of July picnic," he wrote in his book *Teed Off*.

Mangum's operations book was regularly revised and revamped. Employees were held accountable. They completed forms, made checklists and filled books – documenting tournament operations – that were sent to headquarters each week. Those books served as a blueprint for the advance official the following year so he could have perspective on problems that were handled in the past.

"We turned routine into routine, which left time for real problem solving," Beman said. "I knew I had to organize my own staff and get our house in order before I could ask the sponsors to re-think how they ran their tournaments."

Once he standardized tournament operations and office procedures, he turned his attention to updating the mom-and-pop ways of the tournament organizers.

"Many events failed over the years because they were not professionally managed," Beman said. "It was amateur hour."

Local tournament committees disbanded after the event. There were few full-time, paid tournament directors. Many tournaments were run by civic organizations such as the Jaycees. Volunteers handled day-to-day responsibilities and chose a new volunteer leader every year.

Said Beman: "It was like reinventing the wheel every time you rolled out next year's event."

So Beman assigned the task of creating a tournament sponsor's operation manual to a bright young man, Frank Tutera, who also had worked for Dey. The Tour selected The Colonial and Byron Nelson Classic as his blueprint and shared best practices from various tournaments. Volunteer committees at most Tour events began meeting year-round. Full-time tournament directors and staff were hired.

None of these changes happened overnight. It required a change of mentality, and the confidence of a young leader with big plans and no horizon. And the will to persevere and convince players, sponsors and networks that the Tour could grow to unimagined heights.

The NFL and Major League Baseball, among other sports franchises, already had sophisticated marketing and licensing programs, not to mention their own television production companies. This placed them light years ahead of the Tour. Under Beman's leadership, the Tour quickly closed ground on their rivals, recognizing as they had the importance of creating a fan base much broader than just its own participants. Midway through his original three-year contract, Beman was rewarded with a new, five-year pact extending into 1980. He had begun laying the foundation. Yet much of the heavy-lifting was still to come.

Neal Pilson, former president of CBS Sports, likened the Tour pre-Beman to a country store and marveled at its evolution. "During Deane's tenure as commissioner," Pilson said, "the Tour became the Neiman Marcus of professional sports."

A BLUEPRINT FOR SUCCESS

Sometimes the Tour's fortunes turned on the flip of a coin. Literally.

The year was 1977 and the Tour was head deep in a TV rights fee negotiation with CBS that would determine terms for the 1979-81 timeframe. Beman asked for too much. CBS countered with a much lower figure. Eventually they met in the middle on a three-year deal, which would allow the Tour to earn a sum exceeding its wildest dreams.

All that blocked the path of the Tour securing nearly $20 million were a few minor details. The two parties remained a measly $50,000 apart on the price. Beman had agreed to a final concession during their previous negotiations. This time he expected CBS to give the final inch. "It was a matter of principle," Beman said.

But CBS wouldn't budge. The two sides planned to continue the hemming and hawing over lunch the next day at the famed midtown Manhattan restaurant, 21. Steve Reid, the Tour's television coordinator, briefed Beman on the final details of the agreement. It was Reid who played an instrumental role in what would be a landmark deal for the Tour. Reid had spent a year learning how the networks turned a profit on golf. He demystified everything about the process, from the cost of production to the "make goods" if ratings didn't meet projections.

The Tour was about to enjoy its biggest payday. Realizing the Tour eventually would need to lessen its demands to close the deal, Beman decided to have a little fun in the process. He proposed flipping a coin to determine which side paid the last $50,000. To add some pomp and circumstance to the ruse, Beman secured a silver dollar from a bank for the flip.

When Beman met with CBS president Robert Wussler at the restaurant's bar, Beman took a final stab at brokering the deal, imploring Wussler to fork over that last $50,000. He shook his head and said, "No." When Wussler declared his final offer was on the table, Beman fished the silver dollar out of his pocket and proposed letting fate settle the final tab. Wussler laughed at Beman's brash suggestion. "He thought it was a great idea," Beman recalled. "In reality, it didn't really make a difference whether it came up heads or tails. With the deal we had made we were both going to be winners."

Peter Lund, who later served as president of CBS Sports, supported Beman's notion that this truly was a win-win deal. "Deane wanted to get every last dime that was due him from you as a network, but once he got that, he wanted you to do as well as he did," Lund said. "In some sports, me crushing you is standard, but not in golf and not with Deane."

Seeking an equitable solution became one of the hallmarks of Beman's way of doing business. All these years later, the details of whether Wussler, who died in 2010, chose heads or tails for that momentous flip remain fuzzy. What Beman, the man with the reason to remember most, offers is this: "I know we won."

Beman's victory, however, turned out to be short-lived. It didn't take long for the Tour to realize it would need more than luck on its side at the next TV negotiations. Structurally, the Tour never was stronger. Tournament revenues were at an all-time high. So were purses and the hours of televised golf. But Beman glimpsed a grimmer future headed his way. Interest in professional tournament golf had flattened and tennis, not golf, was the hot participant sport.

These hard truths emerged when Art West, the Tour's director of marketing, presented his television analysis report on Sept. 1, 1979. It was affectionately referred to as the "Red Book," in recognition of the shade of its cover. After spending several months visiting its tournament sponsors, all the major networks, and Madison Avenue advertising agencies, West compiled the 100-page analysis that revealed the Tour's overall combined network ratings for 1979 (the first year of the new

CBS contract) had fallen from 1978. The Tour's ratings had peaked at 7.4 percent of households in 1975 when ABC televised the most events. Through the 1979 Westchester Classic, the overall rating for Tour events plunged to 5.3 compared to 6.0 a year ago. According to the report, at the time there were 74.5 million TV households in America. A rating of 5.3 meant 3.95 million households had viewed the event. One reason for the decline, West noted, was ABC's decision to place the popular show "Wide World of Sports" in direct competition with Tour events. By comparison, in 1978, the show served as a lead-in or follow up to its events.

After being spurned by the Tour, ABC was determined to show the Tour the error of its ways by counter-programming against golf. This wasn't a trivial matter. When then-CBS Sports president Barry Frank realized the network might lose money on golf, he called executive golf producer, Frank Chirkinian, and demanded he cut $100,000 from the $600,000 weekly production budget immediately.

Chirkinian's response: "Impossible."

"I'll make it real easy for you," the CBS Sports chief said to his producer. "If you don't want to do it, I'll find somebody else who can."

When Frank watched the telecast of the Tour event from home that weekend, he couldn't detect a difference. He called Chirkinian, golf's master of television storytelling, the next day to find out how he pulled off his trick. "I'll never tell you, you son of a bitch," Chirkinian barked at his boss.

NBC Sports' executive producer Don Ohlmeyer endured much of the same frustration trying to broadcast a sport with significantly higher production costs. He groused to Beman, "How about I just write the Tour a check for our rights fee so we don't lose any more money."

Beman faced an untenable situation. The Tour relied on 30 percent of TV dollars to cover its administration costs and the remaining 70 percent went to the TV fund, which was distributed to tournament sponsors according to the size of their purses and whether they were a televised or non-televised event.

"The decline in television ratings may be a single year phenomenon. It may reflect a growing long-term trend or it may reflect a general decline of interest in TV sports," read the Tour's internal analysis of golf and its events. "The suspicion persists, however, that it reflects a flattening of the golf growth curve, and that it is in the interests of the Tour to address golf's slowing growth directly and develop tournament golf into more of a spectator sport."

However the Tour couched it, Beman knew he couldn't ignore that TV ratings were trending lower. Beman told the board to brace for a lower rights fee. "We were almost completely dependent on TV revenues," Beman said. "We weren't in control of our own destiny. Ratings and television revenue were driving the bus."

As part of his effort to resolve the rating woes, Beman sought a diversity of opinions. He ordered an internal staff analysis of the Tour and golf. He hired an outside consulting firm to gauge public attitude toward the Tour. The results? Fans perceived players as selfish, aloof, and unappreciative. As prize money increased, players weren't responsive to fans, sponsors, and pro-am participants, according to the consultant's study. To better understand the golf fan, the Tour surveyed its galleries. Families were few and far between, and young fans were mostly absent. (Less than 1 percent of galleries was younger than 18.) "It would court disaster if that trend continued," Beman told Detroit's Adcraft Club in May 1979.

One of the Tour's core problems was it had a narrow fan base. Only the ardent golf fan was willing to walk 4-5 miles to see just a fraction of the shots hit that day. The evidence suggested that golf had not kept pace with other professional sports in terms of marketing, promotion or spectator innovations; nor had the Tour developed any significant revenue sources besides TV rights fees, which, in 1980, accounted for nearly 80 percent of all Tour revenue. (The other 20 percent was comprised mostly from player entry fees and sponsor fees. The latter were raised to $8,000 in 1975 to help finance the Tour's operations.)

"We tried to frame it in the simplest terms: How do we stand in the marketplace with other sports?" Beman said. "What are our problems in competing for the attention of people who want to look at entertainment and sports? And what's our longterm future with young people?"

While Arnold Palmer and Jack Nicklaus enjoyed worldwide popularity and commanded top dollar for endorsements, the Tour itself had, unlike the NFL and NBA, little brand identity. Faced with these unpleasant facts, Beman developed a vision for a broad effort to grow the game. On Nov. 30, 1979, Beman called a special meeting of the board at a West Palm Beach, Fla., hotel to discuss the state of the Tour and golf. On a secondary level, they discussed the marketing of golf and the Tour as a spectator sport on television and to ticket-buying fans. Beman briefed the group on the current situation. His staff distributed copies of a royal blue covered book, forever known in Tour circles as "the Blue Book," containing the internal staff analysis, the 51-page report from Lexikon, the consulting firm founded by sports marketer Steve Lesnik (and later renamed Kemper-Lesnik Communications), and recommendations for immediate action in 1980.

"Our purpose was not to provide the tournament policy board with a few problems, a few objectives and a few 'pat' solutions," Beman wrote in an introduction to the analysis. "We feel that the broadest analysis of the state of the game is in order at this time. Only through a full understanding and discussion of every possible aspect of the game can we develop the kind of strategy necessary to build for the future."

The Blue Book reads as a veritable blueprint for the future. As Beman flipped through its contents, he ticked off proposals to address golf's shortcomings. "An electronic scoring system, junior courses, junior clinics, a statistics program," Beman said, a faint smile turning the corners of his mouth.

One of the top items on the agenda was creating an official statistics program that would develop "story lines" to engage fans. Until then, success and proficiency on the Tour had only been measured by tournament earnings and scoring average. "We wanted to be able to identify players by specific aspects of their performance," he explained. "Who is the best putter? Who is the longest hitter? Who hits the most greens?"

The Tour's statistics program, launched in 1980, allowed golf fans to compare their own statistics, such as driving distance and putts per round, against the performance of their favorite pros. It gave fans another reason to become invested in its main characters. Beman loves to cite how Calvin Peete's name became synonymous with accuracy, thanks to the statistics program. In the first year stats were compiled, Peete finished second to Mike "Radar" Reid in driving accuracy and tied for third in greens in regulation. He won both categories in 1981 and dominated the categories for much of the next decade. "I doubt Calvin Peete would've received the personal recognition as a superior ballstriker if we didn't have the stats program," Beman mused.

When the program began, scorers accompanying each group recorded the statistics and official statistician Bryon Ferguson compiled the raw data by hand. Enter the computer age. In 1983, the Tour negotiated a deal with CompuServe, a home computer information service that later became the first major commercial online service in the U.S. The stats helped gain additional coverage in newspapers' sports section, especially in agate on Tuesdays and Wednesdays when there was little else in golf to report.

"That was a PR man saying we're fighting for space in the newspaper and we have to get more," Lesnik said. "We measured it and it made a huge difference. I often say that I wish I had patented that."

Another innovation that would revolutionize the fan experience was the electronic scoring system. While commuting to the Tour's New York City office in early 1974 before he assumed his full-time duties, Beman made an important discovery that led to its creation. When he arrived at New York's LaGuardia Airport, Beman headed from the concourse down a few steps to catch a cab. He stared at the large flip-disc marquees that provided travelers with updated information, and made "a little click" every time it changed automatically.

"I've always been able to perceive things and put different things together," Beman explained. "A thought crossed my mind, 'Wow, if we had that on every hole you could be anywhere on the golf course and know who was leading and who was chasing and what hole they were on in relation to your position.' "

So, on his next trip, Beman met the airport manager and pumped him for intelligence. He recognized that unless the

Tour made it easier for the casual fan to understand who was winning and what was at stake, the Tour had little chance of growing its fan base. The modern scoreboard jumped to the forefront of his agenda. Beman made the first formal presentation regarding an advanced scoring system in mid 1975. He explained that the old IBM scoring system, used strictly at No. 18 green, required too much power to be used throughout the course. But he had stumbled upon a solution. "It so happens that it only takes a millisecond of power to flip all the discs to say something else," Beman recalled. "You could even run them off golf cart batteries, which is the way we ran most of them."

That's how electronic scoreboards established their presence at Tour events. Though it took several years to perfect the technology and secure sponsorship, the modern scoreboard became a reality at the 1981 Players Championship.

Beman thumbed through the pages again and the list went on. A sponsor/player relations department, a logo change, PGA Tour highlights and a promotional film, an annual awards banquet. Then Beman's smile broadened. "Senior Tour," he said. "It's in here."

Having seen the success of the Legends of Golf in 1978 and '79, Beman recognized what the potential of a Senior Tour could mean for the Tour and all its players. "There were only so many weeks that the regular tour could play tournaments," Beman explained. "The Senior Tour could take golf to more cities and expand the interest in tournament golf. Senior golf was in that book."

Green ink underlined key passages. Scribbled in the margins are Beman's handwritten notes. He switched to a blue pen to indicate board members and the proposals they favored.

"We identified a slew of solutions. It was an accumulation of a lot of the things we thought we could do," Beman said. "None of which was a home run. Each was a bunt or a single."

Reminiscing on the significance of this meeting, Beman expressed surprise that so many ideas from a single board session were not only executed but remain staples of the Tour's success to this day. "If we could point to one moment when we turned it around," he stressed, "not just for the Tour but for the game of golf, then this would be it."

Several of the ideas, admittedly, were borrowed from other sports. Beman looked at what other professional sports were doing, especially the NFL. He observed how important a role NFL Films had played in the league's success. Just as the NFL formed a lasting relationship with the United Way, the Tour partnered with The March of Dimes, a relationship that provided the foundation for one of the Tour's early promotional campaigns. In 1978, Steve Reid left the Tour and founded Reid-Dolph Productions, a television programming company, and the Tour became a client. The Tour lacked the financial resources to start its own production company. In time, PGA Tour Productions, which the Tour formed in 1985 (headed by future WNBA commissioner Donna Orender), would play a vital role in delivering the Tour's message.

Beman proved to the board that the Tour needed to broaden its revenue base and shield itself from the volatility of TV ratings. After much debate, the board committed $580,000 annually to support a four-year marketing initiative. "Over the years golf was never really marketed," Beman said. "I think there was a fear that we would cheapen the game by marketing it.

"But I was always confident golf could be marketed" and kept, he said, as "the pure game we all love."

Beman understood that the Tour wasn't competing against just baseball and football, but also against movie theaters, parks and picnics. Tour events had to become family adventures. So they started marketing trading cards, organized junior clinics, gave away free tickets for kids at McDonald's, built kid-friendly courses called Wee Links, and launched other junior programs.

"There were no instant miracles," Beman said, "just a lot of little things done consistently over a period of time."

To the groans of many who said such actions cheapened the rich heritage of the game, Beman pressed on. It was during this time that the Tour also made charity a centerpiece of its existence.

The Tour's legacy of charitable work originates with a $10,000 donation given at the 1938 Palm Beach Invitational – a golf era dominated by Byron Nelson. "Lord Byron" retired after his memorable 1945 season, but his involvement in the game never wavered – the HP Byron Nelson Championship, which added his name to the tournament moniker in 1968, will always insure that legacy. Nelson's greatest achievement, he said, was not his 11 straight Tour victories or his five major titles, but rather his charitable work for the Salesmanship Club Youth and Family Centers Inc., a non-profit organization dedicated to enriching the quality of life for children and their families for more than 80 years. A few years before his death in 2007 at age 93, he said: "People stop and tell me how the Salesmanship Club saved their life. It's very rewarding."

Since 1973, the overall charity proceeds of Nelson's tournament exceed $116 million – more than any Tour event. "The Salesmanship Club stood out as a shining example of how a tournament should be run," Beman said. "They marketed golf in their area better than anyone else. They became the blueprint for future Tour events."

Beman visited Dallas in 1978 to observe the operations and structure of the Salesmanship Club and the tournament. He and his wife, Judy, took a helicopter to the Club's youth camp in East Texas, far from the city's lights. After witnessing the importance of the tournament to the community, the nexus between professional golf and charitable endeavors became clear to him.

Beman resolved that all future Tour events should be organized and operated for charitable purposes. Beman made charity a matter of policy, part of the fabric of the Tour, by encouraging tournaments to restructure as 501-c3 organizations. Beman also believed that emphasizing charity would help the Tour retain the support of volunteers, whose work was essential to tournament success.

"I perceived that golf would become as big as the other sports and that prize money would double and double and double again," he explained. "Once the money got big, I didn't think volunteers would continue, in many cases, to take their week's vacation to help the players come in to their city and get rich."

One hundred percent of tournament net proceeds flow directly back into the communities where the events are played. That is one of the primary reasons for the Tour's success and acceptance in so many communities, according to Beman. "It gives the volunteers that are so necessary an additional reason, not just because they love golf, but because they're benefiting their community," Beman said.

He added that if the Tour had to pay minimum wage for its army of volunteers, the payroll would bankrupt the purse. Volunteers oversee countless tasks from herding galleries to parking cars to keeping score. Some never get to see a shot all week, and yet they wear smiles on their faces. Their commitment cemented Beman's belief that for a tournament to be successful nationally, it first had to be successful locally. "The corporate sponsor and TV are vital, but without volunteers and a strong community base, then you've got nothing," he said.

In late 1979, the Board passed a policy requiring all PGA tournaments to support a charitable initiative and, preferably, to organize as a 501-c3. Beman proclaimed that he wanted charity to be the leading money winner on Tour every year. He said it so many times that soon it became a Tour slogan. Indeed, every week charities such as The First Tee of Connecticut from The Travelers Championship, St. Jude's Research Hospital from the FedEx St. Jude Classic or the Evans Scholars from the BMW Championship are the big winners. Proceeds from Tour events annually benefit more than 3,000 local charities. Through its philanthropic efforts, the Tour in Beman's day bragged that it generated more money for charity each year than all the other major sports associations combined. "When the other sports want to raise money for charity, they host a golf tournament," Beman said.

The Tour's annual combined charitable contributions grew from less than $1 million in 1974 to more than $30 million in 1994. The Tour and its tournaments total giving eclipsed $1.6 billion in 2010. Behind those staggering numbers are the stories of individuals whose lives are being made better thanks in part to the Tour's support. "The PGA Tour is not just in a community one week a year," explained two-time Players Championship winner Hal Sutton. "We may leave after a week, but our presence is felt all year long."

Said Beman: "The charity connection with golf wasn't conjured up by a public relations guru to paper over some image problem with the game of golf or our players. It's a binding commitment to the communities, volunteers, and corporate

America that the Tour had to stand for more than just a bunch of pros making a lot of money."

Beman also realized that the Tour's progress depended on cultivating relationships with corporate America. He sold them on a simple premise: Corporations could enhance their image by raising money for charity. "It set us apart from every other sport," said three-time Tour winner Howard Twitty.

The Tour's charitable association proved an asset again in 1986 when Congress proposed tax legislation that would eliminate deductibility for business entertainment expenditures such as sports tickets and promotional packages. "It would have been a serious problem for a number of our sponsors," said Tim Smith, the Tour's deputy commissioner and chief operating officer.

The Tour collaborated with the Sponsors Advisory Council and American Golf Sponsors to invest in a major legislative effort in Washington to preserve tax deductions for businesses who purchased tickets to sporting events. To better publicize on Capitol Hill the Tour's contributions to local charities, the Tour hired the consulting firm of a young Virginia lawyer. His name? Tim Finchem.

Finchem, who co-founded National Strategies and Marketing Group in 1984, already had handled a feasibility study on the burgeoning TPC network for the Tour and developed the corporate membership model for TPC Avenel in Potomac, Md. By 1987, the Tour was Finchem's second-largest client and it recruited him to join the staff full time. Before coming on board, however, Finchem helped orchestrate the Tour's effort to persuade Dan Rostenkowski, a longtime member of the U.S. House of Representatives and Illinois Democrat, to champion a special exemption in the Tax Reform Act of 1986 to protect the Tour's sponsors. Rostenkowski understood the relationship between the Tour events and charity from his experience competing in various pro-ams. Rostenkowski went to bat for the Tour. It didn't hurt that Marty Russo, Rostenkowski's close friend and fellow congressman from Illinois took up the Tour's cause. As the chairman of the House Ways & Means committee, Rostenkowski played a key role in advancing the legislation's language that protected the charities in cities across the country. Golf tournaments were specifically mentioned in the House Committee's report. The Senate Finance Committee later approved it, too.

"We had tournaments in almost every state in the union," Beman said, noting more than 75 events were played at the time between the two tours. "Lots of congressmen and senators were contacted. Their communities were going to be directly affected."

But just as importantly the proposed legislation would have had a devastating effect on college athletics and football bowl games, who rely on businesses to purchase tickets.

"The Tour had the ear of the major decision makers on Capitol Hill, but almost every congressman and senator was contacted by the college coalition on this issue," Beman said. "Fortunately, we had a lot of company."

It was determined to be good public policy to protect tournaments' ability to aid their communities. When the Reagan Tax Act of 1986 passed, the Tour discovered it had another problem: Its player retirement plan was in jeopardy. To Capitol Hill, Beman trekked again.

The tournament policy board had established the player retirement plan at its May 11, 1982 meeting in Fort Worth, Texas. "The idea for the retirement plan came out of the previous work I had done in the insurance business," Beman explained. "Once we got our nonprofit status I knew there was this provision in the tax laws that permitted a nonprofit association to defer pay to its employees. The question was could players who were not employees, but still performing a service to the Tour by playing in tournaments, defer some of their pay?"

Turns out they could. But the question remained: Would the players go for it? The first time Beman explained the benefits of deferred compensation at a players' meeting in 1980 a Tour member stood up and blurted, "Why don't we just play for it?" It was a view shared by others.

"There were people dead-set against deferred comp," remembered Twitty, a player director on the Tour's board when the deferred compensation plan was a topic of discussion.

Gaining approval for a plan that wouldn't jeopardize the Tour's 501-c6, tax-exempt status also would prove no small feat. Beman credits Victor Ganzi, then a partner in the tax department at the New York office of law firm Rogers & Wells, for masterminding a plan that would pass muster. The Tour's first request for a deferred comp plan was rejected despite an initial positive reaction from the Internal Revenue Service district office. While the Tour was preparing to re-file, Ganzi designed a similar plan for another of his clients, the LPGA, taking into account the Tour's failure.

When the LPGA's plan passed, it amounted to a policy reversal by the IRS. In light of the LPGA ruling, the Tour re-submitted and was approved on its second try. "The Tour was always entitled (to the plan)," Ganzi said, noting the first ruling was of a technical nature. Ganzi and the Tour staff devised a performance-based plan that rewarded players with one deferred compensation credit for making a 36-hole cut. After the 15th made cut, the value of the credit doubles.

"The cut provision was the linchpin that helped get us approved by the IRS because you had to actually provide a service – namely, play in the tournament – and you had to perform to get deferred credits," Beman said. "The double cut offered an incentive to our best players to compete more often because you had to play more to get more." The deferred compensation plan sheltered the amount accruing each year in players' accounts from current taxation and permitted tax-free growth of the amounts set aside until the players began to receive monthly benefits – in most cases, when they turned 50. Under current rules of the Tour's plan, players are vested in the so-called cuts plan after they have played a minimum of 15 official events annually for five seasons. (Seasons need not be consecutive but the gap between two qualifying seasons can be no longer than five years.)

But there is a drawback to the Tour's non-qualified plan. Though there is no funding limit, players' money must be held as general assets, making the Tour's retirement funds – at least in theory – vulnerable to creditors. The deferred compensation plan has another limitation, too. It can't be used to provide financial assistance to old-guard players who built the Tour and played for little prize money. Creating deferred compensation was another step in the Tour's evolution. Beman had reorganized the Tour as a nonprofit, increased television revenue and established a retirement plan. Now he needed to find a way to fund it.

In 1983, when the average purse was just under $400,000, the Tour plowed $1 million into the fund and 113 eligible voting members of the Tour began earning credits for each cut made. At the beginning of each year, the policy board designates a pool of money for the retirement program to be divided among qualifying players. Initial funding came from one of three sources: tournament entry fees, general funds, and pro-am money. In the years to come, money was never siphoned directly from the TV fund, nor did its deferred compensation plan compromise purse size. Instead, revenue from marketing and licensing agreements and business ventures, such as the TPC network of golf courses, determined annual contributions.

When the new '86 Reagan Tax law threatened to close the provision the Tour originally used for its deferred compensation plan, the Tour petitioned the IRS to delay implementation while it sought a remedy. Congress passed an amendment in late 1988 that exempted the deferred compensation plans of the Tour and other entities that relied on a volunteer workforce – as long as all of the nonprofit's net proceeds were contributed to charity. "We convinced the same group of people that the new law would hurt the people who make it possible for communities to raise money for local charities," Beman said.

The Tour's performance-based retirement plan is universally regarded as the most lucrative in sports and the envy of all professional athletes. It's so good that even a marginal Tour veteran is likely to be "Set for life" – as a 2001 *Golfweek* cover headline blared.

"It didn't seem like much in the beginning but when it all plays out, it's pretty amazing," said Jay Haas, the Tour's all-time leader in cuts made with 592.

"I'd love for someone to say it was a mistake now," Twitty added. "They'd need to be committed." In recent years, Beman noted, a number of retired players have thanked him, acknowledging that the long-term investing and compounding interest have ensured their golden years will be lived quite comfortably. Indeed, some of the players will make more from their retirement plan than they ever earned in official money.

"The deferred comp plan wasn't put together for Jack and Arnold," Beman said. "To be superstars they must have somebody to beat. It was designed for the players who were on the Tour for an extended period of time and made his living and career there. They ought to have real security behind them."

The plan's impact speaks volumes of Beman's vision to better the Tour and the welfare of its members. All of them.

"There are some obscure players who are going to live comfortably because they made so many cuts," said Pat Reilly, past president of the PGA. "These are the same guys who criticized Deane because they were the marginal players. They felt Deane took care of the top players. The top pros felt he took too much care of the mediocre. In reality, he took care of everybody."

LEADING TV BY THE HAND

t's been said that Deane Beman put the Inc., in PGA Tour. By making golf the sport of corporate America, Beman ushered the game into the modern financial era. Purses jumped from slightly more than $8 million when he took over to more than $100 million on three tours 20 years later.

"He raised the Tour from a weekly carnival show to a legitimate business enterprise," said Jim DeLeone, an agent to Tom Weiskopf, Ed Sneed and other touring pros during Beman's tenure. "Do you know how much Tom's check was for winning the 1973 British Open? £5,500. That was the equivalent of $14,300."

DeLeone credited the Tour's financial gains to Beman's ability to marry the Tour, television, corporate America, and charity.

What soon became clear to Beman was that corporate sponsors could get more than an image boost by associating with the Tour's charities. They could get additional national media exposure, too. Beman didn't invent the corporate title sponsorship – the Kemper Open, named for the insurance-provider, and the Buick Open both pre-dated him – but he was the first to realize its potential.

For the most part, networks refused to plug the title sponsor. They habitually dropped the corporate name. So did newspapers.

"Eastern Airlines would beat me over the head," recalled Art West, the Tour's director of marketing from April Fool's Day 1979 until April Fool's Day 1992. "I told them we didn't control that aspect of it. (The network would) call it the Doral Open unless they bought air time. The network wasn't going to give away free ads."

Soon the rules would be re-written. The 1960s and '70s was the golden era of the celebrity host. Bing Crosby, Glen Campbell, Sammy Davis Jr., Joe Garagiola, Jackie Gleason, Dean Martin, Ed McMahon, Danny Thomas, and Andy Williams all had their names attached to Tour events in 1980. But by 1989, when Williams ended his 21-year association with the San Diego event, Bob Hope was the only celebrity whose name still was connected to the Tour. "It went from Dean Martin to Dean Witter," said *Golfweek's* Jeff Rude.

The celebrities infused golf with a sense of cool and played a role in attracting a broader audience to golf. In addition to acting as the event's figurehead, Williams and the other celebrities typically served as the primary entertainers at the pro-am parties. "Andy Williams singing 'Moon River' always brought a climactic ending to the show," said Tom Morgan, executive director at the time of San Diego's Century Club charitable organization.

But as popular as they were, celebrity hosts didn't lift television ratings enough and couldn't anchor a long-term TV business model. In one of his least appreciated contributions, Beman changed the conventional thinking of golf on TV, which was shown sporadically and limited to an abbreviated weekend telecast of usually no more than nine holes. The reason? Golf was the most expensive sport to broadcast because the cost associated with laying cable over a golf course compared with a stadium or arena was significantly more. "Until we found a way to underwrite that production cost, getting a substantial rights fee was a problem," Beman said. "First we had to solve the networks' financial problems."

Beman convinced corporate America to pay the freight. In return, they received substantial brand exposure outside of commercial breaks. In the new model, Beman eliminated the networks' risk, guaranteeing not only the production costs, but the rights fee it paid. In addition, the Tour left the network 40 percent of the inventory to sell for profit. This spurred networks to expand coverage of golf, bringing the sport into the television mainstream and leading to skyrocketing purses. The Tour's TV rights fees increased more than 2,000 percent from $2.8 million at the start of Beman's tenure in 1974 to $69 million in 1994. "Beman was the first commissioner to solidify the foundation of his sport with corporate sponsorship," veteran sports TV producer Don Ohlmeyer said.

The TV strategy's brilliance was in its simplicity. If the TV networks embraced a corporate sponsor, the Tour would guarantee that the title sponsor would purchase enough advertising to make the deal profitable for the network.

"Occasionally he had to lead television by the hand and say 'This is good for you. Trust me,' " said Neal Pilson, former president of CBS Sports. "It was good for television and we did trust Deane, and it all worked out."

Indeed, the Tour's success in television can be traced back to a strategy borne of economic necessity in 1982. Beman's prediction that the Tour's lower ratings would result in lower rights fees during the next TV negotiation proved true. "We had our teeth kicked in," Beman said.

Its TV rights fees from the networks dropped by $1.5 million beginning in 1982. Negotiations with NBC reached a stalemate. Ken Schanzer, who has spent more than two decades with NBC rising to president of NBC Sports, was in his first year with the company and he was instructed to raise the profile of its golf package by acquiring the rights to a major. (Schanzer did say he would accept The Players as an alternative.) Otherwise, NBC refused to pay what the Tour was seeking. "The negotiations got testy," remembered Chip Campbell, the Tour's point man on the television negotiations.

Beman thought NBC and its president of the sports division at the time, Arthur Watson, were being unreasonable. Beman had as much say in telling Augusta National and the governing bodies that controlled golf's four majors which TV network to associate with as he could tell them where to play.

"I always attempted to recognize and respect the people who helped us get there. CBS clearly helped us get to where we were," Beman said. "To extract The Players from CBS and give it to NBC was a little too much trading money for your loyalty and integrity."

After weighing its options, the Tour pitched CBS on forging an alliance for near-exclusivity of the Tour's TV package. CBS's Pilson jumped at the marketing potential of becoming the home of the Tour and shook hands with Beman on a deal that virtually eliminated NBC from covering the Tour. Beman emphasized: "We didn't try to throw NBC away. They precipitated the situation."

According to Campbell, Beman insisted that they owed NBC a personal explanation. Here Beman picks up the story. "So we walked across the street, and we're in Watson's office (on the 15th floor) and I said, 'Boys, we've been asking you for years to be reasonable with us on rights fees. As far as I'm concerned you guys are out of business except for the Bob Hope tournament. (NBC had an exclusive deal with anything on TV with Hope.)' "

"It was a difficult, curt meeting," said NBC's Schanzer. "He was essentially kissing us off."

A few days later, Beman was attending the pro-am at the Manufacturers Hanover Westchester Classic when Pilson phoned with troubling news. The CBS board, he said, rejected the deal. Beman was irate. Smith called back and demanded that Pilson honor his verbal commitment. Pilson disputed his obligation.

"On what grounds?" Smith asked. He's never forgotten Pilson's reply.

"Well, we didn't all turn around in a circle and give each other a peppercorn," he said.

"Which was a reference to some ancient British common law," Smith explained. "What he was saying is they had an 'out' and they were taking it."

Beman was left with little choice but to return to NBC and offer the network its package back. "We went hat in hand," Beman said.

"He was a different person than he was at the last meeting," Schanzer said. "This time he said, 'I'm at your mercy.' "

Smith and Campbell contend it was Beman's finest hour. His mea culpa and longstanding relationship with Watson salvaged the deal, save for a marginal cut in the rights fee. "Instead of putting a foot to his throat we made a pretty fair deal," Schanzer said. "Deane was grateful and he never forgot. For the next decade, I don't think we had a meeting that Deane did not refer to that day."

In an ironic twist, during a later television negotiation, CBS informed the Tour that it could no longer broadcast The Players Championship in March because of its contractual obligations to the NCAA college basketball tournament. Pilson requested to move the tournament to May. This time Beman balked. Now Beman was in a position to hand the tournament to NBC and increase the Tour's rights fee. "It was a very convenient way of not disrespecting what CBS had done but at the same time giving NBC what it wanted," Beman said.

NBC began broadcasting the tournament in 1988, and has treated The Players Championship with the same devotion as a major. Years later, after Beman had retired, NBC's Schanzer persuaded the Tour to move The Players Championship to its current date in May sandwiched between its coverage of Triple Crown horse racing. Pilson had departed CBS, but the date shift didn't go unnoticed.

"Those of us from CBS," Pilson said, "could only laugh when the Tour did move The Players to May because we tried real hard to get them to do that."

* * *

Back in 1982, Beman's TV deal with CBS reduced the number of events it aired from 18 to 12, and the refusal of NBC to add to its golf package left several tournaments without coverage. These were the days when ABC still wouldn't answer the Tour's calls. Having an event televised was a mark of prestige and part of the promotional effort for the host city. Beman knew he had to find a way to finance the growth of televised golf at a time when a hard line was drawn between advertising and the event television coverage.

"The networks had policies against mentioning commercial entities during the telecast," Beman said. "Only during the commercial breaks was that allowed."

The networks' firm stance prohibited their announcer crews to mention the name of the corporate sponsor linked to an event. For example, the Wickes-Andy Williams San Diego Open was shortened to the San Diego Open or the Andy Williams – but rarely was referred to by its full name.

The networks were vigilant about preventing free sponsor advertising, going so far as to complain to the Tour about players wearing company logos on hats and clothing. Their blood boiled over deals such as those crafted by Amana, a refrigerator manufacturer, which beginning in 1971 paid U.S. Open champion Julius Boros and several other pros "tee up money" to wear the company logo on their hats during tournaments. TV's objection fell under the provisions of program practices. "That was a hurdle," Beman said.

In the aftermath of the 1980 TV negotiation that reduced the number of televised tournaments, some of the events that were bounced sought their own coverage. To get back on TV through syndication or cable, tournament organizers courted corporate sponsors to front the money to buy time on TV. Campbell presented a package to tournament organizers calling for the sponsor to assume 40 percent of the telecast advertising time. This eliminated the Tour's risk in producing the event. "This paved the way to lay off the complete risk of the production and ultimately the rights fees to the commercial sponsor," Beman said.

The cable networks showed little concern for program practices. The appeal of a sponsor fronting the dollars for programming trumped all. The Tour's first direct experience with the promise of this model occurred at the 1982 USF&G Classic in New Orleans. The Tour bought broadcast time on ESPN. USF&G, the Baltimore-based insurance company, paid $452,000 for 40 percent of the TV ad time. Then the Tour sold the rest of the inventory. The Tour received significantly lower rights fees from cable but with corporate sponsors funding the television component, purses continued to grow.

Beman termed the Tour's first foray into the TV syndication arena in New Orleans a disaster. Rain washed out play on Friday, forcing the broadcast of the tournament to be shown on tape-delay. Yet after it was all said and done, even without the benefit of a rights fee, the Tour still netted $150,000, and learned that the title sponsor didn't prevent the sale of the rest of the inventory. Actually, quite the opposite occurred.

"With a sufficient amount of the marketplace pre-sold, it created a demand equation for the rest of it," Schanzer said. "If you have 100 units to sell and 60 are already accounted for, it makes it easy to get value for the remaining units. So the value proposition is not only for the sponsor. It also helped create a marketplace. It's brilliant."

The Tour realized there was substantial extra value to stamping a corporate name on the event. Even though it was netting lower ratings on cable, the corporate sponsor more than made up for the lost exposure because its name gained almost immeasurable publicity through mentions in local TV reports and newspaper coverage.

The approach was refined in subsequent deals. "The lights went on here," Beman said. "I reported to the Tour's board on May 11, 1982, that this was a terrific learning experience for us. If we can overcome the program practices, the corporate sponsor gets its name in the telecast, the network gets its production costs, and we get a bigger rights fee. If we can sell the rest of the advertising on there, we can make some big dollars. Applying that to the networks, it's a bonanza. It takes us out of the ratings game for negotiations and takes us into a whole new horizon for golf on television. It overcomes the huge negative that golf has on TV – low ratings, high production costs.

"I wish I could say we sat in a room and said, 'Hey this is what we have to do,' but it was a step-by-step process of solving individual problems and recognizing the successful model you see today."

None of these developments escaped the networks, who reached similar conclusions after observing the Tour's cable efforts. Though its audience still paled in comparison, cable's reach grew rapidly, and it was a potential rival unencumbered by program practices. It was gaining programming, and already costing networks money.

Not to be overlooked was the fact that TV's margins in other sports were shrinking. They faced intense pressure from the NFL, NBA and MLB to pay more for their rights. "We didn't pound on the table and say you have to change your program practices," Beman said. "The networks' came to the realization if they didn't, they were going to lose a profitable product that covered a lot of air time."

As the Tour became more sophisticated selling corporate titles, it began measuring the value of sponsorship. In addition to the television commercial inventory, the sponsor received an in-program CEO message, leaderboard mentions, bumpers, and other promotional graphics. The Tour calculated the cost of a 15-second spot on the local evening news and multiplied it by the number of major markets that existed and then estimated the number for a secondary market and multiplied that by all the secondary markets. The Tour also took into account the value of cable coverage, from the likes of ESPN, and tournament stories in golf magazines. They evaluated the cost of a newspaper buy, too, because the title sponsor had its name splashed on every sports page in the country.

"You couldn't buy an ad on the front page of the sports section. We were getting their name in places they couldn't even buy," Beman said. "The corporate sponsor got a bargain. Once you started to evaluate the return on investment, it was an easy sale."

In 2011, a corporate sponsor pays approximately $7 million to $8 million for a FedEx Cup season event with network TV, according to the Tour. The title sponsorship generates as much as $25 million in advertising value through its combined media exposure, the Tour said. (Because of the Tour's international broadcasting rights, a multinational corporation reaps as much as $35 million in total media value all for the same investment, according to the Tour.) "Whenever we sold golf, we stressed that the sum of the parts was greater than the whole," said Gary Stevenson, the Tour's director of marketing from 1987 to 1995.

For Beman, the new business model represented an escape from the Tour's dependency on ratings. In preparation for the next TV negotiations, the staff pitched to major corporate sponsors the value of having only one name to the tournament. Instead of the Buick San Diego Invitational, the tournament would be known as the Buick Invitational. "It wasn't going to be a convoluted name," Beman said. "There was only one name to call it. The corporate sponsor had to get the most value. It put up the money to guarantee the television."

Beman concedes the model wasn't an overnight bonanza. It was a steep, uphill climb that took 3-5 years of transition before it gained widespread acceptance. The first time the Tour helped a tournament land a corporate sponsor was in 1984, when the

Tour's marketing staff helped the Hartford Jaycees cut a deal with Canon. Before long it began functioning as a natural clearinghouse matching corporate sponsors with tournaments. By the late 1980s, a corporate sponsor was all but mandatory for a tournament to appear on TV. Beman told the networks: "Hey listen, this is good for everybody. We want to make sure you make a lot of money in golf. If you make a lot of money, we'll make more than we ever dreamed of."

The Tour had devised a formula for distributing television revenues – the bulk of the rights fees it collected were cycled back to tournament sponsors and used for the huge purse increases. The amount the tournament sponsor received was based on the purse size and whether the tournament had TV coverage. The higher the tournament's purse, the more television revenue it received.

The agreements reached with CBS and NBC produced in total nearly $60 million in revenue over the next five years, about a 30 percent increase over its previous deal. They covered the years 1984-88 in the case of CBS and 1984-86 for NBC.

"Deane would get fired up for the negotiations," Stevenson said. "There was one time when we were in negotiations with a network and we had all the right information and it was rolling. We had a break at lunch and he came over to me and he had that little Deane Beman smile on his face and he said, 'You know what, Gary? We're not selling here. We're enrolling.' And he shot an elbow to my ribs."

Purses would continue to rise. Beman surmises that the Tour crossed its last hurdle in 1984 when Arnold Palmer requested that the Bay Hill Classic be named the Hertz Bay Hill Classic. Palmer's own company had been purchased by NBC's parent company, and so the network agreed to change the name beginning in 1985.

"This was the last nail in the coffin for program practices for NBC," Beman said. The network now was among the converted.

Soon, only a handful of tournaments without commercial billing remained. Some of the Tour's most venerable events were among the holdouts, and suffered the consequences. CBS juggled its lineup dropping The Los Angeles Open in 1986 because it lacked a corporate sponsor to buy the advertising units.

"The L.A. Open in 1986 – that has such a nice ring to it," tournament chairman Ted Grace told *Sports Illustrated*. "What would I do with all the mugs and sweaters I have at home if I changed it?"

Then in 1987, CBS substituted the St. Jude Classic for the Western Open because the Memphis event signed FedEx as a title sponsor. "These moves got the attention of every tournament," Beman said.

By the time the Western Open was played later that year in July, Beatrice had become its title sponsor, and Nissan came on board as a presenting sponsor in L.A. (It secured naming rights in 1989 and exclusivity when the city's name was dropped from the title in 1995.)

Not everyone welcomed the new era of corporate sponsorship. It "cheapens the game, takes pride away from the club and the city, and destroys (an event's) history," said *Golf Digest's* Dan Jenkins. He applauded the decision of Kathryn Crosby, widow of Bing. She cut family ties to the Pebble Beach tournament known as the Bing Crosby National Pro-Am, when AT&T offered to co-sponsor the tournament for $750,000, *The Los Angeles Times* reported in April 1985. "Bing never would have permitted such exploitation of his name," Mrs. Crosby said in a statement at the time. "They are determined to transform the Old Clambake into just another corporate sideshow for the PGA (Tour)."

Of her charges of commercialism and exploitation, Beman said, "There have been some proposals made to the tournament's foundation that would raise more money for charity. I would not characterize that as money grabbing."

As Beman later expressed it, "She instigated a cause célèbre and savaged us." This incident turned out to be the exception rather than the rule. Before long, a waiting list of title sponsors emerged. In 1987, the Tour recruited Centel Corp., a Chicago-based telecommunications carrier, to sponsor the Tallahassee Open. Centel's CEO Jack Frazee agreed to do so with the understanding that if sponsorship of the company's hometown event, the Western Open, became available, Centel would be given first crack at it. Which it was, and Centel assumed the title sponsorship of the Centel Western Open in 1990.

It proved a solid investment. At the time, Frazee said Centel spent approximately $20 million on print and TV advertising without realizing a significant return in name recognition. When he reallocated $12 million a year into a golf sponsorship platform, Centel's name recognition climbed from 35 percent to 90 percent, according to a study conducted by an outside firm. "We were kind of the poster child for what golf could do," Frazee said.

Beman's masterplan of growth through corporate synergy led to runaway profits. In fact, it wasn't long before ABC took notice of the Tour's success. Its president, Roone Arledge, was infamous for never returning phone calls. Beman had tried him on several occasions without ever hearing back. That wasn't too surprising, considering Arledge had vowed that ABC would never air another Tour telecast.

Beman and Smith were in New York for a meeting when Smith flipped through *The Wall Street Journal* and read that Arledge was scheduled to address ABC affiliates at the Century Plaza Hotel in Los Angeles. Beman was sitting next to Smith doing paper work. Unbeknownst to Beman, Smith dialed the hotel and asked to be connected to "Mr. Arledge's room." The distinctive voice of the ABC chief answered.

Smith handed the phone to his boss and whispered, "It's Roone." Beman grabbed the phone and said, "Roone, Roone, where did I find you?" Arledge had answered from his bathroom suite. "We've got him in a compromising position," Smith thought.

Beman was a thinker, observant and inquisitive, the kind of person who dissects and analyzes the smallest details. At the same time he was a cool, self-contained man.

"Deane was so good in high stakes, high-stress situations," Smith said. "It was the same skill that enabled him to make all those clutch putts. He was smooth as silk. He said 'Roone, it's been ages since we've talked. I know we've had our differences but we've come up with a way for golf to be very profitable for ABC. I don't want you to say no until you've heard us out. I apologize for any misunderstandings in the past, but I miss you.' "

Initially the Tour had to underwrite telecasts through a

"time-buy," but in the end, Beman got ABC back into Tour golf. The return of ABC after a seven-year absence dating to 1978, in effect, closed a circle.

The model the Tour developed under Beman worked then and it works now, Pilson said.

"He enabled television to provide extended coverage of golf compared to what it was in the mid 1970s," the former CBS Sports president said. "We have Thursday-Friday golf, prime time golf, golf on multiple channels, and there's Golf Channel itself. All of these in one way or another, Deane was responsible for and helped bring to fruition."

In recognition for his contributions to television coverage of golf, Beman was inducted into the Sports Broadcasting Hall of Fame in New York City in 2009.

"In golf when the tournament is over, there's only one winner," Beman said during his acceptance speech. "In the game of sports broadcasting I was able to convince your great players that if they would let me bring to the game corporate sponsors, we could all walk off the 18th green as winners."

Beman transformed golf from the most expensive sport to produce to the most profitable – at least, that was certainly the case for CBS. A 1987 *Forbes* article noted that at the time the networks' earned upwards of $1 million per televised tournament. Sponsors maximized their exposure. Charitable contributions grew significantly. And the Tour was no longer at the mercy of ratings.

"The difference between a 3.2 rating and a 2.4 is a 25 percent drop. It seems like a disaster when you read about it in the press," Beman said. "But when your spread on the investment paid by the corporate title sponsor is $7 million v. $25 million in value received from all the extra advertising and promotion outside the telecast, the ratings would be nice to have, but should never be a deal breaker. That's what the press still don't fully understand."

Beman revolutionized more than just the way fans watched golf on TV. The concepts that he championed in the landmark 1979 board meeting fueled the game's greatest period of growth. There was one final initiative that pre-dated the meeting and would soon play a huge role in diversifying the Tour's revenue: the opening of the first Tournament Players Club. Its advent redefined the notion of spectator-friendly, and with it, changed course design principles. In its very first year as host of the Tournament Players Championship in 1982, TPC Sawgrass would make quite a splash. All it took was a dollar and a dream.

A DOLLAR AND A DREAM

I t didn't take long for the Tournament Players Championship to deliver a signature moment in its inaugural year at its new permanent home, the TPC Sawgrass Stadium Course. With the 1982 tournament outcome still in question, Jerry Pate made a move to seize it and ensure fans would never forget it.

Only a day earlier, his orange Wilson Pro Staff golf ball was in virtually the same spot in the 18th fairway of the TPC – a course that drew admiration as well as floods of criticism – and Pate pulled his 5-iron into the lake. This time Pate choked up on a 5-iron. He swung easy. The ball streaked toward the flagstick, drew gently and stopped within 2 feet of the cup, clinching victory and proving that the course rewarded brilliant shots.

"Well, what can you say?" said CBS' Ken Venturi, a PGA Tour player-turned-broadcaster, the pitch of his voice rising. "Shades of the U.S. Open in Atlanta when he hit a 5-iron next to the stick."

As Pate, the 1976 U.S. Open champion, marched to the green under the lowering sky of a beautiful spring day, applause reverberated from the 30,000 fans in Pete Dye and Deane Beman's stadium course. Pate smiled for those watching back home. He mugged for the camera and gave the first hint of what soon was to come at the lake enjoining the 18th green. He asked, "Do you think I ought to throw the commissioner in?"

"Why not?" CBS's hand-held cameraman Dave Finch asked.

There was more. "Pete Dye will go for a swim today," a jubilant Pate promised.

Earlier he had warned the course architect's wife, Alice,

that her husband would join Pate if he reenacted his infamous victory lap. A year ago, Pate plunged into the lake by the 18th green after ending his winless drought in Memphis.

Dye's TPC course – where desire and disaster often converge – proved a valiant test. It was Dye's most potent cocktail yet of his vast powers of visual deception, but it was hardly regarded then as the cherished shrine it is today. Players moaned that it was too hard. It wasn't for Pate.

"What about the alligators?" the cameraman wondered.

Pate didn't answer. He pointed toward the green and said, "I wasn't trying to beat the field. I was just trying to beat Pete Dye today, and I believe I got him!"

He smiled as he drew closer to the green. "Listen to the spectators," said Vin Scully, the CBS anchor.

"That's the loudest applause I've heard since I've been in the game and rightfully so," Venturi gushed.

In preparation for aquatics, a crush of photographers staked out the 18th green to capture the shot for posterity. Some knelt near the water's edge. True to his word, Pate didn't disappoint. After signing his scorecard to make the victory official, Pate returned to the 18th green for the trophy presentation. He said to the commissioner, "Come here, Deane, I want to show you something." Pate slipped his left arm around Beman's shoulder and guided him to the edge of the 18th green, then hurled the commissioner into the lake feet first, arms sprawled above his head in a V.

Once Beman went in, Dye knew he was next.

"While Deane was in midair I looked for Pete, and he was hiding behind some people," Pate said. "But when he saw me coming for him he just about went in by himself."

Last but not least, Pate dove in.

"If this isn't right out of... Animal House," Scully said. "And with that, there's no other way except to go to Brent Musburger in New York."

The celebration was great theater, and punctuated what is considered the baptism of "stadium golf." As one of the cornerstones of Beman's vision for the Tour's growth, TPC Sawgrass provided a home for the touring pros and a site for their championship.

In a land coup on par with the purchase of Manhattan from the Indians, Beman bought for $1 the 415-acre TPC Sawgrass property from a developer, who had fallen behind on mortgage payments. Unlike Manhattan, this deal turned into a home run for both parties.

Constructed as a tribute to golf fans and an unforgiving struggle for players, it delivered on both accounts. With a finishing sequence worthy of Steven King, TPC Sawgrass kept the television audience on the edge of its seat. Show a picture of the 17th hole to almost any golf fan, and they can instantly identify it.

It also helped change the Tour's financial fortunes. The creation of stadium golf became the prototype for a network of more than 30 TPC courses designed to host professional tournaments It changed course design and tournament venues forever.

"The significance of Dye's achievement in designing (TPC) Sawgrass cannot be overstated," wrote golf architectural critic Jay Flemma. "Without question, Sawgrass is the most important course built in this country between Pebble Beach (1919) and Bandon Dunes (1998)."

Beman said it turned out to be a billion-dollar idea.

"They say, 'Success has a thousand mothers; only failure is an orphan,' " Beman said. "This success story had a number of parents."

* * *

Commissioner Joe Dey understood that the Tour needed its own championship on par with what the U.S. Open had come to represent for the USGA and the PGA Championship for the PGA of America. It fell to Beman to make it a success.

"Try to imagine football selling itself without the Super Bowl or baseball without the World Series," Beman said. "That's what we were asked to do."

Dey envisioned the Tournament Players Championship, as it was originally called, as a climax to the summer golf season. He wanted it to rotate around the country; each year one of the Tour's best sponsors would be rewarded with hosting the event in its local community. The first Tournament Players Championship was held over Labor Day weekend in 1974 at Atlanta Country Club in Georgia, during Beman's rookie year as commissioner. The event offered a $250,000 purse. It didn't take long for the media to ask whether the tournament was expected to rival the majors, if not become one.

"Before the first putt has been stroked, the first hotdog sold or the first complaint made about the rough, it has been billed as golf's Super Bowl," wrote *Golf Digest's* Dwayne Netland. "This is quite a burden for any unborn event, no matter how noble its blood, but if the grandiose plans materialize, the Tournament Players Championship may become the sport's fifth major event."

Lee Trevino quipped that the TPC should be substituted for the Masters in golf's Grand Slam. Jack Nicklaus, never one to withhold his thoughts, said: "It is a major event within our own Tour. It is the wrap-up of our Tour, the climax – it is our World Series and a most significant event on our Tour."

But a major? Nicklaus didn't give it a ringing endorsement.

"Its scope is too narrow to gain the status of major championship," he said. "Not one person in Britain or Japan considers this a major championship. They don't even consider our PGA as one. It's at the bottom of the scale."

Nicklaus joked that he won the title in Atlanta in 1974 "just in case" it became a major. After withstanding a fierce challenge from J.C. Snead and delays caused by six summer thunderstorms, Nicklaus tempered his stand with a condition.

"I thought about this during the week and in discussion found a way that this tournament could gain major status," said Nicklaus, who won three of the first five Players Championships and its Joseph C. Dey, Jr. Trophy. "If we took our Tour and started to cooperate with the tours in other areas and make a worldwide tour, then this would be the championship of a world tour and could likely gain a major status."

When the question inevitably was posed to Beman, he chose to be more circumspect.

"We don't have 100 years to wait, like the British Open, to gain this prestige," Beman said at the time. "Mine isn't to say that this is a major tournament, but to try to make it one."

He quickly realized that the fledgling tournament needed to shed its interloper status. The event needed its own place in the sun, its own city, its own identity. The reason? Other tournament hosts didn't embrace it as much as Tour officials hoped they would. Said Dale Antram, a longtime Tour executive during Beman's tenure: "It was less a bonus than an imposition. There was a sense that this was *the Tour's* deal, not *our* deal."

Beman became acutely aware of that attitude in 1975 when he arranged the staging of the Tournament Players Championship at Colonial Country Club in Fort Worth, Texas.

"I thought, 'This is going to be wonderful,'" Beman said. "It was one of my favorite courses. You have Ben Hogan and his 'Alley' and the heritage of a course that hosted the 1946 U.S. Open. What a super thing for us. But The Colonial was their baby. They didn't embrace our event the way they would if the U.S. Open had been played there again. We didn't have that stature yet."

First, Beman moved the event from its late summer date to the first quarter. In its original slot, the tournament had little visibility, getting "lost" following the last major, the PGA Championship, and competing against baseball's pennant chase as well as the kickoff of the NFL season. In addition, Tour events in the first quarter earned the highest television ratings and received the highest rights fees; Beman thought placing it within the first quarter would boost its importance. Beman controlled the tournament schedule and could have commandeered any date of his liking to bolster the Tour's signature event. Instead, he determined to marry the Tournament Players Championship to an existing event, where it could develop a permanent home.

"We needed to have a partnership with a community that would commit itself as much to the championship as we would commit to the community," Beman explained.

The tournament nearly ended up in Orlando, where the annual Tour stop was struggling. Beman had designs of associating the tournament with Arnold Palmer in Orlando. This was in 1976, shortly before Nicklaus hosted his first Memorial tournament at Muirfield Village. But the Orlando tournament organizers refused to relinquish the Citrus Open name. Beman also worried that a deal with Palmer would invite too much involvement from his powerful management firm, IMG.

That March, Beman's 13-year-old son, Darby, was on spring break and joined his father in Florida during the week of the Greater Jacksonville Open for some father-son bonding on the golf course. Beman asked tournament officials where they should play. If Beman was in the mood for a challenge, they suggested, he should go to Ponte Vedra Beach and play Sawgrass Country Club, a relatively new layout that was mired in bankruptcy. Beman and his son drove down Beach Boulevard – the only way to get to Ponte Vedra Beach at the time – to State Road A1A, then a two-lane road. They continued another seven miles and on the left they stumbled upon the golf resort and residential complex. On the way, they passed a couple of condominiums, a few homes and nothing else.

"It was desolate," Beman recalled. "You could shoot a gun down any fairway and not hit anybody."

This former hunting retreat in northeast Florida turned out to be the geographical center of the rest of Beman's life as commissioner.

*   *   *

Ponce de Leon, the Spanish explorer best known for his pursuit of the legendary "Fountain of Youth," is believed to have landed April 2, 1513 on what later would become Ponte Vedra Beach. Seeing no suitable harbor, he sailed south and stopped at St. Augustine, our nation's oldest city.

The National Lead Company built the first nine-hole course for its employees along with a log clubhouse and polo field in 1922, which in 1937 became the Ponte Vedra Inn & Club. When the postwar mineral market dried up, the National Lead Co. launched the resort community and rechristened Mineral City as it had been known, Ponte Vedra in 1928. The following year, the state began work on a road along the shoreline from Ponte Vedra Beach to St. Augustine, which sped up development of the resort community.

In 1942, ownership decided to unload the resort. As the story goes, the resort's manager, Jimmy Stockton, was approached by his bosses, who suggested he buy the place. Stockton shot back, "I can't come up with that kind of money." But anxious to cut their losses, they asked him, "How much can you afford?" Stockton purchased 13 miles of oceanfront property and the resort for $625,000.

As America's economy boomed following the war, Ponte Vedra Beach resumed its evolution in the 1950s as a resort community centered around golf. Golf designer Robert Trent Jones Sr. was commissioned to expand the existing Ponte Vedra Inn & Club golf course to 27 holes. At No. 9, a par-3, he built an island green.

But for all its efforts, Ponte Vedra Beach failed to match the development pace of South Florida as a tourist destination and remained very much a sleepy beach community. Developer James Stockton Jr. broke ground in 1972 on the 1,100-acre development known as Sawgrass. Stockton later said the name was "growing wild like that sawgrass on the property," and he chose it after "tossing and turning" one night. Sawgrass opened in 1974, the same year Beman assumed leadership of the Tour.

Beman and his son started their round on the front nine. When they reached the fourth hole and spotted the Atlantic Ocean in the distance, Beman turned to his son and said, "This is a special place." Impressed with the course, Beman cut the round short at the turn and hustled back to speak with tournament officials. Beman thought the 18-hole Sawgrass complex had the makings of an outstanding venue for the Tournament Players Championship.

The Greater Jacksonville Open was considered the step-child of what pros dubbed the "Winter Tour." It didn't have a popular course like Doral or Harbour Town. The Jacksonville event skipped from Selva Marina to Hidden Hills to Deerwood, where it was being played at the time. It didn't have the celebrity appeal of Jackie Gleason, who hosted the south Florida stop at Inverrary CC. Nor did the Greater Jacksonville Open have network television coverage. But Beman admired the commitment of the volunteers and the way the tournament had become an integral part of the fabric of the Jacksonville community.

"I have a germ of an idea," Beman said to the tournament's organizers. "Would you be willing to give up your whole identity and form a partnership if we could put the Tournament Players Championship here permanently?"

They agreed to listen. So Beman made another trip to Jacksonville and met with John Tucker, who helped revive the Greater Jacksonville Open in 1965. During the visit, Beman negotiated a three-year deal with Florida Publico Charities, the local newspaper's charitable arm, and guaranteed the tournament a minimum charitable contribution of $100,000, more than it ever had raised before. On May 18, 1976, the Tour's policy board approved the move of the tournament to Sawgrass CC. The club's ownership invested $250,000 in changes to the golf course. That summer, Beman enlisted an old friend, architect Ed Ault, and Tour member Gardner Dickinson to make the Ed Seay-designed course tournament tough. Beman checked on the course seven times. On one of those trips, he met with officials at Atlantic Bank. The country was in the midst of an economic downturn, and some Ponte Vedra developments teetered on financial collapse. Developer Jimmy Stockton Jr. had given the bank the deed to the Sawgrass property in lieu of foreclosure, and the bank was trying to unload the resort. Beman wanted to buy the golf course. He was intrigued. He saw an underutilized asset with plenty of room to grow. He made his interest known without hesitation. Soon he negotiated a deal to buy the amenities from the bank for $1.8 million. It included the course, clubhouse, tennis facility, swimming pool, a 10,000-square-foot office, a maintenance facility with five acres of land, 28 beachfront units and an option to buy more than 600 feet of oceanfront property. They had an agreement in principle.

"I was completely convinced that this was going to be a bonanza for the Tour," Beman said.

But first he had to convince the Tour's board, and he knew that wouldn't be easy. The Tour operated off a shoestring budget. It rented office space, owned 20 walkie-talkies, and its biggest investment to that point had been an IBM Selectric typewriter. "I believe the only assets we had at that time were three Budweisers and a can of beans," joked Jerry Pate.

Beman visited each board member individually before the summer board meeting to brief them on the potential purchase.

At the Nov. 17, 1976 meeting, Beman presented his case. Summoning all his powers of reason and persuasion, Beman trumpeted the benefits of ownership and tried to soothe their concerns. He explained he could sell the beach units and recoup half of the Tour's upfront costs.

Beman could sense the board's hesitation. Concerns that the Tour was getting away from its core purpose of staging tournaments were raised. Was it wise to get into golf course ownership? The board members all had heard horror stories of fortunes lost in golf course development projects. Raymond Floyd, one of the four player directors on the board at the time, took the most assertive stance. He sounded a cautionary note, suggesting that rather than making a rash decision the Tour should wait until after the first tournament was held there. The board agreed.

Beman tried another approach at making a deal for the Sawgrass course. He persuaded Marriott Hotels to buy the property and build an oceanfront hotel. Marriott then would extend an option to the Tour to purchase certain amenities, including the course. This would give more time for his board to assess the success of the venture before committing to a purchase. But the deal between the hotelier and bank collapsed in early 1977. It was a bitter setback for Beman's vision to grow the Tournament Players Championship.

"I was devastated," Beman recalled. "But it turned out Raymond did us a huge favor."

* * *

In 1976, the Tour moved the Tournament Players Championship to Inverrary CC in South Florida and made it the centerpiece of the winter season. The Tour subsidized the television costs for the event's first two years at Atlanta and Fort Worth, but given its early season date it would become a profit center.

The tournament's move to Sawgrass in 1977 had the potential to be its permanent home. The event's letterhead billed it as "the first major of the year." Indeed, the largest purse on Tour attracted such a stellar field that Trevino quipped, "We couldn't have a better field if they raised the dead."

Set less than half a mile from the Atlantic Ocean, Sawgrass was designed to be a Scottish-style links in Florida and "resemble Troon, if Troon had palms and ponds," wrote Ron Whitten in *Golf World*.

In March, Sawgrass could be one of the windiest places on earth. On Friday, March 18, 1977, winds huffed and puffed out of the west, gusting to 40 miles per hour. More than three dozen interviews conducted with players, officials, and journalists who were there that day provided details such as blown-over hospitality tents, overturned portable toilets and sky-high scores.

"If this was an airport, it would be closed," joked John Schlee to the *Jacksonville Times-Union and Journal*.

Beman's son, Darby, witnessed J.C. Snead's straw hat blow off his head on the fourth green, bounce a couple of times and collide with his ball, costing him a two-stroke penalty.

"Playing this course," complained Ben Crenshaw, "is like walking through a field of land mines."

During a delay, Watson sent caddie Bruce Edwards over to make sure no one was trapped inside a portable toilet that had toppled. But the best indication of the strength of Friday's wind occurred by the 15th hole, where an anemometer was installed to measure velocity. Even the instrument blew over.

Some players just gave up. Cesar Sanudo hit two drives into the water at the 9th, then walked off before his third try landed. "This is the first time I ever withdrew while my ball was still airborne," he told reporters.

Art Wall couldn't clear the water hazard off the 10th tee against a 40-to-50 mph west wind. Trevino cackled that they should make Beman hit from its back tee and not let him leave until he cleared the 210-yard carry. Admittedly, Beman was angry with the field staff for using the new back tee box. He didn't need this kind of snafu during this delicate launch of the Tour's most ambitious undertaking. Beman banned the back tee on No. 10 from use ever again.

In all, 11 players withdrew that day, including Homero Blancas, who refused to sign for his 91. Gibby Gilbert signed his card "ROB," which stood for Ran Out of Balls. They were not alone in the carnage. Don Bies shot 80 and never lost the honor.

In all, 47 players carded 80 or higher. The average score of 79 was the highest recorded since the final round of the 1972 U.S. Open at Pebble Beach. The cut came at 155, 11-over par. "Guys came back from the airport because they made the cut after all," said esteemed golf writer Dan Jenkins, who enjoyed the suffering. Another reporter tabbed it "Black Friday." And yet somehow, Gene Littler and Bob E. Smith bettered par with 71.

Beman embraced the spectacle. He took his turn on barber Paul Mahla's chair in the center of the locker room fielding all the complaints. Crenshaw and Gary McCord held court as the players entered the locker room. One by one they were ushered into the barber chair and the grilling began.

"Your attention, please," Crenshaw said in mock imitation of a media official. "We have Jim Colbert in the interview area. Jim, tell us about your 88."

Laughter soon reigned. When the tournament moved across the street, the barber shop chair came with it. A plaque commemorates its place in tournament folklore.

Underscoring the notion that misery indeed loves company, players tallied a worst-ball ringer score, adding the highest number posted on each hole. Fred Marti dashed back and forth from the scoreboard to check on the travails of those still suffering on the course, where the average score in the afternoon was 81. They roared with approval when John Lister made eight on the par-3, 15th hole.

"Hot dog," Tour player Bruce Lietzke reported to everyone in the locker room. "That gives us 131." By the time Colbert arrived as one of the final finishers all they wanted to know was if he made any 8s, 9s, or 10s. Anything below eight already was covered.

Mark Hayes won the tournament when leader Tom Watson limped home with a 41 on the back nine. Hayes carded 289, one-over par, the highest-winning score on Tour since the '72 Open at Pebble Beach, and the only over-par winning score in 1977. In the first two years at Sawgrass, no one broke par for 72 holes. "I didn't win," said Nicklaus, the champ in 1978, "I survived."

"From now on," Jenkins wrote in *Sports Illustrated*, "when something terrible happens to a touring pro, he will no doubt say he got Sawgrassed."

Despite the gale force winds that became a Sawgrass trademark, the first tournament there was considered a rousing success. Sensing an opportunity, Arvida Corp., a leading real estate development company, swooped in and bought the property. In time, Arvida turned a tidy profit, Beman said. Soon after, the media trumpeted the course as the "Pebble Beach of the East." In November 1977, *Golf Digest* placed Sawgrass on its list of "America's 100 Greatest Courses" (where it remained until 1989).

Beman disregarded the board's pessimism pertaining to course ownership. He believed that the Tour needed to own the course where the Tournament Players Championship was held. It had a better chance of creating a unique identity if it was held at the same venue annually. Beman was still confident of his eventual success. He soon encountered another major roadblock when Arvida rejected the Tour's offer to purchase the golf course for $800,000. The developer made the decision based on poor experiences it suffered after selling amenities at other properties it owned. Beman argued that this was different. The Tour could bring national and international television advertising and promotion to the development annually.

"You sell your real estate and we own the course," he pitched. "We both win."

Still the answer was a resounding no. But Beman did not go quietly. First he panted overtures by phone. Then he arranged a dinner meeting with Arvida's chairman, Chuck Cobb, on the Friday night of tournament week. After placing their order, the two men launched into a discussion that shaped the future of The Players Championship and the Tour's business practices.

Beman again offered to buy the golf club, promised to host the tournament there and reminded Cobb of the promotional value to Arvida's surrounding real estate.

"You don't really care about the golf course. It will be good for both of us," Beman said. Cobb, a sportsman himself – he was an alternate member of the 1960 U.S. Olympic track team – summarily rejected the proposal. Beman pushed on. He laid out all the reasons the Tour needed to own Sawgrass CC. Foremost, he said that he planned to build the infrastructure to make the Tournament Players Championship what he thought it should be, and he wasn't willing to invest that kind of money into a golf course somebody else owned. (Incidentally, when Arvida Corp. bought Sawgrass it hired Seay to undo much of what Dickinson had done to his design.) Cobb's rebuttal was direct and to the point. "I know your board wouldn't let you buy it before. Nothing makes me believe you'll be able to sell your board on buying it now," he said. "You'll still be here in 15 years."

"That got my goat," Beman recalled. He rose from the table and excused himself for a bathroom break. Beman never carried much cash in his wallet, but on this occasion he had a crisp $100 bill. In the bathroom, he slipped the bill out of its fold and tucked it in his pocket. Beman returned to the table. Growing impatient, he made one last stab at a deal: "Listen, it's getting late, and I've got work still to do," Beman said. "But I'm real serious. If we are going to build a major inside your gates, we need to own the course. I heard what you said, but what's it going to be? Sell to us, or do I find another place for the tournament?"

Suspecting Beman wouldn't be able to get financing nor Tour player support to buy and build a Tour-owned facility, Cobb looked Beman squarely in the eyes and answered, "You'll never get it done."

Beman said, "I bet we will," and fished the fresh $100 bill from his pocket, slammed it down on the table, swallowed hard and said, "Here's mine. Where's yours?"

"Of course, I didn't have $100 on me," Cobb recounted, confirming the details of the story with a chuckle.

It was a wager that forever changed the face of the Tour. Beman rose early Monday morning after the Tournament Players Championship ended, hired a helicopter, and took off right in front of Arvida's office building on the company's helipad. Thus, he began searching for the future home of The Players Championship. Dick Martin, a tournament volunteer, offered to show him around. Later that day, Beman, his wife, and a couple of staff members landed back on the same helipad at Arvida's headquarters. The message was loud and clear: Beman meant business.

*   *   *

As Beman contemplated the idea of building from scratch a permanent home for the Tournament Players Championship, two important moments shaped his vision.

In the mid 1960s, Beman teamed with Ed Ault, a prolific golf course designer in Maryland and Virginia. None of the courses they planned ever were built, but their conversations cemented in Beman's mind a new way to conceive a golf course.

"That's where the term 'stadium golf' came from," Beman explained. "Ed wanted to put several golf holes in a virtual stadium. He even had roadways – people movers, almost – to move the galleries around. He and I didn't see eye-to-eye on that. I thought it was too much of a departure."

Beman embraced the basic concept and approached the USGA with a novel idea: Why not build a rota of USGA-owned, spectator-friendly courses that could host the U.S. Open and its other national championships, and serve as laboratories for the Green Section's turfgrass research? Joe Dey, then the USGA's executive director, listened, told Beman he would think about it, and nothing ever happened.

"Even though my discussion over lunch with Joe took a couple of hours, it took a couple of minutes for Joe to impress upon me that he wasn't interested," Beman recalled. "Joe Dey just didn't have the vision for what it could be."

Beman filed the idea away. After he became commissioner, the first tournament Beman attended was the 1974 Phoenix Open. Only on the rarest of occasions, such as when he witnessed Marty Furgol win the 1954 National Celebrities Open at Congressional CC as a teenager, had he gone to a golf tournament as a spectator. In Phoenix, Beman stayed outside the ropes to understand the consumer experience. He grabbed a pairing sheet and walked to the ninth green. The gallery was stacked 10 deep. Standing 5-foot-7, Beman craned his neck to see the action. Some fans stood on their tiptoes; others resorted to bringing folding stepladders. As in the days of Furgol, Beman noted a paper periscope outsold all items at the souvenir stand.

"I'm looking through the back of some head trying to figure out who is doing what," Beman said. "I said to myself, 'Wow, can you imagine people coming out here and walking 5 miles to watch this. It's dead flat, you can't see anything, you don't know what is going on, and there are hardly any scoreboards."

Beman, an incurable Washington Redskins fan and supporter of University of Maryland basketball, compared his experience to watching a game at the old RFK Stadium or Cole Fieldhouse. He was accustomed to buying a ticket, entering a stadium or arena and having an assigned seat. Vendors paced the aisles selling refreshments and food so fans didn't have to miss a play. Restrooms were nearby. He could see the entire action and always tell the score. Beman thought, "It's amazing anyone comes out to see golf."

In his view, the poor fan experience handicapped golf's ability to compete in the sports marketplace. He wasn't the first one to come to this realization. None other than Ben Hogan once wondered why spectators trudged along following him because "the prices are inflated, they don't let you in the clubhouse, and you can't see a thing."

Beman soon realized the courses where many Tour events were staged were too small in scale to host the corporate entertainment he envisioned. Corporate hospitality required two or more acres for tents. Sponsors paid top dollar for distant spectator parking sites. Television called for production pads, crane positions and routing for miles of cables. Tournament administration needed headquarter space and dispatching areas for an army of marshals and volunteers. Concessions required a staging area and numerous on-course sales sites.

The average course of 120 to 160 acres barely could accommodate galleries of 10,000 or more. Small galleries equaled smaller purses. So did rising "use fees," the Tour's euphemism for rent. It was at Phoenix that Beman's idea for a stadium golf course took shape.

"Out of this first trip, I convinced myself we needed a modern scoring system so the gallery could find out who was doing what, and we should build some stadium golf courses so people can see," Beman said.

His vision would not be the first golf course designed for spectator convenience. But it would be the most complete.

*   *   *

In 1977, Tour pro Bob Dickson determined no matter how he cooked the books, he was spending more than he was earning as a player. It was time to retire. An amateur sensation, Dickson won the 1967 British Amateur and 36 hours later reported for duty at Fort Bliss in El Paso, Texas. Later that summer, he hoisted the U.S. Amateur trophy, matching Beman's feat of victory in the two most prestigious amateur championships. (Dickson did so in the same year.) Dickson won twice on Tour, but now realized that for the first time in his life, he needed to get a real job. He approached Beman for some advice and listened in astonishment as Beman said, "I have an idea. Come work for me. We're going to build a golf course, and I can use your help."

Beman hired Dickson to look at property for a permanent home for The Players Championship in north Florida. Together they looked at a range of possibilities, and nearly struck a deal to build a 36-hole facility on what later became Guana State Park there. Several holes would have been situated right along a dramatic stretch of beachfront, the Atlantic almost lapping at one's feet. Ultimately, construction of an $800,000 causeway across the Guana Lake nixed the deal.

"It would've been a hell of a place," Beman said.

In the midst of Beman's negotiations for the beachfront property, real estate developer Paul Fletcher phoned Beman with an appealing offer. In 1973, he and his brother, Jerome, purchased 5,300 acres in Ponte Vedra west of A1A from Land Corporation of America with the idea of developing the property. It made them the largest land owners in Ponte Vedra. Most of the development there surrounded the more desirable beachfront property, but the Fletchers didn't buy into conventional wisdom.

The Fletcher brothers already had developed real estate communities around three courses. Baymeadows Country Club in Jacksonville was their first. The Desmond Muirhead design featured Gene Sarazen as a design consultant. They also built courses with golf architect George Cobb in Birmingham, Ala., and Memphis. They understood the value and prestige a golf course could bring to their land. With 5,000 acres, golf was always part of their plan. When the brothers heard that Beman was looking to build his own course, they made him an offer they thought he couldn't refuse: "We'll give you whatever you need for a golf course and a headquarters, if you'll move here to our property," Paul Fletcher said.

Beman's response to Fletcher's offer was typical of his hardnosed approach. Beman replied nonchalantly, "I've been offered 17 different sites around the country, some of them for free, but I'll keep your offer in mind."

When negotiations for Guana stalled, Beman called back and asked with more than casual interest, "Were you serious about giving us the land?"

Across the highway from Sawgrass' 13th fairway lay a large plot of acreage, which Fletcher Land Corp., was developing into the Innlet Beach community. When Fletcher and his right-hand man at the time, Vernon Kelly, showed Beman and course architect Pete Dye around the land it was an impenetrable forest. They noted an impressive array of live oak, palm, pine, sweet gum and magnolia trees. (Dye later tied a white ribbon around those that would remain.) They wore snake boots, followed deer tracks and carried machetes.

"You entered at your own risk," Beman said.

The men stood in a hip-high sea of sawgrass, its tall sharp blades swaying in the light breeze. When Dye grabbed a shovel and dug test holes to decipher the soil, out popped a giant water moccasin.

"It must have been five feet long and as big as your arm," Beman said.

Rather than despairing over the landscape, he imagined what could be, and decided this was the place where the Tour should dig its deepest roots. Paul Fletcher offered his take on Beman's ability to see beyond the here and now.

"I once read about chess players, and what makes a true grandmaster is someone who can look at the board and see it in an entirely different fashion than his opponent," Fletcher said. "That's Deane. He could look at a situation and see three moves ahead."

Beman asked for the southern-most stretch of land, 415 acres in all, more than the Fletchers ever thought he could possibly need for one golf course. The price: $1.

The Fletcher brothers weren't golfers, but they knew that developing a championship golf facility that would host a world-class event would bring new life to the sleepy beachside community.

"Everybody thinks, 'My God, 415 acres for $1? That's the deal of the century,' " said Kelly, who later became president of PGA Tour Golf Course Properties. "It was, truly, but the Fletchers had the vision to realize what the course would mean."

On June 8, 1978, Beman entered into a letter of intent with the Fletchers. Giving away the land presented its own set of challenges. For starters, the land was encumbered by a mortgage with Chase Manhattan Bank, and the Fletchers were behind on their mortgage payment and accruing interest. At a time when its lender wanted the brothers to enhance collateral they seemingly were doing the opposite. Beman went to New York to have lunch with representatives of the bank accompanied by Lew Lapham, chairman of the Tour's tournament policy board and vice-chairman of Bankers Trust. Before lunch, Beman explained to Chase's Bill Butcher that he wanted the bank to release the 415 acres under its mortgage for $1. Butcher looked at Beman, smiled and said, "Let me understand this, we don't have a good loan, we've got a bad loan. We've got 4,000 acres of security, and you want me to give you more than 10 percent of our security for $1?" Beman answered, "Yes, sir. That's what I'm proposing you do."

The banker, Beman noted, couldn't fathom why he should consider such a preposterous proposition.

"Well, we better just go have lunch," Beman said.

He pressed on while they ate in the bank's executive dining room, embarking on the same sales pitch he'd delivered to Arvida's Cobb that hosting a prestigious event and television exposure would add enormous value to the property. By the time they finished, Butcher looked at Beman and said, "You know, that just may work."

Convinced that this was the best chance of recouping its potential losses, the bank released the land. Before Beman signed the deal with the Fletchers, he added one last stipulation. He was impressed with Kelly, an engineer by trade, and he needed a local project manager.

"What is it?" Paul Fletcher asked.

"Vernon comes to work for me to build this thing," Beman requested.

They had a deal. On Feb. 1, 1979, the Tour made out check No. 12302 to Fletcher Land Corporation for "One and No 100."

The Fletcher brothers never cashed the check. It remained on display at their office, a priceless memento. In 2007, the Tour asked to showcase the uncashed check in the new TPC Sawgrass clubhouse. Fletcher consented, but not before he smiled wide and said, "Only Deane Beman would buy 415 acres for a dollar and then ask for his money back."

A GRAND OPENING

The Tour's plan to build its own course began in earnest on April 26, 1977. On that day, the board threw its support behind Deane Beman's vision by approving a $75,000 feasibility study. Bob Dickson, who served as the project manager of the study, already had narrowed the choices down from 20 sites. The Tour hired industry leaders Ernie Vossler and Joe Walser of Unique Concepts Inc., and Bob Dedman of Club Corp to evaluate five potential sites and conduct a specific feasibility study on the Innlet Beach site. Their report was submitted to the board on Nov. 1, 1977. It indicated that the TPC would pay for itself and generate substantial income for the Tour in the future – nearly $12 million in net taxable income over a 20-year period, they estimated. They forecasted the project would still break even over 20 years, even if the projected income was off by some 40 percent.

Once the Tour obtained the land, it solved the important question of where to build. Next Beman faced an equally daunting task: How to afford construction? The Tour's board wouldn't risk any of its assets. Acquiring a bank loan seemed the least of Beman's worries. Several Jacksonville banks supported the Tournament Players Championship. Proud that the tournament was laying roots in its community, the local banks clamored to provide financing. That is until Beman told the banks he required a non-recourse loan, in which the lender can't claim more than the collateral as repayment. Under such terms, the bank would merely regain the land. One by one, they backed off. So Kelly called his personal home mortgage agent at Daytona Federal

Savings & Loan and said, "Listen, do I have a deal for you."

Kelly soon learned the value of star power. He offered to bring Beman to meet the bank's boss and executive team. "They were fired up to meet the commissioner," Kelly said.

Beman persuaded the Daytona Beach, Fla.-based savings and loan bank to approve a $3 million, 30-year loan at 11 percent interest, and the Tour pledged the 415 acres it bought for a dollar as collateral. On July 12, 1977, Beman negotiated a 10-year extension of its deal with Florida Publico Charities to keep the tournament in the Jacksonville community. Of greater importance, Florida Publico agreed to cap charitable dollars at $100,000 annually over the next 10 years and contribute the tournament's receipts in excess of that amount to help finance the new TPC. The Tour received approximately $2.4 million from this source from 1978 through 1982. Beman called this his "backup financing" in case the new venture struggled initially.

Fifty local businessmen paid $20,000 each for a founding membership. In return, they received a 40-year membership – no dues, cart, or range ball fees for the first 20 years – which could be transferred to a family member or sold. And, they were promised their initial investment would be refunded in 2020. With the passage of time, the investors have called it the best deal of their lives. Yet hardly anyone was beating down a door to join when TPC Sawgrass resembled a swamp. Dickson took prospective founding members to the property. They wore snake boots, rubber waders and stood knee deep in mud. They took a leap of faith.

"That was really something in 1978," Kelly said. "The people buying the memberships weren't buying them for the golf experience. They were buying it because they believed it was the right thing to do for the community and because that's what was necessary to keep the tournament here."

The Tour signed 3,000 additional local golfers as associate members at $25 apiece to assure the course of local play, and achieved positive cash flow from Day One. To Beman, this confirmed that the Tour had chosen the right community. Together, these various funding mechanisms helped the Tour cover the $6,355,533 tab for the course, clubhouse, maintenance building, including all furniture, fixtures, and equipment as well as all subsequent capital improvement through 1982. "Not one nickel of the Tour's money was spent there," Beman said.

Beman had briefed the board every step of the way. They humored his quixotic quest. When Beman presented his plan at the Nov. 17, 1977 policy board meeting at Walt Disney World Resort, it appeared he had succeeded.

"They never thought we could get it done, I'm sure," Beman said. "Now all the pieces were together, and everybody at that point was literally shamed into voting for it. There were several players that were darn reluctant. We're calling for the gavel, it's going to get done."

Moments before, Beman had outlined that with a $1 investment for the land, a non-recourse mortgage, 50 local investors, 3,000 associate members, and the income from the tournament proceeds over $100,000, he had satisfied the board's condition that he could build the golf course only if he could do so with no risk to the Tour. He had arguments prepared to counter every objection – except one. Former secretary of state and attorney general William P. Rogers representing the Tour's outside law firm (Rogers & Wells) attended that board meeting.

"This happened to be the only meeting he ever came to," Beman noted.

Decades later, there still is a look of disbelief on Beman's face as he recounted what happened next. First, board member Don Padgett, the PGA's president, raised an objection and called for the second time that the independent directors study and define the objectives of the Tour. Then a player letter was read aloud, which suggested $1 for land might constitute overpayment, petitioning for a players' vote. In an attempt to break the rising tension in the room, Rogers interrupted and took the floor.

Beman recalled: "He said, 'Well, if I could make a suggestion, if it would make everyone feel easier about this, why don't you put it to a vote of the players?' I went absolutely white. The player directors' said, 'Okay.' The rest of the board said, 'Okay,' and it was voted on in 10 seconds."

The blood hadn't returned to Beman's face when he realized the board had just set precedence by sanctioning the first player vote on a business issue in Tour history.

"The Tour is not a democracy like the good ol' U.S. of A.,"

Beman stressed. "The players never had voted directly on any business issue and should never have voted on a business issue. That's what the board is for. Now they are going to have a chance."

Rogers had infused another twist into the ongoing drama. Beman determined that for the future welfare of the Tour he must ensure players voted in the affirmative.

"If we lost that vote, we'd lose the Tour's ability to function as a really good business entity," Beman said. "The players would then want to vote on all business issues, and that would become a bigger problem than the golf tournament."

Said Dickson: "As big as the TPC and the network has grown, it was not a slam dunk at the beginning. Deane had to put on his selling shoes big time to get the players to sign on."

It was just one more hurdle to clear for Beman. He lobbied the players aggressively. The staff compiled a 51-page prospectus, crammed with the objectives and philosophy of the club, the concept and marketing of the membership, capital costs and operating projections, and distributed it to all members. At a 2002 press conference to celebrate the TPC's 20th anniversary, Pate recalled the Tour's full-court press of public relations material.

"We call it information," Beman deadpanned.

"I call it propaganda," Pate shot back, with a smile.

Pate showed the prospectus to his father, an executive with Coca-Cola Co. "He said, 'Son, this is a great idea. You need to support it. Commissioner is doing a great job. Let him run with it,' " Pate said.

Beginning at the 1978 Quad Cities Open and continuing for the next eight weeks, Beman traveled to each Tour stop to persuade players that the course project was in their best interest. He deliberately scheduled these special player meetings at inconvenient times – at 6 or 7 a.m., in the afternoons during pro-ams, when half the field was on the course. Beman did so because he wanted to unveil his plan in front of no more than eight to 10 players at any one meeting in order to give every player personal attention. Beman delivered his well-honed stump speech for building the TPC: "We've helped all these real estate projects to sell their properties, and when they're done, they kick us to the curb and we're on to the next course. Just once, we should be the one's to reap the benefit."

At the end of each informational session, players were asked to vote. Beman is an intense man with piercing blue eyes, capable of delivering a look, which friends say, can exterminate head lice. He told his wife Judy, "I'm going to look them in the eye if they are going to say, 'No.' "

That was hardly necessary. Beman orchestrated it so that the first 12 players that he knew were in favor of the deal signed under "Yes" on the ballot. The 'No' side was blank. As other players continued to vote, they detected an ever longer list of names on one side of the ballot. "The sheep followed the shepherds," he said.

The final vote was 100-3. Several prominent players, such as Jack Nicklaus, abstained. On Sept. 26, 1978, the board gave final consent to build the course, authorized retaining an architect and pursuing founding members. It also approved moving the Tour's headquarters from Bethesda, Md., to Ponte Vedra Beach, Fla.

On Feb. 12, 1979, the Tour held a formal groundbreaking ceremony just off Route A1A, across the entrance to Sawgrass CC. Standing on a patch of dirt in front of a gallery of invited guests, Beman hit the ceremonial first drive off the neck of a vintage MacGregor Ben Hogan model driver he pulled from his closet. The ball skittered into the surrounding palmetto brush. The mishap didn't ruffle Beman. He took a mulligan. "I hit the second shot right on the screws," he said.

What happened to the real first shot? Carolyn Dickson, Bob's wife, thought she was risking her life searching in the rattle snake-infested palmettos. But she recovered the Titleist 2. She presented it to Beman at a 2006 reunion organized by the Tour of the TPC's key contributors. And the mulligan? After a lengthy search, the ball was recovered by Paul Fletcher and presented to Beman with an engraved plaque.

Beman, dressed in a light blue suit, donned a hard hat, hopped onto a Caterpillar D6 tractor and lowered the blade. He even toppled a few saplings. Soon the bulldozers and backhoes began moving earth. A week later, the Tour staff officially moved from Maryland to its new Florida headquarters, working out of two model homes at 100 Nina Court in Ponte Vedra

Beach until permanent headquarters were completed near the Tournament Players Club. Patty Cianfrocca – who has worked for more than 30 years at the Tour, rising to director of tournament operations for championship management – recalled that her first office in the four-bedroom home was its dining room.

"Deane's office was the master bedroom," she said. "The garage had all the copy equipment and a postage meter, and for a P.A. system we just yelled at each other."

Not long after the move, Beman hosted CBS Sports president Neal Pilson and led him into the uninviting wilderness. Beman turned to Pilson, squinted into the sun and said, "We're going to build one of the great golf courses in the world right here."

Pilson recalled being too busy swatting mosquitoes at the time to notice that the land gave new meaning to the cliché "flat as a pancake." He said, "Good luck. We're with you."

Ironically, Beman had resurrected his old laboratory golf course idea rejected by Joe Dey years before and used it to make Dey's last act as the Tour's first commissioner – The Players Championship – reach its intended status.

As *Sports Illustrated's* John Garrity wrote, "It may have looked as if Beman was building a course in a swamp, but he was actually leading the Tour to higher ground."

*   *   *

Pete Dye pioneered a new movement in course design. But like all trailblazers, he still was bound by the inherited prejudices of the past, by the sentimentality of conservative players who despised making bogey, or worse.

In 1969, Dye built Harbour Town Golf Links with Nicklaus, out on the southeastern tip of Hilton Head Island, nestled against the Calibogue Sound. At first, players were disoriented by its layout. After all, they were accustomed to a certain style of course.

"It's different, but then, so was Garbo," Dye said, when he unveiled Harbour Town.

Before long, it evolved into a favorite of the players, including one who would someday employ Dye. Beman ranked Harbour Town among the best competitive golf courses he ever had played, a gem that set a standard for tournament golf courses. One morning, Beman phoned Dye, a former insurance salesman-turned-golf course architect. Dye was a fine golfer in his own rights whom Beman knew from his amateur days. They talked for a long time. When the call ended, Dye walked into the kitchen of his South Florida home and told his wife Alice: "That was Deane Beman. He wants me to build a course for him."

Alice was surprised, and skeptical.

"Oh Pete, you're crazy," she said. "You can't build for Deane. He's particular, he's efficient, he's all the things you aren't. He'll have his hands in there trying to tell you what to do. Don't do it."

She usually offered wise counsel, but on this occasion her husband didn't listen.

To better understand the design concept he envisioned, Beman suggested the Dyes tour Glen Abbey Golf Club in Ontario, Canada, a Nicklaus design that had hosted the Canadian Open. Whereas Nicklaus' layout of Muirfield Village Golf Club in his native Ohio presented a natural amphitheater, here he crafted a central core by constructing spectator mounds where fans could see play on the vast majority of holes. On a winter day, the Dyes flew north of the border. While waiting to go through customs, Alice bought a pack of cigarettes. They rented a car and drove out to the course. It was 25 degrees and sleeting so Alice stayed in the clubhouse and watched curling on television. Fifteen minutes later, Dye returned. A surprised Alice asked if everything was alright, and her husband replied, "I've looked at it and I can do better." They drove back to the airport, where Alice converted her Canadian currency from purchasing the cigarettes. After spending all of one hour in Canada, they boarded a plane and went home.

On May 16, 1978, Dye came to Jacksonville to evaluate the TPC Sawgrass property with project manager, Vernon Kelly and Beman. Afterwards, they grabbed dinner at The Homestead Restaurant, known for its generous portions, perfect for a trencherman's appetite and those with a disdain for cardiologists whining about moderation. "They had the best fried chicken in the world," Kelly said.

Beman pitched his vision for a course layout. He wanted a

design that would favor no one particular style of play. He demanded a thorough examination that wouldn't allow a player to compensate for a shortcoming in his game with unusual skill in another aspect of play. He told Dye he didn't want one side of the course to be tougher than the other. Both nines should begin with a similar challenge because they would have starting times from both nines during the first two rounds of the tournament. There had to be both right and left doglegs. The course routing needed to be laid out so no two consecutive holes ever played in the same direction. With this mandate, wind direction would have a more balanced influence on the field of players. Beman wanted the layout to loop back in proximity to the clubhouse every three or four holes so that fans could return to the clubhouse area more easily. The routing needed to create hubs of activity for viewing for additional fan convenience.

"We can't play in a stadium, but we can make it a better experience for fans," Beman said.

For the four par-3s, the thinking was to have one short one with a high degree of risk, two others, of moderate length that required deft play with medium irons, and one lengthy test with a fittingly larger target green.

The 10 par-4 holes, likewise, would provide a blend of short, medium, and long challenges, each requiring distinctive approaches. Demands for accuracy from the tee would vary with more spacious fairways for the longer holes and precision placement needed on the shorter ones.

Among the prerequisites were a variety of par-5 holes. One was to be short and reachable by almost any pro. Two others, of medium length, would afford skilled and strong players a reasonable option of going for the green in two – but not without the threat of penalty. And the fourth would be a supreme challenge, forcing nearly all players to play it as a three-shot hole.

Beman described how he wanted the closing holes to look, insisting that the final three test players' mettle and tempt them to play aggressively. Beman's final stipulation? He wanted to build the first golf course designed for spectators.

"It should be the best course it can be for the competition, but it has to work for the spectators so we can compete with the other sports," Beman said.

Dye polished off his glass of sweet tea, snatched a placemat, flipped it over, and quickly pencil-sketched a potential course routing for the back-nine. He smiled and assured Beman he understood.

"How about this?" Dye said, and pushed the placemat in front of Beman.

Their eyes met, and the smile that creased Beman's face left no need for words. "Pete Dye embraced Stadium Golf as if it was his own child," he said.

Beman pocketed the placemat. For years, Dye's free-hand sketch hung in Beman's home office. Today, the primitive layout is displayed behind a glass picture frame on the wall at the TPC Clubhouse. "It wasn't something you could take to a bank," Beman said with a laugh.

At the time, that was an issue. Kelly told Dye the bank required a full set of plans for the Stadium Course. Dye said he would take care of it.

"I suppose Deane's bankers must have been afraid I'd kick off midway through the job and they would be left with half a golf course," Dye wrote in his autobiography, "Bury Me in a Pot Bunker."

But on the day the loan was closing, there still were no plans. The bank grew impatient. A distressed Kelly reminded Dye of the deadline. It's been said about Dye that he never met a board of governors he didn't prefer to ignore, or an executive committee whose counsel he would rather not seek. A day later the plans appeared (Dye said Alice drew them) and were handed over to the bank. "They were tickled to death," Kelly said.

The loan closed and the next time Kelly made a construction site visit he and Dye drove in a pickup truck. They parked and started to observe the cut lines from the survey when Kelly realized they didn't have the plans. "Wait a minute," he called out and rushed back to the truck. When he returned with the rolled up plans tucked under his armpit, Dye asked, "What's that?" Kelly caught his breath and answered that he had retrieved the plans. "Put them back in the truck," Dye snapped, a deep scowl on his face. "I don't want to see them again."

Kelly obeyed.

"Pete draws with a bulldozer," said Bobby Weed, who

headed the Tour's in-house course design division for six years before starting Bobby Weed Design.

Restricting Dye to a set of plans is equivalent to forcing a gifted artist to color within the lines. Dye's creativity is unleashed by being in the field, from visualizing features based on the shape of the land, and pacing holes the way a good story unfolds. At TPC Sawgrass, Dye and company didn't follow the plans. They followed the sand.

"This was the darnedest property because usually sand runs in a vein and once you find a seam you can just keep following the seam. But this came in pockets," explained Kelly.

Consequently, the lakes are located where the good sand was discovered, making Dye's plans useless. "This course couldn't be designed on the office drawing board," Beman said. "You had to be on site, boots on the ground."

The other significant construction challenge Dye faced was lowering the water table. At no point does the land rise higher than 5 feet above sea level. "The word swamp never left our lips," Dickson said.

Dye had to design a way to shed water quickly. An afternoon downpour is as much of a summertime ritual in Florida as sweet tea. Drainage was a major hurdle, especially because the completion of A1A effectively dammed the site on the east. Dye often said, "we have to de-water this place." To solve the problem, they built a moat around the perimeter of the course. Technically, it was called a rem-ditch, a network of lakes and canals constructed throughout the property that provided drainage and ample irrigation water.

"We came up with a novel way to provide drainage, security and a boundary for the property all at the same time," Dye joked.

Digging a ditch from the pump station to the property was no easy task. Six months into the project, Beman asked Dye, "Are we on schedule?" Dye answered, "Of course."

In truth, Dye had his doubts. "I don't think we'll ever get this damn place done," he said.

It took a better part of a year to construct a 36-foot-wide canal that encircled the property. (Reclaiming usable land from swamps and marshes by draining the water into lagoons was allowable then but no longer is permitted.)

"Just as an aside, to show how smart Jerome and Paul (Fletcher) were, they immediately began marketing the property as ribbon lake frontage," Kelly said with a chuckle.

In 1979, during the building of the course, crews ran into uncooperative skies. Rainfall fell short of a record by an inch in September. Kelly told his staff, "It's been a bad month but it's almost over."

That night a 100-year storm hit. Heavy rains contributed to pushing back the course's opening a year. After the downpours, Dye used a rowboat with an electric motor to navigate the course. Workers had to patch 60 to 70 washouts. They already had tiled No. 1 green, but when the water finally drained those corrugated pipes had floated over to the spectator mounds beside the first tee. For months, a battalion of workers toiled around the clock. Machines crawled over the earth, grading the future course. Dye was often right alongside the laborers, shirtless, steering a bulldozer, clearing brush, raking a finished green.

To make a sandy-soil base grow Bermuda grass, they dug out a 12-inch layer of undesirable organic soil on top (otherwise known as "muck"), removed the sand below it, and then packed the sand on top of the muck. Dye piled more than 150,000 cubic yards of the debris-like surplus alongside the fairway for spectator mounds. He positioned the spectator mounds on the right side of the hole so the gallery would be looking into the golfers' faces, as Beman had himself observed when he went to see Nicklaus's Glen Abbey course. Yet Dye never envisioned the spectator mounds rising as high as they did. What were expected to be 10-12 feet tall, soon tripled in height. Beman loved it. The higher, the better, he said, so more fans can see all the action.

"People ask how many yards of material did you move? I have no idea," Kelly said. "It's almost inconsequential because we moved everything out there."

Beman knew how to reward his staff and keep them motivated. One time, early in construction he phoned from the Tour's then Bethesda headquarters and ordered Allan MacCurrach, the Tour's chief agronomist, to hustle to the Jacksonville airport to pick up a package he sent. MacCurrach, drenched in sweat and caked in dirt, hung up and complained aloud at the assignment. But he dutifully made the hour-long drive, waited at the luggage conveyor and looked for Beman's package. MacCurrach watched a case of Coors beer circle unclaimed several times. "Finally I looked at it and it was for me," MacCurrach recalled. "Believe me, we really enjoyed that when I got back."

It was a touching gesture, and a window to a gentler side of Beman so often obscured by the toughness that governed him in his quest for rolling over the status quo in this traditional game.

Beman made frequent course inspections. So did Alice Dye, whose opinion often trumped her husband.

"At the end of the afternoon, we're covered with sweat and mud and she comes out all prim and proper, smelling as fresh as a daisy, and she could rip you apart in the nicest way," Weed said. "She would say, 'Now Pete, how are we going to play this? How are the high handicappers going to playing this? How are the thumpers going to play it?' He would say, 'I don't know. What was I thinking? I'm sorry.' And we'd go back to work."

Her biggest influence occurred at the par-3, 17th hole. The plan that Kelly showed the bank called for a small lake to the right side of the target, making for a peninsula green. The area around the green site, however, contained the best pocket of sand for the course. The more they excavated to use on the fairways, the deeper and wider the cavity became. "Pretty soon there wasn't anything left but this little old place to put the pin," Beman said.

The story that follows has become an indispensable part of the Dye legend. One day, Dye stopped his wife and said, "We have a big problem. I only have 17 holes out there."

They drove out and looked over the area. Alice suggested building the green and filling in the hole with water.

"She said to me, 'Throw a bulkhead out in the middle of it and put some sand and dirt on top on it.' A light went on, and that's exactly how it (happened)," Dye said.

The Dyes were quite familiar with the island green Robert Trent Jones Sr. had built down the road decades ago at the Ponte Vedra Inn & Club. They first played it together in 1946. TPC's apple-shaped, island green was 26 paces long and 30 paces wide. Assuming the hole wouldn't be terribly difficult, Dye sloped the back portion of the green toward the water. "Greatest golfers in the world," Dye repeatedly said, "What's too hard for them?"

Alice told him if he left the green as so, she envisioned a backup at the tee with players unable to keep their tee shots on the putting surface. "Ladies and gentleman," she imagined the TV announcer say, "it's 2 o'clock in the afternoon and the first group is still on No. 17 green." Beman insisted that another board be inserted to raise the back portion of the green. Dye added a small front bunker so balls wouldn't spin off the front of the green into the water. "The green needed a little tweak," Beman said.

The 17th was born by accident, a quirky concession to the limits of space, rather than a grand scheme designed to yield ecstasy as easily as agony. It has become golf's most photo-graphed hole, where roughly 120,000 balls a year are fished out of the lake, or an average of three balls for every golfer who plays the course. As one writer put it, this is the water hole that amateurs replenish with tears.

Not every one of Pete Dye's ideas panned out. He convinced Beman and Kelly to have a small herd of goats roam the course as a tribute to the old Scottish custom of having sheep graze in the rough. The Tour's Dave Postlethwait purchased six goats at a livestock auction and penned them off between the first and second hole in what he dubbed "Goat Island." The goats ate the prickly palmetto rough without damaging the fairway grass. "They were better than a lawn mower," Dye said.

"People thought they were so cute that we started letting them out and soon they were everywhere," Kelly remembered.

Being natural climbers, the goats, led by "Old Prunes," the largest of the lot, scaled the railing of the steep-sloping, pyr-amid-shaped clubhouse roof. When word reached Beman he called Postlethwait into his office.

"I thought this isn't good for me," Postlethwait recalled. "Deane started talking to me. 'About them goats...' "

The blood drained from Postlethwait's face. Beman contin-ued, "If someone doesn't get a picture the next time they're atop the roof, I'm going to be pissed off."

He winked at Postlethwait, who breathed a sigh of relief.

Grass wasn't all the goats ate. They also went grazing in the golf carts of unsuspecting golfers. They gobbled candy bars straight from the wrapper. But the most disturbing story unfolded one day before a horrified lunch crowd at the clubhouse. They watched a baby goat drinking from the pond fronting the practice putting green. Out of nowhere, an alligator emerged and flipped its tail, swatting the goat into the water. The goat popped up and swam for its life with the gator in pursuit.

"Everyone in the dining room cheered for the goat to make it to shore," Kelly said. "Somehow that goat swam to the bank and safety."

Soon the goats were reproducing at prodigious rates, recalled Pete Davison, the club's first director of golf. Anytime it rained, the goats huddled under the porte-cochere, and in the morning it smelled like a zoo. When Old Prunes head butted a golfer, a decision was made: The goats had to go. Any thought of giving the goats a reprieve vanished when one of the goats harassed a sponsor's wife. "That was Crew," recalled Judy Beman, laughing. "He took a liking to her."

Added Kelly: "You know, the downside when we got rid of the goats was we had to add eight men to the golf course crew."

*   *   *

When players got a sneak preview of the under-construction TPC course during the 1980 tournament held across the street, the pros reacted harshly.

In his twangy tenor, Tour veteran Miller Barber said, "Mr. Pete, it'll be a fine course once you put the greens in." Of course, the greens were already in place. They were small. It was Dye's ultimate target golf course.

As a Harbour Town devotee, Tom Watson joined fellow pro Leonard Thompson for a look after their second rounds and lashed out with a fresh round of criticism. "We looked at each other and said how could anybody design greens like this?" Watson remembered.

When the negative reports reached Dye, he approached the two golfers and offered to give them a personal tour the next day. "We got to No. 2 green and I said, 'Pete, how do you get a golfer to play this green?' " Watson asked. "He said, 'The best players in the world can play this golf course.' I said, 'Yeah, but what about the amateurs?' "

One player who took exception to the criticism was Nicklaus. Dye gave him a personal tour in a golf cart that ended in darkness. Jeff Rude, who had been gathering player comments for a story in the *Jacksonville Journal*, had been tipped off that Nicklaus was surveying the course and waited in the shadow of the clubhouse for his review. Night closed in around them as Rude jotted down Nicklaus' response: "All those other guys are wrong. Pete's done a great job."

One of the first to play the completed course was policy board member Ed Sneed, who toured the front nine with Beman and the Tour's Clyde Mangum soon after the holes were grassed. Sneed walked off No. 4 green and said, "Deane this may be the hardest golf course I've ever played." Beman laughed and replied, "Ed, you've just played the four easiest holes on the golf course."

Tour public relations director Dale Antram also escorted *Golf World's* Ron Coffman around the course before its official open. A 5 handicap at the time, Coffman shot a 109. Asked if it was the toughest course he ever played, Coffman answered, "It was that day!"

In front of Coffman was the group of Sneed, Tom Weiskopf, and Ben Crenshaw, who carded a 76 and claimed he putted lights out. "It's Star Wars golf," Crenshaw said afterwards. "The place was designed by Darth Vader."

After dumping four balls in the water during a windy trial-run, Jerry Pate said, "If the wind blows, the tournament may have to be canceled because the 17th hole is unplayable."

But with criticism also came recognition for the enormous achievement of building the course. In March 1980, three years after the bet was made, Arvida's Cobb paid off his lost wager by presenting Beman with a $100 bill mounted on a plaque with the following inscription: "To Deane Beman, the man who did what we said couldn't be done. From Chuck Cobb and his associates at Arvida, who bet on the difficulty of the task, not on the capability of the man doing the task."

Eventually, Alice Dye conceded she too had been short-sighted, in her case when evaluating the unlikely pairing of her husband and Beman.

"Boy, was I wrong," she said in retrospect. "Deane was wonderful. He let Pete do his thing."

"Deane stuck his neck out," Kelly said. "If he failed, it was his head."

But Beman brushes aside individual accolades and applauds the team effort. To some, the gesture may seem like false modesty, but it's genuine appreciation for his fellow dreamers.

"This course didn't get built by anybody's book. It got built by grit and ingenuity and solving problems no one ever faced before building a golf course," said Beman, praising the work done by Dye, Kelly, and Postlethwait.

At 9 a.m., on Friday, Oct. 24, 1980, a bagpiper led a host of dignitaries into the grand opening ceremony. The course was dedicated "to all players of the PGA Tour, whose excellence and integrity in competition are the standard by which all players are measured."

In the audience were Beman's predecessor, Joe Dey, dignitaries such as USGA Senior Amateur champion Bill Campbell, Hall of Famer Byron Nelson, Jacksonville Mayor Jake Godbold, and active Tour pros including Bob Murphy, Mark McCumber, and Bert Yancey. The weather had been magnificent all week with sunshine streaming through the clubhouse windows. But on the day of the course dedication, rain threatened.

The ceremony was planned for the lawn, but was moved inside. Attendees crammed into the clubhouse. Dripping umbrellas were stashed in the entranceway. Tour policy board member Hale Irwin spoke on behalf of the players and called it a "dismal day," but a historic one for the Tour. "We have a place we can call home," he said. "Everybody needs a home." Irwin added, "There was some hesitancy on the policy board's position as to whether we should venture into something of this nature...I've always agreed we should. I'm very proud of the decision we made."

Dye said the weather followed true to form of his course openings dating to his first in Ann Arbor, Mich., when half an inch of snow fell – on a May morning. Dye heaped praise on his crew, noting, "A lot of us take the credit but there really are two people who did all the work. One is Vernon Kelly and the other is an associate of mine, Dave Postlethwait, who spent endless hours working on this project."

Finally, the commissioner addressed the audience. Beman had prepared remarks, but ditched them at the last moment after looking out the clubhouse window. "Some 400 years ago, I believe it was on a day just like this in St. Andrews, Scotland on a gnarly, windy day that somebody played the first round of golf," he said. "So it's not inappropriate that we open a new era here at the Tournament Players Club on just such a day."

Those who attended the ceremony still grin as they remember his remarks almost verbatim. Beman refused to allow the weather to dampen his enthusiasm.

"I think with this golf course we're seeing the beginning of Stadium Golf," Beman continued. "I feel that over the next 20 years that most tournaments we know today will be played on facilities specially designed for spectators."

When he finished, Beman turned the ceremony over to Rev. Abraham Akaka from Honolulu to dedicate the course. Beman and his wife had met the soft-spoken Akaka, pastor of the Kawaiahao Church, when he performed a blessing at the first tee of the Hawaiian Open earlier that year. He flew in from "the Big Island" special for this occasion.

"I think of Deane as a prophet and a priest of golf," Akaka said. "A prophet is one who sees the future and helps to bring it into being and a priest is one who nurtures the life of golf that is here."

To christen the affair, Akaka dipped palm leaves in an ancient ceramic bowl, resembling a salad mixer, which Beman held filled with water. Akaka said a prayer and waved the wet leaves in four directions, representing the four corners of the earth. Then he asked the audience to rise, bow their heads and join him in prayer. The blare of bagpipes signaled the end of the ceremony. Fireworks burst in the air, creating a mosaic on a canvas of gray clouds.

Mercifully the rain stopped. Fall chilled the air. Fifteen minutes later, the inaugural group of Beman, Dye, Irwin, and John Tucker, the ceremony's emcee and the first chairman of the Greater Jacksonville Open in 1965, teed off. Irwin carded a back-nine 33 and Beman hit a fairway wood to 3 feet on the final green, prompting golf writer Jeff Rude to deadpan, "Pete, you didn't make these finishing holes tough enough. The commissioner finished birdie-birdie."

Afterward, Dye was asked if the TPC was his best design. He answered with the savvy of a foreign diplomat. "It's a great bit of personal satisfaction to be asked by the Tour members to build their golf course," he said, "but comparing golf courses is like comparing women. The most beautiful one is the one you're with now."

That weekend, Beman played with Jerry Pate and coached him around the course. Beman told him that Dye created visual hazards off the tee that are less severe than they appear.

"If you pay attention, I'm going to show you how to play this golf course. And if you'll just follow my lead you'll probably win this thing," Beman said, referring to the Tournament Players Championship.

His top tip? Dye built a second-shot course with greens so small and undulating, Beman told Pate, that if he decided to layup off the tee, he'd face a more difficult shot than the one he just avoided. "Go ahead and be aggressive off the tee," Beman advised.

Those pros not in attendance were just as curious about the much-ballyhooed course and asked Mangum, the Tour's deputy commissioner and a crusty golf lifer, for a scouting report. He smirked, and with a slow, North Carolina drawl said, "Tick, tick, tick." It was Mangum's sly way of saying danger loomed at every turn – and flirting with it could explode a round.

The course officially was open for play, but the Tournament Players Championship wasn't held there the following March. It needed time to mature. So, the tournament returned for a swan-song at Sawgrass CC. Meanwhile, several of the TPC's greens were softened and run-offs raised to create more pin positions between the course opening and the first tournament at TPC Sawgrass in 1982. Dye didn't appreciate the changes Beman insisted on, but he relented. "It was just on the wrong side of fair," Beman said.

As the first Tournament Players Championship at TPC

Sawgrass approached, the anticipation heightened. Among the blizzard of hype, Peter Dobereiner in his September 1981 *Golf Digest* column may have summed up best what to expect: "On March 18, 1982, a new major championship will be born. In the years that follow, the new championship will grow in stature and, although it may never achieve the cachet of the venerable U.S. and British Opens, it will acquire a special status as the ultimate test of a golfer's character and skill. This much is certain and beyond argument."

Future Commissioner Beman on the shoulders (left) of future USA Today golf writer, Steve Hershey, during 1952 Rec Center football season in Bethesda, Md.

Francis Ouimet (left) with two future PGA Tour commissioners, Beman and Joseph C. Dey.

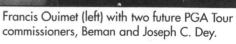

To Deane Beman with all good wishes.
Ben Hogan

15-year-old Deane Beman during an exhibition match with Ben Hogan in 1953.

Amateur Beman holding the British Amateur Trophy (1959) and his second U.S. Amateur Championship Trophy (1963).

Beman as a golf pro getting ready to tackle the Tour (late 1960's).

Policy Board Meeting of the Tournament Players Division of the PGA of America in 1969. Top (L-R) - John Murchison, Dudley Wysong, Sam Gates, Ross Teter, Bill Clarke, Jack Tuthill, Billy Casper, George Love, Warren Orlick, Beman. Seated (L-R) - Joe Dey, Paul Austin, Leo Fraser, Jack Nicklaus.

Barbara Nicklaus, Beman, Jack Nicklaus, after Jack won the 1976 Tournament Players Championship at Inverrary, FL, receiving the Joseph C. Dey, Jr. Trophy.

Joe Black, president of the PGA of America, with Beman at announcement of name change back from Tournament Players Association to PGA Tour on March 17, 1982.

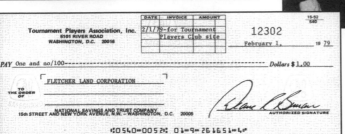

Beman pushes the first dirt to start construction on the Tournament Players Club, Sawgrass (1979), joined by his wife, Judy, and Paul Fletcher. Pictured is the one dollar check to Fletcher Land Corporation for the property.

Stadium golf takes shape as construction nears completion at the TPC Sawgrass. Here, the original first tee. The inset drawing at right depicts Beman's sketch for the first tee design.

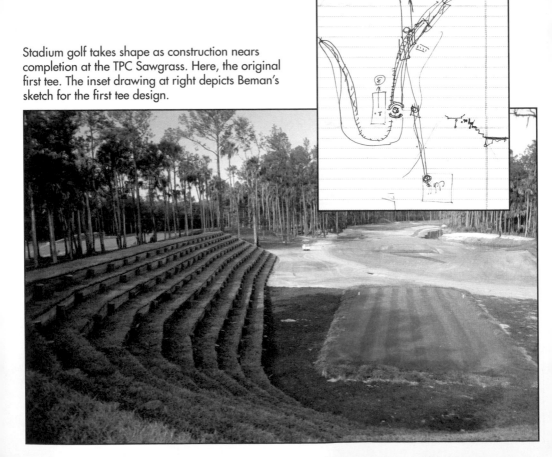

Architect Pete Dye with Beman at Opening Day of the TPC Sawgrass, October 24, 1980.

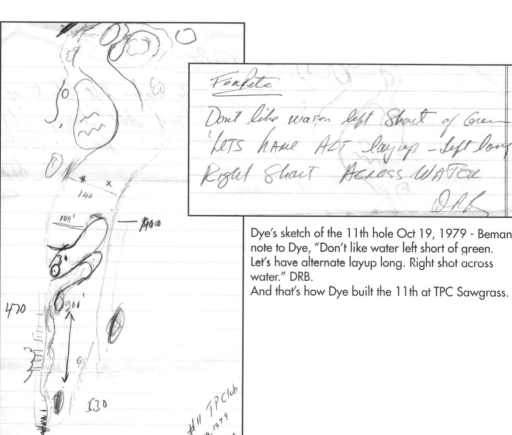

Dye's sketch of the 11th hole Oct 19, 1979 - Beman's note to Dye, "Don't like water left short of green. Let's have alternate layup long. Right shot across water." DRB.
And that's how Dye built the 11th at TPC Sawgrass.

Jerry Pate goes for a victory lap after winning the first Players Championship in 1982 on the new Stadium course. Beman and Dye watch from the water.

Beman and son, Darby, still climbing mountains 30 years after finding Sawgrass Country Club.

Florida GOLFWEEK Cover
October 31, 1985
"Beman Pulls another Rabbit from TOUR hat"

FLORIDA GOLFWEEK's cover provided colorful emphasis to another step of the PGA Tour's growth.

Shell Oil president, Steve Miller (left), Beman and executive director of the Houston Golf Association, Duke Butler, as Shell signs on as title sponsor for the event in 1991.

RJR Nabisco party 1986, San Antonio, with Beman and his "horse" in the armadillo race.

Beman with Del de Windt, who maintained a low single-digit handicap while devoting 13 years of service to the PGA Tour's tournament policy board, including the last 11 as chairman.

Beman visits the Past Champions' Dinner at the 1992 HP Byron Nelson Classic.
Top (L-R) Lanny Wadkins, Tom Watson, Mark Hayes, Raymond Floyd, Bruce Lietzke.
Middle - Bob Gilder, Ben Crenshaw, Craig Stadler, Bob Eastwood, Payne Stewart, Fred Couples.
Front - Jodie Mudd, Beman, "Lord" Byron Nelson, Nick Price.

Beman and Arnold Palmer at the
commissioner's retirement party.
Players Championship week,
March 19, 1995

The Evolution of the PGA Tour Logo

1969 thru Jan. 1, 1976

Used until 1980

Used until 1982

Used Jan. 1 1982 - March 17, 1982

March 17, 1982 - Current

ONE GIANT LEAP FOR STADIUM GOLF

W hen the 1982 Tournament Players Championship dawned, the curtain finally was raised and Beman and Dye's dream of "Stadium Golf" debuted. It was mid-March and their vision of transforming professional golf from a player's game that towed a gallery behind it to a spectator sport that allowed fans to sit comfortably and watch the competition unfold would finally be put to the test. The spectator mounds had been fashioned and refashioned with this event in mind. But would fans surge through the gates and depart voicing their approval? Even Dye wondered how the TPC course would be accepted.

"Then I walked around and saw about 4,000 people sitting to the right of the 18th green and another big crowd on the mound to the left," Dye said. "I thought to myself, 'My God, they work.' "

Defending champion Raymond Floyd proved the course could be handled on pro-am day, when in the company of Dye, he toured the course in 66, smashing the course record by three strokes despite a double bogey at the final hole. Dye provided suggestions where to hit the ball, but somehow they got separated on No. 18. Without Dye's guidance, Floyd hit the ball on a flat area of the green and it bounded over.

Golf World's Ron Coffman walked a few holes with Dye later that day. Whenever someone hit a shot close to a hole and made birdie, Dye declared, "Hole's playable." They watched Nicklaus shoot a 32 on the back nine, his front side of his pro-am round. The architect openly rooted for a low score. "Come on, Jack,"

Dye said to himself. "Shoot 63 and get these guys off my back."

As Coffman and Dye watched play at the last hole, Dye said, "They look like they've been through a real battle. And that's the way it is: they should have to battle."

After witnessing Floyd's round and Nicklaus' strong play, Dye was confident players would embrace his groundbreaking design. He couldn't have been more wrong.

From the very first day the pros screamed that TPC Sawgrass was too penal. Most of the criticism was leveled at the tiny, tilted greens – each was 6,000-square-feet or less. They also were too bumpy, quirky, and contoured. "He took Augusta's greens and miniaturized them," Tom Watson said.

Dye considered that a compliment. "I thanked him," Dye said. "I always felt Augusta's greens were too big."

Nicklaus had praised the layout during construction, but when asked whether the layout suited his game, he answered frankly. "No," he said. "I've never been very good at stopping a 5-iron on the hood of a Volkswagen."

Players were concerned that the championship might turn on the sheer vagaries of fortunes. "They messed up a perfectly good swamp," J.C. Snead added. "This course is 90 percent horse manure and 10 percent luck."

But if players despised it, fans loved it. "The course provides dizzying changes in fortunes for an exciting telecast, excitement for those who, like Romans at the Coliseum, ring the 17th waiting to see how many Christians survive," *Golf World's* Dick Taylor wrote.

The par-3 island green quickly earned its reputation as a hole with no margin for error. Wet or dry. On or off. No hole makes more golfers wince, cover their eyes, or bow their head in shame. Former British Open champion Mark Calcavecchia compared it to a 3 p.m. root canal. "All day you know it's coming," he said, "but that doesn't make it any easier when it's finally time to confront it."

Nightmares, cold sweats, and heartburn became associated with No. 17, a hole Peter Dobereiner wrote is "surely destined to become the most notorious short hole in America. I reckon it will invoke more blaspheming than the 16th at Cypress Point by a ratio of about two to one."

He was right. From its baptism in the first round at precisely 8:59 a.m., when Dave Thore dumped one in the drink, to Len Mattiace's disastrous 8 knocked him from contention in 1998 to the rinsed tee shot of Paul Goydos in a 2008 playoff, the par-3 17th has terrorized even the best golfers. Thore, a 28-year-old pro from Reidsville, N.C., pushed an 8-iron into the water. *New York Times* Pulitzer prize-winning sports writer Dave Anderson was there to chronicle it.

"Congratulations," somebody said to Thore after he posted a 77, "you're the first ever to put it in the water on No. 17 in competition."

"Thank you," Thore said with a smile. "And after I put my next shot on, I was the first ever to three-putt it in competition, too."

Almost an hour later, Doug Tewell drained a 10-foot putt for the first birdie. When the first round ended, 20 balls had splashed into the the lake at No. 17, including two each by Ed Fiori and David Edwards. Fiori had the lead at 5-under, but after paying a taxing price at the treacherous hole he finished with 70.

The Florida wind that usually blew unremittingly each March was little more than a light breeze. Thirty-five players broke par and 21 matched it. Still, at the midway point, the TPC savaged many of the best golfers in the world. Several players destined for Hall of Fame enshrinement someday missed the cut, which came at 4-over, 148. Among those departing were Trevino, who shot the first 82 of his Tour career and didn't turn in a card the second day; Arnold Palmer, Ben Crenshaw and Johnny Miller (149); Lanny Wadkins (150); Nicklaus and Gary Player (151); Chi Chi Rodriguez (153); and Sam Snead (158). Pate, in contrast, was brimming with confidence: "When we got to Saturday, I looked around to see who had missed the cut and said, 'Lord, I only have a few guys to beat.' "

* * *

On March 20, 1982, at 4:30 p.m., America finally got a chance to see what all the fuss was over the course when CBS Sports came on the air. "Welcome to the inaugural Tournament Players

Championship at the Tournament Players Club," CBS commentator Vin Scully began, "a course that smacks of Seminole and Pine Valley and Harbour Town with a distinct Scottish flavor that will perpetuate the memory of two great architects, the late Scot Donald Ross and the creator of The Players Club, Pete Dye. It also expresses the dreams and aspirations of commissioner Deane Beman, relying on the philosophy of target golf, where accuracy and the use of every club in the bag is absolutely necessary."

When the leaderboard flashed on the screen, Scott Simpson held a 2-shot advantage through 12 holes over Brad Bryant, who was two holes ahead of him. A logjam of four golfers shared third place at 5-under, including Pate, who had just found the water with his second shot at No. 18.

"So the leaderboard is about to change a bit," Scully announced.

Even after he shot the day's low round, a four-under 68, Watson continued his assault on the course. "The pin placements are stupid, the greens so severe they're unfair," he said in *The Jacksonville Times-Union*. "They really should be changed, and I'd be happy to drive the bulldozer."

At day's end, Bruce Lietzke, with a 69, moved into a share of the lead at 210 with Bryant. "Whoever wins," Lietzke said, "will have to show a lot of heart and have a lot of guts."

To triumph, Lietzke knew he would have to survive a closing gauntlet of holes that writer Ron Coffman predicted would "someday be mentioned alongside Augusta's Amen Corner or Merion's quarry holes or Pebble Beach's ocean holes."

In 2008, Beman's son Darby – who all those years ago played with his father on spring break when the vision of a permanent home for the tournament in Ponte Vedra took form – stood in the family's den and pronounced, "They can say all they want about Amen Corner but to win The Players Championship you've got to run 'The Gauntlet.' "

A nickname had never stuck for the treacherous closing holes from Nos. 16-18 at TPC Sawgrass. Beman liked it, picked up the phone and told Tour officials he had a name. Later that day, NBC's Jimmy Roberts relayed the story to a national TV audience and christened the stretch "The Gauntlet."

On Sunday at the 18th hole in 1982, Beman enjoyed a private moment of satisfaction. The weather was breezy but pleasant. This was his time, a quiet interlude before the leaders emerged and he would hand the trophy to the champion. Where Beman once imagined "the future of golf" amid crooked pines and palmettos, there now sat thousands gathered to honor it.

Just as Beman had wished, the course's routing moved away from the clubhouse and back toward it on several occasions. The hubs of activity Beman conceived meant fans didn't have to walk several miles to view multiple holes. The finishing hole played in front of one giant amphitheater capable of holding 50,000 people. Every paying customer could witness the winning putt. No periscopes required.

"It's been praised and it's been criticized," Ken Venturi said on camera that day. "Great courses are like great players. They must stand the test of time."

When CBS showed the first leaderboard during the final-round telecast, Lietzke, through 12 holes, owned a one-shot lead over Pate and Bryant with Craig Stadler, Roger Maltbie and Seve Ballesteros trailing by two shots. Hubert Green enjoyed the clubhouse lead at 2 under. Lietzke birdied the first two holes, but slid back with bogeys at Nos. 8 and 9. After a poor chip, Lietzke saved par at No. 14 from 12 feet.

Pate, playing one group ahead of Lietzke, had birdies at No. 3 from 15 feet and No. 7 from 30 to gain one stroke with an outward 35. He sliced his deficit to one shot at No. 12, holing a birdie putt from 12 feet. Two holes later, he grabbed a share of the lead when his 20-foot birdie putt broke left into the center of the cup. Pate pumped his fist. Bryant made it a trio atop the leaderboard with a birdie at 14, but fell back with a 3-putt bogey from 25 feet on 15.

With the outcome still in doubt, Beman went on camera to announce the Seiko Grand Prix, a season-long points race beginning at the Tournament Players Championship and concluding at the tournament preceding the TPC next season. His marketing deals were beginning to take flight. This deal promised more riches to the top-8 finishers; they would share a $350,000 purse with $150,000 awarded to the points leader.

Pate made the serpentine walk to the tee box at No. 17,

the par-3 with a tee shot Maltbie likened to landing a 747 on a cocktail napkin. Moments before, Ballesteros's bid to win the tournament ended there when he missed the green. Wet. Five. Done. Victor Regalado made back-to-back sevens there the last two rounds. Now, it was Pate's turn. The previous two days he hit 9-iron, but this time, with the pin positioned in the back right corner – a small and precarious target – Pate cut an 8-iron. It was perfectly judged, stopping 15 feet left of the hole. Standing on the 17th green, Pate watched Lietzke, his brother-in-law, take a drop after his second shot at No. 16, a cut 2-iron from 241 yards, found the water. The ball skipped off a mound, kicked through a bunker and trickled into the drink. Knowing he was now sitting in the cat bird's seat, Pate canned his slick downhill birdie putt. For the four rounds, Pate birdied No. 17 three times.

As soon as Pate knocked his approach stiff at 18, Beman handed his wallet and watch to his wife. Even before Pate sank his winning putt, Beman knew he was about to get wet.

He and Pate walked toward the water. Pate's left arm rested on Beman's left shoulder, and Beman's right arm wrapped around Pate's waist. They looked like a happy couple. When CBS cut back from a commercial break, Scully asked, "Would you like to see perhaps the wildest moment in the history of any professional sport?" He broke off in mid-sentence to report, "There goes the commissioner, Deane Beman, pushed in by Pate. That splash was Pete Dye. Last is Jerry Pate." Beman's backstroke, Scully quipped, was worthy of the 1984 U.S. Olympics team.

"Deane was blowing water out of his mouth like a whale," the Tour's Vernon Kelly said. "Right after that he developed hepatitis. I swear it was from that damn water."

Beman's spiffy camel hair coat was ruined. A bespectacled Beman forgot to remove his glasses and also left in his breast pocket a handful of note cards upon which he jotted notes. A soaking wet Dye didn't have a change of clothes so he went into the pro shop and charged a pair of tan slacks and a shirt to Beman. Dye still wears the sansabelt pants once in a while.

"They're a little suity for me," Dye said. "They have pleated fronts."

Trophy ceremony emcee Pat Summerall asked Pate, "Do

you have some deal with Jacques Cousteau?"

"I told Pete Dye I was going to make him famous on Friday," Pate explained. "He said, 'How's that?' I told him I'm going to win the tournament and throw you in the lake and I said, 'I'm going to have to drag the commissioner in, too.' "

Beman took off his sport jacket; he stood with his hair wet and slicked back, his shirt unbuttoned at the top and his tie loosened. He feigned that the check for a record-prize of $90,000 had been in his breast pocket, but had disappeared. "It's over there," he said, pointing to the water.

"If all this doesn't make the TPC a major championship," concluded *Sports Illustrated's* Dan Jenkins, "then Jerry Pate, Deane Beman, and Pete Dye can't swim a stroke."

*   *   *

Architecture, it's often been said, is best seen out of one's peripheral vision. The same can be said for golf course design. After the round, Pate needled Beman and Dye's creation at the winner's press conference. Pate joked to the media that he kept his first-place check dry so he could give it to Dye to pay for remodeling some of the greens. Pate was kidding about picking up the tab, but the players he beat thought the course no laughing matter. One year later, Dye's TPC Sawgrass came in for a fresh round of scrutiny. As was often the case, much of the vitriol surfaced during a rain delay that forced a Monday finish.

"It was mutiny," recalled Tour veteran Mark McCumber.

Nicklaus complained that the course repelled good shots. He voiced an opinion shared by many. "I've never seen players talk so freely about a golf course," Nicklaus told the *Jacksonville Journal*. "You hear stuff you wouldn't hear at any other tournament. One hundred and 20 players can't be wrong."

Tom Weiskopf's tirade extended all the way to the players' parking lot. Having likened the course to "playing Donkey Kong out there," he noted players had to climb 50 steps to reach the locker room. "At the bottom of that hill is handicap parking," Weiskopf said. "That's how tough this place is."

Dye listened to the objections and maintained his position that the course wasn't as severe as the players insisted it to be.

"I don't think there's any need to back off on the course, to soften it," Dye said while watching the tournament. "In fact, when they learn how to play the course, we may have to put in some more obstacles to keep them totally frustrated."

Two days later, many of the Tour's leading golfers submitted a letter of complaint to Beman. Hale Irwin, Crenshaw, Nicklaus, Stadler, Watson, and Weiskopf were among those who signed it. The letter listed the course's faults. They also complained that Beman dictated the design of the course without consulting them.

"The first year we played, we just barely got by," Dye said in retrospect. "The second year when they played, they had a revolution out here, and they wanted to kill me."

To appease the protesters, Beman called Dye after the '83 tournament and asked him to tour the course with a player committee comprising Nicklaus, Crenshaw, Irwin, Ed Sneed and Jim Colbert. The "gang of five" accompanied Dye around the course on May 30.

They gathered in the players' locker room at the TPC. While they waited Nicklaus advised his fellow pros, "We don't want to embarrass Pete." Everyone agreed to keep the discussions civil. Suddenly, the doors flung open and in walked Dye, saying, "Hello, everybody!"

Wasting little time on small talk and introductions, Dye took control of the meeting. "Guys," he said, "before we start this meeting can we do one thing?"

Heads nodded in agreement. Dye wanted to go straight to the course. So they mounted up in a fleet of carts, two men to a buggy and drove to the first green, which was widely panned for repelling good shots. Dye pointed to the hump in the green and confessed to riding the dozer and shaping it himself. He explained there was a method to his madness and he took full responsibility. "When I got finished, I stood back and I liked it," he said. "I liked it so much, I did it 17 more times." Dye's mouth turned into a smothered smile. Everyone laughed.

"Guys," Dye said, "we don't have to close the course for anything. We can do these greens one at a time, take the slope down, soften it and be back in business in two weeks."

Dye had broken the tension, but the excoriation continued.

They went hole by hole. "It was a grill and roast session," said Bobby Weed, who as Dye's right-hand man at the time would make the changes to the course. "They asked, 'Why did you do that? I would like to know. What were you thinking?' "

Dye remained tight-lipped and relented. He answered every question. Sometimes he shrugged his shoulders and his comeback amounted to "I don't know what I was thinking. You're absolutely right." He asked for their advice on improvements. "That's good. We can do that," he said.

But, in truth, it was a hard day. Naturally, he had invested emotionally in the work, making it difficult to cede control, and felt dismayed by the course's reconstruction. Months later, Crenshaw, the architectural committee's co-chair, presented a report on the changes to be made to TPC Sawgrass. He went hole-by-hole. When Crenshaw, skipped from No. 3 to No. 5, Curtis Strange yelled out, "What? No changes to No. 4?"

Crenshaw replied, "No, Curtis. We can't change all 18."

It's worth noting that in the years to come many of the most outspoken critics borrowed attributes of TPC's design for their own course projects. Said Beman: "There were comments about windmills and Donkey Kong and the hood of a Volkswagen – we won't mention any names here – but I have since played a number of golf courses by those people who made those quotes, and some of their greens were a lot more severe."

Weed took notes during the session with the architectural committee and eventually he implemented the approved tweaks. From 1983 to 1988, he made subtle changes to the course, removing some of its fangs. In fact, he and his crew started working on the greens Sunday of the final round of the tournament once the last group finished a hole. The crews stripped the greens and altered their slopes. They replaced Bermuda grass with bent and then returned to Bermuda. The original greens were of the old-fashioned push-up type, using native soil. In the summer of 1987, Weed finally built USGA regulation greens.

Crenshaw was wrong. They could change all 18 greens, and they did – even No. 4, to Strange's delight. They also widened fairways and removed hundreds of trees. They took out a pot bunker in front of the 18th green. All the alterations led *Golfweek's* Jeff Rude to declare, "TPC Sawgrass has been tweaked more than Cher."

Said Weed: "One of my biggest regrets of being in the business is I was the one who had to make all the changes."

But Weed chuckles as he tells the story about gaining membership in the American Society of Golf Course Architects. To be considered for this elite fraternity, an architect must have completed a minimum of five projects. Admittance is voted on by one's peers. In touting Weed's merits, Dye remarked, "I think we should let Bobby in on the fact that he rebuilt TPC Stadium Course five times."

Over the years, players' opinions softened as the course matured. Admiration for the layout grew with each passing tournament. Beman said it took 10-15 years longer than he expected for it to be considered one of golf's most prestigious events. "It's the ugly child that you've grown to respect and love," Beman said.

Those who remember the land's transformation from the outback to "a sub-tropical Neverland," to the setting for the elegance of today's Mediterranean Revival-style clubhouse, still marvel.

"You once were more likely to be attacked by a wild boar out there than you were to be served a draught Stella (Artois)," 1988 Players champion Mark McCumber said.

Born and raised in Jacksonville, McCumber understands better than most that the course, the tournament, and Tour headquarters combined to change the city's image as a "Double-A" town.

"I love everything about my hometown but it is South Georgia - North Florida," he said. "We don't have palm trees everywhere. We have a bit of a winter. It's a blue-collar town. It's not Miami Beach. It's not on a Bay."

Yet this is where Beman picked, of all places, to base the Tour. This is where Beman defied the odds.

"You're going to build in an area that at the time you wouldn't want to drive through at night without an extra canister of gas in your car?" McCumber said. "And now it's going to be the home of a high-end golf resort and community and host the best golfers every spring? And by the way, we'll give you these 415 acres for a dollar. It's quite a story."

More than a decade after TPC Sawgrass opened, Jacksonville landed its own NFL franchise. In 1999, the team hosted the Tennessee Titans at home in the AFC Championship game. Duke Butler and his wife, Sheila, arrived at the Tour's luxury box at Alltel Stadium an hour early. Who were the lone other early birds but Deane and Judy Beman. Soon the box and the stadium would be full and the Jaguars would have a chance to reach the Super Bowl. Butler sidled up to Beman and used this private moment before kickoff to share a belief he publicized often: Jacksonville wouldn't have landed a NFL franchise in 1995 if not for Beman. It was the Tour, Butler claims, that put the city on the map.

"If you know Deane, you know he reluctantly accepts compliments," Butler said. "He had a little smile on his face and he replied, 'Could be.'

"He thought about it for a moment and added, 'I might be the reason the Mayo Clinic is here too.' It's the most braggadocio thing I ever heard him say. And he's right."

*   *   *

When some Tour caddies first paced off TPC Sawgrass, they tabbed it Deane's Dream. Ever since, he's been hailed for his foresight. The success of TPC Sawgrass spawned a network of more than 30 courses around the country. During construction, Beman's vision grew beyond just a permanent home for The Players Championship because he was approached by Bob Kirby. The Westinghouse chairman and member of the Tour's policy board presented a prospect for a second TPC in Coral Springs, Fla. Soon the American Golf Sponsors, the trade group of tournament directors, attended an outing during the grand opening week at TPC Sawgrass and were dazzled by the possibilities.

"They saw it. They played it. And they realized what it could mean to their tournaments," Beman said.

Phoenix, Houston and Hartford were among the early suitors. Kelly, who oversaw the Tour's Golf Course Properties subsidiary, contends he never convinced anyone to build a golf course. Here's why: the Tour established a policy that encouraged building new TPCs. They waved incentives in front of tournaments, such as a place to play rent-free. This represented a significant savings – in some cases as much as $300,000 – that went straight to the bottom line. In addition, the tournament organizing committee received the first $100,000 of net revenue from the club. When the tournament poured those funds back into its purse, it also got a bump in television revenue because the formula for splitting the TV fund was a function of purse size. That amounted to another $50,000 the tournament could donate to local charities.

Kelly's ace up his sleeve to developers: Being able to promise the course would host a tournament. If a developer planned to build a course for a hotel, a real estate project or a municipality, it was a fairly easy sell, he said.

"The golf course is kind of a sunk cost. You're going to have to fund the thing in the meantime. Why not give us the money to build the course," Kelly pitched. "It may cost a little more than you were going to spend, but not a lot. You fund the initial operating losses, which frankly, you will have to do anyway whether we are involved or not. But if we are involved, we will give you 80 percent of the revenue we generate until you get back the money you spent on the golf course without interest."

Without having to buy the land, pay the construction costs, or service the debt, Golf Course Properties, the Tour's for-profit arm, would eventually gain control of the facility. Every dollar the developer received from the Tour reduced its option price by a dollar. The terms of the agreement was usually 10 years, and Kelly can't recall a case where the Tour didn't exercise its ownership option (except for the few occasions where the developer went bankrupt). Of course, the Tour shouldered responsibility for operating losses once the development sold out. Kelly also downplayed the notoriety of selecting a signature designer alone. "It will be unique until such time as they build another course down the road, but a TPC with that same architect will always be unique in a specific market," Kelly explained.

For developers, the annual tournament exposure was an irresistible sales tool as was the comfort of knowing the Tour would ensure course conditions were maintained at tournament level. "We did TPC deals more than once with the same partners so I know the model worked," Kelly said.

He fondly remembers the deal the Tour orchestrated with the city of Scottsdale, Ariz., as one of the most memorable. City officials offered a 50-year lease that Kelly considered a win-win proposition for both parties. Beman, however, objected. He wanted the same 100-year term that the city agreed to with the Bureau of Land Management. Fifty years was the longest contract the city ever signed. Kelly told Beman he thought asking for a longer term could be a dealbreaker. But Beman persisted.

All the lawyers were seated at a long conference table at closing. The lease terms, however, still were unresolved. The deal had to be completed the next day because construction of the two courses were financed by tax-exempt bonds, which had been eliminated by the 1986 Reagan tax bill. Time was running out. Kelly called Beman in Florida for his final instructions. Beman gave Kelly his blessing to close the deal for 50 years, but he wanted Kelly to try one more time to improve the terms.

Kelly entered the conference room and everyone turned to him in expectation of Beman's decision. Kelly explained he still required the same terms as the Bureau of Land Management. "A city official threw down his pen in disgust and said, 'We're not even going to be alive in 50 years.' I said, 'You won't be. I won't be. But the commissioner thinks he will be,' " Kelly recalled. "They laughed and damn near fell on the floor. They gave us a 25-year extension, and Deane was happy with 75 years."

The Stadium course model, the only major-league sports venues owned by the players themselves, has fulfilled their promise as homes for bigger galleries. The TPC Scottsdale has become the largest attended tournament in the world, earning the nickname "The Greatest Party on Grass." Weekly attendance annually exceeds 500,000, or more than double the figure at some U.S. Open venues. The par-3, No. 16 is reputed to be "golf's most hollered ground," where crowd capacity – on this one hole – exceeds 20,000 people.

The success of TPC Sawgrass, in turn, influenced future golf architects and led to Dye being hailed as "the father of modern golf course architecture." As one of golf's most influential temples, TPC Sawgrass inspired a generation of target golf courses and started a trend of creating "heroic holes" – with disaster waiting at every turn. Elements of Dye's demonic design became de rigueur: nightmare-inducing carries of water, steeply banked greens, and severe putting surfaces. Railroad ties so proliferated golf course design in the 1980s that Dye ultimately stopped using them.

The TPCs that followed, however, suffered in comparison to the success of Dye's model. The Tour's goal was to create a family of courses as diverse in personality and geography as they were united in ideology. But some players complained that the courses looked too alike and all were patterned after Dye's original. *Golf Digest's* Ron Whitten noted one could detect a watermark in their design that included no uphill shots, no elevated greens, and no trees that could interfere with a spectator's view.

"(TPC) layouts each had their own personality, but all were unmistakably children sired within the same clan," Whitten wrote.

There was no arguing that the TPC network was an unqualified success in the Tour's effort to diversify its revenue streams. A decade after TPC Sawgrass opened, revenue from operations, royalties and licensing fees, management fees, and membership sales totaled $63.5 million – eclipsing revenue from television. The courses' constitute part of the for-profit end of the Tour's business; The Tour owns or has an ownership stake in the majority of the clubs.

But not every TPC resulted in a financial success. Beman took this in stride, preferring to look at the bigger picture.

On one occasion, a Tour member addressed attendees at a players' meeting in the late '80s and noted the TPC Connecticut in Hartford (which opened in June 1984) wasn't meeting expectations.

"Yes, it is true," Beman told him, adding that the Tour had lost approximately $5 million. (Later, when the Tour sold real estate it owned by the course, it recovered its losses). "I won't defend that. I will only say this: I overspent by $5 million there, and I've lost some more you don't even know about, but I've made you about a billion dollars overall and that ain't a bad score."

To arrive at that lofty figure, Beman counted the asset value of the Tour's ownership of properties and net income that has been generated by the facilities and passed through into the players' retirement plan (at the end of 2010, the net cash flow was north of $250 million since the first TPC opened). He also factored the savings gained from individual tournaments playing their championships on TPCs rent-free (a $75 million savings, according to the Tour), and the revenue generated from accommodating more spectators.

"You add all of that up, and the net income to the charities, the net income to the players, and the existing book value assets that the Tour now enjoys, and it is just about a billion dollars and growing," he said.

Beman moved mountains – of swampy muck – to get the first TPC built. There may be no better legacy of his tenure than the course and the tournament that has become such an annual rite of spring.

"It comforts me to know that long after I'm gone players, fans, audiences around the world will still be enjoying these clubs," Beman reflected. "That's immensely satisfying."

A FOX IN THE CHICKEN COOP

As Mark Kizziar turned his rental car on to PGA Tour Boulevard, something looked different this time. It was Oct. 31, 1981, and he was there for a policy board meeting. Kizziar had visited Tour headquarters in Ponte Vedra on several occasions. As vice president of the PGA of America, he had been there for the grand opening of TPC Sawgrass, and for the Tournament Players Championship. When he nosed the car to a stop, it hit him. All the signage had been changed. Where it once read PGA Tour, the signs now were inscribed with the insignia of the TPA Tour. This wasn't a Halloween decoration. Beman had called their bluff.

"That was Deane firing a salvo over the bow of the ship," Kizziar said. "That's just the way he went at it."

At the previous board meeting in August, the Tour had voted to change its name and the PGA directors were none too pleased. PGA president Joe Black called the Tour's board chairman Robert Oelman, chief executive of NCR and a weekend golfer, and requested a private meeting to voice the PGA's displeasure. Black, Kizziar, his secretary, and PGA treasurer Mickey Powell commandeered Beman's office at Tour headquarters for the meeting. If Oelman didn't realize the severity of the situation, he soon did. The PGA officers made no effort to hide their disgust. Powell erupted, "The first thing I'm going to do tomorrow is move that we fire Deane Beman."

"And I'm going to second it so we can get it on the floor," Kizziar threatened.

Oelman listened as they railed about how unreasonable

Beman had been, and tried to head things off. "Gentleman, that's not going to get us anywhere."

In truth, the PGA officers knew they wouldn't muster the necessary votes. But Powell wasn't done yet. He interjected, "I want to make one thing clear, there will always be a PGA Tour and we will run the PGA Tour if we have to, so we might as well get this figured out."

That would come in time. Cooler heads prevailed at the Tour policy board meeting the next morning, but the PGA directors made clear that its drawn-out battle with the Tour was on the verge of mushrooming into another full-fledged confrontation.

*   *   *

Relations between the Tour and PGA simmered after peace was reached in late 1968 with the formation of the Tournament Players Division (as the Tour was initially known). Joe Dey helped smooth over the rough patches.

During a private conversation in the early 1970s, Beman remarked to the Tour's board chairman, Paul Austin, what a tough job he and Dey faced, considering lingering tensions between the players and PGA. Austin smiled broadly and replied that he was a master of avoiding conflict. It was simple, he said. Beman raised an eyebrow and wondered, "Simple?" As if he suffered an allergic reaction to conflict, Austin tabled any topic that he didn't expect would be approved unanimously, according to several former policy board members.

Austin's strategy succeeded in promoting goodwill and shedding the nasty image of warring factions. But it also prevented the Tour from making any significant progress, which Beman likened to "crawling over hot coals." Beman understood this, at least enough to make allowances. "It was right to let the wounds heal, but it was a lost five years from the standpoint of making progress in bringing golf into the world of major sports," he said. "Strategically, Austin wasn't wrong. It was a comfortable place for Dey, who wasn't really a businessman and wasn't a crusader for progress. He was a preservationist."

During Beman's early tenure in the 1970s, the two groups coexisted uneasily, but for the most part, productively and congenially. But tensions flared in the early 1980s when Beman began instituting many of the new programs approved during the Tour's groundbreaking board meeting in late 1979. To Beman, the signs that turmoil lay ahead were always everpresent. When the Tour negotiated a deal in 1975 for Anheuser-Busch to sponsor an event at Kingsmill Resort in Williamsburg, Va., the PGA threw up a red flag. PGA president Henry Poe noted that the PGA pro there didn't own the pro shop. Poe expected Beman to make the pro's ownership of the shop at the Anheuser-Busch-owned resort a quid pro quo of any deal.

"His first thought is 'We have to protect the pro in the golf shop,' " Beman said. "This is almost one-third of my board. This is what I had to deal with on a regular basis."

It was the type of dispute that Austin avoided. Beman ignored the PGA's objections and got the deal done, but it was a harbinger of things to come.

When the PGA's executive committee gave approval to the Tour to form its own independent corporation in exchange first for a 7.5 percent royalty and then for the World Series of Golf, the PGA – Beman believed – in effect sold the Tour to the players.

"But the PGA continued to act as if they still owned the Tour, and the Tour existed primarily for the benefit of the PGA and not for the benefit of the players that were playing," he said. "That was the basic problem."

The PGA resisted Beman's initiatives. Del de Windt, the Tour's board chairman from 1981 to 1993, made certain to remind the directors to act within the bounds of their complex legal and fiduciary duties; nevertheless, having three board members from the PGA was a continuing source of frustration for Beman. In 1974, the PGA objected to the Tour selling a program for the Tournament Players Championship (then played in August) because it would compete for advertising dollars with the PGA Championship program. Trouble was brewing. "We hadn't talked about marketing," Beman said. "We only talked about a tournament annual program. It was a pretty good indication of what I was going to face."

To bolster his argument, Beman mentioned the time he did a slow burn when he discovered that the PGA had sold its foreign TV rights for the PGA Championship along with its domestic

rights to ABC in 1979, without even the courtesy of informing him. In the past, the Tour had packaged the foreign rights
to Tour events and the PGA Championship together. Beman
dashed off a highly-charged letter to the PGA's executive director Mark Cox noting his dismay.

Once Beman started to expand the Tour's marketing and
licensing deals, the two golf bodies became gripped in bitter
political squabbling. It came to a head over what insiders called
"the three letters," and who had ownership rights to the mark,
PGA. Beman, aware that golf had stagnated somewhat during
the 1970s, was confronted with a need for mass marketing revenue, but golf wasn't yet a mass-marketing sport.

"We cannot afford, in the light of several recent years of virtually zero growth in the golf industry, to sit on our hands and
hope for the best," he said at the time. "If we have a genuine
concern for the future of the game, then it is time to apply our
resources and imagination to the job of spurring growth."

Beginning with the policy board's approval of a four-year
marketing initiative in February 1980, the Tour set in motion
a plan to broaden its fan base. Net income from any licensing
agreements involving non-golf related merchandise, such as
soft goods sold through pro shops, were earmarked for junior
golf programs. One of the concerns of the board in approving
a marketing strategy was that the Tour's efforts not harm the
marketing prospects of individual players. The board passed a
resolution clarifying that nothing in the Tour's marketing program or tournament regulations "shall be deemed to restrict
any member's individual marketing rights." It was hoped that
greater public interest in, and support for, the Tour would enhance the individual business opportunities to all members.
Whenever asked to explain how Beman's corporate-sponsor
model benefited players in unforeseen ways, Tour member Jim
Colbert told the story of Cadillac's umbrella sponsorship tele-
vising the Senior Tour.

"It took Cadillac less than a month to figure out they were
showing a bunch of Toyota hats," he said, referring to endorsement deals the Japanese automaker cut with several stars. "So
Cadillac signed Arnold Palmer, Lee Trevino, and Bob Charles
to contracts and created Team Cadillac. At one time, it consisted

of 15 players (including Colbert). That's a real simple thing but when these sponsors came on board they needed spokespeople and it mushroomed from there."

The licensing program's vast potential was spelled out in an October 1982 Tour report, which painted a rosy picture for soft-goods sales. A financial study authored by an independent consultant estimated $2.3 million in sales in the first year and climbing to $80 million per year in five years. Based on 7 percent royalties, the report predicted $5 million to $6 million in licensing revenue.

The PGA expressed reservations immediately. According to the Tour's board minutes, Beman informed the board of a proposed licensing deal for soft goods with Izod LaCoste during the May 7, 1980 meeting in Dallas. "The PGA said, 'Wait a minute, we're not sure we want you to do that,' " Beman recalled. "They said, 'We have a deal with PGA Victor Co., and they have rights to soft goods exclusively.' "

The PGA contended the new initiative might violate its licensing agreement of the initials "PGA" to PGA Victor. According to the PGA, this might restrict the Tour's use of the initials in its commercial relationships. In short order, the Tour's board appointed a committee consisting of Oelman, Black, and player director Tom Kite to examine the Tour's use of the mark. When the board convened in San Diego on Feb. 3, 1981, the status of the Tour's merchandising initiatives topped the agenda. The board agreed that the Tour should be restricted from entering the hard-goods category. After all, the Tour agreed to amend equipment from its bylaws years ago at the PGA's request. But the board gave the Tour the green light to proceed with its other marketing plans assuming the PGA granted permission. Black declared that the PGA letters were exclusive to PGA Victor, and reiterated that the agreement extended to soft goods, too. Rather than gavel it through and risk another legal skirmish, Oelman delayed a vote. In short, the Tour was stymied unless an agreement could be reached with PGA Victor. So began a protracted negotiation.

Dating to the 1968 Statement of Principles, the Tour became a division of the PGA. When Joe Dey signed the 7.5 percent royalty deal, the PGA approved the Tour as a separate entity.

That separate corporation was obligated to pay the PGA for the right to the use of the PGA name. In one of the final stipulations before the PGA officers approved the Tour's incorporating documents, they required the Tour to strike from its bylaws the marketing of hard goods. Beman couldn't understand the PGA's restrictions on the Tour's use of the PGA mark.

"If we didn't have the right to marketing and licensing after paying the 7.5 percent, then what were we paying for?" Beman said. "And if we didn't have the right to marketing and licensing, why did we undergo a protracted negotiation in which we agreed not to market hard goods?"

The PGA claimed that the Tour's licensing agreement for the PGA name was limited to tournament use. Beman pointed to the Tour's charter, which specifically extended marketing and licensing rights, and proclaimed the Tour was ready to expand into these new business ventures. None of this shocked the PGA. As recently as 1977, then-PGA president Don Padgett had proposed a study be conducted to determine what the Tour should be permitted to do. This veiled attempt to restrict the Tour's business endeavors never gained a groundswell of board support, Beman said. Now Black hammered away, charging that the Tour's marketing efforts "diluted its primary purposes."

Meanwhile, Beman continued to seek a solution. In May 1981, the Tour's board signed off on PGA Tour Properties, a for-profit subsidiary. But when Beman asked the PGA to approve registration of its mark, the PGA refused until it got approval from PGA Victor. Beman stewed. Efforts to negotiate proved fruitless. Talks rekindled and just as quickly flamed out. "We had wasted more than a year," Beman complained. "We were getting nowhere, and it became abundantly clear that PGA Victor wasn't going to agree to anything."

With no resolution in sight, the Tour's future was at a crossroads. To Beman, there seemed only one conclusion to avoid another legal battle: change the Tour's name. As the infighting worsened, Beman threatened to do just that. Doing so would free Beman to enter into licensing and marketing agreements on a broad basis. Beman proposed switching the name to TPA, which stood for Tournament Players Association, and would be reflected in the Tour logo too. On Aug. 25, 1981, independent director Del de Windt made a motion, seconded by Kite, to adopt the new name. The board approved the name change by a vote of 6-3. (Independent director Bob Kirby missed the meeting. To no surprise, all three opposing votes were PGA directors.) "It was just impossible for us to fairly compete with other major sports in broad-based marketing without using our branded name with the letters PGA," Beman explained. "It put us at a tremendous disadvantage."

That November, Beman and his executive assistant, David Hueber, attended the PGA's annual meeting at the Boca Raton Hotel in South Florida. Beman had butted heads with PGA officials before, but overnight he had become a pariah following the removal of the "three letters" in the Tour's name. When Beman, flanked by Hueber, entered the hall an icy reception welcomed them. "It was like the Red Sea parted for us," Hueber said.

In introducing Beman when it was his turn to speak, Padgett called him the commissioner of the Tournament Players Division. "Deane corrected him," Hueber remembered. "He said, 'Thank you for that warm welcome, but I'm here as the commissioner of the TPA.' Deane handled it flawlessly."

The Tour removed the PGA letters from its TV logo, the covers of its rules book and media guide, headquarters signage and everywhere else. In its haste to make the change, the Tour forgot to consider the impact on Dentsu, Japan's largest advertising agency at the time, which had secured the exclusive rights to the Tour's logo in Japan. "We got a Telex," Smith remembered. "It said, 'Big loss of face.'"

To make matters worse, a pirate entity had registered the name TPA there. Smith and Campbell hopped on a plane to Japan to apologize and beg foregiveness. Their efforts were unconvincing, at least to their translator, who urged them to be sincere. "I said, 'We are being sincere,'" Smith said. "He told us, 'Be more sincere.'"

Indicative of the finality of its logo switch, the Tour replaced business cards and letterhead and tossed items with the PGA Tour insignia. But the TPA name never truly resonated with players, media, and fans – though one can argue it never was given a fair shake. That's because just when the name change appeared cemented in stone, Beman thought he had a better idea. The PGA was in a state of flux. Cox had resigned and Jim Butz, an interim director, was in charge. Beman still clung to the notion that the two organizations could reunite and become a dominant force for the growth of the game. With the National Golf Foundation floundering too, Beman sought to consolidate power. With the thought fresh in his mind, Beman phoned Black, told him there was still room for dialogue, and offered to meet in Dallas. Black, who formerly played on the Tour and served as tournament supervisor for eight years, invited Beman for dinner at Brookhaven Golf Club, where he was director of golf. There was an ice storm in Dallas that night when Beman met with Black and Kizziar, a duo who Smith likened to the Soviet Union's Mikhail Gorbachev.

"They started détente," Smith said.

Beman didn't have the slightest idea where the talks would lead, but it seemed like the right thing to do. Whether the egos involved would permit a joint effort was another question. The conversation was cordial when Beman began outlining what he had in mind. "I stressed that this is okay for us – we've got TV, and we can build a new brand – but this isn't in the best interest of the PGA members and the game of golf," Beman recalled.

He offered to discuss restoring the PGA Tour name with his board if Black would entertain the idea of reuniting the PGA and Tour under one umbrella with his executive committee. The PGA's acceptance wasn't a condition of the deal.

"Deane was always trying to find a way to engage the club professional in activities because he saw potential," said Jim Awtrey, a PGA pro who later became the PGA's CEO. "I think he'd like to have had it folded in where he could've run all of it. He saw what it was capable of, and at the time it wasn't realizing that potential."

Indeed, Beman could see a world of possibilities. Presently, the PGA had 12,500 members, according to published reports. "If we could galvanize the PGA members – with the Tour's potential impact through television – we could be a powerful force for the good of golf," he reasoned. "It would be in everyone's interest to get that done."

Black's response didn't mince words: "I'll talk to you at

anytime," he said, "but I will absolutely not negotiate in the press....If there is, I'm walking away from the table."

They shook hands and resumed discussions over the course of the next three months. To avoid media attention, negotiations were conducted under the strictest secrecy, beginning at a small community bank in Palm Beach Gardens, Fla., where the two parties met at 7 a.m. on a Sunday.

"We had to give up church," recalled PGA secretary Mickey Powell.

Among the topics they discussed was a joint-marketing venture as well as funding a developmental tour. Over the next few months, meetings were held in Jacksonville, New York, and Washington, D.C. The negotiations heated up at the Bel-Air Summit Hotel during the week of the 1982 L.A. Open. The Tour's board chairman was doing double duty there. As CEO of Eaton Corp., de Windt had business to conduct. When he excused himself to attend to his day job, the two sides remained at an impasse. Beman pressed for control of the marketing entity. He hammered away. Finally an exasperated Black halted the proceedings. All pretense of diplomacy was dropped. "Forget it. That's it," he snapped. "It's 50-50, or nothing."

Sensing Black's hunger for the deal, Beman requested a few minutes to caucus with his team. The minutes ticked by. He returned and struck a deal in principle that re-wrote the 1968 Statement of Principles. Once and for all, it resolved questions concerning the rights of both organizations to the use of the initials "PGA" in marketing. The PGA retained its right to use the PGA mark in connection with the PGA Championship, the Ryder Cup, the Senior PGA Champonship and other PGA-sponsored events. It continued to secure the future television rights fees for those events. The Tour did the same for its tournament schedule and would negotiate separately with the networks. Both organizations agreed to continue joint ownership of the World Series of Golf. The Tour acquired the rights to "soft goods," including slacks, shirts, sweaters, hats, socks, and other apparel; the PGA had the right to license "hard goods," such as clubs, bags, balls, gloves and other items necessary to the playing of the game.

They formed PGA-PGA Tour Properties, a joint marketing

venture, which was responsible for the licensing of both PGA and PGA Tour names and trademarks to corporate clients under agreements that produced revenues or actively promoted golf. As part of the marketing partnership, they created the PGA Tour Inner Circle, an affinity program with a magazine and membership modeled after the USGA's membership program. It was to be headed by the PGA to generate more interest among the general public. The Tour was to receive 50 percent of all net revenue from the Inner Circle. They also agreed to jointly fund the new Tournament Players Series, a secondary tour of 10 tournaments, to be subsidized for a minimum of five years from Inner Circle revenue. The comprehensive agreement provided that both parties contribute their shares of World Series of Golf income and royalties from PGA-PGA Tour Properties (up to $300,000 each year) into the funding of the TPS for at least the next five years. Returning to the negotiations after his business meeting, de Windt stepped from the elevator and met both sides congregated in the hall amidst laughter. "When I left here," an overjoyed de Windt said, "I was sure this thing was falling apart."

Truth be told, there was still one sticking matter. Black had to convince Bob MacNally of PGA Victor to agree to the deal. Black said he sorted through various compromises until the night before the scheduled announcement. Drafts were written and discarded. Revisions were faxed back and forth to re-work the contract with PGA Victor's counsel in Chicago. Eventually, they struck a deal. Beman wondered what differed between now and 18 months earlier? One can only speculate, but Beman has his own opinion. "I believe the PGA used PGA Victor to block the Tour's program in marketing," he said. "The name change forced the PGA to come to their senses."

After months of clandestine maneuvering, on March 17, 1982, one day before the first Players Championship at TPC Sawgrass, a press conference was held at the TPC clubhouse. Black and Beman exchanged pens after signing the landmark agreement, and Beman ordered the PGA Tour name be flashed on all the electronic scoreboards. Ernie Roberts of *The Boston Globe* called it "the most publicized reunion since (Richard) Burton and (Elizabeth) Taylor took place this week."

"That gives us our identity," Tom Watson said of the return of the Tour to its former name.

That evening, Beman invited the principals in the deal to his house for a reception. Kizziar expected to see all of Beman's golf trophies and memorabilia and to listen to tales of his triumphs in the U.S. and British Amateurs. Instead, Beman relished telling the story of how as an eighth grader he scored 128 of his team's 158 points as a running back in the 125-pound division of the Montgomery (Md.) Recreation League. He pointed to the framed photo of his team carrying him, the smallest guy, off the field after they won the championship. Beman sat on the shoulders of Steve Hershey, who grew up to become the longtime golf writer for *USA Today*.

"Deane never mentioned a word about golf," Kizziar said. "All he wanted to talk about was his football prowess and how many touchdowns he scored."

From an early age Beman had become accustomed to winning. In his role as commissioner he fought on the players behalf for every inch, but he also realized in business there had to be room for his partner to win too. He wanted this to be a long-term partnership, where both parties could succeed.

"The PGA was a winner in many respects," Beman said. "At a time when exemptions for club pros and Monday qualifying opportunities to play the Tour were being diminished, TPS gave PGA members a place to compete. We thought we'd win from a long-term, promotional aspect."

Just as importantly, the short-lived TPA name vanished, a footnote for the record books. "I think I have an ashtray with the TPA logo," Powell said. "It's funny every time I see that name."

But not everybody involved in the talks chuckles at the name change. The Tour's board chair, for one, could never generate any enthusiasm for the reversal. "I rue that day," de Windt said. "Many times the Tour is not said in the same breath or written in the same sentence with PGA. We give the PGA all the publicity in the world. That was a big mistake."

Ric Clarson, who joined the Tour in 1980 and spent more than three decades working in a variety of roles, echoed de Windt, saying once the distinction was made Beman had the makings of the perfect brand family: the TPA Tour, the TPC

Sawgrass, and the Tournament Players Championship. "It was totally its own brand with no confusion with the PGA," Clarson said. "To this day there is still some brand confusion with the PGA of America."

Whether the Tour should've changed its names has proved a topic of enduring debate within a small circle of Beman's former confederates. He doesn't disagree with their assessments. His lament notwithstanding, in retrospect, he thinks de Windt and others have forgotten to take into account one crucial footnote in the final evaluation.

"I probably made a mistake changing the name," Beman said. "Part of the agreement that I made in good faith with Joe Black when we put this deal together was that they would explore with the PGA board the idea of reuniting the PGA and Tour back into a single organization. They reneged on that. Had I known they weren't sincere, I never would've changed the name back."

Black listened to Beman's overture, but he said he never truly considered supporting Beman as "commissioner of golf," and never proposed the idea to the executive committee. In August 1982, the PGA hired Lou King, a marketing chief at Amana, as its executive director. (He was behind the Amana hat promotion on Tour.) Beman accepted that the two governing bodies would never be one.

"Del trusted my instincts, but he kept saying we never should've changed the name back," Beman recalled. "The PGA solved its problem of a place for its members to play. It got us to use the PGA name again. It got 50 percent interest in the marketing/licensing venture. At this point, it looked like the PGA got the better of the deal."

Beman waved his index finger for emphasis and amended his comment. "At this point," he said, pausing for effect. "We didn't know how important a role the partnership with the PGA would play in the outcome of the player revolt."

Beman is referring, of course, to the letter dated a little over a year later in May 1983 from Nicklaus, Palmer and a dozen of the most prominent players on Tour. After de Windt distributed its contents to the board members, Colbert picked up a phone and called Kizziar to feel out where the PGA stood in the controversy. "We're going to support what we said we'd do. We're in your corner," Kizziar said.

On this occasion, the PGA backed Beman because they were now his partners. Had the marketing pact not occurred before the player rebellion, Beman is convinced the PGA would have sided with the leading players and sealed his fate. Sometimes you win by losing, he said.

"Would we have been better off if we stayed as TPA? The answer is no," Beman said. "But just because we got lucky, not because we were good."

*   *   *

More than simply settling a dispute, the revised agreement with the PGA was supposed to open up a range of mutually beneficial projects for both organizations. On paper, it was a dream matchup.

"I pitched it as the PGA of America can provide the grass-roots part of the sport and a major championship, and we can deliver the competitive side of the sport," said the Tour's former marketing chief Gary Stevenson.

Beman's idea was to create an affinity program modeled after the USGA member's program that Palmer endorsed. Expectations were high. The Tour and PGA targeted an enrollment of one million amateur supporters of the game within five years. But when King reported on Inner Circle during the May 17, 1983, board meeting, he noted the program's sluggish start. Beman's notes read, "so far a bust." That was no exaggeration. The Tour stated in its 1983-84 annual report that Inner Circle results in the program's start-up phase were "somewhat disappointing." Slightly over 18,000 members enrolled in 1983.

Undeterred, King reiterated his million-member promise. Based on the underwhelming performance to date, de Windt asked in a neutral voice, "Lou, do you really think you can do that?" King responded, "I'm holding up the sign, aren't I?"

"Well, maybe you should consider backing off on the projections," de Windt suggested.

King would have none of it. "Those are the projections," he said, "period."

"He actually said the word 'period,' " Hueber noted with a chuckle.

For 1984, the PGA refocused the program to concentrate on benefiting junior golf. To better market Inner Circle, Nicklaus, Hal Sutton, and other Tour players agreed to participate in TV announcements featured on every Tour telecast, as well as direct mail pieces and pro shop promotions.

"We were giving them our full support expecting that the signups would be at golf course counters around the country, but that wasn't happening," Beman said.

Kizziar called Inner Circle a great idea and underscored Beman's opinion that it floundered because PGA pros failed to embrace their sales responsibility.

"Deane felt very strongly that with all the PGA professionals throughout the country, Inner Circle would create so much revenue for both the PGA and the Tour, and in theory he was right," Kizziar said. "The pros would endorse it, but we just couldn't get them to sell it."

By the Oct. 9, 1984, meeting in Atlanta, Powell conceded that pro shops were an ineffective sales point. Six months later, King reported to the Tour's board that Inner Circle continued to lose money, and he recommended suspending the program by Oct. 1, 1985. Revenue from Inner Circle was supposed to be the lifeblood for funding the TPS. This circuit provided a competitive environment for non-exempt Tour pros. With more and more PGA pros getting squeezed out of Tour events, TPS solved a huge political problem for the PGA leadership by securing playing opportunities for its members. But when PGA professionals struggled against the touring pros, the PGA realized they were bankrolling a program that provided little tangible reward to its members. The PGA cut its funding, and the circuit soon fizzled. Beman would have understood if the PGA pulled back after its five-year commitment expired, but to renege during the circuit's infancy amounted to a serious blow in establishing a secondary tour.

"They should have honored their agreement," Beman said. "We're supposed to be partners in helping to build and promote the game, and any time it is going to cost them a little money they are ready to go backwards."

When asked to explain why the marketing partnership between the Tour and the PGA didn't succeed, Beman chalks it up to different objectives. Marketing the Tour and broadening the base of interest in golf were Beman's primary goals. Producing net income often took a backseat. Admittedly, sometimes the rewards were stacked in the Tour's favor. Properties struck one of its bigger deals with watchmaker Seiko, which became the Tour's official time piece and sponsor of the Tour's new match-play event in 1984. The deal didn't generate any direct benefit for the PGA.

"This was the first signal where the PGA started to feel that all the big deals were going to the players," Beman said.

In the early days of the Tour's marketing program, Properties often traded "hard dollars" – endorsement fees or trademark royalties, for "soft dollars," – the value of promotion, free or discounted goods or services provided to Tour or PGA members. In many cases, the Tour determined the increased national exposure reaped from a marketing program was worth as much or more as licensing payments. Sometimes, the Tour struck deals that required sponsors to buy additional TV ads on Tour telecasts to tie-in to the sponsor's promotions. The PGA soon tired of these one-sided arrangements.

"Those were the seeds of discontent," Beman said.

In another instance, Properties inked a deal with Sheraton, in which the hotelier agreed to pay $50,000 in cash and spend $110,000 in commercial time in support of "Inside the PGA Tour," its weekly tournament highlight show on ESPN. The PGA thought its share should be $80,000 based on the combined value, rather than $25,000, or half of the cash value. It should be mentioned that not all deals favored the Tour. A separate deal with Nikon provided for $50,000 cash and $75,000 in support of a PGA Championship highlight video. "We tried to be fair," Beman said. "We were trying to grow the game. That was to the benefit of everyone."

Even when the game was not growing, Tour purses rose steadily. Strangely, the purses for the four major championships – which garnered lucrative rights fees for Augusta National, the R&A, USGA, and PGA – weren't appreciably higher than the average purse of the Tour's community-based events.

During a board meeting in early 1982, Colbert broached the subject of prize money and TV revenue at the majors. The board directed Beman to meet with the leaders of the organizing bodies of the major championships and negotiate at least a raise in tournament prize money. In preparation for those meetings, on Dec. 3, 1982, Beman wrote a letter to the Tour's 20 leading money winners and the last five U.S. Open winners (not included from the money list). In it Beman asked, "Has the USGA reasonably shared the vast income created by the U.S. Open with the players whose participation is essential to its success?"

Beman recognized that the USGA owned the U.S. Open; but in order to televise it, the USGA must get players to assign their TV rights each year. Beman's proposal requested the purse should be no less than the average of the top 10 purses on Tour. With the USGA's share of ticket and program sales, this didn't seem to be an unreasonable sum. As a matter of fact, Beman noted, in 1982 the USGA charged a $60 entry fee and received 5,000 entries. That $300,000 nearly equaled the prize money paid in 1982 ($319,000). The USGA also should contribute 20 percent of the U.S. Open rights fee to the Tour's television fund, he proposed. "The USGA should be willing to pay you a reasonable share of the proceeds of an event that your talents make successful," he concluded.

Nine players signed the document and two more confirmed their support. "The PGA, R&A, and USGA were all making a fortune and offered as little prize money as they possibly could," Beman said. "I think they felt the winner of a major got huge financial rewards in endorsements, which was true, but what about the rest of the players in the field who were trying to make a living? The winner has got to have somebody to beat."

Beman sought answers that April at Augusta National. He met with the club's chairman, Hord Hardin, former president of the USGA, and a longtime friend. Beman asked first about the television revenue the club generated. Hardin told Beman that Augusta's deal with CBS could be bigger, but unlike the other majors the club only asked for as much television money as it needed to pay the purse. Beman had heard that before. But he was flabbergasted by Hardin's answer when Beman inquired about raising prize money. "He said to me, 'Well, I don't know what to tell you about the prize money. I'll have to talk to our friends at the USGA, the PGA, and R&A. We have our gentleman's agreement that one won't raise prize money without the others,' " Beman recalled. "That 30-second conversation took care of prize money for the major championships forever."

Beman bit his tongue, then went directly to Cox, the PGA executive director who attended Tour board meetings. Beman said, "After all this time and all we've been through, you have conspired to reduce prize money in these events, and it's going to stop. You're going to do the right thing by the players or else I'm going to file a suit against all of you. You'll have the damnedest lawsuit you've ever seen."

The PGA broke ranks with the gentleman's agreement first, raising the PGA Championship's prize money from $450,000 in 1982 to $600,000 in 1983. The USGA followed suit, announcing an increase in prize money from $375,000 to $500,000 – at the time, the largest purse increase in the history of the event. The USGA's then-executive director, Frank Hannigan, disputed Beman's charge of a conspiracy and insisted the increase "was a consequence of our television money rising." The purse increase at the Masters lends further credence to Beman's claim. After a marginal bump from $362,000 in 1981 to $367,000 in 1982, the tournament purse jumped to $500,000 in 1983 after Beman's threat, and to $612,000 the following year. From then on the majors chased the purse of The Players Championship.

Despite the constant clashing, a certain level of mutual admiration existed among the leaders in golf, especially between the PGA and the Tour.

"They would negotiate back and forth until there was blood, and then they'd go over to Deane's house for dinner. It was shocking to me," said Patty Cianfrocca, a Tour employee since 1980. "Deane said, 'That's what we do.' They left it at the door."

Kizziar recalled the time Beman attended a dinner in recognition of Kizziar's service as PGA president at the conclusion of his term in 1984. Kizziar never heard words of praise heaped on him like Beman did that night. "I just thought, who is this guy and what have you done with Deane Beman!" he said. "I'll never forget that. It was a surprise, and it kind of showed a different side of Deane that not everybody sees all the time."

The PGA held plenty of regard for Beman, too. So much so that in February 1987, the association sought his help to bail them out of a bind. That's when the PGA board dismissed King as its executive director. It happened in a matter of two hours. "We were a bunch of club pros. What did we know about firing an executive," said Pat Reilly, a past PGA president who sat on its board at the time. "Our independent directors' told us we didn't handle it right, and we may have some exposure. We met with our lawyers. We couldn't afford for it to be dragged out. We needed to settle this son of a bitch."

After a lengthy discussion on how they could resolve King's termination, only one name emerged who they felt had the presence to prevent this from becoming a firestorm. "I thought of Deane," Reilly said.

It was King who the PGA hired instead of evaluating Beman's proposal of reuniting the PGA and the Tour. And yet Beman never considered turning down the request. He jumped on a plane the next day. When Beman arrived, he grabbed a yellow legal pad. He jotted down parameters of high and low figures that he was approved to offer King. If a wrongful termination suit was filed in court, the PGA officers knew nothing good would come of it. King and Beman met at a condo the PGA owned near its headquarters in Palm Beach Gardens, Fla., and in one hour Beman made the deal. King's resignation was announced on Feb. 26, 1987.

"Lou was happy, we were happy, end of story," Reilly recalled. "Some of the past officers were ticked that we used Deane. They felt they could've done it. But Deane was on the periphery. He wasn't toxic.

"Does he get any credit for that? Hell, no. Except from the people that were there and understood the potential for disaster. I don't want to make Lou feel bad, but he got the low end of the deal with us."

Two months later, Jim Awtrey was promoted to deputy executive director, marking the first time a PGA professional had held the association's top post. Awtrey described his first years on the job dealing with Beman and the Tour as "conflict management." Before long, the two organizations, which already had divorced and kissed and made up, would reach amicable terms to split for good.

* * *

The marriage of the Tour and the PGA endured its next rocky period in the late 1980s. The marketing partnership struck in 1982 failed to reap the benefits both parties envisioned. Soon Properties would reach a tipping point.

A seemingly minor difference of opinion preceded the breakup of the partnership. In November 1987, Beman sent a memorandum to the Tour's board describing the background of a disagreement that arose with regard to the rights of both organizations to television and, specifically, to the production of home video cassettes.

The PGA planned to market a home video called the "PGA's Greatest 18 Holes." But the Tour was in the process of marketing its first home-video product through an exclusive distribution deal. The Tour asserted that the 1968 agreement between the two organizations assigned to the Tour the exclusive right to engage in golf-related television activities (except for the PGA Championship, Ryder Cup, PGA Senior Championship and similar PGA-owned events). Not wishing to set a precedent or waive what it considered its exclusive rights in the area, the Tour rejected the PGA's video. (The Tour permitted the PGA to sell a video version of its teaching manual and to market instructional videos.)

The crux of the conflict can best be summed up in the PGA's rebuttal: It argued that the Tour's exclusive rights was limited to the area of co-sponsored or Tour-owned tournaments. Otherwise, the PGA contended, it had the right to produce televised golf events, and it intended to pursue that as a business activity. Eventually, the PGA and its business partner, IMG, released the video as "Golf's Greatest 18 Holes," and removed the PGA's mark. Discussions between the Tour and PGA failed to resolve the larger issue, and the parties exchanged "legal briefs" supporting their position in February 1988. In agreeing to disagree, the PGA said it would submit any proposed TV projects to the Tour and asked the Tour to do likewise for any "general TV" projects that it intended to pursue.

In following that protocol, a Sept. 11, 1990, letter informed the Tour that the PGA's Grand Slam of Golf, formerly a non-televised, one-day fundraiser for charity, would become a nationally televised, two-day, 36-hole event with a $1 million purse.

The Grand Slam of Golf already had stirred trouble between the two sides once before. Originally known as the Round of Champions, this charity event featured the winners of the U.S. Women's Open, LPGA Championship, the U.S. Open and PGA Championship. In February 1979, the PGA petitioned the Tour policy board for permission to re-brand the event as the Grand Slam of Golf and substitute the two female winners by spotlighting the champions from golf's four men's majors. Beman opposed the PGA's plan on the grounds that it was scheduled for Aug. 7, and would adversely affect the Tour event in Hartford that week. "It further glorified the four majors," he argued, and urged the player directors and independent directors to vote it down.

When the PGA learned of Beman's objection, it lobbied the Tour's independent directors. Kizziar said the PGA pitched the Grand Slam of Golf as a one-day fundraiser supporting the PGA Junior Golf Foundation, and promised that it would never hold the Grand Slam for a purse nor would it air on national TV. Its future came down to a vote of the Tour's policy board. "For the first time in my recollection, we prevailed," Kizziar said. "The three independents voted with us, the players went against, and the vote was 6 to 4."

But after pledging in 1979 to keep it a simple charity event, the PGA reversed course and pursued its made-for-TV project. Nine days after receiving the PGA's Grand Slam of Golf bombshell, the Tour responded. The Statement of Principles clearly restricted the PGA to operating the PGA Championship, the Ryder Cup, the Senior PGA Championship, and a handful of club pro events (listed on Exhibit B of the 1982 Basic Agreement). The Tour charged that the PGA violated the Basic Agreement by reinstituting the World Series of Golf in its previous format and labeling it with the Grand Slam of Golf name from Exhibit B. Beman was incensed. This was a more egregious betrayal than when the PGA sold its international TV rights without telling him.

"It wasn't a tournament. It was just a television exhibition that took television money away from the players, cheapened the competition, and downgraded the value of our tournaments," Beman said. "I thought it was both destructive and reprehensible."

Beman made no effort to hide his disgust. He called Kizziar and said, "Where do you want your subpoena sent?"

Kizziar listened closely as Beman's voice crackled over the line from Ponte Vedra. Kizziar understood Beman's demand for an explanation of the PGA's ambush tactics. "We had given our word as officers of the PGA," Kizziar said. "Some years later, the people in charge at the time – whether they didn't take the time to read the minutes or to ask a question, I don't know – they broke our agreement. Deane had every right to do what he did in that instance, in my mind."

Beman's Oct. 12, 1990, letter to then-PGA president Reilly served as a notice of default. In it, Beman noted that since 1969 the Tour had paid more than $12 million to the PGA to be the entity that conducts professional golf competitions and for exclusive broadcast rights. The Tour also annually released players' television rights for the PGA Championship, which he said was producing more than $3 million annually to the PGA's bottom line.

"Surely, (the Grand Slam of Golf) is contrary to, and not permitted by, the spirit and letter of the Basic Agreement," Beman wrote. "This breach on the part of the PGA will constitute a material breach resulting in the PGA's license to the Tour becoming permanent without the obligation on the part of the Tour to provide any further consideration."

Awtrey and his staff offered a far different slant. The development of the Grand Slam of Golf was no different than the development that had occurred with respect to any number of Tour events since 1982. "Your thesis appears to be that such development is permissible on the part of the Tour but somehow impermissible on the part of the PGA," wrote Gary Crist, the PGA's general counsel in a missive to the Tour.

To grow the PGA's assets, Awtrey realized the association needed more events on television. When he assumed his post, the only event the PGA owned that generated a rights fee was the PGA Championship. The Ryder Cup, as recently as 1987, was a "time-buy." That had to change. To Awtrey, this fight, then, was all about the future. "I wasn't going to back off," he said. "For a couple of years, it was conflict management. It was nothing personal. We had some serious private discussions. Deane fought for his brand, and that's why the Tour is where it is today."

Ironically, Beman had recruited Awtrey to join the Tour's operations staff in 1987. A few months later in June 1987, Awtrey was promoted to lead the PGA and sat across the table from Beman in the next round of negotiations between the two partners. Hot anger gave way to cold reason. The Tour batted about the possibility of a lawsuit, but another drawn-out battle seemed unappealing.

"I don't think anybody was interested in going to the mat legally," Beman said. "I think the PGA knew that, which was strategically in its favor in pushing the envelope."

After the initial furor subsided, they agreed the partnership wasn't working. The PGA wanted to conduct its own marketing and build its own brand, and it was in the best interest of both to have an orderly termination of their partnership. "Deane saw it was headed for litigation," Awtrey said. "When that happens nobody really wins. So we sat down and renegotiated the whole agreement."

Experience had taught the PGA that Beman's belief in a win-win deal usually amounted to "Beman wins twice." Whatever reservations the PGA harbored that it might get out-negotiated by Beman again, the association was convinced it had to regain the rights to market the PGA's brand. Beman's attention wandered to the Ryder Cup. It was hardly the international spectacle it is today or the cash cow it has become, but Beman recognized its potential. No sooner had Beman inquired about acquiring the Ryder Cup did objections come flying back. "The solution to be able to move forward and market was so much more important at that particular time," Beman said. "Getting a percentage of the Ryder Cup rights fees was the best that could be done under the circumstances."

The new agreement was based on negotiations conducted over several months, coming to a head in the summer of 1991. It superceded all prior agreements between the Tour and PGA. In return for receiving the right to broadcast the Grand Slam of Golf and market and license its own brand, the PGA relinquished its half ownership stake in Properties, and agreed to pay 20 percent of both the Ryder Cup and Grand Slam of Golf rights fees. Best efforts would be made to ensure that the PGA maintain purse levels of the PGA Championship and Senior PGA Championship at a level at least equal to the fourth highest purse, and under no circumstances less than the top 10 purses on the respective tours. The Tour also acquired the PGA's 50 percent stake in the World Series of Golf for a payment of $1.2 million. "The PGA gave up too much," Kizziar said.

The PGA made one other seemingly minor concession. They agreed to reduce its members on the Tour's board, in phases commencing in 1993, from three to one and allow the addition of one more independent director. To Beman, the changes gave him and the Tour the autonomy they had always craved.

"For all those years, I had three board members with their foot on the brake," Beman said. "By the time I decided to retire, it paved the way for half the politics to be gone."

Awtrey reasoned the player directors could outvote the PGA directors every time. To oppose the Tour on a policy issue required rallying the support of the independent directors. "In my mind, we still had an individual on the board so we still had representation," Awtrey said.

But several past PGA presidents who served on the board disagreed and claim the PGA directors wielded considerable influence and say their role was diminished to an honorary voice at best. On July 31, 1990, Beman and Awtrey signed a letter of intent. The PGA board approved the new agreement a week later; the Tour's board did the same at its November meeting. After more than two decades of wrangling, the Tour and the PGA – with the casual stroke of a pen – dissolved their marketing partnership and went their separate ways.

THE ULTIMATE MULLIGAN

On Jan. 16, 1980, a landmark meeting laid the formal groundwork for the Senior PGA Tour. Sam Snead, Julius Boros, Gardner Dickinson, Bob Goalby, Don January and Dan Sikes attended an informal session with Deane Beman and several members of his staff in the conference room at the commissioner's office in Ponte Vedra Beach. Based on the ratings success of the first two Legends of Golf, these men, who became the founding fathers of golf's fountain of youth, had the vague notion there might be a market for a limited schedule of senior tour events. They were looking for a little diversion, a reason to get out of the house, a chance to see old friends and compete again. They asked Beman to put his organizational expertise behind the formation of a new tour, a tour for the 50-and-over-set.

The success of the Legends, a two-man team-event that resembled an Old-Timer's baseball game, hadn't escaped Beman. Months earlier, he included the concept of a Senior Tour in the November 1979 "Blue Book," which gave birth to many of the Tour's most influential innovations, as a way to expand interest in the game.

"I was convinced that it was going to be successful and I was also pretty convinced that if we didn't do it somebody else would," Beman said. "I felt a responsibility to these players who were the pioneers of the PGA Tour."

The aging pros met the first week of February during the 1979 Senior PGA Championship at Walt Disney World Resort and brainstormed. They named Sikes chairman and Snead honorary chairman of what they called the senior advisory council. Leo Fraser – the former PGA of America president who had made peace with the players back in 1968 — offered to host the first "official" senior event at Atlantic City Country Club. The pull of competition was undeniable. It was the players' oxygen and they were squirming without it.

When the skills of professional golfers declined, often so did their nest eggs, if they ever had stored one. Without a retirement plan, most Tour players in their advancing years took jobs after their playing careers faltered. For many this occurred in their late 30s; playing into one's late 40s was rare (Snead was an even rarer exception, who remained competitive into his late 50s). When they left the Tour, most players attempted to capitalize on their names and reputations and remain in some capacity in the golf business. Many took club professional positions. Others specialized in teaching. Some played corporate outings or became course owners. Still more found jobs outside of golf. You didn't want to run into Bert Greene, a Tour regular in the 1960s and '70s. He became a highway patrolman in Mississippi.

The players first approached Beman and his staff shortly after the 1979 PGA Senior Championship.

"They said, 'Deane we've been playing this Legends of Golf thing and we kind of like having a hotel key in our pocket and making some money,' " recalled Dale Antram, who was in charge of the Senior Tour administration during its formative years.

There was little affection between the founding players of the Senior Tour and Beman. Dickinson and Sikes both wanted to succeed Joe Dey as Tour commissioner and resented Beman. These players didn't like it when Beman replaced Sam Gates, their handpicked lawyer, or when Beman tried to restrict their lifetime privileges when the former major winners were no longer competitive. The indignities didn't stop there. Doug Ford had written, and Goalby had signed, the memorandum to Beman shortly after he took office demanding job descriptions and salaries of each employee, and his estimated budget for the first year of operation. Beman remembered, too, how some of these players passed a rule when he turned pro reducing unlimited sponsor exemptions a first year player could receive to three (unoffocially known as the "Beman Rule"), which forced Beman to earn his card at Q-School.

"I didn't kowtow to those guys," Beman said. "They thought it was their sandbox and they didn't want anyone playing in it."

At first, the players organized the concept of the tour independently. On one occasion, Goalby had gone to Ponte Vedra by himself to discuss the idea with Beman and his staff. Despite being outnumbered 26 to 1, "including the secretaries," Goalby minced no words when the meeting ended. "We're going to go on with this whether you take us or we have to go somewhere else," he said.

In spirit, Goalby remained defiantly independent. In truth, he wanted help. Goalby knew that Beman's staff was doing a splendid job growing the Tour and that no one was better equipped to get a senior circuit off the ground. But the seniors did, in fact, pursue other partners. Goalby, Dickinson and Sikes pitched the possibility of senior golf to Joe Black and Mark Kizziar of the PGA. Though interested, the PGA officers knew that the Statement of Principles, the agreement between the PGA and Tour signed in 1968, forbid the PGA from running a full-fledged circuit anymore. That didn't stymie the players from moving forward with their vision of an over-50 circuit.

"I hope it goes," January told *Florida's Golfweek* in December 1979 after winning the Senior PGA Championship. "I think there's a need for a senior tour. Not a whole bunch of tournaments, maybe eight or 10."

Despite the hard feelings that existed between the founders and Beman, each party had its self-interest in working together. And so meeting after meeting was held to finalize details. Sikes lived in Ponte Vedra near Beman, which made for convenient informal discussions. To a great extent, the players who were instrumental in the formation of the Senior Tour were the same ones who directed the separation from the PGA more than a decade before.

"I have great respect for these guys," said Hale Irwin, the all-time leader in both victories and earnings on the Senior Tour. "They were the forerunners who set the table for me to enjoy the regular tour and later the Senior Tour."

When the players met again with Beman in January, the posturing continued. Beman had reasons to be intrigued – a survey of Tour players who would be eligible for a Senior Tour showed overwhelming support for the development of such a circuit – but he put on his best poker face. Beman didn't have a list of demands, just one make-or-break condition.

"The deal was this: Either you play all of (the tournaments) or none of them," Beman said. "There wasn't going to be any in between. We were not going to have the same problem we had on the regular tour."

The problem Beman referenced had to do with guaranteeing a representative field for the sponsor, or to be more precise, the inability of players to commit to play soon enough to provide sponsors' adequate promotion.

"This was a new product and you don't sell a new product with half the package empty," Beman said.

On April 18, 1979, the Tour issued a news release announcing that letters had been sent to senior professional golfers seeking their commitment to play in six events. The enclosed statement of intent to be signed by the players read:

> "I am willing to commit to play in six Senior Tour events co-sponsored by the PGA Tour in 1980. I understand the PGA Tour will use this commitment to go to cities and sponsors with the idea of creating a six tournament Senior Tour in 1980. The Senior Tour will be limited to players 50 years of age and older. I further understand that a committee with a majority of the members being Senior players will be formed to help create the rules, format, exemptions, eligibility and other regulations of the Senior Tour."

An internal memo from Labron Harris Jr., the Tour's director of tournament operations, to Beman dated May 7, 1979 noted that 55 commitment forms had been mailed. By that time, 29 players already had signed up while three players, including Dow Finsterwald, expressed reservations because of possible conflicts with their club pro duties. (Ken Venturi said he would be willing to play as long as he didn't have a conflict with his TV broadcasting obligations.) Three players declined to participate: Jackie Burke Jr., Henry Picard, and Byron Nelson. Among those who didn't respond initially: a soon-to-be 50 Arnold Palmer. But the commitment list grew and so did Beman's interest in making the circuit a reality.

Not every one was so sure of the concept. While lobbying the Tour officers to support a Senior Tour, Goalby recalled Jack Nicklaus telling he and Snead, "They're not going to let you old farts play."

Once Beman gained the players' assurance to play in every tournament, he gave them his complete support. In a memo to the tournament policy board he wrote that the financial support needed to underwrite purses for six events amounted to $800,000. Another $200,000 was required to cover expenses to conduct the events. Therefore, the Tour sought $1 million from a corporate sponsor to bankroll the Senior Tour. At the Sept. 24 board meeting, Beman reported that potential deals fell through "for varying reasons" with R.J. Reynolds and American Express. The Tour's board approved the Senior Tour creation on Jan. 22, 1980. Before the six founding fathers went their separate ways at the airport following their advisory council meeting, Boros made a statement that underscored their enthusiasm.

"Boys, I don't care where we play or how much we play for, just so long as it gets me out of the house 10 weeks a year," said the 59-year-old, three-time major winner.

Everyone broke out in smiles.

When the Tour's board convened less than a week later and discussed the Senior Tour, Beman faced stiff opposition.

"I don't think this is going to work," said Del de Windt, the chairman of the Tour's policy board. "Nobody wants to see a bunch of washed up guys 3-putt and shank it."

Truth be told, the Tour didn't have much money to invest in the Senior Tour venture. Some board members objected to subsidizing its tournament purses, but ultimately they agreed to finance its administration.

"I thought it was a pretty good idea," said Irwin, a player director at the time. "This could be an annuity for the older guys who helped start the Tour. But we couldn't deal it out of the deck of cards we had. There wasn't a lot of money to be thrown around."

Beman cobbled together a budget of slightly more than $700,000 to launch the Senior Tour. The Tour's board approved the creation of the Senior Tour on Jan. 22, 1980. Golf's greatest mulligan was born. It would become successful beyond anyone's wildest dreams.

"In the beginning, it was magic," Goalby said of the senior circuit. "For about 10 years we were just trying to keep up with its growth."

From its humble beginning in 1980 with two tournaments spread five months apart and purses totaling $250,000, the Senior Tour morphed into a full-fledged circuit. A decade later, it hosted 40 tournaments in a year-long affair, offering more than $25 million in prize money.

* * *

If the Senior PGA Tour was born in 1980, then it was conceived on April 30, 1979, during the final round of the Legends of Golf.

The Legends was the brainchild of golf great Jimmy Demaret and TV producer Fred Raphael, who deserves credit for coining the name. In a story told and re-told by Raphael, he was enjoying dinner Friday night during the 1963 Masters with Gene Sarazen, the first golfer to win the career grand slam. Sarazen, the affable host of Raphael's popular series "Shell's Wonderful World of Golf," excused himself to check his tee time the next morning. When Sarazen returned, he proclaimed to Raphael, "Tomorrow morning at 10:52, the old legend will tee off with the future legend," referring to Arnold Palmer. The word 'legend' stuck with Raphael all those years.

Raphael had shopped the concept of a two-man, best-ball format tournament for some of the great names of yesteryear – minimum age 50 – to the television networks and was denied at every turn. But when Don Ohlmeyer was hired as executive producer of NBC Sports he asked for all the rejected proposals from the past three years. He reviewed them in a single weekend and determined the Legends was better than much of NBC's current programming. He struck a deal.

For the first Legends of Golf in 1978, Demaret made a few phone calls to his friends and rustled up a field of 20, including two amateurs. The players ranged in age from 48-year-old Peter Thomson to Sarazen, who at age 76 was the oldest. The event made its debut at the Onion Creek Country Club in Austin, Texas. Appearing on national television as a player for the first time, Sarazen birdied his first two holes and shared the lead after 27 holes with his younger partner, Goalby. When NBC's Bud Collins asked The Squire what he was doing there, Sarazen replied, "This is the place for all the former masters to come."

Wrote *Sports Illustrated's* Dan Jenkins: "At first it was like packing up a museum and taking it on the road...the only thing modern about the Legends was the prize money."

The $400,000 purse, the largest in golf at the time, was another reason the legends leaped at the chance to come out of retirement. It ensured a record-payday, with the winners splitting $100,000. No one in the field had earned so much in a single season. The best-ball format guaranteed even the last-place twosome would share $20,000. Paul Runyan, the Tour's leading money winner with $6,767 in 1934, pocketed more for finishing last in the Legends than he ever cashed for winning a tournament.

In that first year, Raphael said he received the best kickoff possible when Sam Snead, wearing his trademark porkpie hat and putting sidesaddle, partnered with Gardner Dickinson to win. Originally intended as a "one and done" event, the Legends was repeated in 1979 because it was such a rousing success. Roberto DeVicenzo and Julius Boros defeated the odd couple team of tempestuous Tommy Bolt and taciturn Art Wall in a six-hole, finger-wagging, birdie-fest of a playoff that carried into primetime.

"I'm telling you, this baby may go on forever," said NBC commentator Jim Simpson.

A national television audience watched spellbound as the legends proved they still had game. Palmer recalled that the event raged on as the men's closing dinner time approached at Latrobe (Pa.) Country Club. But no one moved from the grill room to go upstairs and dine until the match ended.

"Sam winning the first one was all I needed," Raphael said. "The next year, we got a six-hole sudden-death playoff. How could it not take off after that?"

But a full-fledged Senior Tour? Demand certainly seemed lacking.

"When I first saw the Legends tournament I thought that's a cute tournament," two-time major winner Hubert Green, at the time a 32-year-old rising star on the PGA Tour, remembered. "When they talked about having a Tour I said, 'There's no way.' If I was a betting man, I'd be broke because I'd have bet everything that it wouldn't work."

*   *   *

Various accounts of the Senior Tour's early days suggest that Beman was reluctant to back the circuit. Nick Seitz, the former editor of *Golf Digest*, once wrote: "I cannot forget... the sunny day in suburban New York City that (Deane and I) combined our collective visionary powers, peered toward the hilly horizon and agreed that the Senior Tour was a silly idea whose time was not likely to come."

Players expressed a similar sentiment best summed up by World Golf Hall of Fame member Billy Casper: "At first, Beman didn't want the Senior Tour to succeed," he said.

Beman did withhold his endorsement initially, but he did so with good reason. This was a classic case of Beman keeping his cards close to his chest. His feigned indifference gave him the leverage he needed to gain player support to build the Senior Tour. In reality, he was thrilled to have a solution that would keep aging champions productive. As for what he shared with the press? Beman didn't care for "spinning" a story, and was often reluctant to explain the complexities of his future plans. He didn't have the time. He cared more for substance than style.

In any case, Tour records show that Beman pioneered the concept of the Senior Tour before the players approached him. At the Dec. 17, 1978, board meeting Beman requested permission to conduct a feasibility study on the Senior Tour, which was completed in late spring of 1979.

"We were pretty ahead of the curve," he said.

Before the Senior Tour's emergence, only a few special events catered to tournament professionals over the age of 50, most notably the Senior PGA Championship. Without a better option, established players continued to play the PGA Tour well after their skills had eroded. An internal Tour staff analysis noted growing concern that this practice was undermining the credibility of competition.

"The pending Senior Tour," read the report, "while still not yet a fact is an attractive solution."

A few years earlier, Beman tried to fix the issue of players playing past their prime and failed. The policy board attempted to narrow the lifetime, unlimited exemption that spared all pre-1970 winners of the U.S. Open and PGA Championship from having to qualify for tournaments. Under the new rule announced in November 1977 and scheduled to take effect in 1979, that privilege would not be automatic. Past champions would have to earn an annual minimum ($10,000 for each of the first 15 tournaments entered) or else return to Monday qualifying to earn a spot in the field. (It wasn't just the major champions who were abusing the rules, Beman noted. All tournament winners prior to 1970 were given a lifetime exemption to the tournament where they won.)

"An exemption that was unlimited in duration and had no relationship to current abilities was unreasonable," Beman said at the time. "It denied someone else the opportunity to compete."

It was a controversial move because it was bound to upset several prominent major winners. It did. Sarazen, Snead, Boros, Burke Jr., and Ford – their names engraved on nearly 200 Tour trophies – were among 13 plaintiffs who sued the Tour in state district court in Houston on Jan. 13, 1978.

One of the plaintiffs in the class-action suit, 1957 PGA Champion Lionel Hebert, told *Time Magazine*, "I resent anyone in this era telling me that what I won, they're going to take away. They're going to have a hell of a fight doing it."

Hebert could've been Exhibit A in favor of the rule change. He never finished in the top 60 on the money list after 1966. He entered 30 tournaments in 1976, but played so poorly that he survived only six cuts, never finished higher than 34th place, and earned a total of $2,381. Other targets included Jerry Barber and Ford. Beman charged they were guilty of abusing the privilege of their exemption.

"They didn't like the new rule and they didn't like me," Beman said. "I was looking out for the future of the Tour. I respected that they had won the PGA Championship 25 years ago but I also knew they were playing and missing the cut every week and taking the spot of someone trying to make a living."

On Jan. 17, 1978, Burke Jr., winner of the 1957 Masters and PGA Championship and co-owner of Champions Club in Houston, and Hebert attended the Tour's board meeting at Pebble Beach. Burke had little reason to complain; he had retired at age 34 to run his club and wasn't among the players trying to extend their careers. But he objected on principle.

"I won three things: a cup, a check, and a lifetime exemption," Burke said. "It's a gentleman's game and that's what I won. Snead won it. Ford won it. Dave Marr won it. The prize money wasn't anything. It was the lifetime exemption that was really worth something. I couldn't have built my club if I didn't have that."

But Burke conceded that several of the past champions competed well past their time.

"You've got to get out of the tree at some point in your life and go to work," Burke said. "I quit the Tour at 34. I won 15 tournaments but you couldn't support three kids on what you earned out there."

In the final analysis, this was a fight Beman couldn't win, and maybe didn't want to win. The stiff opposition from those he respected forced a reappraisal of his own beliefs. Beman met with Burke in Houston on June 3, 1978, before the start of the hearing. Afterwards, he phoned Burke and relented: "I agree with you. It's a gentleman's game and we just have to act like gentleman."

Beman and Houston Attorney Tom Alexander reached an out-of-court settlement suspending the application to change the Lifetime Exemption rule. The players withdrew the suit. There was no monetary exchange. The Tour members retained their exemptions and agreed to self-police their use of the designation.

"We ended up punting," Beman recalled. "Players were divided. Some said they earned (the lifetime exemption). Others felt get rid of them. The better players who were exempt could care less. They knew they could beat the old guys."

The conflict took a personal toll on Beman as well. It strained his friendship with Burke, which dated back to the 1955 U.S. Open. The two didn't speak for several years.

Coincidentally, Demaret, who was Burke's partner in Champions Club, conceived The Legends of Golf in the office they shared. When Beman watched the event on television he recognized its potential as a place for the Barbers, Heberts and Fords to play. If Beman couldn't eliminate the lifetime exemption, creating a senior circuit that past champions could claim as a league of their own provided an alternative solution.

"It was a gift from heaven," he said.

The Tour hired a staff and committed significant resources to the Senior Tour. According to Beman, the Tour invested approximately $8 million during the first decade until the senior circuit became a self-sufficient entity.

When the Senior Tour made its debut at the Atlantic City Senior International in June 1980, its 50-man field comprised 20 players on the all-time money list, 20 players on the all-time victory list, six Monday qualifiers and four sponsor invitations. From those earliest meetings, the founding players agreed that the Senior Tour would have to trade on the reputations and images made by PGA Tour players over their long years of activity regardless of their specific ability to compete in the present. Gallery favorites Snead, Boros and Bolt – all 60 years of age or older and in the twilight of their careers – were the catalysts.

"Without those three, we wouldn't have gotten out of the starting blocks," Goalby said.

One superstar was conspicuous in his absence. In the champions' locker room at Augusta National in 1980, Goalby and Ford made their pitch to recruit Ben Hogan. It was Tuesday and Hogan was at the Masters for the Champions dinner later that night. Goalby asked Hogan about his intentions for the Senior Tour. "Hogan said, 'Oh my game isn't for display. I don't play well enough and I'm not going to do that,' " Goalby remembered.

He nodded that he understood and moved on to another subject. Here Ford picks up the story. "So Goalby and I went to play and when we finished Hogan was still sitting there in the locker room relaxing. Well, I started up again, 'Do you think you can play a little just to help us get it going?' "

Hogan took his fist and slammed the table, making the

glasses atop it jump.

"'God damn it, I told you I'm not going to play any senior golf,' " Ford recalled Hogan yelling. "That was it. We didn't say anymore about it."

Later on at the Champions dinner, Hogan made a short speech and reiterated what he had said earlier to Goalby and Ford. He cracked that he was going to leave senior golf to Snead.

"Sam chimed in, 'I'm going to play them all, Ben,' " Goalby recalled. "Sam had a big smile on his face. Snead loved to play. He loved to compete, to be out there with the guys. That was his life. He loved golf."

Snead played at the June kickoff but withdrew after his front nine. He holed out from the sand to win a skills competition prior to the event at the Atlantic City Senior International, but wrenched his back. So did Boros during a pre-tournament clinic he conducted. Toney Penna, at age 74 the oldest in the field, summed it up to *Golf World*: "Sure we have aches, but I'm breathing and with friends."

On June 22, 1980, Texan Don January changed putting styles three times during the final round in Atlantic City before he managed to overtake overnight leader Mike Souchak. For winning the first Senior Tour event, January collected $20,000 of the $125,000 purse.

"It seemed like a damn fortune to us," Goalby said. "Now they'd spit lead nickels at that."

Five months later, Charlie Sifford won the second event, the Suntree Senior Classic. Afterwards, he said, "The Senior Tour is the greatest thing that ever happened to me."

Soon, golf fans were seized by nostalgia. The Senior Tour's novelty certainly helped the circuit's popularity at first. But its appeal endured because the tour enabled golf's biggest names to age gracefully. In other words, it allowed the public to hold on to its heroes. The Senior Tour grew at a dizzying pace, from two events in 1980 to five in 1981, to 11 in 1982, 18 in 1983, 25 in 1984, and so on. It was hailed as the most successful sports start-up of the '80s.

"It was like attending your 15th high school reunion," wrote veteran scribe Bob Drum in *Golfweek*. "The faces you saw were not the current ones but the faces of youth, your own youth."

*   *   *

Ask any of the original graybeards on the fledgling Senior Tour and to a man they will say that Brian Henning was the circuit's unsung hero. To be accurate, they would call him by his nickname, "Bruno." (The Bruno Award is given to an individual judged to have made special and outstanding contributions to the Champions Tour; he was its inaugural recipient.)

Henning, a South African, came to the U.S. for the PGA Tour's Qualifying School in 1968, but failed to earn a card. As the commissioner of the South African Tour, he traveled to the States during the Masters and U.S. Open to encourage players to compete in South Africa's winter pro series. It was during the Tournament Players Championship in 1977 that Henning informed Beman that he and his family were considering emigrating, and inquired about a job with the Tour. Beman suggested he send a resume in case a position opened. Henning never heard back about a vacancy but that didn't stop him from moving to Dallas, where he worked as an assistant pro at Bear Creek Golf Course, a 36-hole public facility, for club professional Gary Dee.

Several years later in 1981, Dee's wife, a flight attendant, rushed home from work on a winter night and couldn't wait to call Henning. It was after midnight, but she had to share her encounter in her first-class cabin. In a breathless voice, she said, "You're not going to believe this."

Jolted awake, Henning listened as she recounted how she overheard two men talking golf and mentioned that her husband was a professional. When Beman introduced himself as the Tour commissioner, Dee said, "Oh, you must know our dear friend, Brian Henning." Beman nodded and wondered, "Where the hell is he?"

By the time the flight landed, Beman handed her his business card and asked her to have Henning contact him. Henning called that next morning. Beman asked if he was still interested in working for the Tour. "Hell, yes!" Henning said.

A week later Henning and his wife met Beman for dinner in Dallas and listened to Beman describe the job of leading his latest undertaking, the Senior Tour. Beman said he intended to interview a few other candidates, but promised he would get back to Henning soon. Three weeks later, Beman had Henning visit the Tour's headquarters in Ponte Vedra Beach. Beman introduced him to a few employees. "I want you to spend some time with each of them," Beman requested.

"Are you offering me the job?" Henning asked. When Beman told Henning the position belonged to him, Henning smiled and said, "Why don't I go back to Dallas and pack up my clothes and I'll get to know them as soon as I get back."

Henning started working that Friday. For the next 22 years, Henning started every tournament morning by singing "Oh what a beautiful morning" over his walkie-talkie radio. As administrator of the Senior Tour, Henning visited golf-starved cities such as Syracuse, N.Y., Lexington, Ky., and Melbourne, Fla. Henning presented a simple pitch: Guarantee a $125,000 purse and he would deliver the 50 best senior players in the world.

"They thought I was kidding," Henning said. "With 50 players you could sell 200 pro-am spots. At $1,000 a pop, that's $200,000; even at $500 in those early days that's $100,000. Plus, the tournament organizers kept the gate money and whatever else they could sell in sponsorship and advertising. It was all yours. They jumped at it."

As big a selling point as the golf itself was the chance to interact with the players. No sport let the fan get as close to the legends of the game. The two-day, pro-am gave the sponsors real value. (Until 1987, one of the pro-am rounds counted as an official tournament round.)

Players attended 3-4 cocktail receptions a week at the club, member's homes, wherever they were told to go. Sponsors threw draw parties the night before each pro-am, an awards party afterwards, and a party or two in-between just for giggles.

"I told the guys to get your coat and ties on and go to every damn one of them," January recalled. "Don't all sit at the same table. Spread out and meet the people. They did. They took it to heart. They made it a success."

Goalby remembered one time 49 of the 50 players in the field appeared at an unofficial party. What about the one no-show?

"One guy was sick," Goalby said. "Art Wall."

To his enduring credit, Snead played every tournament during the first four years. He still was accorded star treatment. On the few occasions when the seniors appeared on television, directors insisted Snead receive plenty of air time regardless of his tournament standing. Snead, however, couldn't walk 18 holes anymore. "All I ask, Sam, is don't take the cart on the greens," Henning pleaded.

"Snead was 67. He wasn't a kid," Goalby recalled. "It wasn't easy on him. He'd say, 'We don't have to do that again tonight do we?' I'd say, 'Sam we really need to. You don't understand. We have to sell this thing. We've got to make it work.' He'd do it. We'd get him to say a few words. He was a big hit."

A typical pro-am draw party introduction of the legendary Snead would begin with Goalby, in his best carnival barker voice, saying, "Here he is ladies and gentlemen, the winner of more than 80 Tour titles. A man who can still pick the ball out of the hole without bending his knees. A man who can still kick the top of a door from a standstill. A golfer who's playing in your own backyard this week on the Senior Tour, please give it up for Slammin' Sammy Snead." On a good night, an indulgent Snead and Lionel Hebert played trumpet. Miller Barber played bass. It harkened back to their regular tour days when Venturi would join them and play drums. Their makeshift band performed after tournaments in hopes that community sponsors would invite the pros back the following year to play golf again. On the senior circuit, vocals were lacking. "None of us could keep a tune in a bucket," Barber said. No one complained. And word spread.

"I was getting calls from all over the country," Henning recalled. "Come visit us and tell us about the Senior Tour. What do we need to do? Off I'd go to sell another event."

The Senior Tour worked because it was one part competition, one part nostalgia, and one part television show.

"We were very careful to make it a different product," Beman explained. "We weren't pretending these guys are as good as the other guys."

Henning and his staff made sure the courses were more benign. They moved up tees, widened fairways and slowed the greens.

"I remember Al Besselink came up to me after the first round of the very first tournament and he said, 'Make it easier. Nobody wants to see Bessie shoot 78,' " said Labron Harris, who oversaw the senior circuit's inaugural season.

The Senior Tour organized smaller fields, hosted 54-hole events and eliminated cuts so all the legends would be there for the gallery to see on Sunday. The changes enabled aging superstars to maintain their dignity and allowed fans still to witness their skills.

"The Senior PGA Tour is a golfing phenomenon, an over-the-hill-gang circuit whose success has mystified the critics and surpassed even the most optimistic of supporters," wrote *Golf World's* Ron Coffman.

For all of their efforts, the Senior Tour still coveted another marquee name to recruit the idea of an over-50 circuit to the public and, most critically, to corporate sponsors. It turned to Arnold Palmer, golf's first telegenic personality.

Palmer was reluctant to participate initially, in part, because he didn't like the idea of three-day events. He insisted on four rounds of competition, even if it meant counting the pro-am round. Palmer got his way and the second pro-am day became an official round. Three tournaments into the new format, Palmer approached Henning and said, "Bruno, I screwed up." Palmer realized that amateurs and pros didn't mix well in the heat of competion. Before long, the Senior Tour resumed 54-hole events.

Palmer relished winning again and became a regular on the senior circuit. Attendance skyrocketed. Palmer impacted senior golf in other ways, too. The USGA, for example, had established 55 as the minimum age for its first U.S. Senior Open in 1980. But with the Senior Tour choosing 50 as its cutoff, and realizing Palmer wouldn't be eligible for another five years, USGA officials reversed course and lowered its age limit to 50 beginning in 1981. Palmer was crowned champion that year.

"It was the Arnold Palmer of old," wrote Jack Berry in *Golf World*, "who gave the senior movement its greatest boost since Serutan."

Soon the question shifted from "Will the Senior Tour work?" to "How many events could it stage?" In the beginning, the players designated 10 tournaments as the maximum.

"When they started playing," Beman said, "they found how much they missed the competition and camaraderie and they said, 'Let's play more.' "

But once the Tour expanded to 18 events in 1983, players complained it was maybe too much. During an advisory board meeting, concern was expressed that they were "going to kill the goose that laid the golden egg." But they couldn't say no. Antram recalled the number of events swelling: "(Don) January calls and says, 'Deane, I've got this guy who wants us to play for $300,000. We better add this one, too.' "

The PGA's Mark Kizziar, who served as a board member in the early years, and organized a senior event, The Tradition, remembered asking Palmer during one meeting, "What are you going to do when somebody offers you a million dollars for an event? He said, 'What are you smoking? That's never going to happen.' "

There was another legitimate reason to push onward. Other organizers, including the sports management behemoth IMG, began to realize the potential of senior golf and pitched their own tent.

"We weren't leading all the wagons," Beman said. "The rest of the world of golf wasn't sitting on their hands waiting for the PGA Tour. It was going to be a race to see who was going to control senior professional golf. We did have the right structure, we had the commitment of the players, but our job was to find other sponsors and convince these independents that they were better off to be affiliated with the Senior Tour."

Henning advised the players, "Gentleman, there are others who want events and if we don't take them someone else is going to run them, and we won't have control. So let's keep going."

The Tour staff also reminded the players that all the money it raised would support the purse (and later player retirement fund); an independent promoter would demand a return on investment. Expansion and growth continued in 1984 with more than 24 tournaments on the Senior Tour schedule, offering in excess of $5 million in prize money.

Getting its first television deal proved to be the turning

point for the Senior Tour. In a meeting at the 1981 World Seniors Invitational in Charlotte, an IMG event, Beman informed the players that he had canvassed the TV networks and none were interested in offering a deal. The seniors' questioned Beman's dilligence in securing them air time, suggesting that he was preoccupied with what they called the "junior tour."

"It became a contentious matter," Beman said. "They thought they were getting short-changed on television."

With little progress occurring, the players asked for permission to seek their own deal.

"Do these guys actually think they're going to get a TV contract?" asked David Hueber, Beman's executive assistant at the time.

In a letter to Goalby dated Oct. 3, 1983, Beman granted the players' request to seek a qualified independent representative to solicit corporate advertising support.

"While it's our opinion that no conflict of interest exists," Beman wrote, "this will have the effect of eliminating the perceived conflict and may produce the results we all want: more exposure for the Senior Tour and more dollars for the (television) fund."

In early 1984, a handful of players flew to New York City at their own expense and met with Ohlmeyer, the former NBC Sports executive producer, and Ray Volpe, the ex-LPGA commissioner. "It wasn't easy to get Snead to spend his own money," Goalby said. "But he loved senior golf. He said, 'I'll do anything to keep this thing going.' "

Goalby had worked as an NBC golf analyst for more than a decade. Ohlmeyer had "greenlighted" the first Legends of Golf and recognized the potential of senior golf. He launched Ohlmeyer Communications Co., in 1982. Snead, Goalby, Boros, January, and Ford met at The Masters Club at New York's LaGuardia Airport with Volpe and Ohlmeyer. During his LPGA tenure, Volpe orchestrated a sponsorship deal with Mazda Motors USA and sensed the automaker might be interested in expanding its association with golf. Ohlmeyer sat on ESPN's board and thought the fledgling network might be interested in expanding its live programming. When the two parties adjourned they had the framework for a deal. Suddenly, the seniors went from barely able to get newspaper ink to national cable TV exposure. Mazda Motors of America paid $200,000 to underwrite production costs for eight events in 1985 on ESPN, and offered a season-long $300,000 jackpot for players. Goalby recalled receiving calls from friends saying they had seen Snead on the tube and didn't even know he still was alive.

"Getting on television was the catalyst that moved the Senior Tour from a series of cocktail parties and exhibitions to a full-fledged tour," Beman said.

Eventually, Beman sold corporate sponsors on the notion that the Senior Tour was a marketing vehicle targeted at the over-50s set, who liked watching golfers their own age. This demographic audience came out in droves to follow their favorites. Fueled by its success, the PGA Tour created a separate logo and licensing program to market the seniors. Other major sponsors jumped in. RJR later replaced Mazda and sponsored the first $1 million event, The Vantage Cup. (In 1990, Cadillac became a television underwriter. Company officials at the time said the move was the best investment they ever had made in sports.)

The Senior Tour helped grow interest in professional golf in new, smaller markets. Initially, tournament organizers of PGA Tour events objected to the seniors entering their territories. Once the seniors found a home on television, they made inroads into bigger markets, too.

"The regular tour sponsors realized senior golf was here to stay and they couldn't be the only 7-11 in town," Henning said.

By 1985, the Senior Tour was large enough to merit its establishment as a division of the Tour. That meant the creation of a distinct and separate operating and financial entity, with Senior Tour net revenue going to fund a newly created Senior Tour retirement plan. To help grow this fast growing circuit, a Senior Tour division board was formed consisting of three independent directors, three player directors, and the immediate past president of the PGA of America. The division board was later expanded from seven to nine with the addition of another independent director and player director.

Field size grew from 52 to 72 and eventually settled on 78, resulting in increased opportunities for a wider range of Senior

Tour hopefuls. Each year a new crop of former stars and colorful characters lead the 'youth movement.' Boros and Snead gave way to Palmer and Player, who made room for Trevino and Nicklaus. Yes, when Nicklaus turned 50, he officially became one of the "old farts" on the Senior Tour.

"It was like a living museum," said *Golf Digest's* Jaime Diaz, "and you could see the history of the game in living color."

And yet these museum pieces became fresh-faced rookies again, the new kids on the block.

"Why would I want to be out there with all those young guns?" Lee Trevino said in his rookie campaign in 1989. "No sense playing the flat bellies when you can play the round bellies."

Many of the players won more than they ever did in their prime. It took Chi Chi Rodriguez more than 25 years to earn $1 million on the PGA Tour. He needed just three years to do the same on the 50-and-over circuit and reached the benchmark in 1988, joining Barber, January and Gene Littler, who also accomplished the feat. Charles Coody, the 1971 Masters champion, also prospered. From the time he cashed his first Tour check in 1963, Coody earned $1,187,762 through 1982 on the PGA Tour, and made $428,926 in his final 10 years leading up to his 50th birthday. But during his Senior Tour career, Coody earned $4,037,785, including more than $3 million during his 50s. Talk about being born again.

These players weren't alone. In 1990, just 10 years after the circuit's formation, Trevino became the first player to earn seven figures in a Senior Tour season. In 1993, all but three exempt players had won more money on the Senior Tour than they did on the PGA Tour. Jim Colbert, winner of eight tournaments, was the 38th golfer to surpass $1 million in career earnings on Tour. He achieved the feat on the same golf course where 17 years earlier he cashed his first paycheck as a touring professional for $537.50 at the 1966 Texas Open Invitational. In a Tour career spanning 21 years, he made a total of $1.5 million. In 1996, at age 55, Colbert eclipsed that figure in a single season on the Senior Tour.

"If the Senior Tour had started in 1970 instead of 1980, I'd be a multimillionaire," Tommy Bolt lamented.

When the Senior Tour had blossomed to 41 events and the average purse surpassed more than $1 million, Kizziar sent Palmer a note that read, "I told you so." Several pros, including Walt Zembriski, a former high-beam steel construction worker, turned ordinary Tour credentials into senior success. In 1988, Zembriski became the first man who never won on the Tour to win on the Senior Tour. John Brodie, the former San Francisco 49ers MVP quarterback, turned in a stellar second career on the senior circuit. One of the most popular pro-am draws, Brodie even won a tournament. "I can't compare this to anything I've ever done," Brodie beamed after recording a victory in his 157th event spanning seven years.

This second act grew so lucrative that professional golfers counted the days to age 50 with the enthusiasm of a young man about to turn 21. One major champion even was carded like a young hotshot trying to sneak into a bar under-age with a fake I.D. When Gary Player first appeared in the Tour's media guide in 1957, his birth year had been listed mistakenly as 1936. One year later, his birthday was corrected to Nov. 1, 1935, and remained that way until the error re-appeared in the Tour's 1970 media guide. This clerical error was printed and re-printed through 1978. After Player won the Masters at what then was considered the advanced age of 43, the error was rectified in the media guide in 1979 for good. The age discrepancy never concerned Player until he neared age 50 and Senior Tour officials questioned his eligibility. Alastair Johnston, his agent at the time, had to present Player's birth certificate to Beman as proof.

"It was a gold mine for these guys," Johnston said.

When the first wave of stars started to push 55 and beyond, they wondered what was next.

"I don't know what I'm going to do when all this stops," January told *Golf World* in 1983. "I've been able to dodge work all these years. I don't know anything except golf. Maybe they'll have a Super Senior Tour by then. We'll play just one day."

January wasn't far off. In 1987, the Vantage Super Seniors was added for the 60-and-older set, helping to keep some of golf's most glamorous names active even longer. They played in the regular tournament proper and competed in a two-day "tournament-within-a-tournament" for a separate purse. (January won another 35 times in the over-60 events.) Senior golf grew to such heights that some wondered if it might one day upstage the regular tour. Beman, however, didn't fret.

"I always was convinced it wouldn't because whether it's the LPGA, the seniors or the regular tour, the more exposure golf gets, the more golf grows," Beman said.

Inevitably, the question became what would Beman do when he turned 50? During his vacation time, Beman qualified for the 1986 British Open at age 48. It marked the first significant tournament that Beman had entered since the 1973 Walt Disney World tour stop in Orlando. He played the Irish Open and a couple of other European Tour events in preparation. Beman chalked it up as a "personal challenge," but it led to speculation that he might resign as commissioner to play the Senior Tour he helped create.

"I think he was secretly fiddling with the idea of leaving office and playing golf again," speculated Duke Butler, a former Tour executive. "He is a competitive golfer first and foremost. It's in his DNA."

In retrospect, Beman said he believed he could've been successful on the Senior Tour. But he couldn't walk away from the challenges that awaited him as Tour chief.

"Even if I had wanted to we were still pushing uphill," he said. "Golf technology was starting to become a big issue and I felt very strongly about it. I knew what was happening could hurt the game."

That's not to say he didn't dabble in senior golf once he turned 50 in 1988. Beman competed that year with partner Al Geiberger in the Liberty Mutual Legends of Golf, then an unofficial event that didn't affect the money list. As *Sports Illustrated's* Jaime Diaz wrote, "No commissioner of a major professional sport in America had ever competed with or against the same people he could slap a fine on, or penalize a few shots."

"I don't think I scared too many people," Beman summarized at the time.

Nevertheless, his decision to compete rankled some of his fellow players.

"It was small and petty," Diaz recalled. "I didn't understand why anyone felt there was a conflict. All he wanted was to be in the arena again."

Among the barbed comments, Rodriguez delivered the most humorous, noting Beman's wisdom in pairing with Geiberger, senior golf's hottest golfer at the time: "I want a smart commissioner," he told *Sports Illustrated*. "If Deane had picked [86-year-old] Gene Sarazen, then I'd worry."

Less than a month later, Beman abandoned plans to play any more Senior Tour events.

"I simply do not have the time necessary to prepare for competition if I am to continue as commissioner, and I intend to do that," he said.

But it didn't stop him from playing competitively during his vacation time. Not to be forgotten, Beman was the 54-hole leader of the 1990 Senior British Open (which was unaffiliated with the Senior Tour). For several months in preparation, he beat balls daily at 6 a.m. at the back range at TPC Sawgrass before going into work. But a driving rainstorm on the final day derailed him; Beman shot 80 and lost by a stroke to Player, who rallied from five shots back. In a show of sportsmanship that also reflected the strength of their friendship, Beman and his wife joined the Players at their victory dinner celebration that night.

"How could you not?" said Judy Beman. "I know Deane was disappointed but it was quite a feat to come from behind the desk and play so well."

Beman blamed his failure on his glasses, which he never had worn playing golf in bad weather. When he returned home he promptly was fitted for contact lenses.

"I didn't play enough golf to play in anything but good weather," Beman said. "I should've just taken my glasses off. The wind was blowing the rain sideways so you couldn't see the ball land anyway."

His staff back in Ponte Vedra had crowded around a TV set at the TPC Sawgrass clubhouse to watch the broadcast and agonized over his fate.

"It could've been another career-changing moment," Butler said. "The business lucked out again like it had in 1969 (when Beman finished runner-up at the U.S. Open). (The defeat) kept him in office another bunch of years."

*   *   *

Many professional golfers still count the days before they can join the senior circuit, but there's less of a need today to get a second chance at golf. Most of the top name players graduating to the Senior Tour have earned a lot more money than the early pioneers of the senior circuit.

"They don't need it and damn sure don't need getting beat up," Beman said. "When they do play, they're not having as much fun because the Senior Tour competition is at a very high level."

It also has lost much of its cachet. Palmer, Rodriguez, Trevino, and others who popularized the Senior Tour in the 1980s and 90s have succumbed to the verdict of time.

"I'm like a 1967 Cadillac. I've changed the engine twice, rolled back the odometer and replaced the transmission," Trevino said. "But now all the tires are going flat, and it's time to put it in the junkyard."

The pioneering spirit of Boros, Ford, January, Sikes, Snead and Goalby is a distant memory, but they remain proud of what they brought to the game.

"I won a Masters and 14 tournaments and I'm proudest of my Senior Tour involvement," said Goalby, who spent 16 years on the Senior Tour policy board.

Goalby chuckled when the Senior Tour in 2002, renamed the Champions Tour, instituted what it termed "fan friendly" policies in order to rejuvenate interest.

"All of that is great. But there's no way they are as friendly as we were back in the day," Goalby said. "We had to be. It was a matter of life or death."

FIXING AN UNEVEN PLAYING FIELD

W hen Deane Beman turned pro in 1967 he successfully navigated fall Qualifying School. All it earned him was the privilege to enter Monday qualifying. In January 1968, with a mortgage, borrowed money from friends and four kids in school back home, he arrived at the season's first event in Los Angeles to find that there were so many players competing Monday that he was assigned to Riviera C.C., one of three courses in use. They all were vying for two available spots at each course into that week's L.A. Open at Rancho Park Golf Course. He shot 68 and got in. Beman knew Monday qualifying up close and personal.

So did Gary McCord. When he turned professional, he finished second behind Ben Crenshaw at the Tour's 1973 Q-School. McCord's first qualifier happened to be the L.A. Open, too. He was assigned to Los Serranos Country Club, where 180 hopefuls battled for one spot. "Your picture was on a milk carton if you didn't shoot 65," McCord said.

For Beman, McCord and so many others, this was a way of life. At the time, the top 60 money winners from last year's money standings were exempt from qualifying each week. So were top 25 finishers in the particular tournament from the previous year, and anyone who made the cut at the most recent tournament. For everyone else, Monday awaited.

"Perhaps nowhere in the annals of the Games of Man has there been a competition to equal the tense, raw-nerve combativeness of this one-day event. Or the heartache. Or the joy," wrote *Golf Magazine's* John Ross, a former Tour official who regularly witnessed these heart-breaking shootouts first-hand. "It wasn't for a championship, but the players weighed each stroke, each stratagem as if it were the Masters, the U.S. Open, and the PGA, all rolled into one. This was a chance to make it, and it wouldn't come again until – well, next Monday, if the money held out."

Before long, McCord became one of the rabbits, a term established players used to describe non-exempt players who had only this desperate route to qualify for a spot and jump from week to week trying to get their shot at the big show. McCord thought there must be a better way. There were a host of reasons to abandon the present system. The life of a non-exempt player was a gypsy experience at best. Those who failed had to hang around until the next qualifying round. They would find a course near the next tournament and scare up a game playing each other for what little money they had. Meanwhile, they incurred the same travel and living expenses as the exempt players. The very players who could least afford such financial tolls were the ones most burdened by the system in place. "It was an ever-evolving trip down the toilet was what it was," McCord said.

Occasionally, a "Second Tour" event was held for the non-qualifiers but the meager prize money offered in these events seldom offset the players' expenses. When they did qualify for a Tour event, they played first to make the cut so that they could play the next tournament. "The system cried for a better alternative," Beman said.

Yet change wasn't embraced by many players. "The devil you knew was better than the devil you didn't," Beman said.

That changed, beginning in 1983, when the Tour introduced the All-Exempt Tour, virtually eliminating the regular ritual of Monday qualifying. (Four open spots still exist.) Every Tour member who finished in the top 125 on the previous year's money list carried exempt status into every open tournament on the circuit. Each Tour player earned a rung on the priority ranking system – with tournament winners from the previous year near the top and Q-School grads towards the bottom – that was used in selecting tournament fields. Over the years as the new system gained acceptance, McCord earned the reputation as the father of the All-Exempt Tour.

Beman recognizes McCord's contribution, but has a different take on its creation. An All-Exempt Tour had been years in the works, dating to Joe Dey's term as commissioner. Beman championed the idea in several phases but he couldn't sell it to the players. That's where McCord excelled.

Said Beman: "Gary deserves a lot of credit for convincing the guys that it was a better idea."

Beman mostly was troubled by the inequality the existing system created. Sixty players could arrange their lives. The rest of the field couldn't plan their schedule, earn outside income by playing pro-ams or corporate outings on Monday and Tuesday, and didn't even know when they were going to get home to see their wife and kids. Monday qualifiers viewed a tournament through a different lens. First they had to qualify on Monday. Then they concentrated on making the cut on Friday (and earning exempt status next week). Finally, they played the weekend to make money and earn a top-25 finish (and an invite back next year).

Some players complained that Beman was almost too sympathetic to the Monday qualifier's plight and pushed the Tour towards socialism. *Golf Digest's* Dan Jenkins termed it "tyranny from the bottom." But Beman disagreed. "It has nothing to do with socialism and everything to do with a level playing field."

A 1987 *Forbes* article called Beman "the John L. Lewis of professional golf," comparing him with the benevolent dictator hailed by coal miners for providing higher wages, retirement and medical benefits. "(Beman's) created a powerful trade union for the players. Good for the rank and file, no doubt, but what about the sport?" the article wondered.

Turns out it was pretty good for the sport, too.

*   *   *

Some say the modern-day Tour can be traced back to time well spent during a rain delay at the 1928 Texas Open. Of course, tournaments were held before then – the first U.S. Open was played in 1895 and the Western Open dates to 1899. Golf historians say the evolution of an informal tour began in the early 1920s when the first resort boom hit the sunshine belt of Florida, Texas, and California. It was during a storm that forced a Monday finish in San Antonio that Scot Tommy Armour called a players' meeting and the structure of a tour took form. According to Art Stricklin, author of "Links, Lore, and Legends: The History of Texas Golf," Armour had been elected as president of the Professional Touring Golfers' Association of America, and introduced a local lawyer who helped adopt the tour's bylaws and articles of incorporation. One year later, the circuit consisted of 12 tour stops.

At that time, all anyone had to do to join the PGA was pay $5 dues and an entry fee, and scrawl his name on an entry slip. After World War II, entry was restricted to PGA members, amateurs, and approved tournament players. To become a PGA member, you had to be employed at a club. To become an approved tournament player, it was necessary to convince your local PGA section that you had playing ability. They then nominated you for playing status. Starting in the mid 1930s, qualifying rounds became an accepted practice of the tour as the size of fields expanded. With qualifying came the first exemptions. Bob Harlow, tournament bureau manager at the time, suggested that sponsors exempt better players to avoid asking them to qualify, and possibly, insulting them. Exemptions were granted based on performance in the PGA Championship and U.S. Open.

Into the early 1960s, qualifying rounds were only required during the winter tour, which was a haven for club pros escaping the cold winters of the North.

"We were like birds," said Jackie Burke Jr., of the pros who taught in colder climes. "We just headed south."

As golf grew in popularity, many participants in the qualifier clearly didn't possess the skill to compete. To separate the wheat from the chaff, in 1965, the tour held its inaugural Qualifying School at PGA National Golf Club in Palm Beach Gardens, Fla. Q-School was even more of a life or death situation than it has become. Those who didn't make it had few competitive options until next year. That wasn't a problem for John Schlee, the medalist. Another player in the field was Jim Colbert, who remembered having to prove to his PGA section that he had enough money to support himself for a year.

"In those days that took $12,000. You'd go to class for three days and learn how to dress, how to act and then play a little golf. I think there were 49 of us there," Colbert said. "They told us there would be 17 cards. You could've knocked me over. I thought we were all getting cards." Colbert tied for 17th and earned the final card. He qualified on Monday for his first Tour event in San Diego at Torrey Pines North. Of the 156-man field, 50 made the cut and only the top 25 finishers cashed a check.

"The Monday qualifier was tough," Colbert said. "Any PGA club pro in America who could play a lick would come out during the winter." In golf, a pretty good player can beat the leading money-winner in an 18-hole contest on any given day.

By 1968, it was necessary to hold two schools a year – one in the spring and one in the fall (the card was valid for 6 months). Intended as an improvement, this modification only further stacked the deck against players outside the top-60, who had half the time to establish a higher status. By 1971, the Monday qualifying rounds were overcrowded and a Friday preliminary qualifying round was instituted for all non-Tour members who wished to try out on Monday. The qualifying system was onerous to administer, too. Many times the staff had to prepare three golf courses and oversee three Monday events. Not to mention that the Friday pre-qualifier turned up all sorts of players. One time a competitor shot 86 and asked Mike Crosthwaite, the Tour's director of sponsor-player relations, "Do I get a gift certificate?"

Another time, Crosthwaite recalled running out of daylight at the qualifier for the Kaiser International Open in Napa, Calif.

No one wanted to come back the next morning. So Tour pro Dave Newquist pulled his van around, shined the high beams and they held a putt-off on the practice putting green for the last two spots. "That was what it was like," Crosthwaite said.

Moreover, this was becoming a financial burden for the tournament sponsor, who had to absorb the cost of using a pre-qualifying, qualifying and tournament course. Nominal entry fees failed to offset the expense. Joe Dey tried in vain to resolve this problem during his five-year tenure as commissioner, which began in 1969. Dey convinced a number of tournaments

– among them the Florida Citrus Classic, Kemper Open, and Byron Nelson Classic – to offer a satellite event for secondary players who didn't qualify for the main field. In 1968, the tour, besides its major tournaments, had only two $5,000 satellite tournaments. In 1972, the tour listed 18 satellite events with prize money totaling $254,000 for those touring pros unable to qualify for the regular tournaments.

"If all sponsors could be induced to put a portion of purse money toward such events a large problem would be solved," opined *Golf World's* Dick Taylor.

Purses for these 36-hole affairs typically ranged from $10,000-$35,000 and were subsidized from the overall purse, resulting in less prize money for the top pros. It also meant fewer dollars could be raised for local charities. Tournament sponsors proved incapable of funding the satellite tour.

"If a tournament put money into a second tour event, it diverted money away from the purse in their main event, which could hurt the field," Beman explained.

So the satellite events soon died out. In July 1970, a proposal was presented to the policy board to use satellite events (renamed Second Tour events in 1972) as qualifying rounds for next week's tournament. Dey requested that the player directors and young players advisory council review the matter and report back to the board. It's unclear whether they ever did. But in February 1972, the topic resurfaced. The board minutes detail the appointment of a committee consisting of player directors Gene Littler, Dale Douglass, tournament director Jack Tuthill and Dey to study the commissioner's recommendation for a plan using Satellite tournaments as qualifying rounds and thereby eliminating Monday qualifying rounds.

In August 1973, Tuthill reported the results of a member survey on the topic: 114 supported continuing qualifying rounds and 51 favored abandoning Monday qualifying and using second tour events as qualifying rounds. Based on the lack of player support, the board agreed with Tuthill's conclusion that no action should be taken. Dey's effort came to a screeching halt. When he stepped down in February 1974, Dey listed the defeat of his qualifying changes as one of his greatest regrets.

"Monday qualifying is not the best means. It is not

commensurate to the tour operation," he told *Golf World* after he announced his retirement. "It is bush."

Beman had played in the system and realized its shortcomings were too long to list. "When I became commissioner I knew the system was unfair for anybody other than an exceptional player," Beman said. "The system was tilted. So early on I was looking for a way of bringing change to what I thought was a considerable flaw in our competitive system."

Just months into his tenure, Beman formed a committee consisting of himself, player directors Colbert and Bob Dickson, and PGA director Henry Poe to explore the idea of reviving a second tour. But the reality of more pressing concerns delayed any progress in his first year on the job. In July 1975, the committee pursued the cause again. It submitted to the Tour's board a 15-page study. One scenario proposed increasing the number of exempt players to 140. "This ensures that anyone with a reasonable rate of ability has exempt status," the study said. It also suggested the Tour host mini-tour events that would serve to qualify players to the major events. The question, however, remained two-fold: "How is the Tour going to find the courses and how is it going to raise the prize money?"

In October 1975, another report focused on finding an economically viable system that would give all players an equal chance to play "free and easy" once the competition got underway. The revised report suggested an exempt player tour could be instituted in 1977. The plan proposed five review periods that would drop 12 players from the "Major Tour" and add 12 players from the "Second Tour." Under this system, the Tour would host a second tour lasting 4 weeks in length, and enabling a player dropped from the major tour to rejoin it within a 60-day period. Player entry fees of $1,500 would be the primary source of income to fund the second tour. It remained a topic of discussion at future board meetings, but minutes indicate that no action was taken on the idea.

Efforts resumed during the August 1976 board meeting with discussions of reviving the Caribbean Tour, a popular winter series that attracted many club pros before folding in the late 1960s. Beman visited with the old leadership of the circuit in the Dominican Republic, Costa Rica and Venezuela but talks stalled and then faltered. "That was just one of our failures to get a second series of tournaments going," Beman said.

Though efforts proved fruitless, Beman, noted that this time period marked the beginning of the arduous task of evaluating whether the Tour could be better structured. Players began entertaining the idea, too. On Jan. 17, 1977, Dale Douglass outlined his thoughts for an All-Exempt Tour in a letter to the policy board. But a groundswell for change had yet to arise.

For the next two years, discussions of fixing the qualifying system languished as Beman expended his political capital building TPC Sawgrass and moving the Tour's headquarters to Florida. That is until May 22, 1979, when player director Bob Murphy presented to the board a detailed plan for 100 players to compete on the regular tour, 150 players on a qualifying tour, and the elimination of Monday qualifiers. At the end of the season, 40 players would be promoted and demoted based on their standing on the two money lists. Explaining his plan's importance and the hardships of Monday qualifying, Murphy noted, "You can shoot 71 five straight weeks and never get into a tournament."

"I think it's a good idea," Jack Nicklaus said publicly. "It would relieve the crush. It would provide opportunities for more players. It would take golf to cities which don't have it, to regions of the country which don't have it, and it would create new stars. Somebody would come along and win six tournaments on the second tier and would arrive on the major Tour as an accepted 'name.' "

Arnold Palmer, on the other hand, called it a bad idea. "We would be drawing a line we don't have to draw," he said in *Sports Illustrated* when Murphy's proposal was the hot locker room topic. "The minute you designate something minor league, you've got an uphill battle."

Though the media scribbled down the opinions about qualifying changes from Palmer and Nicklaus, such proposals didn't really affect them. This was a matter for the marginal player. He may have dreaded Monday qualifying, but he still knew he was one step away from a breakthrough. A second tour meant he potentially was two steps away. Against this backdrop, Beman needed to persuade these players that they were missing the larger point. To whip up interest, the Tour's statistical wizards calculated the percentage of official money won by the top 100 money winners between 1976 and 1978. The evidence was staggering. Of the nearly $27 million combined prize money played for during the three years, the top 100 won more than $23 million, or 86 percent. To tell the players that few of them were prepared to earn a living at the highest level rang hollow, but the magnitude of the numbers resonated. "It was a reality check," Beman said.

On Oct. 2, 1979, Labron Harris Jr., director of tournament administration, sent Beman a memorandum briefing him on the Qualifying Tour test program for 1980. It included a budget, eligibility criteria, possible event sites, and a proposal to potential sponsors. Even sponsor agreements had been drafted. The trial-run targeted four consecutive tournaments – The Colonial, The Memorial, the Kemper Open and Atlanta Classic – to hold opposite events and assess the feasibility of a two-tour structure in the future, perhaps for implementation as early as 1981.

The "Championship Tour" would consist of approximately 30 events with prize money of at least $300,000. The fields would be made up of top 100 money winners from the preceding year, the roughly 20 major winners awarded a lifetime exemption, and sponsor invites. The "Qualifying Tour" was designed to prepare younger players for the Championship Tour through weekly competition and also serve as a place where a player who wasn't eligible for the Championship Tour could refine his game and play for modest prize money.

The Qualifying Tour would consist of approximately 30 events with prize money of at least $100,000. The fields would be made up of Nos. 101-180 on the preceding year's money list, 40 new players from the Qualifying School, the players granted a lifetime exemption, and sponsor invites. As an incentive to play in the trial events, money earned was to be counted as official prize money. Another proposal that was considered: the top five money winners of the four qualifying Tour events combined would receive exempt status on the Championship Tour for one year.

"Instead of 43 cities, professional golf would be available to 60 cites," Beman told *Golfweek* in May 1979. "And another 150 players would be able to play each week."

Beman heard from several camps. Opinions varied and sentiment shifted.

"While it may break a few eggs, I think the potential omelet is all to the good," wrote former Tour policy board chair Lew Lapham. "All of us have been over this ground in the past several years, one way or another, and as I see it, sooner or later the bullet has to be bitten. I'm for biting."

"We tour members still remember the previous unsuccessful attempts to get sponsors for a second tour," wrote Tour veteran Kermit Zarley in August 1979. "If a deep recession sets in, this may not be the time."

"I believe in what you are trying to do," Nicklaus concluded in a typed letter to Beman on Sept. 25, 1979. "However, financing it and sustaining it over a period of time is going to be difficult. I wish you good luck with it."

Zarley and Nicklaus had reasons for concern. But the plan for financing the Qualifying Tour seemed adequate. It relied on dipping into the Tour's television revenue from its domestic TV rights fee. According to the proposal, "there will still be a surplus of over a million dollars available in TV funds to subsidize the Qualifying Tour."

After all the effort and debate, the two-tour concept seemed on the verge of winning approval. But it failed again. The reason? Too many players remained noncommittal. During the fall of 1979, the Tour conducted a player survey to establish interest in the four Qualifying Tour events and the results were lukewarm at best. Of the 365 members at the time, 136 responded, 44 declined to commit (including 18 who would have been eligible) and 92 committed to play if eligible. However, only 56 players who weren't in the top 100 money winners for 1979 (and thereby eligible) committed to play in the 1980 trial-run. The same issue that derailed Dey's effort six years earlier had stalled the creation of Beman's attempt at an All-Exempt Tour, too.

"You're never going to get the turkey to vote in favor of Thanksgiving," is how Monday qualifying veteran Mike Donald, explained it. "Guys didn't want to be demoted."

Beman recommended that the project be dropped. To "spin" the decision positively, Beman told the *Houston Chronicle* "the players are more interested in competition than they are security. I can't fault them for that." Beman still clung to the idea that the All-Exempt Tour was needed, but in hindsight, he observed that the delay might have been a blessing in disguise that allowed the Tour to focus on the creation of the Senior Tour.

"We did a lot of work on the All-Exempt Tour, but when it came to players actually committing so we could go out and find somebody in the community to put up the money to do it, the players came up empty," Beman said. "Instead we became fully engaged now in developing the Senior Tour, which had widespread player support. If the players had decided to fully support it, our staff and financial resources would've been overwhelmed in trying to make both successful at the same time. Both may have failed."

Two more years passed before player sentiment shifted. This time the momentum to push the All-Exempt Tour through would come from one of its own.

*   *   *

In the early 1980s, Gary McCord was a struggling Tour member, barely eking out a living. McCord made the top-60 only once in nine seasons between 1973 and 1982. He was a perennial rabbit, a Monday qualifier who jumped from event to event hoping to earn a spot that week. In that role, he played a key part in the extinction of the rabbit on Tour.

McCord pointed to a Monday in Miami at the 1981 Doral Open when he began to entertain the possibilities of a better way. Warming up on the range beside him were past champions Miller Barber and Frank Beard. "I was amazed at how many tournament winners were trying to qualify," McCord said.

The result that day was another failed Monday for McCord. When he got home, he counted the collective wins achieved by the Monday qualifier field, and the number surpassed 50. Over the course of the next month, he poured over stats from the last few years and made an important discovery: In 1980, 69 percent of the Tour – comprising 93 exempt and 210 non-exempt players – qualified through Monday events. Even more revealing: Based on his estimated annual minimum earnings needed to break-even after expenses, McCord calculated 76 percent of Tour competitors couldn't make ends meet. He resolved that the number of exempt players should increase from 60 to a figure closer to 144, the typical size of a full-field event.

"I didn't have an exact number," McCord said. "I took the idea to Joe Porter. He was the first non-exempt player elected to the policy board (in 1977). Joe was loud and had a lot of opinions. I called him up and told him I wanted to share this idea with him."

Porter had left the Tour and settled in Phoenix, where he went into the real estate business. Before he did, Porter played for more than a decade on Tour and he served a two-year stint on the policy board. "It was fun for me to be able to match wits with these titans of industry," Porter said. "It was one of the best experiences of my life and really gave me the confidence to go into business once I quit playing."

Porter was intrigued. He invited McCord to stay at his home. McCord spent much of the day wading through data, pondering various scenarios and waiting for Porter to get off work so they could calculate the supporting numbers late into the night using the computer at Porter's office. Once McCord formed the semblance of his plan, he weighed his options. He remembered how players Phil Rodgers and Fred Marti had proposed a similar plan during Joe Dey's tenure as commissioner and handed it off to Dey to generate the requisite support. That didn't work. Neither did Murphy's effort with Beman. McCord decided no one could champion his plan and rally the troops better than himself.

"I wanted it to be like a labor union uprising," McCord said.

He pitched it to his guys, "the Monday's Children," at the 1981 Tallahassee Open held in mid-April. Since most of the players were staying at the Holiday Inn that week, McCord asked the hotel's general manager if he could use its conference center as meeting space. He then posted flyers at the course and told anyone he ran into – from players sitting by the pool to those practicing on the putting green – that he had a new way to play the Tour. His hook: Find out how you can plan your schedule in advance. Word spread. "Over 100 guys showed up," McCord said, brightening at the memory. "I explained it. Some guys liked it, some guys didn't."

They took a show of hands and the majority favored McCord's plan. So McCord called Crosthwaite, the Tour's director of sponsor-player relations, and explained it to him. When Beman caught wind of the concept, he invited McCord to make a pitch in front of the full board the week of the Houston Open. He made his presentation on April 29, 1981, a day McCord later commented to *Golf World* would go down in history. "It won't be like Oct. 12, 1492 and Christopher Columbus," he said, "but it should be significant."

First, McCord listened as a member of the Tour staff presented the case for what tentatively was called the split tour. Given that top players tended to compete in approximately half the events anyway, the idea was to divide the Tour's existing 44 events into two leagues much like an American and National league in baseball and allow the sponsors to draft all the players. The four majors, Tournament of Champions, Players Championship, and World Series of Golf would be the equivalent of all-star games featuring the best players from both leagues. The season would conclude with the World Series of Golf in September, giving the players a fall hiatus to compete overseas until the new season kicked off the next year. This led to a heated discussion. The end result: the split tour failed its first test.

"While most liked the idea of a defined season, no one, especially the leading players, would relinquish their right to pick and choose when and where they play," Beman said. "We could never get over that hurdle."

Two alternatives were proposed. McCord presented next. He suggested raising the number of exempt players to 170 based on the previous year's official money list. Monday qualifying would be eliminated. At the end of the year, the bottom 26 would be dropped and the top 26 at Q-School would be promoted.

Beman listened with great interest. "Gary was a bright guy. I was delighted to transfer the initiative to him so this revolutionary concept we believed in would come from the players rather than from us at headquarters," Beman said. "It was ideal. We did not discourage the notion that this was coming from the players. It was a strategic decision on my part."

In addition to McCord's proposal, 51-year-old Don January proposed an old idea with a new twist. He recommended cutting the Tour to 25 official events with a minimum purse of $400,000. If a tournament couldn't afford that purse size it wouldn't be an official Tour event and official events would be the only place the 170 members of the All-Exempt Tour could earn official money for next year's standings. Unofficial money, he suggested, from lower-profile events would spend just as easily. January's plan was named the "Super Tour."

"We need to streamline the Tour," January told *Golf World*. "We talked about this in 1959 but it was voted down. Hell, the All-Exempt Tour was voted down a few years ago. But we need a change."

Beman promised that the board would evaluate all three proposals at the next board meeting on May 26 during the Kemper Open. Over the next few months, interest in the All-Exempt Tour gained momentum. Veteran Charles Coody, who noted that only the top 50 were exempt during his rookie year in 1962, attended a players' meeting later in the summer when talk of 125 exempt players had emerged. "I thought, 'My gosh, that's way too many people to be exempt,' " he said. "If you could play a lick, you could make the 125."

Some thought 125 was too high, others insisted 100 – which had been Murphy's figure in 1979 – was too low. The top players didn't care. Either way, they were in.

"The only guys who cared were fighting for the last spots. They got it pushed through," Coody said.

The board formed a committee consisting of Colbert, Tom Kite, Hale Irwin, the PGA's Mickey Powell, and board chairman Del de Windt. The committee settled on increasing the number of exemptions to 90. McCord said he couldn't sell it. That hope dashed, they pushed for 100. Beman thought this was the right number. McCord countered with 135. Support from the marginal players was the key to the All-Exempt Tour's approval. With the memory of previous failed proposals still fresh in their minds, they compromised at 125.

"Make sure the guy we're kicking off isn't better than the guy coming in. That was my criteria," McCord said. "I said,

'Let's take 5 years to figure out what the right number should be.' I was never sold on the No. 125."

At the next board meeting, player director Ed Sneed reviewed the latest list of modifications. The board recommended increasing the exempt figure from top 100 to top 125 on the money list, in part, because the original study was based on a field of 144. Increasing the field to 156 created 12 additional spots. Moreover, the development of the Senior Tour hadn't been considered in the original proposal. The prospect of an expanded Senior Tour would attract a number of players exempt in multiple categories, creating room for the additional exempt players.

Still, there was opposition. Powell commented that the moves would further shrink the opportunity for PGA members to participate on the Tour. Beman and Sneed noted that the format more than doubled the number of exempt players and statistics proved that exempt players had a more realistic chance of competing successfully on the Tour. The field staff chimed in that they preferred limiting fields to less than 156 players due to slow play. Sneed said they should eliminate slow play rather than playing opportunities. Having heard the arguments for and against, de Windt moved to modify field size from 144 to 156 and change the exempt list from top 100 to top 125.

PGA president Joe Black asked to postpone a vote on the All-Exempt Tour until there was a resolution of the PGA's grievances to the board. He also reiterated Powell's concern that the new system would restrict access of PGA members to the Tour. De Windt, chairman of the Tour's restructuring committee, responded that the concepts of the All-Exempt Tour had been passed in principle during the last board meeting. Furthermore, the Tour had conducted 14 player meetings in which 99 players attended, and there was strong support based on a 156-man field and an exemption for 125 players. (Many of the leading players, however, did not attend these meetings.) Player support weakened assuming a field of 144 and exempt status for the top 115 on the money list.

For those reasons, de Windt contended the decision shouldn't be postponed because such a delay could jeopardize the planned implementation in 1983. The discussion then shifted to the remaining modifications to the All-Exempt Tour proposal. They confirmed reducing the number of rounds at Q-School from eight to six and offering 50 cards and ties. There would still be four open qualifying spots into most Tour events. Independent director Bob Oehlman called for a vote to approve the modifications. The motion was made by de Windt and seconded by Howard Twitty.

Black again pounded at the same theme, requesting that the Board defer action on the All-Exempt Tour until there was an agreement reached between the PGA and the Tour policy board regarding what he termed "the status of the Tour's mission." After more discussion, they concluded they should not defer this matter. They assured Black his arguments would be taken into account and they would study any particular contentions or grievances the PGA wished to submit to the board. Finally, the time came to vote. The board approved the All-Exempt Tour by a vote of 7-2, with only Black and Kizziar dissenting. (Powell chose to abstain.) At last, Beman thought, Tour competitions would be a fair fight.

* * *

"Rabbit Monday" died at the 1982 Walt Disney World Classic, the last official event of the season. Now Mondays were like Tuesdays and Wednesdays for the top 125 players on Tour. In January 1983, a Tour press release noted, "the dreaded ritual of Monday qualifying has been eliminated."

Meanwhile, some members of the media mourned the rabbit's extinction: "The passing of the Monday qualifier takes away a large chunk of the romance of tournament golf – the heart-tugging, white-knuckle drama that seldom got more than a line or two at the bottom of the sports pages, but was such a significant thread in the fabric of the game," wrote John Ross in *Golf Magazine.*

But for those players who no longer had to endure it, they missed it about as much as a lingering cold that won't go away. Fourteen would-be rabbits, including 11 of them who had won tournaments, enjoyed their finest campaign in the inaugural year of the new format. Not everyone found immediate success.

Without the pressure pushing him to make the top 60, McCord failed to make even the top 125, finishing No. 131 on the 1982 Tour money list. He missed by less than $1,500. But McCord hardly was upset.

"The worst thing in the world would be if I created (the system) and then got to be one of the entitled," he said. "I remember sitting there at TPC Sawgrass after I got my card back (at Q-School) and saying, 'It works.' No one could cry favoritism."

What few argued was that the system allowed more players to set a schedule, playing events that suited their game, and compete aggressively without the fear of Monday qualifying. Scoring improved. "Beforehand, we were never comfortable," McCord said.

Not everyone agreed the new format made for a better Tour. It has caught its share of flak. The prevalent complaint is that it promotes mediocrity and winning takes a backseat to earning a fat check and keeping your card. Lee Trevino said at the time, "It took the fear out of the game."

CBS executive golf producer Frank Chirkinian argued that players lost an important training opportunity. "Every week the rabbits learned three things," he said. "First how to qualify, then how to make the cut and finally how to win. All of that is lost."

Nicklaus agreed with those who thought it bred complacency, but on the other hand, he told reporters, "It has given stability to a man's lifestyle."

Others expressed serious reservations that it ruined the pure, free enterprise system of pro golf. Raymond Floyd complained in a 1987 *Forbes* article that the All-Exempt Tour turned a capitalistic system into a socialistic one. Watson told *The Washington Post*, "What we have now is a closed shop, plain and simple."

Whatever reservations the board harbored toward allowing too many exempt players, the figure has survived intact. "We thought we could reduce the exempt number later," Colbert said, "of course, that never happened."

To this day, Colbert contends the number of exempt players is too high. "I see too many players hanging on," he added. "They're going to make a big check if they can make two pars. That's not what the Tour is about. Before, there was a much bigger premium on winning."

Echoed Powell: "I think it's too many. My number was 90. The Tour could be much more competitive than it is. Getting the number (lower) was too low a priority. Deane wasn't going to win that battle and lose the war. He didn't think small."

Beman, however, never subscribed to the criticism he heard that the new format created a welfare state. "The priority wasn't to get to 100," Beman said. "It was to achieve an equal competition and expand opportunity. It wasn't important whether it was 125 or 115 or 100. The right figure would take care of itself."

All these years later, even McCord is amazed there have been no significant changes. "It was a better system for our time and place in sports," he said. "I wish I would've copyrighted it because every tour in the world plays by that format now."

STRIKE ONE. STRIKE TWO. HOME RUN!

B y the late 1980s, Deane Beman's vision for the PGA Tour was coming into focus. A network of TPC's dotted the country, corporate America lined up for the privilege to be associated with Tour events, and the media celebrated the Senior Tour as the sports start-up of the decade. The riches the players now competed for was the most obvious measure of success, but it was hardly the most telling. Beman was a man devoted to making the existence of the Tour member a better one. He cast about for ways to extend the Tour's reach. Some gambits – such as "grow the game" initiatives Family Golf Centers and Wee Links – fared poorly. While his detractors delighted in his failures, Beman took them to heart.

"Sometimes you fall in love with your own ideas," Beman said. "Most ideas need day-to-day nurturing, management, and capital. We had a small staff and not a lot of money. Some of my ideas that I thought would take over the world of golf didn't leave the impact I predicted."

None of it stopped Beman from pursuing new ventures. He was a fountain of ideas. The Tour's Steve Reid coined a memorable saying around headquarters. He told colleagues the first time Beman pitches an idea, forget about it. The second time he proposes it, make note of it. But if he mentions it a third time, then you better plan on executing it. Beman never abandoned the idea of a developmental tour. He believed the Tour should provide a season-long proving ground for the stars of tomorrow, a competitive environment where pros either moved up or moved out, and a place to lessen the blow of missing at Q-School.

"We made several half-hearted attempts to launch a developmental tour," Beman said. "Those efforts failed because it was never a high enough priority. A good leader must decide when to fold them, when to retrench and try again and when to be bold and press for an ultimate conclusion. In the late 1980s, I realized now was the time to do it."

Having persevered to introduce the All-Exempt Tour, the developmental tour was the final piece to an intricate puzzle. It took several tries and many years to find the right fit, but once the pieces fell into place it would provide playing opportunities for pros, as the saying goes, "from cradle to grave."

* * *

Coinciding with the debut of the All-Exempt Tour in 1983 was the launch of the Tournament Players Series, a joint venture between the Tour and PGA of America that emerged from the renegotiation to the Statement of Principles in 1982. It called for no less than 10 events annually for five years. Fields consisted of 50 PGA pros, 50 touring pros, and 50 open spots. At the same time, there was a movement to lower the minimum age of the Senior Tour to 45. But the proposal faced stiff opposition from the current crop of senior players. As a compromise, players age 40-45 were made eligible for the TPS and 10-15 spots were reserved to give them another place to compete.

Many of the players that backed the All-Exempt Tour did so with the promise that the Tour would underwrite a series of developmental tournaments for the non-exempt players. They didn't want to be banished to the mini-tours, which traditionally are set-up like a poker game – every one antes up and whoever wins gets most of the pot.

"There had to be another tour," said veteran Tour member Gary McCord, the lead player advocate for the All-Exempt Tour. "I told the board, 'I'm not going to kick my guys off the Tour and there's nowhere to play.' Instead of one tournament for all year (Q-School), there should be another tour."

The TPS debuted in 1983 with nine events worth a total of $1.675 million. It gave the rabbits a place to develop their skills. Some crossovers from the Tour, major winners such as

Gary Player, George Archer and Bob Charles and future major winners such as Paul Azinger, Jeff Sluman, and Bob Tway filled out the fields. Russ Cochran won the first event, the $150,000 Magnolia Classic at Hattiesburg (Miss.) CC, and finished first on the money list to earn exempt status on the Tour the following season. But from the start the chemistry of the TPS circuit didn't work.

"The three constituencies – novices looking for seasoning before going on to glory on the Big Tour, journeyman Touristers whom glory eluded looking for a place to get some, and club pros looking to share anyone's glory – have as much in common as oil and water," wrote Larry Kieffer in *Golfweek*.

An even bigger problem emerged: the PGA backed out of its financial commitment. The TPS cost the PGA $500,000 a year, and it was seeing little return on investment. In its first year, Inner Circle – managed by the PGA and designed to be TPS's primary funding source – lagged below expectations.

What began as a way to provide playing opportunities for PGA members lost importance when the lack of success of its members on the TPS became clear. Before long, the PGA reevaluated whether supporting the TPS was the best use of its financial resources. At the May 1984 Tour board meeting, Beman argued that for the TPS to succeed, it must expand beyond 10 events. For the first time, the PGA made it known it was unwilling to finance any expansion. In fact, PGA president Mark Kizziar said the association was considering pulling out of its original five-year deal. Instead, they wanted to conduct their own series of tournaments strictly for PGA pros, even though the Statement of Principles forbid the PGA from doing so. Beman saw no reason to stand in the way of such a modest proposal. The Tour granted the PGA permission to launch a club pro series. More disconcerting news came when a PGA update to the Tour's board revealed that the Inner Circle program still was underachieving and losing support. After this discussion with PGA officers, Beman realized the TPS wouldn't succeed under its current format. "It was the first signal that the PGA wasn't permanently committed to this," Beman said.

So what to do? "It was going to require a subsidy," Beman said. "We were not unwilling to fund TPS because I always had a vision for an All-Exempt Tour backed by a TPS or a series of tournaments so if you missed your card you had a place to learn how to be successful. I always thought that was important."

Faced with subsidizing the circuit alone, Beman decided to rescue the TPS by staging revenue-generating pro-ams. He suggested restructuring the tournament format after the Senior Tour model, reducing the field size and holding a two-day pro-am in conjunction with tournaments. Under this scenario, the field size would be cut to 52 players, 25 of which would be age 40-50 to guarantee some name players for the pro-am, along with 12 from Q-School, 12 PGA club pros, and three open qualifying spots. Kizziar supported the concept and agreed to take it to the PGA executive committee. However, the formula, which depended on the support of older name players to attract enough interest in the pro-am, proved to be flawed. The grizzly vets refused to commit in advance to play in the lower-purse events. "The constituencies for whom it was designed are losing its enthusiasm," the Tour's Steve Rankin told reporters at the time.

Beset with sponsorship issues it flickered out. At the May 1985 meeting, the board approved a phase-out of the TPS after its third season. A few events continued opposite short-field invitationals and some were converted to Senior Tour stops. "TPS died like the second tour died," Beman said. "If the Inner Circle worked, we could have funded it no problem, but there wasn't readily available money to throw a couple of million bucks at the TPS. It was too big of a financial burden."

Despite the failure, Beman's conviction that a developmental tour was needed never wavered. His capacity to overcome past setbacks fortified his belief. "The disappointment of the failure of a particular plan can never stand in the way of your ultimate objectives," Beman said in reflection. "We just had to find a better way of making it succeed."

*   *   *

When it came to launching a developmental tour, Beman tried, tried and tried again. In the years that followed the TPS failure, corporate sponsors began to realize the value of title sponsorship and this presented a fresh avenue for Beman to underwrite tournament purses.

On March 7, 1988, the tournament policy board met in Ft. Lauderale, Fla., and authorized the staff to investigate Beman's concept of a new tour that would increase the number of professional playing opportunities for young players and expose new markets to golf. His detractors asked Beman the same question: What makes you think the result will be any different than the TPS? It was a legitimate concern. Beman knew if he could just get an umbrella title sponsor, the burden of prize money wouldn't fall on local communities. This time he would reinvent his developmental tour concept with a stronger financial structure.

But first, Beman contemplated a surprising development. At the August 1988 board meeting, he reported that he had been contacted first by an LPGA member and subsequently by one of its officers about the possibility of the Tour assuming control of the administration of the LPGA. Beman indicated he could respond only to a direct proposal from the LPGA's board, and that it would be a matter for the Tour's policy board. Sensing that the LPGA would divert attention and resources from its core responsibilities, Beman recommended against the Tour pursuing consolidating women's golf under the Tour's umbrella.

"We weren't mature enough yet," Beman said in retrospect. "It wouldn't have been an asset. It would've been a liability."

Especially since Beman was about to embark on another attempt to revive a developmental tour. At the same meeting, the board approved the concept of a new tour to launch in 1990, provided the Tour could secure a corporate title sponsor. Beman found a willing partner in Minoru Isutani, owner of Cosmo Worldwide. According to published reports, the Japanese tycoon paid $58 million in 1988 for the Hogan Golf Co., makers of golf equipment and apparel. Beman pitched sponsoring a 30-event circuit to boost the company's brand awareness and show its support of developing the stars of tomorrow and PGA professionals who would make up the fields.

"Mr. Isutani paid more for Hogan than he should have paid," Beman said. "He was buying the name. He was buying a brand. I convinced Isutani and his advisors that the only way out of his bad investment was the Hogan Tour – that it could build the importance of the brand in 30 different sections of the country. He understood the enormous collateral value of having a name on an event. They bought it. Now we wouldn't have just a fledgling couple of events. We'd have a whole tour."

But it wasn't that simple. Once again Beman's long time dream nearly imploded before it even got off the ground. The stumbling block this time was a familiar foe. "The PGA tried to muscle in on the deal," Beman said.

By now, though, Beman was no longer surprised by such tactics. The Tour had allocated spots in every tournament for PGA members to play. Part of the rollout of the Hogan Tour involved Beman speaking to the various PGA sections and generating goodwill for Hogan. Excited over the prospects of a deal, the Tour began coordinating meetings with PGA sections across the country to explain the new circuit and how they might benefit from it. Sections could earn revenue through entry fees for hosting the qualifying tournament. But Beman's jurisdiction only ran so far and the PGA took exception to the Tour talking directly to its sections.

"Deane needed the PGA club professional forces to get enough mass to get the Hogan Tour launched," the PGA's CEO Jim Awtrey said. "I personally felt that it was the only time we would be able to negotiate because we were needed."

Beman didn't need a partner like the one that reneged on TPS. He objected to the PGA's sudden interest in helping make a developmental tour successful now that Beman had lined up an umbrella sponsor. The PGA jeopardized the whole relationship. The Hogan Co. entered into a business arrangement with the express purpose of gaining the goodwill of PGA members and growing Hogan equipment sales. Company officials hadn't signed a contract yet and already the PGA was attempting to interject itself into the deal. The Hogan Co. wondered if it was jumping into the middle of a dispute between the PGA and Tour rather than into the makings of a formidable marketing vehicle. Beman worried that the Hogan Co. was having second thoughts.

"For 15 years we're trying to put together a developmental

tour and we haven't been successful yet and now we have a real shot at an umbrella title sponsor," Beman said. "If we had lost the Hogan Co. because of the PGA's interference I would've filed a lawsuit and it would've been a big one."

It never came to that. On Dec. 12, 1988, in a meeting in Maui, HI, Beman agreed to a handshake deal with the Hogan Co., for it to become the title sponsor of the new Ben Hogan Tour. The terms of the five-year agreement were $3 million annually to purses and another $4.2 million in operational subsidies over the life of the contract, for a total of $19.2 million.

Still unresolved was the none too simple matter of telling Ben Hogan. As author James Dodson details in his book "Ben Hogan: An American Life," when Isutani came to pay a call on the legend whose name he had purchased, Hogan was blunt. He reportedly shook the man's hand before sitting down to lunch at Shady Oaks CC, leaned toward his guest and said, "You've just bought the family jewels, Mr. Isutani. Please don't screw it up."

Some say Hogan didn't use the word "screw" or bother with the formality of using "please." What's certain is Beman remembered that Isutani feared Hogan, then chairman of the Fort Worth, Texas-based golf equipment manufacturer bearing his name. "In fact, I was asked to tell Hogan because Mr. Isutani was afraid to do it," Beman said. "He owned the name of the company. He could do what he wanted with it. But his staff preferred I go to Fort Worth to tell him."

So Beman went there to see the golfer he idolized during his formative years, the legend he had played 14 holes with as an aspiring teenage golfer in 1953. Beman didn't go alone. With a sense of awe undiminished with passing years, Steve Rankin – Beman's executive assistant at the time – held Hogan in the highest esteem. "On bended knees he pleaded with me, 'Let me go with you.' He loved Hogan," Beman said. "He had pictures of him on his wall. So I agreed to take him with me."

Beman shared the depth of affection Rankin and others felt toward Hogan. Beman said one of his great disappointments was when Hogan declined to attend the grand opening of TPC Sawgrass. But on this occasion, Beman had an exclusive audience. They entered Hogan's office. Beman's former lieutenant, David Hueber, recently had been wooed away from his CEO post at the National Golf Foundation to become CEO of Cosmo Worldwide. He was there too. Beman explained the agreement the Tour had struck with Isutani, and the number of spots promised for PGA pros on the new circuit. He added that club pros who no longer were competitive on the Tour now would have a place to play. Hogan couldn't have been more pleased. "If there had been such a tour when I was starting out to play I would've been successful 10 years before I was," Hogan said.

Before they parted, their discussion drifted to golf equipment. Beman never has forgotten what Hogan said about the golf ball. Beman had overseen the implementation of the one-ball rule on Tour in 1979, which prevented players from switching from a surlyn to a balata ball, or vice-versa, depending on conditions, during a round. Most pros at the time used a softer balata-covered ball for its better spin characteristics. But Hogan revealed to Beman that he enjoyed the advantage of the 2-piece ball, and if he were playing the Tour he'd surely trust the more durable, longer-flying surlyn ball. Beman thought he'd unearthed some incredible story for the annals of golf history. He could see the headlines now, "Ben Hogan chooses a surlyn golf ball in competition!" With a look of astonishment, Beman asked him why? Hueber noticed Hogan's lower lip begin to rise and almost purse with indignation. Beman pitched forward expecting Hogan to impart a secret no one else knew. Hogan replied simply, "Because it's better."

"He looked right at me," Beman said. "He didn't look at your nose or your ear. When Hogan looked at you he looked right through your pupils to the back of your brain. I said, 'Ben, why is it better?' He answered, 'I'm not going to tell you.' He got up. That was it."

"We knew the meeting was over," Rankin said. "It was as unnerving an experience as I've had, but we've chuckled about it for all these years since."

The Hogan Co. and Tour publicly announced the formation of the 30-event series of $100,000 tournaments on Jan. 4, 1989. (One tournament was played for $150,000.) *The New York Times* golf writer Larry Dorman still marvels at this accomplishment.

"At face value, he had just sold a tour for guys who aren't good enough to be on the PGA Tour," Dorman said. "Why should we care? But it turned out to be an integral part of creating a new generation of Tour caliber talent."

A few weeks later, the Hogan Tour's staff started taking shape with the selection of Bob Dickson as its tournament director. Hogan's Hueber and Dickson had teamed to find cities for the now defunct TPS, and were reunited to launch the latest attempt at a development circuit.

In June, the Kentucky Section of the PGA agreed to co-host the Ben Hogan Elizabethtown Open, the first event co-sponsored with a PGA section. The first 28 tournaments had been announced in brief press releases. On Oct. 9, 1989, a press conference was held at Shady Oaks near Fort Worth, Texas to announce the completion of the 30-event schedule and the eligibility requirements for the 1990 Ben Hogan Tour. A press conference was something Hogan hadn't participated in since, he said, "I don't know how long, if ever." With grace and good humor, Hogan, 77, at the time, gave the tour bearing his name the final seal of approval. He looked regal in a dark grey suit, red tie with blue stripes and a white pocket square. Sitting behind a table on a stage, Hogan looked out through a pair of gold-framed glasses. Beman spoke first.

"When we began the impossible task the 1st of April to develop the Ben Hogan Tour without one site committed there were a lot of people – some on my staff – that thought it couldn't be done by the end of the year," he said. "I set a goal that by Sept. 1, I wanted all 30. I'm not disappointed that we missed it by a few weeks. The 29th and 30th tournaments officially will be announced today."

The Ben Hogan trophy was unveiled. Above it hung the Hogan Tour logo – its silhouette of a golfer swinging was unmistakably Hogan, down to his trademark ivy cap. At tournaments, the iconic image of Hogan's 1-iron to the 18th green at Merion in the 1950 U.S. Open was splashed on posters with the tagline "The Next Generation of Champions."

Beman boasted that the new tour would rekindle interest in professional golf in parts of the country where the Tour no longer visited, such as El Paso, Texas, and Texarkana, Ark. "I saw a picture of Byron Nelson in the grill room there," he said.

Before fielding questions from the floor, Beman couldn't resist taking the rare opportunity to pose the first questions to Hogan. "The commissioner doesn't get too many privileges. He gets all the problems," Beman said. "From your standpoint, Ben, why do you think this type of competition is important?"

Hogan paused, measuring his every word, before delivering his answer. "If you have competition you're trying all the time. Every shot," he said. "You're trying to win. You're not trying to beat someone purposely. You're trying to shoot the lowest score."

Next, Beman asked Hogan to explain his interest in supporting this new initiative. "I think the Hogan Co. and Ben Hogan is obligated to put everything they can back into the game," Hogan said. "I've enjoyed every second of it. It's very important to me that I put something back into golf and repay my dues."

The voice of *Golf Digest's* Jerry Tarde sang out from the back of the room with the first question from the press corps. He wondered if the camaraderie that used to exist when players traveled together in Hogan's day would be a positive for the new tour.

"It's a wonderful thing, the camaraderie," Hogan began. "Three fellas including myself rented the second floor of a house on Sunset and Gower Street in Hollywood, Calif., in 1931. Dick Metz and Ky Laffoon joined us...It was one of the most enjoyable times I've ever had. I now feel sorry for the cafeteria we used to go to. You could eat all you wanted to for 35 cents. Soon after we left there, the cafeteria had to go out of business. I'm sorry about that. We were hungry kids."

Any sign of the intense expression in Hogan's eyes from his playing days had disappeared. With a smile on his face, he continued to paint a picture of a lost era. "It was the greatest feeling in the world to have friends and compete," Hogan said. "When one tournament was over we couldn't wait to get to the next one to go through the same routine. I'm sorry we don't have that right now, but we might have it with the new tour. They're going to get that enjoyment that we had.

"When I started it was in Pasadena, Calif. The Pasadena

Open had a $3,500 purse. First was $1,000 and last was $50 for 12ᵗʰ place. We were trying to get the $50 so we could buy gasoline to get to the next tournament."

It would be nine more years before, through sheer will and persistence, Hogan would win an individual tournament. First he went broke trying to make it on Tour in the 1930s, dropped off, raised enough money for another bid and became one of the greats of the game. How many prodigies have gone undiscovered, he was asked, for lack of financial support or competitive opportunity?

"I assure you there are many," Hogan said. "In fact somewhere out there today is a young man like I was, battling to stay in competition long enough to get a break. I want to help him."

Hogan compared competing on the developmental tour to earning a Master's degree in tournament golf. "That's what this tour is like," he said. "If you get your Master's degree, you use it to go out on the regular tour."

In his final statement at the press conference, Hogan remarked, "I'd like to be re-born so I can start on that tour myself." And he smiled again.

As attendees were filing out of the press gathering, Beman leaned over to Hogan and made a promise he intended to keep: "The Ben Hogan Tour is going to work. You're going to be proud of it."

* * *

Even the most optimistic person couldn't have foreseen the success of the Ben Hogan Tour, when it debuted in Bakersfield, Calif., on Feb. 2, 1990, a mere 54 weeks after Beman assigned Dickson the task of launching it. He had been working as a Senior Tour rules official when Beman approached him with an ambitious agenda.

"Just imagine being told, 'OK, go out and start me a 30-tournament tour,' " recalled Dickson, the man who put the nuts and bolts of the new endeavor together. "That had never been done before. You start with 3-4 tournaments, then go up to 6-8. Boom! We had 30."

And yet when the time arrived, the tour was ready to host regional qualifying at four locations. The 72-hole Qualifying finals had a starting field of 132. An unknown from Arkanasas named John Daly hit the ball a country mile and won the Hogan Tour qualifying tournament held Jan. 1-5, 1990, at the Grenelefe Resort (West Course) in Haines City, Fla. Tour membership was awarded to the low 35 scores. The Hogan Tour was composed of the top 80 finishers who failed to qualify at the 1989 PGA Tour qualifying tournament, and the top 35 finishers in the Hogan Tour's qualifying tournament. Fields consisted of 132 players for the 54-hole events. (Most tournaments expanded to 72 holes in 1993.) The demand for such a developmental circuit was illustrated before the first tournament when a field of 264 teed it up in open qualifying for eight spots in the tournament proper.

Overnight rain didn't diminish the enthusiasm in Bakersfield, that inaugural tournament day. There hadn't been professional golf there since the 1950s. A bagpiper led the players to an opening ceremony, where Beman hit a ceremonial tee shot and was given the key to the city. "This is not just a new tour that will be here for a while," he said. "We're committed that this tour is going to be here forever."

Due to a close family illness that had turned serious, Hogan was unable to attend. Excerpts of a letter he wrote apologizing for his absence were read to the audience. "Nothing would please me more than to be able to attend all 30 events," he wrote. "At my age this is impossible."

But Hogan had participated in a promotional shoot conducted by PGA Tour Productions. When asked his advice to the new crop of aspiring tour pros, Hogan answered in four words: "Watch out for buses."

Hogan was nearly killed in 1949 when the car he was driving home to Ft. Worth after the Phoenix Open collided head-on with a Greyhound bus on a foggy highway east of El Paso. Like relics of an earlier time restored, the fringe players dotting the developmental tour drove from tour stop to tour stop much the way the pros did in Hogan's day. In addition to traveling by car, players doubled up in economy motels and ate fast food.

"Players lived like caddies back then," said Jerry Foltz, who played the Hogan Tour its first year and later became a commentator of the circuit on Golf Channel. "We used to sleep four guys to $30-a-night rooms with nasty shag carpet. A nice restaurant was a place where they waited on you. Wives caddied for their husbands not because they wanted them to, but because they couldn't afford one."

Long before live scoring on the Internet and Thursday-Friday TV coverage became ubiquitous, the Hogan Tour delivered additional exposure of professional golf to smaller markets much the way the Senior Tour once had. Hueber took particular pride in spearheading the tour's stop in Fort Wayne, Ind., at Orchard Ridge Country Club, where his father had once been a club professional. Events were staged in all regions of the country, beginning in California and moving east visiting 23 different states. "At the Dakota Dunes Open," recalled Foltz, "we slept in Iowa, ate in Nebraska and played in South Dakota."

If a player drove to all 30 tour stops in 1990, the Hogan Tour's crack media relations staff estimated he would have logged more than 13,000 miles. Golfers embarked on this quixotic journey so that someday they would walk to the first tee bursting with confidence.

On a cold, blustery day at Bakersfield Country Club where players dressed in ski caps and volunteer scorers wore ear muffs, Mike Springer's confidence soared. He shot a final-round one-under-par 71 to better the field by two strokes and earn $20,000 for winning the tour's first event. Two months earlier, Springer, 24, sat dejected in a golf cart to the side of the large scoreboard at the TPC Woodlands, the Associated Press reported, after shooting a 13-over-par 85 in the fifth round of the finals of the Tour's Q-School. It all but ended the former college All-American's hopes of earning his Tour card for 1990. His father attempted to console him, and reminded his son that if he played well enough tomorrow, Springer could still acquire playing rights on the new Ben Hogan Tour.

Now the PGA of America's Pat Rielly was handing Springer an oversized paper check, the biggest payday of his young career. (He never had won more than $9,000.) "Mike, you can hand that check over to your wife like most of us do," Beman joked.

Springer and his wife, Crystol, parked their belongings in

storage, purchased a van and clocked most of the tour's 13,000 miles. A top-5 finish on the Hogan Tour money list afforded an automatic promotion to the regular tour the following season. Springer capped off a storybook season with bookend victories, shooting 65 in the final round of the last tournament of the season – the Ben Hogan El Paso Open – and finished fourth on the money list with $82,906, to punch his ticket to the PGA Tour.

He wasn't the only one who chased a carrot, hoping to avoid a dreaded date with Q-School. After not being fully-exempt into each Hogan tournament at the start of the year, Jeff Maggert headed for the Australian Tour, which he'd played in 1989. A win in his second Hogan Tour start shifted his focus to earning his card through a top-5 money list finish. He won again, topped the money list with $108,644 in 22 events, and was named Ben Hogan Player of the Year. Neither the trophies nor the accolades rivaled the sense of accomplishment of earning his PGA Tour card. "It meant everything," he said.

Maggert had missed three times at Q-School and was beginning to wonder if he would ever get to prove himself in the big leagues. The next year when he played The Colonial, he made sure to meet Hogan at the Tuesday night champions' dinner. Maggert shook his hand and thanked him for supporting the developmental tour. Maggert became a multiple tournament winner, played on three Ryder Cup teams and one Presidents Cup squad, and didn't have to attend Q-School again until 2009.

The top five money-winners – Maggert, Jim McGovern, Dick Mast, Springer and Ed Humenik – qualified for the big Tour the following year. They also were slotted in front of the players who finished in the top 50 at final stage of Q-School. "Now that we had a full series of events, I thought that (sustained excellence on the Hogan Tour) was a better indicator of how well a player would perform on the regular tour and not just how he would play one week in the finals of Q-School," Beman said.

Finishers Nos. 6-10 on the final money list were exempt on the Ben Hogan Tour if they failed to make it through the final stage; Nos. 6-20 on the Hogan Tour money list got to skip the first two stages of Q-School; Nos. 21-50 were exempt from first stage. The final stage of the PGA Tour Qualifying Tournament at La Quinta, Calif.,validated the caliber of competition on the

Hogan Tour as 22 of the 49 players receiving their 1991 PGA Tour cards were Hogan Tour members. "These guys are your future Jack Nicklaus and Arnold Palmers," said one of the veterans of the bunch, Joe Jimenez. He pointed at a few young players. "One of these guys is going to be one of the best. You don't know which one it is."

He was right. At age 25, Daly became the first Hogan Tour graduate to win a major on the PGA Tour thanks to a stunning victory at the 1991 PGA Championship. David Duval and Tom Lehman cut their competitive teeth on the circuit before they each won a major and reached No. 1 in the Official World Golf Rankings. In short order, the tour proved to be a fertile farm system. But was the tour built to last?

Amid the lingering good feelings from the developmental tour's successful launch, a pall was cast over its future when the Hogan Co. decided to sever ties with the tour in 1992. There was legitimate cause for concern. Drowning in debt from his disastrous purchase of Pebble Beach Resort, Isutani unloaded the Ben Hogan Co. to another independent investor, William Goodwin, Jr., chairman of CCA Industries of Richmond in 1992. When Goodwin met with Beman at Tour headquarters, he refused to honor the contract. Beman reminded him that their contract had two more years to go. Beman was informed by his legal staff that even if the Tour sued, at best, they would receive "liquidated damages."

Without an umbrella sponsor the Tour couldn't possibly sponsor a series of secondary tournaments without losing money. By the next board meeting, Beman assembled a presentation to convince the board that the developmental tour must be salvaged. "It wasn't just a promotion," he explained. "It was an integral part of the whole fabric of the Tour. It was the final step in creating a total system for bringing new players into the Tour and preparing them on how to survive."

He told the board if it wasn't committed to subsidizing a circuit then it would fail. Beman recommended appropriating $1.6 million for administration costs as a substitute for the underpinning of the Hogan Co. He proposed discontinuing the $100,000 purse subsidy immediately to help finance the 1993 season. If he didn't find a replacement umbrella sponsor, the developmental circuit's prize money, he projected, would dip from $5 million to $2.8 million. The Tour asked the PGA to contribute the $500,000 it earned in entry fees to help with funding. After all, many of its members were playing on the circuit, and it was generating goodwill with the local PGA sections. The PGA refused, agreeing to a 50/50 split of entry fees. The board approved the plan. "It was the kind of fantastic commitment the Tour made for the future of the developmental tour," Beman said. "It was the right thing to do."

Fortunately, such measures never were needed. From June to September, the Tour's business development staff scrambled to find a replacement sponsor and landed a big fish. Nike debuted as the tour's umbrella sponsor in 1993. Purses topped $6 million for the first time in 1995, doubling in the tour's first five years of existence. The tour has gone through a few other iterations – a short stint as the Buy.Com Tour (2000-2002) and since 2003 as the Nationwide Tour. Beman, for one, thinks sponsorship of the developmental circuit is the best bang for the buck for a corporate title sponsor. According to the Tour for an investment of $12 million in 2011, a corporate title sponsor for the developmental tour receives nearly $60 million in value.

"If I was a company putting money in golf, the (developmental circuit) would be the product I'd buy," Beman said. "It's the best deal going. For dollars spent, they get more residual value than any sponsor of the Tour, with the exception of FedEx (which sponsors the season-long competition on the PGA Tour)."

* * *

The Nationwide Tour was founded to serve as a proving ground for up-and-coming golfers. It has grown into so much more than that. Today, PGA Tour fields routinely consist of more than 50 percent former Nationwide Tour graduates. It has spawned marquee names such as major winners Daly, Lehman, David Toms and Ernie Els. Recognizing the talented players on the Nationwide Tour, the Tour increased the number of money list exemptions from five to 10 in 1993, to 15 in 1997, to 20 in 2003, and to 25 in 2007. The ultimate goal is to finish among the top 25 and be promoted without having to endure Q-School's six-round pressure cooker.

"It's the best route back to the land of milk and honey," Foltz said.

To compete on the Tour itself, they must make it against the best players in the world. The developmental tour provides a proper setting to refine skills in a true tournament environment where they can learn to cope with pressure, develop a winning attitude and gain the confidence necessary to succeed at the highest level. The difference in the caliber of play between Tour players and the unheralded stars of tomorrow has become nearly indistinguishable.

While the Nationwide Tour was designed for younger players, it features a number of veterans of the Tour who are trying to resuscitate their careers or prepare for the Champions Tour. As if these players need any additional motivation, the allure of the Nationwide Tour also has grown stronger thanks to the increase in prize money. In 2008, for the first time in the circuit's history, two tournaments offered $1 million each in prize money. The downside of such lucrative purses? Players can make a good living on the circuit and never graduate. That limits the number of younger players who might really develop into Tour caliber talent if they had a place to learn how to compete.

"My feeling about a player is he should have a reasonable period of time to develop his talents and then if he can't make it to the big show, he ought to go home and get an honest job," Beman said.

Through its first 20 years, the Tour's developmental circuit – minor quibbles aside – has lived up to the promise its founders envisioned. "Third time around," Beman said, noting the past failures with a chuckle. "Some visions take a while to get right."

BIG SCOREBOARDS FOR SPECTATORS, BIGGER PURSES FOR PLAYERS

I t happened in 10 minutes. All on account of an article Beman read in *The Wall Street Journal* and some fast thinking on his feet. In the time a foursome takes to negotiate a par 3, Beman engineered the most lucrative sponsorship agreement of his tenure, a 10-year, mega-million deal with RJR Nabisco.

In truth, the deal was years in the making. He shook hands on the framework of the unprecedented deal in the winter of 1988, back when $200 million really was a lot of money. Well, that's still a lot of cookies and crackers. No less than *The New York Times* called Nabisco "the most powerful player in professional golf's money boom."

Only eight years earlier, Beman created the Tour's marketing department with the express purpose of licensing the new Tour logo – a silhouette of a golfer striking a pose. The logo replaced the knock-off of the "Union Pacific" shield, and more importantly, symbolized opportunity for new revenue.

As Beman wrote to the players, "the new Tour logo was not designed just because we wanted something pretty. We wanted something to sell – something that said 'golf.' " Thus began the brand-building of the PGA Tour.

Beman recognized that the economic base that supported televised golf was small. A plan to promote and grow the sport didn't exist. And to make matters more challenging, golf's governing bodies were more interested in pursuing their own agendas rather than uniting to popularize golf.

Beman, however, remained undaunted. He envisioned a

marketing machine driven by the Tour that not only would elevate professional golf but nurture the game for all.

"It adds to the exposure of golf to the public," Beman told *The Florida Times-Union* in early 1981. "Eight to 10 years from now, our marketing program will produce 15 to 25 percent of the prize money. Right now it produces zero, but it eventually will make us less dependent on our No. 1 source of income, which is television."

Early marketing and licensing deals, such as an agreement that made Gatorade the Tour's official thirst quencher and positioned its creamsicle-colored coolers on the tees, involved modest sums. (The Tour often accepted less direct money if advertisers would buy TV time on its telecasts.) Once the Tour's marketing program took off, it opened doors for other revenue-producing departments such as PGA Tour Productions and Tournament Players Clubs.

"We believed our destiny was tied to creating more value in golf for the corporate world than they could buy in any other sport," Beman said.

Not everybody agreed with the way Beman made golf the sport of corporate America. His critics accused Beman of selling the Tour's soul to the highest corporate bidder.

"To put a commercial name on a tournament was like selling Jesus T-shirts at the foot of the Sistine Chapel," Beman remarked.

Beman seized on the chance to forge partnerships with corporate America. He increased the number of weekly pro-am teams from 48 to 52 creating an additional 16 places for amateurs to rub shoulders with Tour players. The Tour kept eight spots, which it used to entertain potential clients, and local sponsors received eight more places to sell and raise money for its bottom line. The Tour created an annual event called the CEO Open, a multi-day tournament held in far-flung locales such as Jamaica, British Columbia, and Spain. The destination tournaments became must-play events for golf aficionados and savvy corporate marketers, pairing prospective clients with current partners already delighted with their relationship.

"We found it was more credible for a fellow CEO to convince a potential sponsor of their return on investment than for our staff to do it," Beman said.

Before television and sponsorship made staggering purses commonplace, tournaments scrambled to raise the most prize money to lure the best fields. Tournament prize money totaled $13.4 million in 1980, "nice dough, if you could get it, but not exactly the treasure of King Tut's tomb," wrote E.M. Swift in *Sports Illustrated*.

No event raised the stakes like the Panasonic Las Vegas Pro-Celebrity Classic (as it was known in its debut year). Jim Colbert, who had assumed residence in Sin City, helped broker the deal, which involved 19 hotels and the Las Vegas Convention Center as sponsors. When discussions commenced in 1981, Colbert met with Harry Wald, president of Caesars Palace, who laid his cards out quickly.

"What's the richest tournament in the world?" he asked. When Colbert told him a half million dollars, Wald said, "I think we can safely double that."

But when the deal reached the Tour's board, it hit a snag. Player director Ed Sneed objected to counting the entire $1.052 million purse as official earnings. Flabbergasted, Colbert demanded an explanation.

"He said, 'It's going to throw the money title out of whack. Everybody will have to play there,' " Colbert recalled. "I said, 'Duh, that's the point.' (They settled on $750,000 official money, which was three times the purse of several events.) Nobody really liked Vegas's 5-round, pro-am format but they sure liked the purse. We'd play in the streets of Laredo (Texas) for $1 million."

Other tournaments scrambled to keep pace. By 1987, 40 tournaments were contested for more than a half million dollars. By 1990, the million-dollar figure was a benchmark for at least 34 events. From 1980 to the end of the decade, annual prize money made a quantum leap, surging from $13.4 million to $40 million.

But Beman didn't chase every buck. The Vegas marketers dreamed up a promotion to pay the golfer with the low round at its tournament the first three days a prize of $7,777. On the final two days, the tournament proposed awarding the low scorer $11,111. It was an obvious play on rolling 7 and 11 in craps at the casino. The board rejected the promotion, protecting the

Tour from a direct association with gambling. The search for appropriate business partners, however, was relentless.

"When we made a sales call if we saw a pro-am plaque on the wall we were pretty happy," said Henry Hughes, who oversaw the Tour's marketing department for several years during a 25-year tenure with the Tour. "If we saw tennis racquets in the corner we knew we were in trouble."

As purses soared and the names of celebrities and cities were wiped from the tournament marquee, some of golf's more tradition-bound moguls found Beman's promotional tactics to be troubling. At the 1988 Masters, tournament chairman Hord Hardin, who stood square in the face of change, pronounced that rampant commercialism was ruining golf. If purses continued to escalate exponentially, Hardin feared that one day players would skip the Masters if it was flanked by events with exorbitant purses. Hardin considered it his duty to preserve and protect the Bob Jones tradition of all that is noble in golf, and talk of a commercial sponsor was verboten.

"I don't visualize us having the Pizza Hut Masters," he said.

Three days after Hardin voiced his concerns he announced the purse for the 1988 Masters – a cool $1 million. Hardin's viewpoint personified the reluctance of the golf community to capitalize on commercial exploits and Beman's decision to break with the status quo. Beman knew the Tour needed more corporate support and new approaches to generate interest among non-golfers. The Tour's internal study from November 1979 estimated that 80 percent of tournament galleries consisted of participants in the game. "The 15 million golfers in the U.S. are not enough to support a television package such as ours," the report said.

Beyond his promotional and public relations endeavors, Beman proposed that the electronic scoring system would be the single biggest improvement in making golf more of a spectator sport. "Golf is 25 years behind the times in giving information," he told *The Boston Globe* before its debut. The Tour arranged a sponsor preview of the system at the 1980 Tournament Players Championship at Sawgrass CC. An electronic scoreboard crudely hung from three palm trees behind the 18th green. To make matters worse, it malfunctioned early in the tournament during the demonstration, forcing Art West, the Tour's director of marketing, to shut it down temporarily.

"We had to smuggle a part in through customs from Canada overnight," West recalled.

The Tour had pursued a sponsor for the electronic scoreboards for years. West sold the concept, despite its early kinks, to RJR's chairman J. Tylee Wilson; the Vantage cigarettes brand agreed to underwrite the electronic scoreboards.

They proved to be RJR's entrée into a relationship with the Tour, which Beman characterized as a "stepping stone approach." The original 10-year, $12 million pact RJR signed with the Tour in 1981 represented the Tour's biggest sponsorship deal to date. Each week the Tour's operation staff trucked the 20 portable scoreboards and 18th hole leaderboard to the next event to provide spectators spread over many acres with up-to-the-minute reports and scores. The boards debuted in March 1981 at The Players Championship, the first of 22 events that year, and expanded to 30 tournaments the following season. Before long they were fixtures at all Tour events.

"I thought (electronic scoreboards) were essential," Beman said. "It goes back to my own experience at Phoenix, my first time outside the ropes, when I found it almost impossible to follow what was happening in the tournament.

"This simple technology had a direct effect on broadening the base of the game."

Developing a relationship with a blue-chip brand was a boon for Tour business and got the electronic scoreboard project off the ground, but it took on greater importance when RJR bought Nabisco for $4.9 billion in 1985. At the time, it was the largest merger ever to take place outside the oil industry.

The Tour set out to expand its deal with RJR so that it would cover the entire company, not just the Vantage brand. Working in their favor was the fact that Ross Johnson, president of Nabisco and the man whose products filled every pantry in America, loved golf, understood its values, and appreciated the wholesome image that the pros projected. Shortly after RJR bought Nabisco, Johnson engineered a coup, retired Wilson, and assumed control of the company.

"It was a merger of equals but as often happens, one party

takes control of the ship," said Tour deputy commissioner Tim Smith. "Ross Johnson just took over, and that was a blessing for the Tour."

That fall, the Tour entered into a three-year agreement with RJR's Vantage Cigarette and Nabisco Brands Inc. It created a season-long $2 million bonus pool – the largest such player bonus pool in sports at the time – for the top 25 players in the final points standing to divide. Points were awarded to the top 25 finishers in each tournament. The Vantage Cup awarded $500,000 to the player who accumulated the most points during the year-long competition.

Billed as one of the largest promotions in sports history, the RJR Nabisco deal meant an infusion of $6 million into the Tour. It included an intriguing charity component too. The Nabisco Charity Challenge, a team competition, offered $2 million for charity, based on the earnings of the five-man teams drafted by the 41 participating tournaments. (The Doral-Eastern Open didn't partake because of its supporting charity, the Cancer Fund, and requirements to use the Vantage cigarettes electronic scoreboards as part of the sponsorship.) It was an early version of fantasy golf. At a Nov. 14, 1985, player draft meeting at the Mandalay Four Seasons in Dallas, each tournament picked a five-man team to represent its event. The Greater Greensboro Open selected Lanny Wadkins with the first pick and the Honda Classic chose Mark Calcavecchia with the last of 205 picks.

"Deane wanted to make the Nabisco Charity Challenge draft as important as the NFL draft," said Ric Clarson, a Tour marketing executive for more than a decade under Beman. "It didn't get there, but it wasn't for a lack of effort."

Vantage Cup points earned by each player also were credited to his team's account; the team accumulating the most points earning a $500,000 bonus for the local charities involved. RJR Nabisco also debuted a $2 million advertising campaign touting the Tour's charity work that resembled the NFL's marketing of its involvement with the United Way.

"There was a lot of creativity in (Deane's) organization," Clarson said. "You might not get that impression at first. But the more you worked with him, you realized he had hundreds of ideas, and he's not scared to put them to the test."

The Vantage Cup also encouraged more top pros to support a wider range of tournaments and enabled fall events to attract better fields. The Vantage Championship in San Antonio, which offered a $1 million purse the last weekend in October of 1986, guaranteed the winner of both the individual and team charity championship would be determined at the event. To promote a Texas-sized flavor, local organizers arranged a barbecue feast, gave alligator cowboy boots as gifts, and, of course, held their own armadillo races.

"Armadillos aren't too fast as evidenced by the amount of road kill on Texas highways," joked Chip Campbell, former Tour director of communications who became a sports marketing executive at Ohlmeyer Communications and managed the Nabisco account.

Each armadillo has its own handler, who races his creature a distance of 10 to 15 yards in an enclosed track. Once the armadillos are off and running, handlers can't touch them. So, how do they encourage faster performances?

"Well, you blow on his butt, that's how," Campbell said, explaining why a few adult beverages are often consumed before races. "Even without the aid of alcohol, there was old, dignified, formal Deane down on his hands and knees blowing on that animal's ass all the way to the finish line. He wasn't about to let that 'sumbitch' lose...and he didn't."

The Vantage Championship in San Antonio that week was a success. But afterwards, RJR Nabisco complained to Beman that the tournament organizers were "nickel and diming" them on the bill. T. Wayne Robertson, who was in charge of RJR's sports marketing, requested Beman resolve the issues. Beman was in California and returning to Florida. He decided to stop in San Antonio on his way and scheduled a meeting with the tournament organizers at an airport conference room. The committee was seated around the table when he arrived. Gen. John Roberts pitched forward in his chair at the head of the table and spoke first. Holding a list of expenses at least 20 long, he said, "We're glad you're here. I'm sure we can come to a meeting of the minds on these expenses."

"General," Beman interjected, "we have a huge misunderstanding of the agenda and I apologize for that."

The General looked puzzled. "The misunderstanding," Beman continued, "is you think I'm here to mediate this problem when your tournament has made more money than you've ever dreamed of making at a golf tournament. What I'm really here to talk about is whether or not there's ever going to be professional golf in San Antonio again. RJR Nabisco is the best client you've ever had and the best client we've ever had. So make it right to their satisfaction."

Beman rose from his seat and stated that he expected a message that the matter would be resolved to the satisfaction of RJR Nabisco by the time he landed in Jacksonville. "Gentlemen, I've got a plane to catch," Beman said. "Nice to have seen you."

Beman walked from the room and boarded his flight. Golf in San Antonio met his deadline, and has become one of the Tour's top charitable contributors.

Not everyone appreciated all of the finer elements of RJR Nabisco's sponsorship. Some of the players objected to the Tour's association with tobacco. Joe Inman, chairman of the Tour's players advisory council, requested if players who didn't want to be associated with endorsing smoking could have their names removed from the electronic scoreboards. The Tour's board rejected the idea. Aligning the regular Tour with Nabisco and the Vantage brand with the Senior Tour, whose players were delighted to have a sponsor, solved that problem. One year later, the season-ending San Antonio stop was renamed the Nabisco Championships of Golf. The purse doubled to a record $2 million and the format changed to invite only the top 30 players off a points list.

"The tremendous money of Nabisco, and the ingenuity of Beman, has created a true season-ending climactic event that golf needed so badly and never had before," wrote Charley Stine in a 1989 commentary in *Golfweek*.

"One of Beman's long-sought dreams came true," wrote *Golf World's* Brett Avery. "The Vantage Championship was golf's equivalent to the Super Bowl or World Series."

In 1987, bonus-pool payouts counted as official money, the first time in Tour history that players were rewarded for season-long consistency. One year later, at the 1988 Nabisco Championships held at Pebble Beach, Curtis Strange and Tom Kite were tied at the end of regulation when they ran out of sunlight.

Duke Butler, then executive director of the Houston Golf Association, counted Strange among his tournament's five-man charity team. If Strange won, the Houston Tour stop would earn the $500,000 first-place charitable contribution from the Nabisco Charity Challenge. So Butler postponed his flight and stayed for the Monday finish. He accompanied Strange to dinner in Carmel that night and drove his man to the course for the playoff in the morning. Strange said he was too nervous for breakfast. Between the title and the season-long, bonus-prize money, this promised to be golf's biggest one-day haul. The Tour's player of the year honors likely hung in the balance, too.

On the second hole of the sudden-death playoff, Pebble's infamous par-3 17th, Strange struck a 4-iron to 4 feet, made birdie and beat Kite. Swept up in the moment, Butler flung his arms skyward and ran on the green to join Strange in celebration.

Having skipped breakfast, Strange's stomach growled. He asked Butler to order him a cheeseburger and a six-pack of Budweiser. "That's what you're going to eat for breakfast?" Butler asked incredulously.

The victory made Strange the first player in history to win more than $1 million in a year ($1,147,644). In an earlier era of smaller purses, Arnold Palmer required 14 seasons to eclipse $1 million in career earnings. Now golf's new "Million Dollar Man" dove into a cheeseburger and a six-pack of beer, and belted out Whitney Houston songs on the radio as he and Butler enjoyed the scenic route to the San Francisco airport.

*   *   *

After Pebble Beach hosted the Nabisco Tour Championship in 1988, Beman informed Butler that he wanted to rotate the event to some of the country's most venerable venues. High on Beman's short list was Champions Club in Houston. Beman enlisted Butler to approach Jackie Burke Jr., one of the club's owners. As soon as Butler mentioned that he had spoken with Beman, Burke interjected, "What does that little dictator want?"

A decade had past since he and Beman squabbled over the lifetime exemption status awarded to major winners, but a chill still remained in their relationship. Yet Burke listened and was intrigued at the possibility of hosting the pros again for the first time since 1971.

So Burke met with Robertson, the RJR Nabisco sports marketing executive whose sport of choice was Nascar. In addition to favoring the company's sponsorship of the Winston Cup series, he knew little about golf. To make matters worse, Robertson's flight was delayed, pushing back their meeting. "Jackie Burke did not care to waste his time talking about Richard Petty and car racing with anyone," Butler said.

Robertson carried a $200,000 course rental contract in his briefcase. They managed to reach an agreement. "I won't have anything to do with the cookie-and-cracker salesmen," Burke told Butler after Robertson had departed.

Soon, another sticking point emerged. According to Butler, when George Mitchell, the owner of the TPC Woodlands as well as the developer of The Woodlands community, read in the paper that Beman was considering moving the Nabisco Championship to Houston, he was livid. He called Butler and demanded any tournament in town be held at his course. After all, he supported the Tour as host of the Houston Open, and he paid a pretty penny to the Tour to license the TPC mark. All of this was true. So Butler and Robertson conducted a site visit, driving in Robertson's rental car around the cart path of the back nine of the TPC Woodlands. Beman and Butler arranged a phone call with Mitchell the next day. In short order, Beman convinced Mitchell that what mattered most was the tournament coming to Houston would be good for the city.

"He turned an angry billionaire into okaying the tournament going to another club in his backyard," Butler said. "That's how good Beman was."

What remained uncertain, however, was the relationship between Beman and Burke. Could their friendship be repaired? Butler took it upon himself to reunite the two proud men. During a tournament association social at Beman's home prior to the 1990 Players Championship, Butler invited Beman to play with him and Burke later that spring when course renovations at Champions would be completed. Beman agreed and told him to make the arrangements. On the morning of

May 2, 1990, following a players' meeting in Dallas, Beman flew to Houston to meet with Burke and Butler and play golf at Champions. Earl Elliott, a Champions member and volunteer chair of the 1969 U.S. Open there, joined as the group's fourth. Over breakfast, Burke asked Beman if he had been playing much. In fact, Beman had squeezed in 36 holes a day over the weekend at Augusta National with the Tour's board chair, Del de Windt. Beman acknowledged he even was experimenting with a long putter, knowing full well he'd get some grief. He was right.

"You made every putt you ever hit in your entire life," Burke said. "How are you going to do better?"

It didn't take long to find out, Butler recounted. Starting on No. 10, Beman rolled in a 40-foot birdie putt. On the next hole, he canned a 30-footer. On No. 12, another birdie putt disappeared, this time from 25 feet. Burke had seen enough. "It's not that (long) putter that should be illegal, Beman," he said. "It's you."

Beman shot 5-under 30 on the back nine that day at the same course where he had finished runner-up at the 1969 U.S. Open. More importantly, he rekindled his longstanding friendship with Burke in three holes. Later that year, Champions GC and Burke played host to the cookie-and-cracker salesmen at the 1990 Tour Championship.

*   *   *

As the Tour's partnership with local communities and corporate America grew seemingly unabated, RJR Nabisco stood out from the pack as the Tour's "sugar daddy." Beman sought to net an even greater share of RJR Nabisco's annual marketing budget. During the debate over how much to ask for, the Tour's Kay Slayden advised Beman that Johnson's "a big whale, who thinks big. We should ask for more." He was right. As the authors of the best-selling book "Barbarians at the Gate: The Fall of RJR Nabisco" noted, Johnson's motto was "A few million dollars are lost in the sands of time."

Few invested as heavily in sports marketing as Johnson. When Campbell, who left the Tour in 1985, oversaw Nabisco's golf marketing division, he controlled nearly a $40 million annual budget. In addition to its support of the Tour, Nabisco paid for a relationship with the LPGA and negotiated deals with individual members of "Team Nabisco," which included Jack Nicklaus to Nancy Lopez.

Perhaps the best story of Johnson's use of athletes didn't even involve a golfer, but rather tennis legend, Rod Laver. According to Campbell, Laver's contract required that once a year he and Nabisco president Jim Welch hop on a jet and head to Bentonville, Ark., home of superstore goliath Walmart, for a doubles match. Welch partnered with Walmart founder Sam Walton against Laver and Walton's wife. Walmart's order for Nabisco products would jump 15 to 20 percent without fail whenever Laver and Mrs. Walton won their match, Campbell recalled.

Beman courted Johnson with his usual intensity. He also understood that Johnson wasn't afraid to spend money. If the Tour was going to endorse the "Nabisco Grand Prix of Golf," to the game's fan base, Beman wanted to ensure his money's worth for the players. In what became an oft-told story at Tour headquarters, Beman pulled the purse strings perfectly. Whenever the two leaders met, Beman played coy: "Maybe we shouldn't talk about this because I'm not sure you can handle it." Johnson took the bait. He answered, 'What do you mean? We've got one of the biggest advertising budgets in the country.' "

Beman needed $2 million more annually to underwrite the Super Seniors 60-and-over events among other programs, but thinking big, he sought $4 million from Johnson. Beman asked: "Are you sure you can afford it?" Johnson replied, "Goodness, is that all? That's nothing."

In short order the deal grew by leaps and bounds. One morning in early 1988 as Beman read the daily newspapers, a plan formed in his mind. Litigation and legislation was taking a heavy toll on RJR's ability to market its product. Beman's idea would give Vantage a chance to get ahead of the curve. Later that day, Beman was scheduled to play golf with Ed Horrigan Jr., chairman of RJR Tobacco, at The Vintage Club in Palm Springs, Calif. Beman read an article that had caught his attention in *The Wall Street Journal* speculating that legislation could be passed in the U.S. to ban cigarette advertising and promotion associated with sports. This had the potential of changing the sports marketing landscape; Canada already had proposed a date terminating tobacco's sponsorship of sports there. One of the stipulations of the ruling in Canada would allow existing contracts to be grandfathered in. Beman proposed to Horrigan that the Tour and RJR Nabisco sign a 10-year evergreen contract on the chance that such legislation might be approved.

"If something that was beyond our control restricted RJR's ability to advertise, this contract would protect our interests a lot longer than our existing agreement," Beman said. "It just made sense."

Beman's pitch won him over when he said, "Ed, I think you can outfox them if you do an evergreen deal with us."

Beman also indicated to Horrigan that the Tour's board was unlikely to approve a 10-year, rolling agreement with RJR's tobacco division unless Nabisco also entered the same kind of agreement too.

"Oh yeah," Beman recalled Horrigan replying. "Ross (Johnson) will do this for me."

It didn't take 10 minutes for Horrigan to be convinced, Beman said. It's uncertain what Horrigan said to Johnson, but he gave the deal his blessing. Members of the Tour staff met in New York with Campbell and his team to hammer out the details. The Tour's board gave the deal its seal of approval on Aug. 16, 1988.

"The greatest coup we ever pulled was getting that evergreen contract," said West, the Tour's former marketing director.

Yet even the success of the marketing programs drew criticism. Some observers feared that professional golf was on the verge of becoming a slightly more genteel form of the Daytona 500. Beman slapped the Tour logo on everything from cruise ships to car rental firms. He even tagged entire countries, such as the Bahamas, as "official golf destinations."

"We have so much commercial tie-in, it's like jamming it down the fans' throat," Ben Crenshaw told the *Houston Chronicle* in 1986. "We might be overdoing the marketing now. Enough is enough."

Marcia Chambers of *Golf Digest* noted that Beman's greatest fault might be that he's too successful. In support of her argument, she quoted a disgruntled Tom Watson.

"I respect Deane for doing what he set out to do – increasing the purses of the players on Tour," Watson said. "He did that. But he also created an albatross of bureaucracy on Tour. There are so many people involved and under salary to the Tour. I don't know how many, but everytime I go down to [Tour headquarters] it looks like a new wing or a new building has been added for administration."

To hear such talk from the very men he helped make rich baffled those who negotiated the deals with Beman. Don Ohlmeyer, who orchestrated much of the Nabisco deal for Johnson, considered them ungrateful.

"The players in the professional golf tour should kneel down every day, face wherever Deane is reposed, and thank the lord for the spadework he did in making the Tour what it is today," he said.

As Tour revenues soared, the money was redistributed to the players in the form of bigger purses and larger deferred compensation payments. By June 1989, *The New York Times* wondered, "Are golf purses out of bounds?"

"Long after skeptics predicted that the Tour would kill the goose that laid the golden eggs, the goose keeps producing more and more, with no end in sight," wrote Gordon White Jr. in *The New York Times.*

Golf Digest's Dan Jenkins fretted that prosperity was killing the Tour. Nearly on a monthly basis, he churned out the most biting criticism of Beman's regime.

"Jenkins was all over me, like ugly on ape," Beman recalled. "Any suggestion of commercialism was met with tremendous resistance. It gave him fodder for his humor, which can be devastating."

One sample doesn't quite do justice. Here's a collage of the barbs Jenkins' aimed squarely at his favorite foil, Beman, and his business practices.

"Nobody knew the PGA Tour was for sale until (RJR Nabisco's) Ross Johnson bought it," Jenkins wrote.

"What a country. Apart from inside trading, what other profession permits a self-employed man to make $200,000 – and up – for achieving absolutely nothing?"

Jenkins couldn't resist poking some fun at the players too.

"Imagine the (players) surprise when it finally sinks in on them someday that, thanks to Deane Beman, they have become the auto workers of sport."

Not to be forgotten is one zinger Jenkins loved to recycle: "It looks as if the only cure for what's ruining pro golf is a good old depression."

Being commissioner required a thick-skin and Beman had one. He also had a unique determination. From his stint as a pro in the late 1960s and early '70s, he knew life on Tour was "a subsistence existence" for nearly all except a handful of players. This perspective never left him. When a writer wrote that being a member of Beman's All-Exempt Tour "meant never having to say I'm hungry," he took it as the highest of compliments. He set out to raise professional golf's standard of living. Beman was proud that he had.

"*Golf Digest* kicked us in the rear every time we did promotion and tried to interject commercialism in golf, but they sold advertising in their magazine right behind the editorials," Beman said. "They didn't care that there was an advertisement opposite what they wrote, nor did they care that every time you picked up a magazine three leaflets fell out hawking something. They didn't care a wit about that.

"If Jenkins really felt so strongly about the sanctity of non-commercialism and his thinking was consistent, he would have refused to write for a magazine that sold advertising. They should have to earn all their revenue from subscription sales like he wanted the Tour to exist only on ticket sales. Oh no, you can't sell corporate hospitality or naming rights. It just didn't make any sense."

Beman wasn't the only one who recognized some of the inherent hypocrisy. Charley Stine, editor of *Golfweek*, wrote a story detailing a conversation he had with the publisher of another golf publication who objected to the Tour simultaneously promoting junior golf and cigarette smoking. The publisher condemned the practice, saying it was inappropriate considering junior golfers often idolized Tour players. Stine then informed the reader that the aforementioned publisher delivered his lecture while puffing on a cigarette.

Interviews with several former Beman staffers indicate that Beman did worry that the promotional requirements promised to Nabisco would undercut some of the game's traditions. Tour executive Henry Hughes recalled the time Beman enlisted him to attend the 1990 Nabisco Championship and observe what the Tour could do to raise the tournament's stature. When Hughes parked his car at Champions Club, a person costumed as Mr. Peanut welcomed him and arriving fans.

"I remember thinking, 'I believe Mr. Peanut may be at his last tournament,' " Hughes said. "I didn't think that was the image Deane wanted to promote."

Mr. Peanut soon was reassigned to the players' family party where the children were nuts for him.

"Nabisco was the biggest deal we'd ever done," Hughes said. "That in itself says, 'What did you have to do to get it done? How many pro-am spots did they get? How many free tickets?' I always cautioned people and said, 'Those numbers are bigger than you'd ever seen before.' "

Every request, however, was evaluated through the same prism. During Beman's tenure as commissioner he based his decisions with two goals in mind, Campbell said: "Protecting the integrity of the Tour, the players, and the game and increasing the earning potential of the largest number of players possible (not just the big earners). I think he succeeded at both, although they were sometimes in conflict."

When push came to shove, Beman didn't back down. Instead he found solutions. Such a situation developed when Nabisco insisted "Nabisco points" serve as the measure of success and eligibility for the Nabisco Grand Prix rather than the official money list. Beman wasn't fond of the idea but agreed to a compromise: make each dollar earned worth one "Nabisco Point." In the end, it didn't harm the integrity of the Tour's official money list.

"I know Ross Johnson respected how Deane stuck to his guns and risked losing lots of money," Campbell said.

The Tour's record 10-year, $200 million deal with RJR Nabisco turned out to be short-lived. In December 1988, leverage buyout specialists Kohlberg, Kravis and Roberts paid $25 billion for RJR Nabisco. The barbarians crashed through the gates three months after the Tour signed its 10-year, evergreen deal. After the largest corporate buyout ever, RJR was burdened with debt. Thirteen months later the company's new brass slashed its marketing budget, which *Advertising Age* estimated at $814.5 million in 1988.

The drumbeat that RJR wanted out of its deal grew louder and louder. Rumors spread. On Jan. 12, 1990, the Tour and RJR Nabisco announced they had reached a contract settlement. The decision came less than 18 months after the parties signed the 10-year, evergreen contract.

"We were one of the first contracts to go," Beman recalled. "We were very fortunate to have that long-term contract because there was a 180-degree shift in the corporate objectives."

Under the revised deal, RJR eliminated the $2.5 million season-ending Nabisco Championship (the richest tournament in professional golf); the $1 million individual bonus pool for the top 30 money winners on the Tour; the $1 million charity competition; and sponsorship of the Tour's statistical programs, beginning in 1991. Electronic scoreboard advertising remained intact temporarily. The move did not affect the $4.15 million in prize money, team charity programs and statistical programs that RJR invested in the Senior Tour.

"The umbrella has folded," was how *Golf World* led its report. Neither side would disclose the size of the settlement. Several media outlets reported that the settlement was rumored to be worth $8 million. In actuality, it was much more. The $21 million buyout funded the Tour's reserves for a future rainy day. Gary Stevenson, the Tour's director of marketing at the time, said the settlement provided the Tour an underpinning to market and grow the sport.

"That check paid for a lot of stuff for a lot of years," Stevenson said. "That long-term, evergreen deal had as much to do with the success of the Tour as anything."

Case in point, after the RJR deal ended, Beman decided that the Nabisco tournament kept players active after the PGA Championship and was critical to its success. Building on the tournament's momentum, in 1990, the Tour considered naming it the PGA Tour Championship. The PGA objected on grounds that such a moniker would create confusion with the PGA Championship. Despite the PGA's misgivings, the board approved naming the season-ending event the Tour Championship.

Establishing a prestigious Tour Championship grew in importance. To do so required a special venue. Beman already had taken the event to established, renowned courses such as Pebble Beach, Harbour Town, and Champions Club. Beman thought Pinehurst No. 2, the famed Donald Ross course, ranked among golf's most historic places.

"I came up with the idea of Pinehurst much the same way I came up with the idea of Shinnecock when we were attempting to raise the status of the World Series of Golf," Beman explained.

In Bob Dedman of ClubCorp, Beman found a willing cohort interested in adding to the luster of one of golf's crown jewels. Beman enlisted Hughes and Stevenson to go meet with Dedman at Pinehurst. The deal points weren't favorable. The Tour had to purchase the TV time on ABC and guarantee a room allotment at Pinehurst Resort. It bundled its inventory of rooms, pro-am spots, and TV time into four packages.

"Imagine trying to sell this in the fourth-quarter against college and pro football for an event that used to be named for Nabisco," Stevenson said. "Now the Tour Championship is a meaningful season-ending event. And as a result of seeing how the players received Pinehurst No. 2, the USGA took the U.S. Open there and it got back in the rotation. That's because Deane said, 'We had to play at a great venue or it will never be important.' We had other options. Believe me, there were other resort courses that offered to pay us a fee."

In 1991, Buick asked about assuming title sponsorship of the Tour Championship. The Tour passed on the deal and decided that the Tour Championship should not have a corporate title (Buick settled for the San Diego tournament instead).

Some detractors say Beman didn't create enough wealth for the players because he believed that a healthy Tour was a "balanced" Tour, Stevenson said.

"He was incredibly good at balancing the interests of all the constituents," Stevenson said. "To me, that's the hardest part about being the commissioner. He's the union and management under the same roof."

With the passage of time even Nick Seitz, the longtime editor of *Golf Digest*, has cooled his hard-line stance against the Tour's commercialization.

"When Deane was trying to get the purses up, I have to concede that was the only way to go," Seitz said.

So did Crenshaw, who told *The Florida Times-Union* in March 1994, "No one would second-guess the benefits from going arm-in-arm with corporate America...The formula has been successful."

That may be an understatement. During an era in which golf emerged as the sport of corporate America, Beman never forgot where to draw the line: "We brought golf into the modern world of big-money sports without selling out golf's core values of respect for the rules, respect for your fellow competitor, and respect for the game."

HOLDING THEIR FEET TO THE FIRE

Early in his tenure as commissioner, Deane Beman was invited to Minneapolis for a sports business forum. Commissioners of several sports, including baseball, football, basketball and hockey were among the participants. Seated around a table drinking coffee and Cokes, they made small talk as they waited for the event to begin. Suddenly, NFL commissioner Pete Rozelle turned to Beman and asked, "What are you doing here?" Without skipping a beat, Beman said, "Because the PGA Tour is worth more than all of you guys." Rozelle's face scrunched into a look of confusion and he responded, "What do you mean?" Beman answered, "Well, the PGA Tour has 47 franchises – we call them tournaments – and we own them all. You don't own any of your franchises."

That wasn't the only advantage Beman possessed over his counterparts in the room. Pro golf presented a squeaky-clean image that proved an invaluable asset when courting corporate America. In an era when athletes in other sports often were making headlines for the wrong reasons, the gentlemanly game of golf remained above reproach. "To the other envious commissioners, it must look as if Deane Beman is running the Good Ship Lollipop, ruling a land somewhere over the sports rainbow where bluebirdies fly," wrote Jim Murray of *The Los Angeles Times*.

At the same Minneapolis conference where Beman first met Rozelle, Major League Baseball's commissioner, Bowie Kuhn, dished advice to Beman on dealing with player-disciplinary action. Kuhn believed that Beman needed to let the players know that he couldn't be challenged. "Find an issue that you can really lay the hammer down on somebody and establish your authority," Kuhn instructed.

Beman bobbed his head as a sign of understanding, but he completely disagreed with Kuhn's player-relations philosophy. Instead, Beman established a personal policy that made disciplinary action a private matter between the commissioner and the player.

"Once the commissioner takes action then the player has a whole litany of opportunities to appeal and defend himself," Beman explained. "If you announce something from up high, you have damaged the player and you may not be right. You try to have all the facts in advance, or there might be mitigating circumstances that haven't come to light, but until the process is over and completed, a player is at a huge disadvantage.

"I never wanted to promote problems. I wanted to promote what was good."

For instance, on one occasion, a Senior Tour player was accused of marking his golf ball improperly on the green. Beman took the allegation seriously. He went to the player's home and sat with him and his wife. He explained that he wasn't charging him with any violation, but he had received reports from multiple players making the same allegation (inching the ball closer to the hole). He gave the player two choices: take a voluntary break from the tour for a specified period of time or a full-fledged investigation into the charges would be launched. "You will be under scrutiny," Beman explained, "and I will find out if what is alleged is still happening." The player elected to take a hiatus. Even now, Beman declines to divulge who stood accused of committing this inexcusable offense. "I feel just as strongly about (privacy) today as I did when I was in office," Beman said.

Not everyone appreciated Beman's approach to meting out player discipline. Some felt he lorded his authority and acted as prosecutor, judge, and jury. Ken Green resorted to calling him "Beane Demon." Mac O'Grady said he was "a thief with a capital T." Seve Ballesteros described him as "a little man trying to be a big man." Others settled for "Mean Deane" or simply the "Czar of Golf." Players whom Beman had fined, reprimanded or admonished for swearing, throwing clubs or other boorish on-course behavior muttered more than a few unkind words about the commissioner.

At the start of the 1979 season, Tom Weiskopf asked for permission to wear the beard he grew during a holiday season spent hunting. Beman warned him he'd be fined. So Weiskopf shaved. But he wasn't happy about it. Weiskopf was quoted as saying, "Beman ran a baby-sitting service."

"We've had four Presidents who had beards," Weiskopf told reporters. "What Beman is doing is stereotyping us into one type of person."

But that episode produced few fireworks compared with the ink and attention given Mac O'Grady's defiance. O'Grady could've been known as one of the great rags-to-riches stories in golf. Able to play both lefty and righty, he was a self-taught player who once lived in a cardboard box in Los Angeles and attempted Q-School 17 times over 11 years before earning his Tour privileges for the first time at age 32. "He was Quixote with a 9-iron, a glorious passionate madman chasing the impossible dream," wrote Dave Kindred in *Golf Magazine*.

But O'Grady's legacy was tarnished and reduced to that of Tour eccentric, known mostly for his brash comments of the commissioner. *The New York Times* columnist Dave Anderson called O'Grady "golf's most controversial personality – Patrick Henry with a golf glove." The Tour slapped O'Grady with a $500 fine for "conduct unbecoming a professional," for allegedly using profane language to a volunteer courtesy car driver during the 1984 USF&G Classic in New Orleans. O'Grady denied the allegation, refused to pay the fine and charged that his First Amendment rights were violated.

"I'm just defending my principles," O'Grady said, "as a citizen of this country."

O'Grady also charged that the commissioner was guilty of the "arbitrary" application of tournament regulations and threatened to sue. His failure to pay his fine within 30 days would result in a suspension, according to tournament regulations. After consultation with the Tour's outside legal counsel, Beman docked the money from O'Grady's winnings at a subsequent event rather than suspend him. This action prevented a major antitrust suit involving restraint of trade, which would cost the Tour hundreds of thousands of dollars. "Now all he had was a claim in small claims court," Beman said.

The majority of the membership understood the reasoning behind the deduction, but they didn't necessarily agree with Beman's tactics. Tom Watson sent Beman a letter supporting O'Grady's claim that he was denied due process. In fact, O'Grady was given a proper hearing. According to Tour regulations, a minor penalty only can be appealed to the commissioner, who upheld his ruling. But as O'Grady continued his assault of Beman, sympathy for O'Grady waned. He appeared on "Late Night with David Letterman" and called Beman a "thief, crook, embezzler and a few other things." Several players met with O'Grady at the Los Angeles Open and encouraged him to work within the system rather than in the media. According to Tour player Morris Hatalsky, O'Grady agreed not to publicly criticize the commissioner anymore. The very next day, however, he verbally attacked Tour member Jim Colbert and trashed Riviera Country Club. His vow of silence didn't last long toward Beman, either. After the third round of the 1986 Doral-Eastern Open, O'Grady reportedly stood next to a flower garden and likened Beman to a dictator.

Beman asked tournament director Jack Tuthill, a former FBI agent who joined the Tour staff in 1960, to intervene because many of O'Grady's incidents involved the commissioner. Since O'Grady had opened his case to public scrutiny, Beman made an exception and reported to the media his response to O'Grady's allegations. Following his outburst at Doral Resort, a letter was hand-delivered to O'Grady along with a notice of proposed disciplinary action for a major penalty under tournament regulations. On June 14, 1986, one day after O'Grady notched his first Tour victory, Beman assessed a six-event suspension, a $5,000 fine and one-year probation against O'Grady – at the time the most severe punishment handed down by Beman.

"We have rules that we have inherited. They have been handed down by the players for the players. I'm in charge of enforcing those rules," Beman told the press. "The integrity of the Tour and the game of golf itself has been attacked, and I cannot allow one individual to continue such destructive statements without taking serious actions."

Beman allowed O'Grady to bypass his appeal to the commissioner and go directly to the Tour's three-man appeals panel of Tour policy board chair Del de Windt, PGA president Mickey Powell and Joe Black, a former Tour player, official and past PGA president.

"Now O'Grady will get his full due process," Beman said to his staff. "But he may not like it."

The Tour assembled a videotape with interviews of the witnesses to the incident and USF&G tournament director Tommy Wulff. Hatalsky, a Tour players advisory council member, stated that after viewing the videotape "the facts shown tended to dispute much of what O'Grady had said, including his denial that he had been out of line in his comments to the lady volunteers."

When his appeal was denied, O'Grady went to Federal Court in San Diego. He lost there, too.

"It was Mac v. Authority, his favorite fight," said Gary McCord, O'Grady's friend and occasional pupil in a 1998 *Golf Digest* profile of O'Grady. "Someone in authority said, 'No, you can't do that,' and Mac said, 'Watch me.' "

O'Grady filed a $12 million antitrust lawsuit against Beman and the Tour, contending the suspension deprived him of his right to earn a living. In denying a preliminary injunction, U.S. District Court Judge Edward Schwartz called the O'Grady suspension a "fairly routine disciplinary action by a properly constituted authority for comments that I think under any reasonable interpretation would be damaging to the (Tour's) reputation....Mr. O'Grady would better serve himself by polishing his clubs and golf balls...and leave off his temptation for verbal engagement."

After the judge ruled that his case didn't constitute a restraint of trade, O'Grady withdrew his suit later that year and paid his fine.

"I view it as a wasted year of my life," said Tim Smith, the Tour's deputy commissioner during the O'Grady feud, "but it was important that the Tour prevailed."

A crippling lower-back injury forced O'Grady into semi-retirement, and he disappeared from the Tour scene with a whimper in 1989. In later years, Smith remembered making reference to O'Grady and Beman's personality clash. Beman couldn't hide his irritation. "Mac O'Grady's impact on the Tour and on my career is like a small pimple on an elephant's ass," Beman said. "It's meaningless."

Another of Beman's long-running disputes occurred with Spaniard Seve Ballesteros. No golfer epitomized the spirit of European golf like Ballesteros. Quite simply, he did for golf on the Continent what Arnold Palmer did for golf in America. Beman and Ballesteros had a tenuous relationship. They quarreled over the rules governing eligibility of foreign players. As a condition of membership, all players had to accept the Tour's conflicting-event release, which restricted them from competing in a tournament staged simultaneously against a Tour-sanctioned event unless the commissioner granted a waiver. It was a crucial rule to protect the Tour's tournament sponsor and its field. To retain membership on the Tour, a player must compete in a minimum of 15 Tour events. No hard and fast rule existed but as a guideline, for every five tournaments played in the U.S., a Tour member was allowed to play one international tournament.

At the time, an international PGA Tour member did not require permission to play an event that was considered part of his "home country's circuit." For instance, Japan's Isao Aoki could enter a Japan Golf Tour event without seeking Tour approval. But Ballesteros' home country, Spain, had no tour of its own; it hosted a handful of tournaments under the European Tour banner.

In a June 1983 letter, Ballesteros petitioned Beman to let him claim Europe as his "native country," and allow him to play the European Tour without having to seek an official release. To the PGA Tour policy board, "Europe" did not constitute a "home circuit." Beman turned him down, saying that making an exception to the regulations would anger Tour sponsors and players. Beman asked Ballesteros for his input on what a fair number of PGA Tour events would be. Then Beman offered a compromise, modifying the regulations to make Tour membership a more attractive proposition.

In what became known as "the Seve rule," Beman still required foreign members to play 15 Tour-sanctioned events to retain their Tour cards. As long as they met the minimum requirement, they could play elsewhere without asking permission. Ballesteros could continue his globetrotting ways and play to his heart's content in Europe and Japan, where he reportedly commanded appearance fees of $125,000. At first, Ballesteros gave the new rule his blessing. Then he didn't honor it, called it "silly," and demanded it be revised.

"The world according to Seve Ballesteros is one in which he can play golf where he wants, when he wants and, often, for whatever price he wants," *Golf Magazine* wrote in a special report, "The Ban on Ballesteros."

In the beginning, Beman was accused of showing favoritism to one of the game's rising stars. Two days after winning the 1978 Greater Greensboro Open, Beman tried to entice the 21-year-old Ballesteros into becoming a Tour member. He declined, but some foreign players were irate. After all, international stars such as Graham Marsh, the winner of the Tour's 1977 Heritage Classic and titles around the globe, and Peter Oosterhuis, winner of four consecutive European Tour Order of Merit titles, had not been granted the courtesy.

Beman appreciated Ballesteros' immense talent, but Nicklaus and Palmer were unique talents, too, and neither received special rules. For instance, the week of the 1985 Houston Open, Ballesteros, Nicklaus, Watson and Greg Norman were invited to play in a Skins Games in Australia. To partake in this payday, the players needed a release. Losing this much star power in Houston surely would diminish the field. Beman granted their release, but with one stipulation – he required each player to play Houston once within the next 3 years. One year later, Nicklaus kept his word and made his first start there since winning the Masters. (Ballesteros needed an extra year, but made good on his promise and played there in 1989 and 1990.)

"Deane was an enforcer as commissioner, and his philosophy protected the sponsor and, in some ways, saved the Houston Open," said then executive director of the Houston Golf Association, Duke Butler, whose duties included overseeing the Houston Open. "Having those titans got us a title sponsor." (In 1986, the Independent Insurance Agents of America signed for 5 years.)

In 1984, Ballesteros joined the Tour as a member for the first time. He played his 15 Tour events and finished 52nd on the money list while topping the European Tour's Order of Merit. But one year later, Beman and Ballesteros locked horns. By the British Open, Ballesteros had competed in only seven Tour events and, concerned about burnout, he indicated to Beman he likely would fall short of the quota. Nevertheless, he wanted to retain his card.

Beman advised the Tour's 10-member policy board, which rejected Ballesteros' appeal. By September, Ballesteros had played nine Tour events. Beman spoke to him at the Ryder Cup and warned him he was in danger of losing his playing privileges. The 1983 provision stated he who "fails to honor the commitment...shall not be eligible for reinstatement to Tour membership for one calendar year." He also wouldn't be able to compete in any Tour-sanctioned events for one full year. On Oct. 31, 1985, the Tour revoked Ballesteros' membership, saying that it was more important to support the Tour than "the wishes of an individual player, however prominent he might be."

Words were exchanged between Beman and Ballesteros, both in letters and in the press. John Hopkins, *The Times* golf correspondent, titled his column, "The Man Who Tweaked the Tail of the King of Spain." Ballesteros volleyed back after Beman issued the suspension: "It is a thoughtless decision that can only harm international golf," he stated. "If that is their decision they are making a terrible mistake." Only later would he feel differently.

Ballesteros placed No. 26 on the 1985 Tour money list, but the Tour edited any evidence of his performance from its record books. The media criticized Beman for the move. According to Tour policy, Ballesteros wasn't allowed to play any of its sanctioned events in 1986, including at Doral, where he represented the resort. But Beman made an exception to allow Ballesteros to defend his title at the USF&G Classic, and later Beman offered him a spot in the World Series of Golf, but Ballesteros declined. Ballesteros also was given a chance to defend himself at a players' meeting during the USF&G Classic. He reportedly said, "I thought I'd lose my actual membership but be able to go back to the previous rule by which I played under sponsors' exemptions."

When his ban was lifted, Ballesteros refused to rejoin the Tour. He termed the rule "anti-social," and claimed it was Beman, not he, who arrived at the 15-tournament minimum. Ballesteros limited his American play to the maximum five Tour sponsor exemptions that a nonmember was permitted, plus the three majors held in the United States, which are not sanctioned by the Tour. "He viewed America as a necessary evil," wrote Alastair Tait in his biography, "Seve."

Opinions varied on whether the treatment of Ballesteros was fair. "He was the proverbial kid at the sandlot who says, 'It's my football, and if I'm not the quarterback I'm taking my ball and going home,' " said Roger Maltbie, a member of the Tour's policy board at the time. "We made these rules to accommodate him, rules he agreed to and then he didn't want to play by them. Sorry, I just don't see what's unjust about that."

Others felt Beman lost perspective about what mattered most and argued that the real losers were the sponsors, who lost one of the game's most compelling draws, and the spectators, who missed seeing his rare combination of talent and heart. "I think the Tour has gone overboard on this thing," Ben Crenshaw told *The New York Times* in 1986. "The paying public deserves to see him."

Watson publicly defended Ballesteros, too, noting the absurdity that a five-time major winner had to play under the same circumstances as a player who never had won a major championship. In the ensuing years, more European players joined Ballesteros in arguing that the Tour's rule requiring 15 starts was too much of a burden on international players, who also were required to play nine times on their home circuit, the European Tour. At the 1989 U.S. Open at Oak Hill CC, Beman met with Ballesteros, Aoki, Scotland's Sandy Lyle and England's Nick Faldo in the clubhouse to discuss the situation. As a compromise, Beman offered to lower the demands to 12 tournaments, but there was a catch. In return, he wanted players to commit to up to three Tour events from a predetermined list. Ballesteros walked out in a huff. "Seve thought he was so important that he didn't have to live by anybody's rules," Beman said.

In October 1989, the Tour's policy board rejected the temporary compromise arranged by Beman. "When you have a policy board that makes decisions, even if you disagree, you are obligated to carry out their policy as your own," Beman said.

Ballesteros never rejoined the Tour. In retrospect, Ballesteros indicated he regretted his hard-line stance. When asked in a 2003 *Golf Magazine* interview what he would've done differently in his career, Ballesteros said, "I would've played in America much more."

"Based on Seve's belated regret and my well worn crystal ball, I would suggest that international players reassess grabbing the guaranteed money available to them around the world and consider if their place in golf history is worth the trade for the easy money," Beman said. "They should not kid themselves about their position on the World Rankings that was tweaked to favor events played outside the U.S."

At the height of his popularity, Ballesteros, like O'Grady, engaged in a war of words against Beman, as if an inexplicable wrong had been done to him. In one of the more amusing press room exchanges, *Atlanta Journal-Constitution* columnist Furman Bisher asked Ballesteros after his second round at the 1986 Masters, "You played like you were on a crusade today. Are you trying to prove something to the PGA Tour?"

Ballesteros snapped, "Did Deane Beman pay you to ask that question?"

Bisher said, "No, it's a legitimate question. Are you on a crusade?"

"Crusade? What is this crusade?" Ballesteros said with a shrug as he fell back on his broken English.

"You ought to know what crusades are," Bisher retorted. "Your people started 'em!"

As writer Dan Jenkins noted, "Seve didn't have a kicker line because, like most everybody else in the press building, he'd never learned that the crusades had actually started in Rome."

GAME-CHANGER

E very year as December turned to January for a new golf season, Deane Beman would settle into a familiar routine. He'd pack his bags and head to Palm Springs, Calif., home of the Tour's West Coast headquarters, known fondly as the Tour's "Western White House."

It was during the Tour's West Coast Swing that Beman remembers his first time hitting a U-groove sand wedge the way a duffer recounts the marvels of his first metal driver.

"It was so dramatically more effective that it felt like cheating," Beman said.

The year was 1986 and Beman tried a Wilson R-90 U-groove sand wedge in the white desert sunlight before the Bob Hope Chrysler Classic. Until then, he never dabbled with the popular Ping Eye2 U-grooved irons because they had too much offset for his taste. (Beman long used a Ping Anser putter given to him in 1973.)

With their propensity to generate backspin from the rough, U-grooves were believed to help wayward drivers negate the typical advantage enjoyed by those playing from the fairway. The shift from grooves shaped like a V to those shaped like a U was made legal by a 1984 revision to the Rules of Golf that went largely unnoticed. Yet its influence on the way the game is played still lingers.

Beman said he instinctively knew that U-grooves had the potential to be a game-changer. "It diminished the value of driving and changed the great balance between distance and accuracy that existed in playing golf at the highest level," Beman said. "I confirmed my feeling by talking to several players to make sure it wasn't just my imagination."

Early on, Mark Calcavecchia was the poster child for the "high-tech pro" and the benefits of U-grooves or square-shaped grooves as they were also called. In the final round of the 1987 Honda Classic, he gashed a shot out of the rough and over water with a Ping Eye2 8-iron at the 16th hole and the ball stopped on the green as if someone slammed on ABS breaks. Calcavecchia made birdie and won the tournament. Some say that shot ignited debate over grooves and even a lawsuit. Tom Watson, Gary Player, Jack Nicklaus, and Greg Norman were among the staunchest critics of U-grooves. "They are hurting the integrity of the game," Norman said.

Player offered analogies to underscore his belief that U-grooves would damage the game. "They don't make the 100-yard dash downhill," he said. "You don't see them changing the size of the boxing ring. You don't see the football changing its size."

On June 23, 1987, the USGA, the keeper of golf rules in the U.S. and Mexico, changed its standard for measuring U-grooves making Ping Eye2 irons – the best-selling model made by Karsten Manufacturing Co. – nonconforming. A lengthy and contentious lawsuit ensued.

Karsten maintained that its grooves violated the USGA's new rule by the mere width of a human hair. To some, this description simplified the complex debate in terms all could understand, but others countered that it was misleading. They noted that a U-groove has twice the volume of a V-groove.

Ping founder Karsten Solheim had raised an important question: How could something seemingly insignificant – the microscopic spacing of grooves on an iron – have such far-reaching consequences?

The fact is the effect has been immeasurable. How much the game has changed still astonishes Beman. After all, they were merely splitting hairs.

"The width of a human hair?" Beman asked rhetorically. "I see this being as wide as crossing the Delaware River."

He would stake his reputation on it.

* * *

During the development of his first set of irons in the late 1960s, Karsten Solheim would ride into the desert near Ping's Phoenix headquarters with son Allan at the wheel of his Citroen. "Go 100 miles per hour," the father commanded. Then Solheim would hold an iron, with a string gauge and scale, out the window to test the club's aerodynamics and measure its stability in the wind.

The son of an immigrant Norwegian shoemaker, Solheim didn't take up golf until he was 42, when his co-workers at General Electric invited him to fill out a foursome. In no time, he became obsessed, chipping shots across the yard into his son John's first baseman's glove. Much to his despair, he found that he shared a problem with millions of other golfers – he couldn't putt. Like many, he blamed his equipment. Unlike most, he did something about it.

Solheim tinkered with clubs. He assembled the working model for his first putter, the 1-A, with two popsicle sticks glued to two sugar cubes. He placed a shaft in the middle of his design, rather than attaching it to the heel. The radical design transferred weight to the perimeter of the club, and the hollow center area created a distinctive "ping" when it struck the ball. Thus, a name for his company was born.

At the Solheims homespun operation, dinner sometimes took a backseat to heat-treating putter heads on stove-top burners. It has been more than 40 years since Solheim's part-time passion became a full-time pursuit. Demand for the Anser putter soared. He left GE in 1967 and incorporated his business as Karsten Manufacturing Corp. John dropped out of Arizona State University to help train the company's first 15 employees. Soon, the leader of the two-man band became an orchestra conductor. "Karsten Way" was more than the street name where the company was headquartered in Phoenix.

In 1969, Karsten Solheim applied the concept of perimeter weighting to irons. By taking the weight from behind the center of the head and redistributing it to the toe and heel, Solheim increased the size of the sweet spot. For his next innovation, he used investment casting rather than forging as a more consistent means of producing irons.

Solheim's new design and method of manufacturing was a boon to the average golfer because they created irons with greater playability. Even off-center hits could achieve reasonably good results.

Ordinary golfers stopped to thank Solheim for making the game easier to enjoy. Former USGA executive director Frank Hannigan sparred with Solheim on several issues but even Hannigan grudgingly admired how Solheim bucked conventional marketing methods and made himself the face of the company. Solheim and his signature goatee graced the company's canary yellow ads, and he drew crowds as big as those watching the pros. At the Masters, tournament officials once asked him to sign autographs farther away from the course to avoid patron congestion.

"It's absolutely nuts in terms of the history of (the equipment) business to make yourself, a funny little guy with a goatee, the central figure as opposed to (a great player like) Arnold Palmer," Hannigan observed. "The other thing he did, which I just loved, is he never used an advertising agency....They do these awful ads, in-house, and they're cluttered and ugly and yellow and they simply should not work. Except they work, because people stop and they think, 'That must be true. How could anybody do something that ugly and lie to me.' "

In an age of conformity, Solheim remained a defiant nonconformist. Ping ascended to unprecedented heights when he introduced a new set of cavity-back irons, the Ping Eye2, which became the Rosetta Stone of modern iron design in 1982. Sales skyrocketed when Solheim modified the club's grooves, capitalizing on what appeared to be an insignificant change in the Rules of Golf.

From 1942 through 1983, the USGA outlined three fundamental requirements for grooves, or scoring, of irons: They had to be V-shaped, could be no more than .035 of an inch wide from edge to edge, and could be no closer together than three times the width of the next groove.

As more manufacturers followed Solheim's lead and began using investment casting to shape irons, true V-grooves became virtually impossible to produce by investment casting (but they could have been milled into the face.) Enforcement of the groove rule became irrelevant. More than 60 percent of clubs on the market violated the rules as written because the bottom of the V tended to smooth out, according to Frank Thomas, the USGA's technical director from 1974 to 2000. The process resulted in more of a U-shape. A redefinition of line shape was needed.

So in 1983, Thomas recommended a change in the wording to the groove specifications in the Rules of Golf to allow for a groove with the shape of a three-sided box. It was one of 20 rules changes adopted in 1984. The revised rule specified a depth and width rather than define a groove by its width, flatness and the angle of its side to the face plane. The new rule permitted grooves to be U-shaped, but with diverging sides and no sharp edges.

When one of Solheim's engineers read this in the Rules of Golf, he rushed to show his boss. Solheim's eyes lit up and he marched straight to the lab. Experimentation commenced immediately on the modification that transformed the Ping Eye2 into the best-selling iron of all time.

* * *

The great debate over grooves has a storied history. Once golfers realized scoring the face of an iron helped them control the ball, numerous patterns – everything from punched dots to grooves to dashes – replaced a smooth face. Experts say grooves first appeared in irons around 1914. The first significant grooves controversy emerged several years later after Jock Hutchison became the first American champion of the British Open in 1921. Hutchinson credited his victory in large part to his self-made set of clubs.

Hutchinson, who was born in St. Andrews before emigrating to America, used clubs with furrowed grooves cut into the face of his mashie, mashie-niblick, and niblick irons (the equivalent of a 5-, 7-, and 9-iron) that could make a golf ball do everything except tango.

To protect the integrity of its tournaments, the Royal & Ancient Golf Club of St. Andrews (R&A) barred the use of corrugated, grooved, or slotted clubs claiming they departed from the "traditional accepted forms and makes of golf clubs" after Hutchinson's triumph. The USGA followed suit on Jan. 1, 1924, when it established the approved cross-sectional shape of grooves for the first time.

The groove issue cropped up again at the 1948 U.S. Open at Riviera CC. Before that tournament all of the MacGregor irons, played by the likes of Ben Hogan and Byron Nelson, had to be buffed down, according to the USGA. It didn't make a difference to the winner. Hogan shot 276 and broke the tournament record by five strokes.

Following that incident, John D. Ames, chairman of the USGA Implements and Ball committee, published a one-page explanation titled, "How to Test Iron Club-markings," in the August 1948 issue of *Golf Journal* that ended with this insightful observation: "It seems too bad that it has been necessary to get down to such fine points in order to insure fair play. Wouldn't it be nice if, as in the old days, we could just go out and play golf?"

Nearly 30 years passed before grooves made headlines again. With play at the 1977 Greater Hartford Open backed up at the second tee, Jerry Heard fished into the bag of his playing partner, George Burns, pulled out an iron and said, "George, these grooves look a little wavy. You may want to get them checked."

The third member of their group, Art Wall, overheard this conversation and after the round, in which Burns shot 64, Wall asked the Tour's deputy commissioner, Clyde Mangum, to examine Burns' Ram clubs. Under an optical magnifier scale, a device resembling a jeweler's loupe, the score lines were discovered to be too wide by the width of "a baby's fingernail." Burns was disqualified. That appeared to be the end of the story except the following week at the PGA Championship at Pebble Beach several pros who played with Ram clubs asked Mangum to inspect their tools of the trade, too. Not just any pros mind you, but Tom Watson, Raymond Floyd, Gene Littler, and Gary Player.

The Rules of Golf don't require such an inspection. It is each player's responsibility to ensure one's equipment is legal.

When examined, the grooves on Watson's entire set, with which he had won the Masters and British Open earlier that year, were declared too wide (.037 instead of .035). So were the grooves on Floyd's irons and half of the irons in Player's bag. Soon other competitors asked for a check, including Nicklaus, whose clubs met specifications. But officials detected more offending clubs. Hale Irwin lost several Wilson clubs and Tom Weiskopf was denied his MacGregor sand wedge. Commenting on the sudden trepidation with groove spacing, Dan Jenkins wrote, "It got to where a man would order a steak and be tempted to say, 'I'd like that within .035 of medium, please.' "

In the meantime, Watson sent for an old set of MacGregor irons he had used to win the 1975 British Open. Only problem being when they arrived, they failed, too. One newspaper head-line blared: "Watson Wins Need an Asterisk."

"Well, I guess I just won the Masters and the British Open," kidded Nicklaus, who had finished runner-up in each event, to Watson on the practice green, according to *Golf World*.

A more pressing concern emerged for Watson as his first round tee time approached. "Anybody got any clubs?" Watson cried on the putting green that morning. "I'll take anything." That's how he ended up playing with a spare set of Roger Maltbie's MacGregor Tommy Armour Silver Scot irons pulled from his trunk. Watson scrambled to hit a total of eight practice shots with them. He rushed to the tee, drove the fairway, and then, using the 6-iron for the first time, stuck it six feet from the cup. He shot 68. Good is good.

*   *   *

To fully grasp the significance of the 1984 rule change and its effect on the game, it is first necessary to understand the role grooves play in the flight of a golf ball. Grooves are inserted in the face of irons for the same reason treads are put on tires. They channel moisture away from the surface, allowing better contact with the road, or in this case the golf ball.

Grass is composed largely of liquid, and when a golf club contacts a ball, the grass between them is reduced to water that is pushed deep into the grooves and out the edges. With

V-grooves, the flight of the ball from heavy grass becomes less predictable often resulting in "flyers," which have little spin and travel unpredictable distances along unpredictable trajectories.

It was Tour consultant Dave Pelz who explained to Beman the reason why. Because a U-groove has a larger cavity than a V-groove, moisture dissipates quick enough so that it doesn't act as a lubricant between the ball and the clubface. If the grooves are smaller and have duller edges, moisture serves as a lubricant between the ball and clubface, causing the ball to aquaplane and reducing spin. With U-grooves, a shot struck from the rough had a better chance of behaving as if it was hit from the fairway – landing softly and dancing to a stop. In theory, and some say in practice, this means a player can bash his drive, knowing that even if he lands in any but the deepest rough, he still can take dead aim at the pin with his approach. However, the benefits of U-grooves are reaped by a small percentage of golfers. Most average players can't generate the club speed needed to produce the same spin as tour pros, and, as a result, can't take full advantage of deeper grooves.

Having already applied scientific principles to the design of golf equipment with heel-and-toe-weighted putters and perimeter-weighted, investment cast irons, Solheim wondered if the grooves on irons could be enhanced. He identified the benefits of using U-shaped grooves – which he once called a gift for golfers – for an updated version of his Ping Eye2 irons. Solheim's use of U-grooves wasn't a secret. The USGA's Thomas said he asked Solheim if he had benefited from the new groove rule during a locker room conversation at the 1984 U.S. Open. As a matter of fact, he had, Solheim replied.

In practice, however, Solheim's grooves had a problem. The sharp edges on the new grooves were tearing up the soft-covered, balata balls preferred by professionals at that time. Players complained and Titleist executives, makers of the most popular balata ball, even contacted Ping representatives seeking a solution. Solheim returned to the lab. To prevent cut balls, he rounded the edge of the grooves. This remedied the scuffing problem. But without changing the groove spacing, the new ratio of groove separation was below the USGA-required minimum of 3 to 1. It was closer to 2.6 to 1.

The Ping Eye2 irons with broadly radiused grooves were introduced to the market in late 1985 before a sample was submitted to the USGA. This action was taken even though the Rules of Golf recommended that equipment manufacturers submit samples of new equipment to the USGA before producing and marketing the product. Solheim believed the modification was insignificant and submitting a sample was unnecessary because the previous Eye2 model had been approved.

The violation of the 3-to-1 distance between grooves on the face of the Eye2 irons was first brought to Thomas' attention by a Tour official questioning the conformity of Scott Verplank's Eye2 irons. As an Oklahoma State rising senior, Verplank won the 1985 Western Open and became the first amateur to win a Tour event since Doug Sanders accomplished the feat 29 years earlier. A week after his Western Open victory, Verplank's practice session at an amateur tournament in Abilene, Tex., was interrupted by a phone call for him in the pro shop. On the other end of the line was Montford "M.T." Johnson, the USGA's chairman of the Implements and Ball Committee.

"He said, 'Don't worry about what anyone says about your clubs being illegal,' " Verplank recalled. "The funny thing was I didn't know what he was talking about." Johnson's declaration should never have been made, Thomas later said. He soon discovered the Eye2 grooves violated the Rules of Golf.

When informed in 1986 that his irons didn't conform to USGA standards, Solheim disagreed and refused to change his grooves. By his measurement – from the wall of the groove rather than the rounded edge – they were within the rules. "This is equivalent to saying the width of a canyon should be measured at the water level of the river that formed it," Thomas wrote in his book, "Just Hit It."

On Feb. 3, 1987, the USGA proposed measuring grooves "between two points, where a plane inclined at 30 degrees to the face of the club is tangent to a radiused edge of the groove." Thomas determined the 30-degree figure was the same measurement applied to V-shaped grooves. In doing so, the USGA abandoned its previous method of measuring groove widths, "the intersecting planes method," which Solheim relied upon to design the Ping Eye2 irons with U-grooves. Under the new measuring standard, Ping Eye2 clubs flunked. The USGA found the grooves to be .031 inches wide, which is acceptable, but the space between the grooves – which is required to be at least three times as wide as the grooves – was too close (only .073 inches).

Karsten said that the distance between conforming and nonconforming grooves under the proposed rule change was equivalent to the width of a human hair, or about 0.005 of an inch.

"That's how close it was," said John Solheim, then a vice president at Karsten.

His father said the USGA was using a rubber ruler and claimed the USGA's method of measurement ignored standard engineering procedures.

"That's one of the things that bothered my dad most of all," John Solheim said.

Nevertheless, on June 25, 1987, the USGA ruled that the 30-degree method (Rule 4-1e) would go into effect Jan. 1, 1988, for USGA competition (the date was later postponed to Jan. 1, 1990) to "make explicit something which heretofore has been implied." Other golf associations, such as the PGA Tour, could impose the new rule if the committee responsible for the competition's conduct adopted it as a condition of play. To allow sufficient time for the average golfer to replace the offending grooves from their bags, the USGA decreed the clubs wouldn't be declared illegal for general play until Jan. 1, 1996.

The USGA's press release noted that "the measurement method will not render nonconforming all clubs with U- or box-shaped grooves." Only the Ping Eye2 irons – with more than 1 million sets sold and a 2 1/2–to-3 month wait list – were singled out. It stated the Eye2 "will not meet the requirements of the Rules of Golf relating to the minimum distance between grooves, unless those irons are modified."

To Hannigan, a USGA staff member from 1961 to 1989 and executive director the final six years of his tenure, the association's decision was difficult but necessary.

"If you're going to make equipment rules that have these very fine lines drawn in them, when you perceive that someone has gone over the line, you either do something about it,"

Hannigan said, "or you withdraw from that field."

In retrospect, it was clear to Hannigan that the USGA botched its handling of the groove decision.

"As soon as I saw the clubs we should have said bang, 'They don't conform and that's it,' " he said, snapping his finger for effect. "We'll take the lawsuit tomorrow."

But Hannigan conceded that the USGA stood by and did nothing for two years. Nearly all Tour players scrambled to add at least one U-grooved club to their bags. By the 1989 U.S. Open, 65 percent of the contestants carried at least one Ping club; 35 percent carried at least one Ping wedge, and 21 percent carried a full set of Ping irons, according to a published report of a survey conducted by a Ping representative.

Hannigan continued. "(The USGA) made a terrible error – and certainly I was part of the decision making process – whereby (Ping) flooded the world with these clubs. So it became an impractical matter, very, very difficult for the USGA to sell golfers in America on the notion that these clubs should be taken away from them at some time. They really had no way of knowing that they were buying – at least at first – clubs that didn't conform by the basis of some thousandths of an inch."

Many industry observers believe that the USGA hoped that by giving pros time to adjust to the new rule and granting an 8 1/2-year grace period to the masses, Solheim would be placated into not taking legal action. The USGA had good reason to wish to avoid a court case. In 1983, it lost a jury trial in San Francisco, in which golf ball manufacturer Polara sued the USGA for banning its self-correcting golf ball.

In a 1991 interview conducted as part of the USGA's oral history of golf project, Hannigan opined that the case was tried, not on the merits, but on the basis of the USGA being a "WASP, male, discriminatory organization."

"(The USGA) was found guilty of that," he said. "And that's… the danger the USGA has or had at going to any jury trial."

Hannigan noted that five of the six jurors for the Polara case were women. They arched an eyebrow when prosecutors pointed out that, at the time, neither a woman nor a minority ever had been elected to the USGA's executive committee. Hannigan's wife happened to be in San Francisco on business at the time of the Polara trial. She witnessed the litigation and reported back: "You have absolutely no chance," and informed her husband that they couldn't have found six people "more alien to the USGA culture."

"They would have found the USGA guilty of anything," Hannigan said. "Sodomy, burglary, anything. It didn't matter."

Ultimately, the judge issued a "judgment notwithstanding verdict," overturning the jury decision. But the USGA paid Polara nearly $1.4 million in an out-of-court settlement. To Hannigan, the message was clear: the USGA was vulnerable at a jury trial.

As a result, Hannigan said there were endless meetings and spirited debate with Karsten Co. for two years in an attempt to resolve the groove matter without litigation. The discussions grew tense. They often revolved around their difference in opinion as to how a groove should be measured. The USGA interpreted the rule one way; Ping interpreted it another.

"So Karsten sent us down an engineer from Boston College which tells you, I mean, tells you right away they couldn't get anybody from MIT," said Hannigan, referencing the acclaimed Massachusetts Institute of Technology.

The meeting proved unproductive, Hannigan recalled. A few days later Ping's outside counsel, Harry Cavanagh of the Cavanagh Law Firm, phoned Hannigan. He listened, his blood beginning to boil as Cavanagh scolded him for berating Solheim on the tape.

Hannigan interrupted: "What tape?"

That's when he learned the Boston College engineer had recorded their meeting with a hidden device in his briefcase.

"That led to us getting an apology from Karsten and the tapes returned," Hannigan said. "Pity the meeting did not take place in New York where such bugging is a crime. Anything goes in New Jersey."

This episode aside, soon it became clear that the USGA underestimated Solheim, an entrepreneur borne with the tenacity to fight city hall. He still clung to the hope that the USGA would come to its senses and insisted reconciliation was possible. But at the 1989 Masters, the Solheims prepared for a legal contest by meeting with Rhode Island-based trial attorney Leonard Decof, of Decof & Grimm, who came highly recommended by Bob Gilder, a member of Ping's professional advisory staff. Decof, who successfully argued several cases before the U.S. Supreme Court, including a landmark case that established the right of medical-insurance policyholders to sue insurers for malpractice under antitrust laws, was selected as lead counsel for Karsten Co. In truth, Karsten Solheim preferred to do almost anything than sit with lawyers.

"My dad did not want to sue," John Solheim said. "He tried and tried but at every turn he ran into a stonewall."

When they remained at an impasse, Karsten Co. filed suit on Aug. 10, 1989. The company claimed the USGA and R&A, golf's rulemaking authority for everywhere except North America and Mexico, violated antitrust laws, slandered the company and interfered with its current and future business. The 27-page complaint filed in U.S. District Court in Phoenix claimed the June 1987 move to alter the 30-degree method – which banned only Pings – "restrained trade in the wholesale and retail sale of golf equipment." The crux of the lawsuit pivoted on the question of how and where to measure grooves.

Sir Michael Bonallack, then-secretary of the R&A, recalled being seated at a dinner banquet after watching the 1989 Walker Cup matches, the biennial competition pitting top amateurs from Great Britain and Ireland against the U.S., at Peach Tree Golf Club in Atlanta. A sheriff tapped Bonallack on the shoulder and informed him he officially had been served with a subpoena. So was William C. Battle, president of the USGA.

"That was very unpleasant," Bonallack told *The Scotsman* in 2006. "The writ said they were suing for $100 million tripled. They have what they call punitive damages in the United States, and it wasn't only the R&A they were suing, but me personally. That got my attention!

"We had good lawyers, though. They showed that the U.S. courts had no jurisdiction over us. We were making rules for golfers outside America."

Indeed, U.S. District Court Judge Paul Rosenblatt ruled in January 1990 that the R&A didn't conduct business in the state of Arizona, and therefore his court lacked jurisdiction. (Karsten could have re-filed its complaint in either Ohio or New York

– locations where the R&A conducted business with IMG and Capital Cities/ABC, respectively.) The judge awarded the legal fees the R&A had spent up to that point.

That didn't stop Karsten Solheim, from taking aim at the USGA, charging the association with "wantonly, recklessly, arbitrarily, unreasonably, and incorrectly" making rules about groove measurements.

Less than six months later, détente between Karsten Co. and the USGA was reached on Jan. 27, 1990 when the two parties agreed to stop splitting hairs. John Solheim missed his first PGA Merchandise Show to negotiate from San Diego with USGA executive committee leaders Battle and Reg Murphy. The hardest part for John was getting his father, who still had reservations, to settle. The elder Solheim was in Orlando at the PGA Show with John's brother, Allan, Babe Hiskey, who was among the first to play Ping irons on Tour and later became a Ping sales representative, and Roy Freeman, who operated Ping's U.K. operation. Hiskey and Freeman were among Karsten's closest confidants.

"If those people weren't with him and convinced him to settle, it wouldn't have happened," John said. "That's why I say the stars were lined up."

After month-long negotiations, Ping dropped its $100 million lawsuit against the USGA when the association agreed to make legal in perpetuity all Ping Eye2 clubs that already had been manufactured. In exchange, Solheim promised to stop manufacturing Ping Eye2 irons that did not conform to USGA specifications by approximately March 31, 1990. Thereafter, all Eye2 grooves would be narrowed approximately "the width of a human hair" and made to meet the Rules of Golf. The conforming version would feature a distinguishing mark – a raised dot for steel or a drilled circle in beryllium copper – in the cavity.

"Karsten changed his grooves, which he said he'd never do, and accepted the 30-degree measurement," Hannigan noted.

The out-of-court settlement culminated after an all-day session at the Hotel del Coronado, where the USGA's 96th annual meeting was held. Outgoing USGA president Battle said the association settled to protect golfers who had bought the clubs and to preserve the USGA's rule-making authority.

In language drafted only an hour before the annual meeting began, Battle announced the settlement at 6:22 p.m. Pacific time in the final act of his two-year tenure. The association conceded that "the dispute has been strictly of a technical nature and there was no competitive advantage to the user of the clubs."

Later Battle added, "Those of you who spent $600 on those clubs can breathe easier."

The more than 400 national, state, district and local golf officials in attendance welcomed the news of the resolution with a standing ovation and "explosion of applause," according to the USGA's executive director, David Fay.

"I'm looking forward to a warm relationship with the USGA with this decision," Karsten Solheim said at the time.

When the lawsuit settled, John was scheduled to take a red-eye flight to the PGA Show in Orlando. Instead he flew back home to Phoenix. "When it was all over I couldn't move," John recalled.

The suit was dismissed with prejudice, meaning it couldn't be re-filed. No money was exchanged. But a few hours after the suit settled, an erroneous story nearly rekindled the feud again.

The front page in *The Arizona Republic* the next day said, "they (USGA) agreed to pay us $5 million, Karsten Solheim told The Associated Press." Later in the story, it reported Solheim spoke from Phoenix when in fact he had left Thursday morning for Orlando to attend the annual PGA Merchandise Show.

During the final round of the Phoenix Open, John held an impromptu press conference to quell the storm of inquiries. AP golf writer Bob Greene explained he had called the Ping plant at night. When he received no answer, he tried an alternate number and thought he recognized the voice as Solheim's and proceeded to interview him. John told reporters the only known person at the plant that night was a security guard, and his name most certainly wasn't Karsten.

SOLDIERING ON ALONE

W hen Deane Beman heard that the USGA had settled with Karsten Co., he absorbed the news with his customary stoicism. Beman wasn't a lawyer but he had studied some of the important principles of antitrust law. From his perch, the USGA had two choices: Settle or lose in court. Frank Thomas, the USGA's technical director, had recommended and the USGA executive committee had approved what Beman considered to be a completely arbitrary new rule on how to measure grooves – and it did great harm to Ping. Moreover, Beman contended the USGA refused to acknowledge that the Tour players had been right all along. U-grooves did make a difference – a big difference – Beman said. "They perceived it as 'Who are these money-grubbing pros to tell us about the rules?' We're the USGA. We make the rules,' " Beman said. "But that missed the point. A U-groove had double the volume to help channel moisture. It was not a matter of the width of a human hair as Karsten's lawyer clearly mouthed to all who would listen."

By the time the USGA and Ping settled, the Tour had started down its own legal path with Karsten Solheim. Rather than discourage Beman, the USGA's failure to see the case through strengthened his resolve. Beman is a man as unyielding as the mighty structure he built. This just meant the Tour would be a proud and lonely voice in the campaign to protect the game. "We felt like we had to save the essence of shotmaking if the USGA wouldn't," Beman sniffed with derision.

Beman contended that U-grooves allowed players who were

long but not necessarily straight off the tee to gain a competitive advantage over less powerful, but more accurate players. To make certain of this contention, he canvassed Tour players. On Aug. 10, 1987, the Tour released the results of its equipment survey, which fielded responses from 172 of 200 competitors. Of those, 73 percent responded that they had used U-groove clubs. When asked the advantage of the club, 74 percent indicated that the grooves provided greater control from wet grass and rough. When asked if the Tour should ban U-groove irons, 60 percent responded in the affirmative.

"Anyone who could play worth a damn knew it made a difference," Beman said. "The problem was nobody at the USGA who had any influence could play worth a damn."

But Beman needed hard evidence to institute a rules change. What he needed was a real scientific test of grooves.

Beman turned to Dave Pelz, the former NASA scientist who was operating Independent Golf Research Corp., in Austin, Texas, and asked him to design a test to apply the theoretical principles of physics to the groove controversy. "Can you measure if players can spin the ball more with U-grooves than V-grooves?" Beman asked.

Pelz said it could be done. Next Beman enlisted Joe Braly, noted as the father of the frequency-matching method for determining shaft flex and Beman's former partner in golf equipment maker Con-Sole. Braly's job was to observe testing and ensure the validity of the raw data. Beman's assistant, Gary Becka, coordinated the project.

Several days after Ping filed its suit against the USGA in June 1987, Beman flew to Phoenix to meet with Solheim. The normally affable Solheim seemed cool and detached, and the tone of their exchange was icy. Solheim maintained, based on his own testing, that U-grooves didn't affect the spin of the ball.

More than ever, Beman understood the importance of removing conjecture. "The motives of the test were pure," Pelz said. "Did U-grooves really make a difference? The players had all these opinions. Deane didn't want to hear opinions. He wanted facts, he wanted evidence, he wanted proof."

In September 1987, Beman wrote a letter to all the golf club manufacturers advising them that the Tour had engaged two independent technical experts – Pelz and Braly – to study the groove issue. The letter asked the manufacturers to provide pertinent information and relevant data. Karsten Co. didn't respond to this request.

In November 1987, Pelz conducted elaborate field tests trying to localize the effect of grooves. At Beman's request, 13 Tour players – John Cook, Mike Donald, Danny Edwards, Tom Jenkins, Howard Twitty, and Tom Purtzer among them – were classified by their average driving distances (four long hitters, five medium hitters, and four short hitters). Each participated for a day or two in the Tour's groove test over a period of 18 days. Beman's staff checked with the National Weather Bureau and chose La Quinta, Calif., as the ideal site because it offered the most consistent weather pattern in the country during the month of November. Beman secured the Stadium Course at PGA West, the Pete Dye design that hosted the Skins Game from 1986 to 1991, and closed the facility for the groove research.

According to Pelz, testing began daily just after dawn, and the participants hit a variety of shots throughout the day: full 7-irons, 90-yard wedges, and 40-yard pitch shots from half-inch fairway lies, two-inch dry rough, and two-inch wet rough lies. Wind speeds were monitored and reported as negligble; testing halted whenever speeds equaled or exceeded 6 mph. Green speed was measured as 9.5 on the stimpmeter, and all greens were measured by laser beam and marked if the surface slope was greater than 2 degrees. Shots that landed in such areas, or missed the green entirely, were eliminated from the data set.

The testing was designed scientifically to prevent the Tour player's personal opinion of the groove controversy from factoring into the equation. For one, the participants didn't know what type of grooves they were using. Pelz pioneered the use of an electron discharge machine. He didn't develop the machine, he said, but he used it for the first time to cut grooves into flat plates. He machined out the face of golf clubs and then replaced those faces with the exact weight. This allowed him to insert a variety of grooves in and out of clubs in a matter of minutes before a player hit them. They were 3:1 V-grooves, representing conventional irons; 3:1 U-grooves, comparable to the "legal" square grooves made by Wilson, MacGregor and others;

2.6:1 U-grooves to mimic the Ping Eye2; and 4:1 U-grooves to identify whether groove width affected performance. The clubs were manufactured to the same loft, lie, length, swing weight and shaft stiffness specifications as the clubs used by test participants in Tour competitions. All 13 players also used their own clubs.

A player struck five shots and then exchanged the club for a different groove pattern. The grooves were indistinguishable to players. "You can't see that fine of detail," Pelz said.

Not only were the pros unaware of the grooves they were hitting, they also couldn't see the putting surface. Pelz's team hoisted four-foot high, black plastic screens in front of all the greens so that golfers couldn't see the ball landing and whether it backed up, rolled on, or how quickly it stopped. A player would swing, watch the ball's flight disappear behind the curtain, turn and hand the club to one of the 44 volunteers helping in the testing. The assistant would wash the clubface, brush the grooves clean, dry the clubface after every shot, and roll a new ball out.

Though Pelz relied on primitive equipment, the scientific nature of the process was impressive. His team measured seven characteristics of every shot – (1) time between impact and first ground contact, (2) distance from impact to first ground contact; (3) depth of divot; (4) length of first bounce; (5) roll after bounce; (6) distance between first ground contact point and final resting point; (7) distribution of the final resting point pattern on the green – using laser equipment to 1/100th of an inch. One individual threw a beanie bag where the ball landed, another volunteer dropped a beanie bag where the ball bounced, and a third person placed a beanie bag where the ball stopped. Then they took a tape measure and determined the difference between the three locations.

Pelz also developed the "divot-o-meter," a tool shaped like a ball that measured the surface of the green and depth of the ball mark. If a ball landed on a wet spot on the green and its ball mark was too deep then that data was invalid.

In the course of testing, Pelz made another discovery: an up-and-coming golfer whom he believed could be the Tour's next world-beater. He fondly remembered this "real casual guy" who hit hundreds of shots and never missed the green with a 7-iron from 168 yards at the par-3, 13th hole. Who was this dead-eyed wonder? None other than Fred Couples, then a 24-year-old, baby-faced newcomer to the Tour with one career victory. "Never made a bad swing," Pelz said. "Some players hit in the water 25 times. I came away from the test amazed not only at the results of the test but amazed at Freddie Couples. He had 'it.' "

Pelz submitted the data to two separate consulting groups, one at the University of Texas and the other at the University of Delaware. Over a period of four months, each university devised its own methodology to analyze the 250,000 data points for shot-performance parameters such as carry, bounce, roll after bounce, total roll and scatter. "You have to be a statistics freak to read it," Pelz said.

In the meantime, on Jan. 30, 1988, at its 94th annual meeting in Washington D.C., the USGA announced the results of its study of U-shaped grooves. "Perceptions of dramatic performance differences attributed to the shape of the grooves was not borne out by the test," said Stuart Bloch, USGA secretary and chairman of the Implements and Ball Committee. With balata balls from high grass, Bloch added, "There was a slight difference, but it was inconsequential."

Beman disputed the USGA findings. He claimed that either the test or the tester was faulty. Becka, Braly, and Beman had observed the USGA's field testing and declared it invalid. "We were concerned they were not making a sincere and proper effort to follow a protocol for their testing," Beman reported to the Tour's policy board.

On April 15, 1988, the university researchers submitted detailed reports to the Tour. Both studies concluded that U-grooves imparted more spin to the golf ball from heavy rough.

"Groove geometry definitely affects players' shot performance," Pelz concluded. "For 3:1 and 2.6:1 box grooves when compared to V-grooves, (they) tend to stop shorter with shorter rolls, and resulting scatter patterns from wedge shots tend to be slightly smaller."

Pelz contended that the results actually understated the groove difference, noting that "flyers" couldn't be measured because they sailed over the green and into the water behind hole Nos. 6 and 13. The test also was conducted on flat greens rather than the undulating greens prevalent on Tour.

In June, the Tour released a five-page explanation of its research, illustrated by charts and color slides. It clarified that strength was not a factor. Results were identical for long, medium and short hitters. The tests found that full 7-iron shots with square grooves carried seven yards shorter than identical shots with V-shaped grooves when hit from dry rough. From wet rough, the U-grooves were less than three yards shorter than V-shaped grooves. U-groove shots stopped rolling quicker than those hit by V grooves, but their first bounce was longer.

"There was no question," Pelz said. " From 160 yards out in the rough, a 7-iron with U-grooves stopped on average 20 feet shorter than the same club with V-grooves."

The disparity between the USGA and Tour results was hard to explain – unless Braly is to be believed: "Someone at the USGA cooked the books," he said. "I can't think of anything else. How can two groups of people with the same question in a finite type of answer and using the same raw data come up with such different opinions? That ain't possible."

Ask Beman and he will say the Tour never intended to be in the rulesmaking business, that it attempted to cooperate with the USGA and R&A. But on May 12, 1988, Beman recommended to the Tour's board that a proposed rule change banning U-grooves be circulated for public comment. Twelve days later the board adopted a rule that allowed only traditional V-shaped grooves in all its competitions.

The Tour's board, members of the Tour staff, Pelz, the Tour's technical advisor, and special guest Tom Watson, met with USGA officials – represented by executive director Frank Hannigan, president Bill Battle, Bloch of the Implements and Ball Committee, and Thomas, technical director – in Denver the night before the Tour's Aug. 16 board meeting. They reviewed the results of the USGA's laboratory and field tests. Battle and de Windt, the Tour's board chairman, met privately too, and de Windt proposed that the USGA consider adopting the rule, which was preliminarily approved by the Tour as a condition of competition, until more testing was completed. Battle offered to present the matter to the USGA's Executive Committee.

He suggested the Tour adopt the USGA's rule that only 2.6-to-1 ratio U-grooved clubs be deemed nonconforming. Further testing would take six months, Battle said, and the USGA wouldn't take action without R&A approval and input from the manufacturers.

During the Tour's board meeting at the Denver Sheraton, the USGA requested a private meeting with the player directors – Mike Donald, John Mahaffey, Roger Maltbie, and Larry Mize – to state its case. According to Maltbie, Hannigan asked for additional time so the USGA could conduct its own testing.

When Beman reconvened with the player directors' he disagreed with their sudden willingness to delay a decision. He deemed the USGA's study incomplete for looking only at the total roll of the ball in concluding the grooves had no material effect. He claimed they should have looked at bounce and roll together if they wanted to understand the essence of the issue.

"Let me tell you something," Beman said. "We don't need confirmation from the USGA, who have made their rule arbitrarily without regard to any reasonable testing. Their findings will only reinforce our study. We should proceed."

Beman also advised against adopting the existing USGA rule on 2.6-to-1 ratio grooves, stating that the Tour's independent test data indicated that such a rule wouldn't solve the problem noted by the players. Maltbie, for one, preferred the USGA to take the lead. "I thought it would serve the greater good if we could forge some kind of working relationship," he said.

At 9:55 a.m., the Tour's board convened an executive session. When de Windt reconvened the board meeting at 11:15 a.m., he announced the Tour's decision to postpone action on the proposed rule until the USGA conducted further player study. The decision was made "for the greater good of golf," Beman told the press.

"Of course, all that happened is it bought time for the USGA to negotiate a settlement, which left the Tour right in the headlights," Maltbie said.

Maltbie said he should've known better. After the meeting, lunch was served on the deck at Castle Pines GC. "One of the USGA committee men – out of respect I'll leave his name out – looked at me and said, 'C'mon Roger, how much of a difference do the grooves really make?' I looked at him and said, 'Are you kidding me? Have you not listened to any of this? Have you not read any of this?' "

When the USGA decided not to ban all U-grooves, the Tour no longer could stand on the sidelines, Beman said. "It was the USGA's first abdication of responsibility," he said.

The Tour's policy board voted to adopt the U-groove ban at its Feb. 28, 1989 meeting. At that time, the Tour's bylaws required a majority of the directors present and three of the player directors to vote on any rule change. To avoid a conflict of interest charge, the four player directors and the PGA officer directors abstained from voting. Each of the abstaining directors had ties to golf club manufacturers. The three independent directors unanimously voted for the rule. They did so under the premise that a professional sports organization has the authority to make its own rules of competition. The effective date of the rule was Jan. 1, 1990. It marked the Tour's first-ever equipment ban.

"The Tour is governed by its tournament regulations and its articles of incorporation," Beman explained. "Granted, they say we'll play by USGA rules unless otherwise modified, but that 'unless otherwise modified' has always been there to give the Tour the flexibility to adjust USGA rules."

Karsten Co. expressed its concerns to the Tour in a meeting on Aug. 14, 1989. John Solheim requested and received the test data the Tour relied upon. In a later deposition, he testified that it took a couple of months to review the data. Based on its own testing, Ping officials reaffirmed that U-grooves didn't affect the spin of the ball. On Dec. 1, 1989, Karsten and nine touring pros – Bob Gilder, Ken Green and John Inman on the PGA Tour and Rafe Botts, Bob Erickson, George Lanning, Deane Refram, Walter Zembriski, and Agim Bardha on the Senior Tour – filed an antitrust lawsuit, seeking more than $100 million in damages against the Tour. Ping alleged the Tour circumvented its bylaws to ban U-grooved clubs from its events.

"The reason they attacked the vote is to create the suspicion with the court that, yeah, there's something wrong here, 'How come 70 percent of their board didn't vote on it?' " said the Tour's general counsel, Ed Moorhouse.

What began as a technical skirmish escalated into a war over the authority to make rules for golf. It had the potential to rock the foundation of the game.

* * *

In the court system, the case became known as Gilder v. PGA Tour, Inc. Gilder, one of the player plaintiffs, wasn't convinced grooves mattered all that much. He objected to his fellow Tour pros accepting a rule that would restrict the use of his clubs.

"The best players were saying that guys with less skill were becoming better players because of equipment," Gilder said. "I thought that was a bunch of bologna."

Gilder called Beman and grilled him about the grooves test. Gilder asked several times for an explanation of the findings in the grooves. Each time, Beman repeated that the test results were significant. "Finally he said it amounted to 2 feet," Gilder recalled, citing the USGA results, not the Tour data. "That's with all the balls that didn't stay on the green being thrown out of the test. I said, 'You're nuts. There's never been a player who can control the ball within 2 feet.' " (Beman doesn't remember the exchange this way, but points out the Tour's tests revealed a difference of 20 feet not 2 feet with a 7-iron from the rough.)

Gilder and Ping had a lengthy history. When Solheim initially struggled to persuade pros to switch to his cavity-back irons, he seeded his product with players at the college level and hoped they graduated to the pros. Gilder, who had used the clubs since the early '70s when he was a student at Arizona State, was Solheim's first convert to make the Tour.

Ping's complaint, filed on behalf of Gilder and eight other players, sought injunctive relief and alleged the actions of the Tour and its directors' violated sections 1 and 2 of the Sherman Antitrust Act, violated Arizona's antitrust laws, and interfered with the company's and the pros' business relationships. The complaint also charged the Tour's independent directors – de Windt, Roger Birk and Hugh Culverhouse – with breaching their fiduciary duties and sought to hold them liable for their allegedly tortious conduct.

The legal action against the Tour effectively became a struggle for control of professional tournament golf. It revolved around whether the Tour had the right to regulate the rules governing its competition, especially if new equipment altered the character of the game or artificially enhanced the skill of players. Major League Baseball, for instance, had banned metal bats from its game, and its rules prevent a baseball from being aerodynamically engineered to help the pitcher.

After Karsten filed its suit in Phoenix, Beman gave two days' notice to Tour board members of a special meeting to amend the bylaws and enable the Tour to re-pass the groove rule challenged by Karsten. On Dec. 5, 1989, all 10 members of the Tour policy board met in a special session. To make the groove vote valid, the Tour rewrote its bylaws so that a quorum or majority vote wouldn't be required when there was an abstention (partcularly if there could be a conflict of interest), and that player members on the policy board didn't have to be part of the vote if there were abstentions. The three independent directors then voted 3-0 to ban U-grooves, effective Jan. 1, 1990.

Two weeks after the birth of his first child (a son), Moorhouse traveled to Phoenix for the preliminary injunction hearing, which got underway on Dec. 15. At the beginning of the hearing U.S. District Court Judge Paul Rosenblatt revealed he was a golfer and he used Ping clubs. He listened as Gilder testified that switching equipment would impair his playing performance and harm his endorsement opportunities. Gilder stated that he "liked the design and dynamics" of the Eye2. Richard Smith, an Arizona State University economist, testified that a correlation exists between a consumer's choice of golf clubs and a professional's choice of clubs. Karsten claimed its market share of the iron category had dropped from 28.2 percent to 20.9 percent, and that sales of all Ping equipment had suffered a corresponding drop since the enactment of the U-groove ban.

When Beman stated his case, he testified that the issuance of the preliminary injunction would have "dire consequences for the Tour." In cross-examination, he acknowledged that of the affidavits presented in support of the V-groove rule, Palmer (Arnold Palmer Golf), Nicklaus (MacGregor), and Watson (a royalty contract with Ram), had interests in equipment makers. The plaintiff said their ties would affect their credibility. To avoid such conflict of interest was the very reason the Tour had re-written its bylaws permitting the player directors not to vote. Beman claimed Ping's legal team challenged the Tour on both sides of the issue. The court would have to decide if the board's second vote without the players was valid, according to the new bylaws.

When considering a petition for a preliminary injunction, courts engage in a balancing test, weighing the interests of plaintiff and defendant while also considering the public impact of granting injunctive relief. According to Judge Rosenblatt's summary, he took into account the likelihood of the plaintiffs' success at trial; the threat of irreparable harm to the plaintiff if the injunction was not imposed; the relative balance of this harm to the plaintiff and the harm to the defendants if the injunction was imposed; and, the impact on the public.

After a three-day evidentiary hearing, on Dec. 24, 1989, Judge Rosenblatt issued a preliminary injunction stopping the Tour from implementing the ban. Rosenblatt ruled the Tour's policy board vote establishing the ban circumvented its bylaws. He determined Ping's hardship of retooling and abandoning a ready market for its Eye2 U-grooved irons would be far more serious and damaging than the Tour's claim that its rule-making authority would suffer and possibly result in a loss of confidence in its ability to govern itself. The court also concluded "there was a reasonable possibility of success on the merits and there was a great possibility of irreparable harm."

In the dark of night, Becka and Beman flew back to Jacksonville on the Tour's plane following the issuance of the temporary restraining order. Disgusted by a ruling he termed unfair and improper, Beman fretted that the case now would drag at least another year and possibly much longer. There was another negative ramification, too.

"The Tour is now going to be put in the same position as the USGA in which thousands of golfers will be purchasing (allegedly) illegal clubs," Beman said. "This was a huge disappointment."

He didn't utter a word the entire flight, from wings up to touch down. Becka recalled that Beman finally spoke when the two men got in their car at the airport. What did Beman finally say?

"Nothing fit for print," said Becka, laughing.

* * *

On Dec. 28, the U.S. Ninth Circuit Court of Appeals in San Francisco declined the Tour's request for an emergency hearing and stay of the injunction, prohibiting the Tour from implementing the U-groove ban on all three of its tours at the start of the 1990 season. (The appeals court later upheld the injunction in June 1991.) Given that Karsten Co. settled with the USGA, Beman felt Solheim should try to do the same with the Tour to "restore tranquility to the game." In a Feb. 20, 1990 letter to Solheim, Beman extended an olive branch, urging the use of binding arbitration rather than the court system to resolve the matter by mid-June.

"We wanted to end it," Moorhouse said. "It was costing us money and it was a distraction to the Tour."

Solheim, however, expressed his desire to take his lawsuit before a jury in federal court. For one, arbitration doesn't allow for the same level of discovery and, of course, there was no recourse from an unsatisfying decision. In general, most litigators strenuously recommend clients avoid arbitration. One of Ping's attorneys, David Van Engelhoven of Cavanagh Law Firm, likened arbitration to a risky gamble. "You might as well go to Las Vegas and put your money on red," he said.

When Golfweek's James Achenbach asked Decof to describe his legal strategy, Decof responded, "First of all, you have to listen to everything and understand everything. Then you can get aggressive." Solheim followed up his victory in the appellate court with an amended complaint, adding to the list of defendants the Ben Hogan Co., and the Tour's two experts – Braly and Pelz.

Decof had unearthed several seemingly explosive gems to attempt to show the Tour and Beman conspired or agreed with one or more persons to interfere with competition. Without a conspiracy or agreement that unreasonably restrains trade, there can be no antitrust violation. Decof planned to show that

Beman didn't ban U-grooves to protect the game from technological change but rather as part of a conspiracy with top players to help Ping's competitors. In particular, Decof focused on the Tour's signing of a lucrative deal with the Ben Hogan Co., to become the title sponsor of the Tour's new developmental circuit.

This claim appeared to have its own holes. Initial discussions with the Ben Hogan Co. concerning naming rights commenced in the fall of 1988, more than five months after the adoption of the Tour V-groove rule. Furthermore, Hogan's best-selling iron at the time was the Edge, a U-groove club. The company also sent a letter to the Tour, along with several other manufacturers, objecting to the adoption of the V-groove rule.

Still, Decof was primed to expose Beman's supposed hidden agenda. In his deposition testimony, the USGA's Thomas stated that Beman had a preconceived outcome of the tests. He testified that Beman told him, "All you have to do is find differences to prove our point, or words to that effect."

Asked for his version of their exchange, Beman doesn't deny he said "words to that effect," but commented the Tour conducted the test to the best of its ability to discover if a difference between grooves existed. Beman said of Thomas, "He was supposed to be the keeper of the gate there, and he wasn't man enough to own up to it. He did everything he could to cover his own ass. When the Tour stepped up to protect the game, he and his cohorts did everything to undermine our efforts."

Decof planned to show a jury that the experts the Tour used to conduct tests were biased and that the procedures were inadequate. To discredit Pelz, Decof cited Hannigan telling the USGA Executive Committee that he felt Pelz was hired as a means of "sanctifying the perceptions" of those believing that U-grooves made a difference in play. (Pelz, who had his own club-making company for several years, previously had sued the USGA over a nonconforming putter and lost.) In the complaint, Karsten charged the Tour's independent testers, Pelz and Braly, were his competitors. The complaint also maintained that the test was "improperly, incorrectly and unscientifically designed, performed and statistically analyzed...in order to achieve the desired result," and that the policy board was not informed of these flaws when it voted. Decof also planned to show that the Tour's three independent directors – board chairman de Windt, Culverhouse, and Birk – violated their duty to "exercise reasonable diligence in gathering and considering all material information available to them."

Karsten's legal team subpoenaed the records of Howard Taylor, the University of Delaware statistics professor, who contributed to the public report. The lawyers latched onto an unpublished sentence in the researcher's records that said, "... in truth, no one knows for sure whether there is a meaningful difference between 3:1 U-grooves and 3:1 V-grooves." When he read the line, Van Engelhoven requested that the school's clerk copy the document immediately.

To Moorhouse, the statement, when taken in the context of the remainder of the paragraph, simply acknowledged the reason for the test to be carried out. But for the plaintiff, it became a critical piece of evidence.

"That phrase was repeated many times in our pleas and presentations to the court," Van Engelhoven said. "Look, they may say they have their reasons and statistical data, but when their experts are talking amongst themselves, they are saying, 'In truth, we don't really know if there is a difference between these two things.' It makes you think there might be another reason for this."

Beman thought this argument rang hollow. "The number cruncher probably wasn't a golfer and he clearly wasn't a Tour player," Beman said. "Sure, he did analyze the data and recorded the results and came up with what Pelz had summarized. But how could he know if it changed the way golf was played?"

Decof also picked apart the credibility of some of the Tour's most high-profile witnesses. During a deposition, Nicklaus admitted that he wasn't trained as an engineer, had no expertise in aerodynamics, and wasn't qualified to give technical expert testimony on the effect of U-grooves. Watson conceded that while he was the co-author with Hannigan of a book on The Rules of Golf, his name had been slapped on the cover for marketing purposes. Next Decof outsmarted Kite, who had claimed during Ping's injunction hearing that everyone should have to play the same equipment in order to level the playing field. Decof asked Kite to describe the clubs used by two-time U.S. Open champion Andy North. To compensate for his lanky figure, North's clubs were extra long, the shafts extra stiff, and the grips extra thick. Decof took aim again asking Kite of medium-build if he could play with North's set. "No way," Kite replied unequivocally.

As the plaintiff attempted to discredit the Tour's list of potential witnesses, a new figure emerged as a key cog in the Tour's case. For additional expert analysis, the Tour turned to "baseball's Newton," Robert Adair, the Stirling Professor of Physics at Yale, and hired him to do a report. When he was president of baseball's National League, A. Bartlett Giamatti, who previously served as president of Yale, appointed Adair "physicist to the National League." The result of his study was "The Physics of Baseball," a book that explained the science behind the crack of the bat and the curve of the ball. Professor Adair compiled an elaborate physics analysis that compared grooves to tread on tires, and would show the jury that the notion that grooves didn't matter because the size was the difference of "the width of a human hair" was patently false. Maledon contends Adair would've been an effective witness. "The jury would've loved him," said Bill Maledon of Osborn Maledon, the Tour's outside legal counsel.

Besides poking holes into the Tour's argument during discovery, Decof scored an early victory in the court of public opinion. Players were alarmed by a videotape of a deposition Beman gave under questioning by Decof. The contents of any deposition are confidential for 30 days. Then each party can advocate to keep its contents, or portions of it, confidential. If the other side disagrees, they negotiate. According to Van Engelhoven, none of Beman's deposition was marked confidential. The Tour's lawyers either didn't designate any of its parts or committed a costly oversight. So the prosecution presented certain snippets to the players with great fanfare.

In the segments, Beman admitted that the players' retirement fund, which had a market value of $41.5 million in 1993 according to the Tour, could be tapped to pay damages if the Tour lost the lawsuit. Beman informed the players that indeed the Tour's retirement fund was vulnerable and conceivably could be used to defray damages. For the Tour to operate as a 501-c6 in which the players aren't employees, the player retirement plan assets must be pooled in the Tour's general assets.

Understandably, this revelation didn't sit well with the players and conjured up fears of losing their nest eggs. Some of them lashed out at Beman publicly. Tim Simpson, who played with Ping equipment for most of his career, made one of the strongest anti-Beman statements. "Deane's lost sight of the reality that he works for us," Simpson said. "Deane basically has a total dictatorship, and he just flatly has too much power. He has to be kept in check better than he is. I'm certain the Tour is going to lose the lawsuit, and in my opinion, Deane should be replaced."

Beman soldiered on, waging his solitary argument. On March 8, 1990, Tour officials flew to Phoenix to meet with Karsten Solheim and his counsel. The Tour made another settlement offer. Solheim thought the proposal was laughable and rebuffed it. He thanked the Tour for coming to meet with them and politely asked them to leave. Tim Finchem, then deputy commissioner, reported back to Beman, "He won't budge."

A year later, the Tour persisted, exploring with Solheim the possibility of permitting a 4-to-1 U-groove if it performed at the same level as a V-groove. Beman was less concerned with shape than performance relative to the traditional 3-to-1, V-groove. Solheim dismissed the possibility. In October 1991, Beman renewed efforts to settle the litigation, pledging to allow a mutually acceptable independent third party to determine the appropriate spacing of the U-grooves. Solheim rejected these overtures too. Even efforts by the Tour's insurance carrier failed.

When peace talks failed, the Tour got feisty. It petitioned the USGA to share its settlement documents from its groove case with Ping. When the Tour threatened to file a contempt of court, the USGA relented. That's how the Tour's legal team uncovered a memorandum from Hannigan, which revealed that the USGA's Executive Committee actually had once voted to ban U-grooves. One individual at a time, Hannigan convinced committee members to rescind their votes. Beman said Hannigan's argument boiled down to this: Would you rather be right or irrelevant?

It had been feared by many in golf that a jury verdict against the USGA in its lawsuit with Karsten Co. would undermine its role as enforcer of the Rules of Golf. The Tour's efforts to ban U-grooves raised fresh concerns that the USGA's rule-making authority may be weakened if the Tour won its case.

The Tour also discovered a correspondence between a former Ping employee and the USGA that documented how the Eye2 ended up violating the groove configuration.

"Karsten knew it," Beman said.

Instead of making a new mold with wider grooves and spacing them to conform to the 3-to-1 ratio, Solheim simply widened the grooves. A Tour representative purchased 100 sets of Ping Eye2 irons and sent them to an independent lab for inspection. Every set was deemed illegal.

"Karsten was an engineer at heart," Beman said. "His philosophy amounted to 'If I can make a better golf club – regardless of the USGA rules – I ought to be able to do so because I'm helping players. I'm the good guy.' That's how he thought."

The Tour answered back on Sept. 26, 1991, with a $100 million counterclaim in Florida Federal Court against Ping, (PGA Tour, Inc. v. Karsten Manufacturing Corp.) contending the company had "knowingly and willfully" supplied clubs for years that were illegal and subverted the rules of competition. Solheim's lawyers moved to dismiss the "frivolous" counterclaim. Decof argued that the 100 Eye2 sets weren't new and the Tour couldn't prove the Eye2 irons were sold in nonconforming condition. A federal judge in Florida denied Ping's motion to dismiss.

"Ping now faced the possibility of being branded as cheaters in a game where integrity is everything," Beman said.

Beman suspected that Solheim's sudden eagerness to return to the negotiating table reflected his fear that his company's reputation could be seriously damaged by the allegation that Ping's dominant market position was obtained by building illegal clubs. Ping's trial, however, scheduled for April 1993 in U.S. District Court in Phoenix and projected to last up to five months, pre-dated the Tour's suit slated for September.

For all of its confidence, the Tour had reasons to want to settle, too. So much was at stake, and as Beman noted, facing a jury trial presented its share of risks. In March 1993, Judge

Rosenblatt denied the Tour's motion to dismiss the case and held that Karsten Co. could seek punitive damages at the trial. The judge's 38-page opinion declared that a jury was entitled to hear the major issues raised in Karsten's complaint. Based on the record of evidence, the judge said, a jury could conclude that the ban was "more about power, politics, and money than grooves."

If a jury found in favor of Karsten Co. and awarded the full $100 million claim – in antitrust verdicts the figure is trebled – the Tour's liability insurance would cover only a fraction of the payment. And that didn't include possible punitive damages. Beman argued the debate shouldn't be about money, but rather the right thing to do. "The money is worth nothing to the game of golf if it isn't used to preserve it," he said.

So far, the Karsten legal victories had been procedural. At last, the legal issues would be tested, Moorhouse said. It is common practice in cases involving complex litigation to rehearse a case on a test jury. Beman had faith that a jury of peers would side with the Tour if its legal team could present the case in easily digestible terms.

"Any adult that drives a car knows when you wear your tires down so the tread is only half as deep as it was when it was new and you hit the breaks in the rain, the car is going to skid," Beman said. "The jury wouldn't have to understand golf and its nuances."

The Tour's legal team conducted a series of mock trials. One lawyer defended the case for Ping and another lawyer presented the Tour's defense to 10-12 would-be jurors, who served as a focus group. Afterwards, Finchem cautioned that the mock trials dramatized the challenge they faced in convincing a jury to care about how the game had been played with traditional V-grooves. Especially since the jury lived in Phoenix, where Solheim, the wealthiest self-made man in Arizona, was celebrated as a hero. (Solheim's net worth in 1993 was estimated at $500 million, placing him among the 400 wealthiest Americans by *Forbes* magazine.) At a briefing during the 1993 Players Championship in late March, Finchem described the challenges the Tour faced and reduced the Tour's chances of winning at trial to 50-50. "What they (Ping) have going for them, and they know it, is that to the average golf and lay person it is very difficult to accept these groove configurations make much of a difference," Finchem said.

Many of the writers who chronicled the game proclaimed Beman's legacy on the line, saying a potential defeat could overshadow everything else he had accomplished. The April 1992 cover story of *Golf Digest* posed the question "Can Beman Survive?" In the face of mounting pressure, both sides sensed that the other had grown more eager to make a deal. Conversations renewed in the form of face-to-face meetings, telephone calls and facsimile.

Even as settlement talks rekindled, the two sides remained at an impasse. As the trial date loomed in early 1993, Moorhouse moved into the Hilton Suites near Maledon's Phoenix office and communicated with Beman each night via phone. The two sides continued to thrash out a deal. Moorhouse's second son was born in March. This time he missed the birth. On April 5, the trial was continued until April 20, marking the third trial delay that year.

Moorhouse returned to Florida. Meanwhile, Maledon had prepared his opening statement. Soon the jury would be selected. As the eve of the trial neared, Beman relented on the U-groove ban in exchange for Solheim acknowledging that the Tour had the right to make its own rules. This compromise came with its own condition: the Tour agreed to create a special committee consisting of five individuals unaffiliated with the Tour or any manufacturer, which would make recommendations concerning any equipment rule the Tour wanted to implement that deviated from the USGA's Rules of Golf. Two committee members must have engineering backgrounds; the others according to Decof, would be judged on "independence, impartiality and reputation."

Such procedure comforted Solheim, who felt he had been denied due process by the Tour. Decof said an independent committee "protects Karsten as well as the golf industry from arbitrary practices." In addition, the settlement agreement stipulated that in the event the USGA adopted a rule prohibiting U-grooves, the Tour would have the option to follow the rule.

Beman and Finchem shared a rented house in Augusta, Ga., for the Masters. They faxed documents back and forth to

Moorhouse and Ping's lawyers during marathon negotiating sessions, and pored over proofs of a revised agreement.

"They had this crappy fax machine where they were staying," Moorhouse recalled. "It would take several times to go through and so I'd call and read the documents to them over the phone."

The conditions seemed reasonable. Ping's U-grooves remained legal in Tour competition; Beman got his independent equipment committee, the Tour retained the right to make its own rules, and no Tour money was paid to Karsten.

"What else was there to win?" Beman said.

Negotiations closed April 12, 1993, with a four-point agreement that terminated the original suit and countersuit 1,228 days after the original was filed. Both sides reaffirmed the USGA as the rule-making authority in the United States, governing the amateur and professional games, a status that had been threatened by the Tour's position.

"We applaud the Tour's proposal to remove the V-groove rule," USGA executive director David Fay said. "We think all of golf is better served by having a truly independent rule-making body, and that's the USGA."

Fittingly, the settlement agreement was signed over the fax. According to the book "Karsten's Way," Solheim said, "Can we say it's finished?" Beman replied, "Yes, Karsten, we can say it's finished." The two sides delayed an announcement until April 14, giving Solheim's legal team the opportunity to acquire the necessary player signatures for the settlement agreement, and Tour officials' time to brief its players at that week's Tour stops, the MCI Heritage Classic and Senior PGA Championship. Beman spent a day at each site fielding player questions. Three days after Chip Beck was second-guessed for laying up at the par-5, 15th hole of the Masters while trailing Bernhard Langer, Beman had his own explaining to do.

A confidential letter from Beman to Tour players said proceeds available from the Tour's officers' and directors' liability insurance "have been or will be distributed to Karsten and the PGA Tour to defray the costs of litigation. No PGA Tour funds are involved in the settlement of the case." The Tour's insurance carrier, Landmark, a subsidiary of AIG, reimbursed the Tour approximately $3.5 million in legal expenses as well as paid an undisclosed sum to Karsten Co.

Several Tour members expressed shock that the Tour settled, including Peter Jacobsen, a member of the Tour policy board, who told *Golf Digest*, "It felt to me like we had a three-shot lead with six holes to play and we turned to our opponent and said, 'Let's call it a tie.' "

Finally, the grooves debate was over – or so it appeared. In truth, the controversy would continue to haunt the game for nearly two decades.

*   *   *

In the aftermath of the suit, portraying victory was a matter of public relations spin. Ping ran a full-page ad that read: "The real winner is the game of golf."

"I don't think there is a winner or a loser," Beman told the media. "Clearly, in order to reach an accommodation like this, everybody has to give a little."

It didn't take long for revisionist history to begin. On its own weekly television program, "Inside the PGA Tour," the Tour made no mention of withdrawing its ban on U-grooves. Instead it declared it had "achieved its goals" in settling the litigation. "This is a new form of goal achievement," *Golf Digest's* Marcia Chambers wrote.

Overall, the media branded the Tour the loser. "It's always bothered me because we really didn't lose," Moorhouse said.

A *Golf Digest* editorial opinion wrote that "Deane blinked and Karsten winked," and the settlement allowed Beman to turn "a potential disaster into a mere defeat."

Steve Pike, writing in *Golfweek*, crowned Ping the victor, noting that ultimately it was the Tour's insurance company that shelled out "in the $9 million range," according to Finchem. "Winners never pay," Pike concluded.

In 2005, Hannigan skewered Beman, penning one of the harshest critiques: "If that was a victory, then Manuel Noriega kicked the hell out of the United States when we invaded Panama."

Through it all, Beman never entertained a second thought

about the way he pursued the case. Not surprisingly, his interpretation of the settlement differs vastly: "We finally did prevail, from the standpoint that the suit was settled and there was full acknowledgement from Ping that we have authority to make our own rules," he said in a 2005 *Golf Digest* interview. "That was an important principle."

Whatever victories the sides claimed, the triumphs rang hollow. Solheim was nearly 82 years old at the time of the settlement. Soon after, he introduced the Ping Zing2, which turned out to be the last model of irons he designed. Kirk Triplett won the Nissan Open with them the week Solheim passed away in 2000.

During its legal wrangling with the USGA and Tour, Ping missed market trends and reacted too slowly to technological advancements, John Solheim conceded. In particular, it converted late to metal and titanium woods, which exploded into one of the game's most lucrative equipment categories. Its market share tumbled and new competitors grabbed a foothold.

Some say Ping has never recovered fully. Ely Callaway – whose company scored with the 1990 introduction of a line of oversized titanium drivers and metal woods dubbed Big Bertha – often claimed Callaway Golf never would have succeeded if it wasn't for those five years when Ping was engrossed in controversy. "That's when Ely said he built his company," said Jim Colbert, who switched from Ping to Callaway equipment during his Senior Tour career.

The damage from the draining litigation ran deep. John Solheim said his relationship with his father fractured during the ordeal: "There was an edge after the USGA agreement."

Even after the lawsuit settled, Beman didn't give up the fight. The equipment advisory committee was formed, and approved by the Tour's board on May 18, 1993. In a confidential memorandum to Tour players, Beman confirmed that they might consider the U-groove issue again. He hinted that any action might ignite another bout with Ping's lawyers.

"If the tournament policy board deems it appropriate to further consider the groove issue, any new PGA Tour rule would have to address the issue of spin rate by regulating other groove dimensions," Beman wrote.

Indeed, he intended to act aggressively. The Tour had initiated its own ball testing under Beman. In 1993 and 1994, the board budgeted $250,000 annually and hired Braly to develop a prototype ball-testing machine that could also be used to test grooves. "Could this be an end-run around the settlement?" *Golf Digest's* Chambers speculated in the July 1993 issue.

But on March 1, 1994, Beman resigned as commissioner, and to his surprise, the Tour never followed through with his plan. Beman's equipment committee was never utilized properly. Before he knew it, the Tour donated the golf ball testing devices Braly invented to the USGA, where they collected dust.

Backing off on the equipment front was the type of indecision Beman, a man of stubborn determination who set the highest standards for himself, lived his life to avoid. "Surprised is inadequate," Beman said. "I was disappointed. It was inconceivable to me that the Tour wouldn't proceed. We spent all this money and we knew we were right. The proof was there for the finding.

"Had I known, I never would've retired."

In the cold light of the years that followed, Beman witnessed the game he loves transformed by technology. It turned out to be his biggest regret.

*   *   *

Deane Beman was sitting at home in Ponte Vedra Beach, Fla., just three miles from Tour headquarters when the phone rang. It was 2008, and Tour commissioner Tim Finchem was calling. He wanted Beman to be one of the first to know that the USGA was about to announce a rules change that affected club grooves. Beman's face stretched with concern. Grooves – it was a subject for which Beman still burned with conviction. He asked his former right-hand man to read him excerpts of the forthcoming press release.

"The revisions are designed to restore the challenge of playing shots to the green from the rough by reducing backspin on those shots," read the Aug. 16, 2008 announcement. "We believe that these changes will increase the challenge of the game at the Tour level, while having a very small effect on the play of most golfers." The rule would debut in 2010 on Tour, and apply to clubs with more than 30 degrees of loft, or anything with more loft than a typical 5-iron.

Shortly thereafter, Beman placed the receiver back on its cradle. Concern turned to relief, then produced a smile. In effect, the USGA was going to turn back the clock in its belated attempt to regulate equipment technology, which radically has changed the way top modern golfers play the game.

When word spread, calls started to pour in to Beman from golf writers who had lived through the "groove wars" that raged during the late 1980s and early '90s. Always looking to stoke new flames even in old controversies, the friendly chats boiled down to the same question, "Did Beman feel vindicated?"

Beman chewed on that question as if it was cud. If nothing else, Beman never was one to mince words. But this was too important an issue to allow himself to be drawn into a process that finally looked like it would get sorted out after more than 20 years of infighting among the USGA, Tour and golf manufacturers, particularly Ping.

"No, I don't feel vindicated," he answered. "This wasn't ever about me. It was about the game of golf and how it would be played in the future. It was about doing the right thing regardless of the cost in time, money or popularity. It was a bedrock issue."

But Beman couldn't resist delivering a parting shot.

"I felt more disappointed in the leadership of the USGA and the Tour for failing their responsibility for all these years to preserve and protect the game I care so much about," he chided. "Because they failed to plug that little hole 'the size of a human hair,' the floodgates eroded. The great players and great ball strikers like Hogan, Nicklaus, Trevino and Norman weep for what it once meant to be a 'shot maker.' "

* * *

It was a typical cold, snowy, January day in 2001 when Arnold Palmer visited the USGA's headquarters in Far Hills, N.J. Palmer toured the Georgian mansion there known as Golf House and visited the equipment test center, where he met the USGA's senior technical director, Dick Rugge, for the first time.

It wasn't long before Palmer wagged his right index finger in front of Rugge's face as if he was giving him a stern lecture and said, "The biggest mistake the USGA ever made was allowing U-grooves in the game."

Palmer was Rugge's childhood idol, yet at that moment, barely six months on the job, Rugge's initial reaction was to inform him he was wrong. "I didn't say that to him," Rugge remembered. "I started to, quite honestly, but realized whom I was talking to and I wasn't going to get into a debate. He certainly knows more about golf than I do."

Instead Rugge politely told Palmer his staff would look into it. "It wasn't a throwaway line," Rugge said. "I was sincere."

Recalled Palmer: "It was a short conversation. He didn't agree with me at first, but after doing a little research, he came around."

Rugge had conversations with several current Tour players. They echoed Palmer's sentiment that allowing U-grooves minimized the importance of driving accuracy in professional golf.

Beman's disgust had marinated for more than a decade. On the eve of the USGA's 2005 annual meeting, Beman sent a letter to USGA president Fred Ridley detailing his concerns about technology's effect on distance and scoring while questioning the USGA's resolve to do anything about it.

"In the next 15 years a new generation of Tour players routinely will be able to drive the ball 330-360 yards, rendering all courses obsolete," he wrote. "Is the USGA going to exercise its traditional mandate to protect and preserve the game of golf? I hope so. If you are unwilling to do so, it is imperative that you make it clear to all concerned that you are dropping the banner we all depended on you to carry and support those who have the courage to pick it up and firmly place it in the ground once again. The time for equivocating has passed."

Unbeknownst to Beman, Rugge proved willing to revisit a contentious topic. He uncovered mounting evidence to support the players' claims. As a result, the USGA publicly announced plans to study grooves at the association's 2005 annual meeting in Santa Barbara, Calif. "We want people to know we're not sitting on our hands," Rugge noted at the time.

Not long after the USGA started evaluating grooves in

earnest, Rugge invited Beman to Far Hills. "He said, 'Deane, (grooves are) the most provable thing we've ever studied here,' " Beman recalled.

On April 11, 2006, the USGA posted an article on its website by Rugge titled "Myths About Golf Equipment and Performance" regarding nine commonly held perceptions about the impact of technology on golf. The first eight were false and Rugge debunked each tersely. The ninth myth: Accuracy off the tee isn't as important as it used to be on the Tour. "That's no myth," Rugge wrote. "It's true. During the '80s driving accuracy was almost as strong a predictor of money-winning as putting. Today it has fallen to the lowest level ever."

In August 2006, the USGA and R&A sent a technical report summarizing the progress of their research to golf club manufacturers. An additional update was published a few months later. On Feb. 27, 2007, after two years of research, lab tests and number crunching, the USGA and R&A issued two reports totaling nearly 300 pages. Their joint-study of spin generation included 30 tables of data and 140 separate graphs. They concluded driving accuracy on the Tour no longer equated to low scoring because golfers were able to hit shots out of the rough and make the ball stop on the green thanks to the size and sharpness of grooves in irons. Rugge asserted that his team benefited from having 25 years of Tour data to use as a baseline. With the introduction in 2001 of Shotlink, which collects and disseminates scoring and statistical data based on every shot by every Tour competitor in real-time, the Tour has measured player performance based on a remarkable number of parameters. (Ping researched the Tour's Shotlink data and discovered that the top-10 players don't play in as many events, which the company says skews data. Ping still maintains there is no correlation between grooves and "anything.")

The reaction to the rule was wide-ranging. Some claimed it was a make-up call for the perceived mishandling of the groove situation by the USGA in the late '80s. "It's like a chair falling off the Titanic," remarked Jack Nicklaus, who has long campaigned for a distance rollback.

Perhaps no one applauded the news with greater fervor than Beman. In a truly ironic twist, the evidence and proof

Beman long searched for would not come from the team he put in place at the Tour, but from the USGA – the very organization that undercut his attempts to rein in technology.

"It took real courage on Rugge's part to embark on any sort of grooves test," Beman said. "I imagine there were groans in the room the first time he mentioned to either the executive committee or staff people that he intended to pursue and resurrect this ugly child."

John Solheim, on the other hand, thought the groove controversy was a dead topic. It wasn't. The Ping family dreaded another fight, a feeling best expressed by the company's outside counsel, Van Engelhoven, who said, "Soldiers don't say, 'Oh great, we get to go fight the war again.' "

Two years later, in a joint proposal with the R&A, the USGA announced U-grooves wouldn't be banned, but clubs would need to meet specifications reducing the size of the cavity of the groove so they performed like V-shaped grooves.

Who says the USGA doesn't believe in mulligans? The 2010 grooves rule essentially returned clubface channels to early 1980s configurations. It marked the first rollback in equipment since the move to a lighter ball in 1931. E. Michael Johnson, *Golf World's* senior equipment editor, likened it to the NFL bringing back leather helmets. Others ridiculed it, saying it was akin to locking the gate after the horse had left the barn.

What it brought was a fresh round of controversy. Even before the rule was finalized, Solheim had written a letter on July 31, 2007, to the USGA and Tour reminding them of their agreements, and warning of the possibility that players might circumvent a new groove rule and use the pre-1990 Ping Eye2 irons. The Tour's out-of-court settlement with Ping, in 1993, and the USGA agreement grandfathering in pre-1990 Ping Eye2 clubs superseded the new regulation.

Solheim's warning proved prescient. In January 2010, Tour pros Dean Wilson and John Daly used pre-1990 Eye2 wedges during the Sony Open in Hawaii. Several others did so at the Bob Hope Classic the following week. Inspired by reading about this loophole, Phil Mickelson dug a 20-year-old Eye2 wedge from his garage, inserted it in his bag at the Farmers Insurance Open in San Diego, and all hell broke loose. Late last year, the USGA declared grooves of a prototype set of Callaway irons Mickelson intended to use nonconforming because they "violated the spirit of the rule." Many interpreted Mickelson's use of the Eye2 as his disapproval of the new USGA regulation.

"I feel like the Eye2 grooves don't conform, but they're approved for play," Mickelson said during his pre-tournament press conference. "All that matters is it's OK under the rules of golf."

Not everyone agreed. Scott McCarron, a member of the Tour's players advisory council, told *The San Francisco Chronicle*, "It's cheating, and I'm appalled Phil has put it in play."

This touched off a war of words. In a post-round interview on CBS, Mickelson hinted at legal action for being accused of cheating. "We all have our opinions on the matter, but a line was crossed and I just was publicly slandered," Mickelson said. "And because of that, I'll have to let other people handle that."

McCarron issued a statement reiterating his stance against the Eye2 clubs, but clarifying that he did not specifically call his colleague "a cheater." McCarron apologized in person to Mickelson, and the golfers spoke for 10 minutes clearing the air the following week at the Northern Trust Open in Los Angeles.

On March 8, a resolution was reached. Effective March 29, Ping waived its rights that prevented the Tour from prohibiting the use – on all its tours, including Champions and Nationwide – of Eye2 irons and wedges that didn't meet the 2010 condition of competition. (Amateurs who play under USGA jurisdiction still could use the clubs.)

"The Eye2 was a sideshow," Solheim said, explaining why he volunteered to close the loophole. "The rule needed to stand on its own to prove that we really didn't need it."

The memory of what his father had endured and how it fractured their relationship also factored into his decision, Solheim added. "I didn't want that to happen again," he said, relating his experience with his father to his relationship with his son, John K., who designed Ping's new conforming groove wedges.

"For the foreseeable future the question of the groove configuration is settled," Finchem said.

At the 2010 Masters, Beman and Solheim crossed paths. Beman stopped Solheim. He shook his hand and thanked him for making a decision he termed "for the good of the game."

"One of my favorite sayings is, 'It's never too late to do the right thing.' And that's exactly what (John Solheim) did," Beman said.

The early evidence suggests the groove change was much ado about nothing. The USGA's Rugge told *Golf World* in June 2010 that it was too early to draw conclusions. "One year doth not a trend make," said Rugge. "One year can be just an anomalous spike in the data. Three years showing the same thing is not a spike." He reiterated this point at the 2011 USGA Annual Meeting in February. But as of early 2011, the new groove rule was roundly panned by the media.

"The groove rule is proving to be one of the least relevant – especially for the trouble it caused – rules ever enacted by a sports body," said Jaime Diaz in a roundtable discussion of writers in late 2010 on golfdigest.com.

Golf World's Michael Johnson noted that he and Diaz rarely agreed on equipment issues, but on this occasion he concurred, "It's been a futile exercise."

The last word on the topic belonged to *Golf World* executive editor Ron Sirak. "I think it was a smokescreen to create the illusion of doing something while not addressing the real issue," he added, "sort of like airport security lines."

*   *   *

When the USGA settled with Ping, USGA executive director David Fay warned, "If any manufacturer believes this is a road map on how to get, in the future, a piece of equipment into play, they are mistaken. It's a road map to nowhere."

The resulting litigation and subsequent out-of-court settlement had a far greater impact on the game than any performance enhancement offered by grooves. Ever since Ping forced the USGA to accept its terms, the ruling body's willingness to use its power to legislate equipment design has been compromised, Beman said. The specter of another potential lawsuit has opened the floodgates to a technological revolution in clubs and balls, he said. He added: "The USGA made a choice to protect its treasury instead of the game."

Beginning in 1996, the average driving distance on Tour climbed at a rapid rate for several years. This surge coincided with the introduction of thin-faced metal drivers that had excessive "spring-like" effect. Thomas, who resigned from the USGA after 26 years in 2000, said Tour pros gained 25-30 yards between 1995 and 2003, "without any increase in skill." Beman lamented if only the USGA had the courage to admit its mistake in permitting U-grooves in 1984, then it would have lead to a more careful analysis of how other technological advancements would affect the game. "The USGA foolishly tried to undo its mistake by changing the way they measured grooves and got smacked down pretty good," Beman said.

Even if the USGA had won its suit, the problem wouldn't have been solved, he argued. While the USGA v. Karsten Co. amounted to the "width of a human hair," the real issue was that a U-groove doubles the area available to channel moisture from between the ball and the clubface compared with a V-groove.

"That is what the Tour was going to present the jury at trial," Beman said. "That is what the USGA belatedly proved in its testing that led to the groove rule change in 2010. And that is why U-grooves make a difference.

"Had the USGA sucked it up with grooves, it would've done it with balls and oversized drivers, too."

If so, Beman believes today's equipment wouldn't be pushing the laws of physics in a battle to make golf shots fly longer and straighter. Golf would be played differently today. Shotmaking would still matter. "They wouldn't be playing with Prince tennis racquets for drivers and prescription balls," Beman said. "A lot of these guys would be cutting greens or working in pro shops."

He fondly recalls when golf used to have a wonderful blend of distance and direction, short and long game, finesse and strength. That balance, he said, is out of whack. It has shifted to a "bomb and gouge" mentality in which players hit the ball as far as they can off the tee. Accuracy is an afterthought. Hall of Famer Vijay Singh turned this philosophy into an art form, wining nine times in 2004 while ranking No. 149 in driving accuracy.

"Can you imagine Ben Hogan playing golf and not having a care in the world about hitting the fairway?" Beman asked. "He's rolling over in his grave."

Beman likened the change in golf to if baseball allowed aluminum bats in Major League Baseball. "The first thing that would happen is that a few pitchers would get killed," Beman said. "They would have to move the pitcher's mound back toward second base – kind of like the new back tees in golf. It would give the batter just enough extra time to knock it out of the park. Billions would have to be spent to build new stadiums. It would be called baseball, but it would be a different game.

"That's what happened to golf with all the new technology in balls and clubs. And we wonder why golf costs so much to play and takes so long to get around 18 holes."

The deck, he continued, is stacked in favor of the player who happens to come out of the womb bigger and stronger. In the process, courses have been stretched like rubber bands or rendered obsolete. Thicker rough, deeper bunkers and slicker greens are required to protect par, all to the detriment of the average golfer who certainly doesn't need more challenges.

"These conditions have driven millions of golfers away from the game," Beman argued. "Unintended consequences can happen when you make a mistake, and it also can happen by failing to take action."

STEPPING DOWN

"It wasn't supposed to be a life sentence," Deane Beman told the press corps.

Just hours earlier on the morning of Feb. 28, 1994, Beman circled a meeting room at Doral Resort & Country Club in south Florida and without saying a word distributed a two-page letter of resignation to the Tour's policy board. "It certainly wasn't on the agenda," Beman later said.

On the 7,305th day after taking office and two days before the 932nd Tour event of his tenure, Beman announced he would not seek an extension of his contract when it expired in December 1995. The timing was no coincidence. Beman did so on the 20th anniversary of his appointment as Tour commissioner.

Beman's decision surprised most everyone. Some players, such as Ben Crenshaw, found out when a Tour official handed them a memo as they finished playing their pro-am rounds at Doral. Beman shared his thoughts on the matter exclusively with his wife, Judy. They agreed it was time.

His job and his life had become indistinguishable. When asked if he tracked the number of miles he traveled annually, he answered, "If I did I would've quit long ago." Judy figured out he was on the road 90 percent of the time during his final full year as commissioner. This was, in part, because Beman invoked a policy to visit each tournament on all three tours at least once every three years. He averaged more than 250 days a year passing through a blur of airports, hotel lobbies, and tournament functions as part of the job. As a result, he developed tennis elbow in the mid 1980s – his doctor said – from lugging his overloaded briefcase to meetings.

Beman worked relentlessly. His executive staff set their watches by Beman's 8 o'clock meetings (5 a.m. for him whenever he operated from the west coast). If he drove his staff like an army, he drove himself like a slave. Late in his tenure, Beman and Tim Finchem, his deputy commissioner, were en route to another meeting when Beman observed that it was the first time in the last 20 years that he could remember waking and noticing that the first digit on the alarm clock was greater than five. "We'd be driving back from the airport at 1:30 a.m., and I might start to doze off," Finchem said. "He'd say, 'Hey Tim,' and whenever I heard those words I knew there was a new idea coming at me. So I'd sit up, and we'd talk about it for another half an hour."

Whatever strain and agony Beman endured, it was worth it to reach this day. But now he wanted his life back. "I neglected things I wanted to do," Beman said. "I decided I only have one life. I thought about retiring a few years earlier, but there were some things I still wanted to carry through."

One of those projects was a place to salute the PGA Tour's finest. Years before, on Sept. 11, 1974, Beman participated in the grand opening of the World Golf Hall of Fame in Pinehurst, N.C. In what *The New York Times* called "the coup of the year," President Gerald R. Ford attended the ceremony and dedication of the building. Two days after Ford was sworn in as president following Richard Nixon's resignation that August, an aide of Ford's phoned to scratch his scheduled appearance at the hall's grand opening. But when Ford caught wind of the cancellation, another call was made with a question of national security: "Is Ben Hogan really going to be there?" the aide asked. Don Collett, the Hall's president, confirmed Hogan would be present for his induction. In that case, Ford would be there, too. Someone had the good sense to seat "The First Golfer" next to Hogan.

For a President with a much-maligned golf game, Ford lived a golfer's dream. He played the first three holes in the company of Jack Nicklaus, Arnold Palmer, Gary Player, and Beman, outdriving the last three off the first tee at Pinehurst No. 2 (only in his late-night dreams could he have hoped to smoke one by

Nicklaus). The President played the middle stanza with Byron Nelson, Gene Sarazen and Patty Berg, and rounded out the side with Sam Snead. With Hogan watching from among the gallery of Secret Servicemen, Ford carded 48 with a closing par, according to published reports.

The inaugural class of 13 inductees honored eight living inductees and five players posthumously. "On one side of the speaker's rostrum were Hogan, Snead and Nelson, in that order, like a row of retired bankers," wrote Dan Jenkins, "while on the other side were Nicklaus, Palmer and Player. Beyond, were Sarazen and Berg. And in memory were Bobby Jones, Walter Hagen, Francis Ouimet, Harry Vardon, and Babe Zaharias."

Berg was the first to be enshrined at the outdoor ceremony. Sarazen soon followed. He gave a light-hearted reflection on those Hall of Famers no longer alive. "I feel lonely up here," he said, reflecting on the absence of his contemporaries Jones, Hagen, and Ouimet. "They're waiting on the tee in another Hall of Fame, expecting me to complete the foursome. But I keep telling them, 'You better go ahead and start, boys. I'll catch you on the back nine.' "

When Hogan delivered his induction speech, he noted a place to celebrate the game was long overdue. "Golf has needed a Hall of Fame for some 50 to 75 years," he said, "and the World Golf Hall of Fame is a tribute to golf and to those of us who play it."

No one in golf really liked the idea that a company interested in selling land and condominiums built and established the Hall of Fame, noted Jenkins, but there didn't happen to be one until Bill Maurer erected the $2.5 million, white-columned shrine.

"Everybody else had a shot at doing it for 600 years and nobody did," said Maurer, head of the Diamondhead Corp., which bought Pinehurst from the Tufts family. "If somebody else wants to build another one, fine. But I like the score I'm in the clubhouse with."

In what proved to be a bad omen for the Hall's future, its leader, Collett, suffered a heart attack just two days after the Hall opened to the general public. (He did recover.) Before long, the Hall itself hemorrhaged money. Its first signs of trouble surfaced when Diamondhead foundered. The company had larger problems to resolve and ultimately went bankrupt, but not before pumping more than $3 million into the Hall – without making a meaningful dent in debts, according to *Golfweek*. Several banks took over. When they searched for a new owner in November 1983, Beman suggested the Tour and PGA assume control of the Hall as co-owners, and offered to stage an annual fundraising tournament there each year. But the PGA had different plans. Its executive director at the time, Lou King, swooped in and took sole possession of the Hall, he said, as a "sacred trust." King looked like a hero. "The Hall of Fame is the PGA's finest public endeavor," wrote Charley Stine in *Golfweek*.

The real reason the PGA stepped in? "We didn't want Deane to have it," said Mark Kizziar, PGA president in 1983-84.

There would be no public reproach from the Tour, but Beman stewed. "I was more than a little disappointed in the duplicity of the PGA jumping in and grabbing what was supposed to be a joint venture for the good of the game," Beman conceded.

The PGA assumed management of the Hall in 1984, along with its collection of golf artifacts and memorabilia, the Hall of Fame building and the 17-acre site on which it was located. The PGA had thought it had snapped up an asset. In reality, it had acquired a liability. "The Hall was bleeding big bucks," Beman said, "and the PGA didn't have a plan for it."

Writer Bob Drum, who had worked as the public relations man for Diamondhead, contended that the Hall failed because it was situated in an out-of-the-way place and not in walking distance of anything but the fourth green of Pinehurst No. 2. "The Hall of Fame in Pinehurst was doomed the day it was built," he wrote.

Drum recounted overhearing a conversation between golfers Fuzzy Zoeller and Lee Trevino on Pinehurst's fourth green during a friendly round. "Why would they put the Hall of Fame where nobody could get to it?" Zoeller wondered.

"They might as well put it on I-95. At least they would get a lot of traffic there," Trevino quipped.

The Merry Mex turned out to be half right. As Trevino suggested, another attempt to build a shrine to golf took root along Interstate-95, 8 miles north of St. Augustine and 22 miles south of Jacksonville, Fla., where an estimated 50,000 cars passed by each day. A swampy landscape would be transformed into a 75,000 square-foot monument of white brick and stucco. A 170-foot tall tower would stand sentinel. Its name? World Golf Village, a place where golf was more than just its middle name. It would be a way of life.

*   *   *

The roots of the Tour's Hall of Fame project date back to August 1983. If the PGA was going to run its own Hall, then the Tour would just build a better one of its own. Beman sought to build it somewhere in Northeast Florida.

Rattled by the thought of a rival, the PGA expressed strong objections. Nevertheless, Beman forged ahead with the Tour's board, which approved the filing of a separate 501-c3 for a PGA Tour Hall of Fame, and an agreement with the city of Jacksonville to build the facility at the intersection of I-95 and J. Turner Butler Boulevard. The land deal, however, cratered. Instead, the location was transformed into a thriving shopping and entertainment complex.

Next, Beman tried to build just south of Jacksonville on a 2,500-acre site owned by a trust, but complications associated with zoning, financing, and constructing an interchange off I-95 proved insurmountable. These false starts, however, didn't deter Beman. "My feeling was you don't fail until you quit and stop trying," Beman said. "When you decide that a project is important and is the right thing to do, you just find a way to make it work."

When the search for land resumed, the Tour briefly flirted with building its shrine near Walt Disney World in Orlando. Some thought the potential of tapping into a robust tourist market made sense, but Beman believed a PGA Tour Hall of Fame needed its own identity.

"He didn't want rollercoasters," said Charlie Zink, the Tour's executive vice president and chief financial officer at the time. "He said, 'This is golf, and it needs to be honored. A golf Hall of Fame can't have mouse ears.' "

It took several years to secure an agreement, but once done, it resulted in the biggest golf course development deal the Tour ever made. Spearheaded by Vernon Kelly, president of PGA Tour Golf Course Properties, the Tour reached an agreement in December 1991 with Billy Dunavant of Memphis-based Dunavant Enterprises, the largest cotton broker in the world.

This vision called for transforming 6,300 acres of swampland into a Hall of Fame, golf courses and golf academy, headquarters for PGA Tour Productions, and residential, resort, and entertainment facilities. Beman and Kelly negotiated a deal with the developer that paid an upfront $1 million royalty and provided for a $12 million subsidy for building the Hall of Fame facility. It also guaranteed $8 million per course to build a 36-hole complex on 400 acres that was given to the Tour, and a royalty on gross property sales. Then the Tour hammered out a separate deal with the state of Florida, which contributed a $2 million dollar annual tax credit over 25 years, or $50 million, through the state's new stadium bill (cleverly expanded to include a sports Hall of Fame). All told, Beman had $80 million at his disposal to build a shrine for Tour players.

Over lunch at the White House, he also convinced U.S. secretary of transportation Sam Skinner to authorize a new highway interchange for the Hall, explaining this wasn't just another real estate development; this would be the home of a nationally recognized monument to golf. Experts predicted one million visitors a year.

Beman read all the lofty attendance projections – based on the number of cars zipping past that corridor of I-95 – and hoped they proved accurate. If road warriors with clubs in their trunks heading to the golf meccas of Sarasota, Jupiter, and Naples, Fla., stopped for one night and visited the Hall, business would be booming. But Beman refused to rely on sunny forecasts. "I wanted to build an asset for golf, not another liability for us to feed," he said.

"There's probably few better ways to go broke than to build a Hall of Fame because it's something that represents your brand," Kelly explained. "So you build it to the highest expense and then you charge the lowest amount to attract the widest audience."

Beman planned for a modest Hall of Fame financed by the developer's $12 million contribution. The Tour would own and operate the two golf courses. The operating income from the golf facilities, along with modest ticket and souvenir sales, would bankroll the Hall's operation. Under Beman's plan, the Hall of Fame should be self-sustaining. The State of Florida's $50 million provided a long-range safety valve. But soon the project grew in scope.

"Now that we had the site and financing in hand, I thought it might be the last chance to make the original concept of a sustainable World Golf Hall of Fame become a reality," Beman said. "I asked myself is it the right thing to do to keep this once-in-a-lifetime project for ourselves, or should we try to share it with the entire community of golf?"

The prospect of bringing the industry together in his biggest deal proved an undeniable attraction. First Beman called his counterpart at the LPGA, Charlie Mechem, and asked the LPGA to join the endeavor. Flabbergasted, Mechem choked back laughter and said, "Deane, this is a historic moment. This is the first time the commissioner of the PGA Tour ever has said to the commissioner of the LPGA Tour, 'I need your help.' "

The LPGA Hall of Fame was founded in 1951, but no physical structure existed. From Patty Berg to Nancy Lopez, the tour's greats – who never had a place to tell their history – gave their immediate and enthusiastic endorsement for the project. One by one, the rest of golf's governing bodies supported the project, which was to be governed by a board of directors of the World Golf Village Foundation (later shortened to World Golf Foundation), a non-profit formed by the Tour. On March 2, 1993, the board approved the World Golf Village and transferred to the Foundation (at the time made up of the LPGA, PGA Tour, R&A, and USGA) the 440-acre site and rights to the state and developer contributed money, which amounted to over $100 million in assets.

Meanwhile, the PGA still was considering its involvement. In the ensuing years, the World Golf Hall of Fame in Pinehurst never achieved financial stability and teetered on collapse again. Its attendance spiked only on rainy days. PGA CEO Jim Awtrey, who inherited this albatross when he replaced King, said the Hall lost $500,000 annually. On July 27, 1995, more than two years after Beman expanded his vision of a PGA Tour Hall of Fame into an industry initiative, the PGA pledged its support and transferred the use of the name World Golf Hall of Fame to the project. "All we were doing was writing checks," Awtrey said.

At the same time, PGA president Gary Schaal announced that the PGA would close the Pinehurst facility on Dec. 1. The land, which was zoned for recreation and cemetery, reverted back to Pinehurst's ownership (ClubCorp of America). "Perhaps a fitting end for a concept that died a slow death," wrote Dick Taylor in *Golfweek*.

And so began the most unique collaboration among golf organizations to support a Hall under one roof – a facility that would honor greats from Tommy Armour to Babe Zaharias. On Aug. 7, 1996, a groundbreaking ceremony was held at World Golf Village. "Men and women, amateurs and professionals, Americans and international stars and non-playing contributors too: No other Hall of Fame anywhere encompasses such a broad spectrum," said Ruffin Beckwith, the first CEO of the World Golf Village and former executive director of the World Golf Hall of Fame.

Construction of the World Golf Village began in earnest two years after Beman retired, but many years after he visualized the concept of a museum and Hall of Fame to encompass golf on a global basis. Opening weekend, May 16-18, 1998, celebrated the building as much as its members.

On a steamy Monday afternoon, reminiscent of the day the Hall had opened in Pinehurst nearly 25 years before, the induction ceremony served as the main event. They grandfathered in 71 members from Pinehurst and the LPGA Hall of Fame to form the foundation of the new facility. Invited guests and fans of the game filled seats and bleachers around the Hall of Fame's "pool of unity."

The Hall of Famers, dressed in blazers and khaki pants – men with Hall of Fame logoed ties, the women with matching scarves – crossed the stage one at a time to be re-inducted. Arnold Palmer, one of 23 returning inductees, hitched his pants before walking to his seat and taking a bow. JoAnne Carner flashed a dimpled smile. Paul Runyan blew kisses from his fingertips. Carol Mann gave a beauty queen's wave. New inductees Johnny Miller and Nick Faldo stood and applauded

"The Slammer," Sam Snead. "The Squire" Gene Sarazen, 96, waved his bucket cap and drew the longest standing ovation of all. Yes, Hagen, Jones, and Ouimet still waited for him to join them as their fourth on the back nine.

Palmer, Gary Player, and Kathy Whitworth, representing the LPGA, offered what amounted to a benediction. Then an honor that stays with a golfer forever was bestowed upon the Hall's two newest members, Faldo and Miller. The moniker "Hall of Famer" eliminated subjective doubt of their greatness.

The retired commissioners, Beman and Mechem, sat next to each other that day and shared in the satisfaction of what Beman's vision had wrought. Getting the Hall built was a victory in itself, but the failure to execute Beman's master plan resulted in a money pit. The "build it and they will come" mantra proved no more successful in the Sunshine State. In its first year, the World Golf Village drew less than half of the 1 million visitors projected to visit the complex. "Those cars may have a husband who likes golf," Kelly said, "but too often his wife doesn't care quite as much and his kids just want to get to Disney."

The World Golf Hall of Fame itself has suffered its share of growing pains. Like its predecessor, rainy days provided the biggest jolt to attendance. Far more tickets were purchased to see movies at the adjoining IMAX Theater than learn about the greats of the game.

What happened to Beman's original master plan of building an asset, not a liability? For starters, they didn't heed his advice. After Beman retired, deals were cut. Compromises were made. Shopping and eating establishments were shuttered or never opened at all. A third-party company built and owned the golf courses, stripping the Foundation of a key revenue stream in Beman's plan. And the Hall used the $16 million originally earmarked for the courses to build a much larger facility up front instead of in two or three phases as Beman intended. In its current form, the Hall is the financial albatross Beman's plan was designed to avoid, losing more money than it once did in Pinehurst under the PGA, according to the Hall's annual nonprofit filing. "We were probably overly ambitious," Kelly said.

The First Tee program also has complicated the pictured,

Beman said. A worthy initiative designed to introduce golf and its character-building qualities to young people and minorities in particular, The First Tee has consumed the lion's share of the World Golf Foundation's financial support that otherwise might have been allocated to the Hall. The First Tee has touched the lives of more than 3 million young people. "Who can say this is a mistake?" Beman said. "There are a lot of smart people at the Tour, and they will figure out how to make the Hall of Fame work."

It might be tempting to grade the Hall an "incomplete" or to assume Beman regrets ever breaking ground on the project. But that misses the point. Beckwith, the man who oversaw the Hall's opening, offers a different perspective.

"I've often been asked why would any organization go through so much pain and anguish if there was never going to be a pot of gold at the end of the rainbow? The answer is simple. That's not why they built it," he said. "The Hall of Fame exists for one reason. Because they could. Deane had the vision to do something for the game and for the players. It's a place to celebrate the game."

* * *

On the day Joe Dey announced he would not seek a new contract as commissioner, the board approved his brainchild – creating what became known as The Players Championship. For those who like symmetry, Beman went out in similar style. When he decided to step down nearly 20 years later, the board approved what would become the capstone of his legacy – The Presidents Cup, an international team competition.

It all began when the Four Tours Championship, a made-for-TV team competition held in Japan and featuring representatives of the PGA Tour, European Tour, Japan Golf Tour, and Australasian Tour, was canceled in 1992 when its sponsor pulled out abruptly. The event had burned through three sponsors already, and a replacement couldn't be found.

As soon as Beman learned of its demise, he advanced the concept of The Presidents Cup. He instinctively understood that a new event never would transcend the history of the

Ryder Cup. How could it? But a new event could earn instant credibility by latching onto the prestige of the highest office in the land. Beman secured the support of Presidents Ford and Bush. With their seal of approval, Beman accelerated his plan to launch The Presidents Cup.

"This was a vacuum that was going to be filled and we better fill it first," Beman said.

Indeed, a race seemed imminent to determine who would capitalize faster on an international event. On Dec. 21, 1993, several months in advance of the public unveiling of The Presidents Cup, IMG issued a short press release with plans to pit the holder of the Ryder Cup (but not restricted to the same team members) against a team from the Southern Hemisphere – consisting of Australia, New Zealand, southern Africa, South America and the Pacific Islands – in a biennial "major international golf tournament." No date, site, or formal name for the matches was announced, but it was planned to debut in late 1994 under the tentative title of the Hemisphere Cup. A $2 million purse was reported. According to IMG's Alastair Johnston, the concept had the backing of a consortium of international television companies, including ABC Sports in the U.S., Sky Television in Great Britain, and Star Television in Hong Kong.

The IMG-backed Hemisphere Cup and Tour-conceived Presidents Cup were designed to be staged in the non-Ryder Cup year and take advantage of world-class players such as Australian Greg Norman and Zimbabwe's Nick Price, who were ineligible for the Ryder Cup, which is restricted to players born in the U.S. and Europe. Beman realized that part of his membership could never participate in the Ryder Cup. There was a cry of "What about the rest of us?" The phrase stuck, and the U.S. opponent became known as "the rest of the world."

It was no secret that Beman had long sought to control the Ryder Cup. Until the 1990s, the Ryder Cup was a public relations asset and a financial liability. A student of world golf, Beman foresaw America's dominance of golf ending.

"The rest of the world was awakening to golf," Beman said, "and I thought that type of international event...frankly, I thought if I could get control of the Ryder Cup, I envisioned making it a three-way match with the rest of the world."

Among his few laments, Beman never could negotiate rights to the Ryder Cup from the PGA.

Tour executives quietly touted The Presidents Cup concept and over the next six months studied the feasibility of such an event. When the Tour's board returned from a lunch break at its August 1993 meeting at the Hyatt Regency Milwaukee hotel, they discovered a covered easel at the front of the room. Soon the drapes dropped, revealing The Presidents Cup logo and site. "That's the way Deane worked," said player director Rick Fehr. "He took it as far as he could without our approval."

There was a reason behind Beman's tactics. If he suspected an initiative had the potential to be delayed or derailed by the PGA, Beman often conducted much of the preliminary work behind the scenes individually. He would lobby player and independent directors individually – often during dinner the night before a meeting – prior to approaching the board collectively.

"That was one of the problems with having a fox in the chicken coop," Beman explained of having three PGA directors on the Tour's 10-man board (reduced to one PGA member representative in 1993).

On this occasion, the PGA clearly was angered. Awtrey harped on a clause in the revised Statement of Principles contract that in layman's terms said the Tour would never do anything to harm the Ryder Cup. "It was a serious vow by both parties," he said.

Awtrey dispatched a letter to Beman expressing his concern that The Presidents Cup violated the intent of their agreement. Nothing ever came of it. "It's lost in the archives somewhere," Awtrey said. "It took vision and real commitment by Deane to say, 'We're going to do it,' knowing full well that there was a contract there."

Beman offers a different perspective and dismisses the PGA's outrage as hypocritical behavior. "I didn't feel it would diminish the Ryder Cup. And it hasn't," Beman remarked.

"It's a curious thing that the PGA should object to the Presidents Cup because of their proprietary right in the Ryder Cup, but it so freely jumped into the Grand Slam of Golf after joining the Tour in a partnership for the World Series of Golf."

The final proposal was presented at the Tour's next board

meeting in March. Beman said it wasn't an easy sell. Even his staff wondered if overseeing an international exhibition was worth the trouble. On more than one occasion, deputy commissioner Tim Finchem asked him, "Are you really sure you want to do this?"

Beman was absolutely certain that the Presidents Cup was an important longterm project and insisted the Tour move forward. After polling the players, the Tour's board voted that net revenues from the event would be divided equally among the 24 participants. Each could designate a charity as the recipient of the proceeds. Player director Jay Haas joked if he made the team, he'd like to designate the Jan Haas window treatment fund, an obvious reference to his wife, as his worthy charity. Everyone shared a good laugh. But all kidding aside, the message was loud and clear: The players preferred a competition for pride, not profit. "It couldn't be just another big-money, made-for-television event," Beman said. "That's the last thing we needed."

The Tour's board conferred and voted. The Presidents Cup was approved over the PGA's objection by a tally of 8-2. By the time the event was held in September, Beman's tenure was over. It proved a perfect coda to his efforts to grow the game globally. (Beman also took great pride in his role as a board member of the International Golf Association in bringing golf's World Cup to Mission Hills Resort in China, the first major international golf event to be played there.) Beman expressed little regret over his role as an honorary observer at The Presidents Cup. "Tim (Finchem) did the hard work in the trenches to launch the first event," Beman said. "His staff did a hell of a job putting it together under a tight timeframe."

That was no exaggeration. The Tour's Henry Hughes remembered Finchem informing him in March that the Cup would be played in September. "All we were missing was a golf course, a sponsor, the format, and the field," Hughes said. "We had nothing."

Preparations emerged at a frenzied pace. Details of the event, format and dates were revealed April 13. The inaugural competition would be held Sept. 16-18, 1994, at the Robert Trent Jones Golf Club – a private course 35 miles west of the nation's capital – on Lake Manassas in Gainesville, Va. The 12-man international squad was made up of players from throughout the world who were not eligible for selection to the European Ryder Cup team. It consisted of the top 10 players from the Sony World Rankings following the conclusion of the World Series of Golf, and two additional players chosen by the team captain.

While the competition resembled the Ryder Cup, there were significant differences. Presidents Cup matches could not end in a tie, and daily pairings were determined at a press conference where the captains alternated choices rather than the Ryder Cup's blind draw. The Presidents Cup also featured three days of match play – four-ball, foursomes, and singles – with a total of 32 matches. (The matches have been contested over four days since 2000, and two additional matches were added beginning in 2003.)

Playing the first Cup outside of Washington D.C. and having Presidents Ford and Bush in attendance created international appeal. For the players, there was a White House dinner with President Clinton and a reception at the Australian Embassy. For the leadership of the game, it marked the first formal gathering of the heads of golf's professional governing bodies. The International Forum of PGA Tours offered a chance to discuss their individual problems and concerns, and the world schedule. It was more than a symbolic gesture. This meeting of the minds was instrumental in the formation of the International Federation of Tours, which became the joint-sanctioning body that gave birth to the World Golf Championships.

For fans of international golf, The Presidents Cup was beamed around the world. "I'm told this is going to be televised in 61 countries. I figure they'll be rooting for us in 60 of them," Zimbabwe's Price told the press.

Price played a key role in one of the more comical moments during the first Cup. To create an air of pomp and circumstance, the flag of every country represented in the competition waved in the wind above the procession. When Price looked for his country's colors, he discovered something amiss. He searched out Hughes, and with a voice of concern, said, "I can't believe what you've done. You're flying the wrong one for Zimbabwe."

Hughes face drooped like a limp flag. This couldn't be. His

staff had researched meticulously each one. But little did they know that Zimbabwe had made headlines for another coup the previous weekend. Price said, "We have one about every three months. That flag is now outdated." Overnight, the staff purchased the proper colors to fly.

A much more serious setback occurred when Norman withdrew at the last minute because of surgery complications. He appeared the final day to support his team as chief cheerleader.

Moreover, Duke Butler, tournament director of the competition, regretfully announced a two-hour fog delay in four, half-hour increments. This produced an inauspicious start. President Ford and golf legend Byron Nelson commiserated during the wait. When the first group finally teed off, Finchem quipped to the media gathered around the tee, "Well, we have history now. Balls are in the air."

There were memorable moments made on the course, too. Fred Couples lifted a 9-iron from a fairway bunker to within 18 inches of the cup to win his match over Price, 1-up. It clinched the Cup's winning point. It was a fitting climax to three days of spirited competition in which the U.S. prevailed 20-12 over an international side from various corners of the globe. "This event is here to stay," U.S. non-playing co-captain Paul Azinger said.

International captain David Graham may have said it best for all concerned at the closing ceremonies: "Ladies and gentlemen, it's been a blast. So let's do it again."

And they did, returning to Robert Trent Jones Club, two years later. In 1998, the Presidents Cup packed for Australia, and it has alternated between the U.S. and various spots on the globe (outside of Europe) ever since. It was in Melbourne that U.S. captain Jack Nicklaus made a pronouncement that astonished Mike Bodney, the Tour's senior vice president of championship management. He and other Tour officials are quick to acknowledge that the Ryder Cup has a 67-year head start on the Presidents Cup. But no less than Nicklaus, who has gone on to captain the American side on four occasions, predicted in 1998, that "The Presidents Cup will be bigger than the Ryder Cup."

Former *Golf Digest* editor-in-chief Nick Seitz, whose magazine often was critical of Beman during his tenure, said he prefers the format and atmosphere of the Presidents Cup. "So

I'm not totally stuck in the past," he said. "I think it's a terrific event."

The Presidents Cup profile continues to rise. In 2000, when NBC snared the broadcast rights to the event from CBS, the PGA's Awtrey expressed his displeasure with this arrangement. "I can't begin to tell you how pissed I am about this," he told NBC Sports president Dick Ebersol. To Awtrey, it was unconscionable for NBC to hype the Presidents Cup with the same fever pitch as the Ryder Cup. "Which are you going to promote the strongest?" Awtrey asked. Ebersol promised he wouldn't do anything to hurt the Ryder Cup. To which Awtrey said, "I know you guys, and you're going to do a great job on the Presidents Cup." And so it is. In even years NBC promotes the Ryder Cup and during odd years the Presidents Cup. Said Awtrey: "So now depending on the year, (The Presidents Cup is portrayed as) the greatest event ever played."

As the final bright idea of Beman's tenure, approved on the day he announced his retirement, it turned into quite a last act.

*   *   *

First, John Morris, the Tour's vice president of communications, approached the microphone inside the media center at the 1994 Doral Ryder Open. He informed the media that Beman asked him to read a letter, a copy of which his staff would distribute to them. "While I'll read," he said, "those of you who can, can read along with me:"

Gentlemen,

Twenty years ago today I was appointed commissioner of the PGA Tour. I accepted the challenge because I thought professional golf should be a more important part of the world of sports. As athletes we were poorly paid as only a handful was making an adequate living from the purses, which totaled $8 million.

Today the PGA Tour and its players are respected all over the world. The Nike Tour and Senior PGA Tour are providing opportunities that were not even in our fondest dreams on

March 1, 1974. This year on all three Tours players will compete for more than $100 million, our sponsors will raise more than $30 million for charity and we will have nearly $50 million in the player retirement fund. The PGA Tour is in excellent financial condition with a strong asset base and virtually no debt. By April or May, all television contracts will be renewed through 1998. The recent recession has had no negative impact on the fortunes of our members.

No other professional athlete demonstrates as much respect for his sport or for his fellow competitors as does a golfer. No sport is more respected for its integrity. We can all be proud of what has been accomplished. It has been a distinct honor and privilege to have been able to serve the game for the past 20 years.

As I indicated to the independent directors early last year, I have decided that I do not wish to have my contract extended, which runs through December 1995. I have a strong desire to return to civilian life, and if the old bones are willing I expect to play some competitive golf. Having been much criticized for the TPCs designed by others over the years, I'm going to design a few courses of my own. Judy and I have many interests that require more time to enjoy. Of course, I will assist in every possible way in making the transition to a new commissioner as smooth as possible.

Sincerely,

Deane R. Beman
Commissioner, PGA Tour

All eyes focused on Beman. But one pair was missing. To her everlasting regret, Judy could not be there. Her mother was dying in Maryland. She couldn't be with her husband to lend support. Beman's face revealed nothing of the import of the words that just had been read. He began, "It was 20 years ago

I assumed the position of commissioner, and frankly, I enjoyed every minute of it."

Beman concluded, "I have no regrets at all. It has been a great run. I am here to continue to serve until a new commissioner is appointed."

The media, sensing one of the stories of the year let alone the day had emerged, bombarded Beman with questions. As Beman offered thoughtful answers, the Tour's board chairman, Dick Ferris, interrupted Beman in mid-sentence, saying, "Deane, I think I should say a few words now."

No one knows for sure what compelled Ferris to cut Beman off, but speculation immediately swirled that he was the front-runner to replace Beman.

"He started acting like Melvin Laird or something, like he was in charge," said *The New York Times* golf writer Larry Dorman, referring to President Richard Nixon's former secretary of defense who eyed the presidency.

Ferris delivered a lengthy tribute lauding Beman's many accomplishments, but it seemed insincere as he hogged the stage. When Ferris finally finished, the awkwardness of the moment was only surpassed by the rarity of a round of applause in the media center for Beman. Staffers were livid at how the hastily arranged press conference was handled. "He was sort of shoved out of the way by Ferris," a longtime Beman aide said. "Deane wasn't given his due. He deserved his moment in the sun."

It didn't go unnoticed by Beman, either. "It confirmed that I was glad I was not going to be there much longer," he recalled.

Yet another awkward moment soon followed. After the press conference, Dorman approached Beman and said he would be remiss if he didn't ask about a rumor circulating that a provision in the previous year's out-of-court settlement with Ping required his resignation, and had hastened his departure. Beman glanced at him, surprised by the question. "Not only is that incorrect," Beman said sniffing with derision, "it was never discussed."

Writer John Feinstein, who was among the cloud of reporters circling around, noted that Beman used a rare profanity in his response to Dorman. The rumors were unfounded but they lingered, in part, because Beman refused to quash them. (Lawyers for both parties and John Solheim all confirm that there was no truth to such hearsay.) Beman addressed his abrupt departure only by noting he was "leaving with no dark clouds hanging over his head." This life-changing decision wasn't one he took lightly.

"We'd climbed this huge mountain," Beman said. "It had taken 20 years. I thought we'd achieved my goals. There was no heavy lifting left, and we were pushing the ball over the top and making sure it didn't crash on the way down. It needed to be in good hands to keep it going."

Afterwards, Beman returned to Ponte Vedra and addressed his full staff. What most of them remember was Beman saying, in perhaps, his most revealing comment: "I'm challenged by building something, not particularly by running something."

Of course, several circumstances factored in Beman's retirement decision. Rest assured, it certainly wasn't comedian Bill Murray, who joked, "I demand the resignation of Deane Beman," earlier in the year at the AT&T Pebble Beach National Pro-Am. In a TV interview he said of Beman, "He's just another screwhead too big for his britches." Beman had Duke Butler, the Tour's executive director of tournament operations, privately warn the comedian that his behavior at the tournament was "detrimental and inappropriate" – and if continued, would result in his immediate removal from the tournament. Murray chose to publicize the reprimand.

But there was an earlier incident that he had never before admitted truly hurt his feelings and made him contemplate retirement for the first time. During the Sept. 1, 1992 board meeting, there was an action item to discuss the commissioner's role in selecting golf course architects and consultants for TPC clubs. According to the meeting minutes, player director Peter Jacobsen indicated that a number of players believed that golf course design shouldn't be a part of the commissioner's job description – and he should be restricted to a hands-off role in the design of TPC courses. Jacobsen insisted a process for selecting golf course architects and player consultants be determined that removed the commissioner's influence. The board disagreed. Ferris indicated the commissioner in his role as CEO of the company had accountability for all Tour business and to exclude him from that role with TPC clubs would not be prudent. Beman had grown accustomed to all sorts of pot-shot from players – "I wouldn't have lasted the first week if I let it bother me," he once said – but still, this player attack deeply wounded Beman. "The board backed me up, but it was a slap in the face," Beman said.

Beman also was troubled by a disturbing trend. As the Tour broke new ground in terms of prize money, players were becoming less appreciative of sponsors. He remembered when players lobbied to play in the Monday pro-am to earn $500. For some it had become an unwanted chore. With Tiger Woods on the horizon, Beman feared it would only get worse. "Everyone knew it was just a matter of time before Tiger turned pro. I knew the money was about to explode," Beman said. "Frankly, I didn't want to expend the patience to deal with an emerging group of unappreciative, rich, know-it-all young pros. Someone else would have to manage the success we had achieved."

"He had the air of a man who was tired, drained, and beaten up emotionally," John Feinstein wrote. His assessment was based on a conversation from the previous fall in which Beman reflected on his tenure and the toll it took on his personal life. "I've wondered if it's all worth it," Beman mused. "I know it hasn't always been easy for my family. I've loved the work, I'm proud of what we've done, but sometimes I wish things had been a little easier on them."

Another factor weighed into Beman's decision: Del de Windt, his board chairman of 11 years, announced his retirement on Aug. 31, 1993, effective at the end of the year. The three independent directors all had stayed on until the groove issue was resolved. The two men forged a wonderful working relationship with de Windt shepherding many of Beman's most controversial ideas.

For all of these reasons, Beman said he reached a conclusion in his mind during the summer of 1993. "I double-checked myself in the fall and it became more and more attractive to me," he later said in a *Golf Magazine* interview.

Ferris, a partner and the chairman of Guest Quarters Hotels at the time, was elected de Windt's successor as the Tour's board chair in December 1993. Arnold Palmer handpicked

Ferris to serve as one of the original members of the Senior PGA Tour division advisory board, (he served two terms, including a stint as chairman), prior to becoming an independent director of the Tour's board in 1992. When Ferris accepted the position he asked Beman one question. "You're not going anywhere, are you?" Ferris inquired. Beman responded, "No." Ferris breathed a sigh of relief.

Beman's recollection differs. He doesn't remember that episode. In any event, over the Christmas holiday, after more internal debate, Beman's verdict was final.

At the 1994 AT&T Pebble Beach National Pro-Am, Beman informed Ferris that he wanted to meet and discuss his future. Two weeks later in Palm Springs during the Bob Hope Chrysler Classic, Beman revealed to Ferris his plan to retire.

For the last two decades, Beman had ably leapt from crisis to crisis, the Tour often a simmering cauldron of unrest. Now he believed everything was in place. Television contracts were negotiated, giving his successor some real breathing room. The Ping lawsuit was settled. There was almost no litigation distracting the Tour (though a Federal Trade Commission inquiry of its business practices remained unresolved).

To Beman's surprise, another crisis emerged. The day after Beman made the retirement announcement, the commissioner was back in his office when his assistant patched through a call from Senior Tour member Bob Murphy. He wasn't ringing his old Walker Cup teammate to congratulate him on 20 years of a job well done.

Beman listened as Murphy told him in confidence that he should know that players on the Senior Tour were engaged in purse-splitting. The prearranged sharing of prize money in competition, known as purse-splitting, occurred regularly on the Tour in the 1950s and early '60s. Before squaring off in an 18-hole playoff to decide the 1962 U.S. Open, Arnold Palmer allegedly asked Jack Nicklaus if he would like to split the first- and second-place prize money. Nicklaus declined, and won the title. After rumors swirled that Palmer, Nicklaus and Player had pooled the purse for the 1962 World Series of Golf and split it regardless of the results of the competition, the PGA banned the practice in 1963, and the policy remained in effect when the

Tour was founded in 1968. "Deane didn't have any idea that this was going on (on the Senior Tour)," Murphy said.

The information struck Beman cold. Appearances of impropriety can prove as damaging as the real thing. How concerned was Beman to avoid any semblance of an association with gambling, for instance? Charles Cobb, the Arvida chief who lost the $100 bet that Beman couldn't get TPC Sawgrass built, offered compelling evidence: "I once asked Deane where's the plaque I gave you (commemorating their wager)? He said, 'It's in my garage. We have a strict policy against gambling and as commissioner I don't want to give the slightest appearance that I approve of it.' "

It didn't take long for Beman to realize he had the makings of a major scandal on his hands. The integrity of the competition was at stake.

Murphy continued. He told Beman of an incident that occurred at the United Van Lines Aces Championship, a closest-to-the-pin competition held Feb. 21-22, 1994, at TPC Sawgrass. In addition to Murphy, the contestants included Larry Ziegler, Gary Cowan, Miller Barber, Doug Dalziel, Fred Ruiz, Bob Reith, Bob Goalby, and Ralph Terry. A player approached Murphy – even now he was too much of a gentleman to finger the individual – and informed him that everyone else had agreed to split the purse. Standard operating procedure at such unofficial exhibitions, Murphy was told. But he refused. Murphy said, "I'm not willing to do that, and quite frankly, I didn't know we did such things."

Such brazen disregard of the rules, especially for a made-for-television special airing later that year, shocked Murphy. "I wasn't popular at all that day," Murphy said, and even less so when he won the $50,000 first prize.

"It was not right that we were accepting a check for one amount as the winner on television and in reality getting a smaller check because we were splitting it," Murphy added.

It galled Beman that this occurred right under his nose near Tour headquarters. To make matters worse, this had not been an isolated incident. Beman thanked Murphy for bringing the unpleasant incident to his attention. Still seething, Beman immediately convened a meeting with Finchem and his legal counsel to draw up an attack plan. "We were in crisis mode," Beman said, "and the crisis wasn't me leaving office as far as I was concerned."

Beman demanded an explanation. He started his internal investigation of the situation by speaking with his staff. He called into his office Brian Henning, the Senior Tour's vice president of competitions, who raised his hand in the air and conceded, "I'm guilty. I knew. I didn't think it was my business."

Henning wasn't the only guilty part. Unbeknownst to him or anyone else from the Tour staff, the players had organized a meeting at the 1991 Merrill Lynch Shootout and agreed to split the purse. During the course of the year, on Tuesdays of tournament week, a 9-hole competition was held among 10 players. After each hole the player with the high score was eliminated. If there was a tie on that hole, those high scorers broke it with either a closest-to-the-hole chipping, putting or bunker-shot contest. The 10 Shootout finalists had earned the most money during the regular season series (which offered a weekly first prize of $4,000). The last survivor of the finals would be awarded $100,000 of a $300,000 purse, or so viewers were led to believe.

Before the event got underway, one of the players sidled up to Henning and disclosed the agreement. The player encouraged Henning to enjoy his usual comedic role as emcee of the event. "I said, 'Fine.' I didn't give a hoot," Henning said. "It had nothing to do with me. We played the final and everybody had a ball. It made for a great TV show."

As emcee for the Merrill Lynch Shootouts, Henning laughed and joked with the players. He initiated a running gag on the first tee where just before a player teed off, he interrupted and asked to inspect the player's golf ball. Henning swooped in, swiped the ball off the tee, examined it like a tomato at a market, and gave it to a young fan in the gallery. To those involved, it made for a good TV show. High-fives and hijinks, such as Raymond Floyd hitting an exploding golf ball off the first tee during the 1992 Shootout finals, were part of the performance. "You're short of the hazard," Henning told Floyd as the gallery roared with laughter.

There were other stunts, too, such as George Archer topping a drive off the first tee that traveled six inches.

"Then we'd give him a mulligan," Henning said. "Does that happen in a tournament? We were doing our damnedest to put out the best show and promote the Senior Tour."

Beman heard enough to know he had a problem on his hands. He knew this had far-reaching implications. Before matters had a chance to escalate, Beman made plans to go to San Antonio, where the Senior Tour's Vantage Dominion was being held that weekend.

"I didn't let any staff people handle it," Beman said. "I didn't let Finchem become involved because I didn't want anybody who might be considered the new commissioner to be tainted by this. It was going to be the most unpopular thing that ever happened out there. It was something nobody wanted. I just sucked it up and did it myself."

Beman assembled a list of every player that participated in unofficial events of this nature during the past five years. He interviewed as many players as he could. Every player confessed to his involvement. Like a private investigator, Beman searched for any clues that might reveal this to be a broader concern. He fretted whether players may have struck similar agreements during official senior tournaments or if the practice had spread to regular Tour events, too. It also meant questioning some of his longtime friends and biggest advocates over the years. He sat down with Colbert, who described how Bruce Crampton approached him during his rookie year in 1991 and explained how the purse was split. "Boy, that really went against my grain," Colbert said.

He rationalized his participation "as not wanting to rock the boat as the new guy." Colbert confessed: "I really shouldn't have done that."

The next year Colbert won. Instead of winning $70,000, he collected his $25,000 share of the $250,000 purse. That year Floyd was a rookie. He objected to splitting the purse. He also bowed out early and didn't make a stink. Murphy's 1993 call to the commissioner's office halted purse-splitting for good. "To his credit Murphy turned everybody in," Colbert said. "It was wrong. It was a TV show, and people thought we were playing for real."

Some felt their character was under siege. Archer, for one, shed tears. He cried, "I never cheated in my life."

The following week Beman went to Orlando for the Tour's Nestle Invitational and met with a host of golf writers to address the issue head-on before rumors surfaced in the press. He also wanted to size up their response. "I didn't know if it was going to be possible to get through this," Beman said.

He briefly considered the worst-case scenario: A scandal might destroy the Senior Tour overnight. If he had to suspend a large number of players, one of the alternatives that he considered was lowering the eligibility age of the Senior Tour to 45 – a move that would instantly replenish the field. He also pondered postponing his retirement, or staying on as commissioner indefinitely. In a voice both calm and firm, Beman was frank with the media. "We have a problem, no question," Beman said. "There's a strong indication that errors in judgment were made."

To some, the Shootouts simply were a Tuesday exhibition that needed to be dealt with, but it wasn't impugning the integrity of the sport. "That was a great example of Deane standing on principle, perhaps to his detriment," *Golf Digest's* Jaime Diaz said. "In his defense, he knew that was a very slippery slope, and he erred on the side of being really strict. He knew if he got on the wrong side of that it could snowball."

On March 16, Beman appointed a special outside counsel – hiring the firm of a former attorney general under President Carter – to address the purse-splitting allegations. The investigation confirmed that official Senior Tour events weren't involved, nor was there any evidence that PGA Tour players had engaged in such activities.

"I think Deane is doing the right thing, getting it out in the open," Jack Nicklaus told *Golfweek* at the time. "If that is going on now, it's wrong."

"I take this very seriously," Beman said. "Others might not think so, but I do. There is nothing more important than the integrity of our competitions."

Beman determined that he didn't need to suspend anyone (players were slapped with lifetime probation). The four-week probe into purse-splitting at unofficial events resulted in the greatest mass-disciplinary action in Tour history. Beman levied fines totaling more than $100,000 against 51 players for violations that occurred at the last two Merrill Lynch Shootout

Championships, as well as at the 16 shootouts sponsored by the company and at the United Van Lines Aces Championship. In keeping with his practice, he didn't name anyone individually. He also issued a "hefty fine" against Henning and other staff members who knowingly allowed the purse-splitting to occur.

"The previously announced inquiry into purse-splitting has been concluded to my satisfaction. I have taken appropriate disciplinary action with those players involved," Beman said in a prepared statement prior to the start of the Senior PGA Championship in Palm Beach Gardens, Fla. Several players confessed when confronted by reporters. "I'm as guilty as the next," said Bob Charles.

"You can't argue with City Hall," added Jim Dent.

Privately, many of the players involved thought Beman overreacted.

"I thought he was wrong," Dave Stockton said in 2010. "This wasn't a scandal. We were just putting on a show. Members of the Tour staff knew about it and condoned it. We wanted to have a good time."

Stockton noted the competitive nature of players and compared the purse-splitting to when the low-pro individual prize money was eliminated from pro-am day. "It got to the point that some guys who were going to be playing for a $1 million that week were busting their tail and ignoring their amateur partners to make $500," Stockton said. "In this case, we're playing a made-for-TV event that didn't affect the money list. We could have fun and kid each other."

But Beman recognized the potential danger purse-splitting posed to the Senior Tour. The Tour's outside counsel warned him that in some jurisdictions the players could be charged with a felony. "Some enterprising local attorney general might've loved to parade the players into the court room and asked them if they did this. It could've been devastating to the Senior Tour," Beman said. "I never breathed that word – felony – until the statute of limitations was over, I can promise you that. It was handled in such a way that I didn't forgive anybody, but it didn't become a scandal."

To this day, he says, "You'll never convince me that what I did wasn't the right thing to do."

* * *

When word of Beman's retirement decision spread to the players, reporters beckoned them to compress his 20 years of labor into 20-second sound bytes for the evening news. Glowing reviews of his tenure were recorded in the morning papers. Johnny Miller may have summed it up best: "We took little pot shots at him from time to time, but deep down we didn't want him to leave the job."

Even Beman's detractors conceded he did a remarkable job as commissioner. Doug Tewell, a Ping proponent, echoed Miller's assessment in the *San Francisco Chronicle*: "My greatest surprise is in my own reaction. It is one of remorse and regret that he is leaving."

Said Mac O'Grady: "Do I hate Deane Beman? Of course not. Do I respect his contributions to the game of golf? Yes, I do. Will I always love him for his contributions? Yes sir." For good measure, O'Grady added, "Do I disagree with the way he has violated his fiduciary duties? Yes sir."

Beman never was the sentimental type. One day he indicated to Finchem his intention to step down. Finchem said he was saddened, but remembered Beman quickly shifted the conversation to a bigger-picture discussion of what it meant for the Tour and how best to handle his departure. To this day, Finchem maintains he was disappointed when Beman left. "It really hit me when he told the staff," Finchem said. "I would've much preferred if he stayed for another 10 years. I wasn't lusting for the job. I wanted to run a company someday, but in those days I thought I'd be leaving to run a company somewhere else."

The Tour formed a search committee consisting of Ferris, its board chair, Hugh Culverhouse, a board member and owner of the Tampa Bay Buccaneers, and player directors Fehr and Haas. An advisory panel included Charles Hugel, chairman of the Senior PGA Tour board; Terry Dill, a player director on the Senior Tour; and Schaal, president of the PGA and a member of the Tour policy board.

Among the players, the hot topic of conversation became "Who do you think will replace Beman?" Just as quickly a litany of names surfaced, ranging from former baseball commissioner

Peter Ueberroth to former vice president Dan Quayle, to ex-U.S. Amateur champ Vinnie Giles of Pros Inc., a sports management group, and players such as Hale Irwin, Ed Sneed, and Jacobsen. Neither Palmer nor Nicklaus expressed interest in the job. "One thing is certain," wrote Robert Lohrer in *Golfweek*, "Deane Beman's successor will need the negotiating savvy of a diplomat, the financial acumen of a banker, and the schmoozing skills of a Hollywood agent."

One by one the leading candidates responded with their regrets. "Although flattered I am not a candidate," Ueberroth said. "It is my view that the next commissioner should be an internal choice, as (professional) basketball and football have successfully done with the selection of David Stern (NBA) and Paul Tagliabue (NFL), both of whom took over in a seamless effort to the betterment of their respective sports."

Realizing that golf had grown dramatically from when Beman took charge and that a player may no longer be qualified to oversee the increasingly complex business operations of the Tour, virtually every player under consideration dropped out of the hunt. Irwin told *USA Today*, "It's too big a job now for someone without corporate business experience. I'm certainly not considering it at this time."

Speaking at a March 9 meeting of Senior Tour players, Ferris stated he was not a candidate for the job, either. It wasn't until March 22, that Finchem formally threw his name in the ring for commissioner.

"I'm not lobbying," he told members of the media after a players' meeting prior to the 1994 Players Championship. "I'm going to talk to some more players, and if I get reasonable support, I'll apply."

Finchem was a deputy adviser for economic affairs under President Carter in 1978-79. The Tour had become the second-largest client of the Washington, D.C.-based consulting firm National Strategies and Marketing Group, which he co-founded. He joined the Tour in 1987 as vice president of business affairs. Beman considered Finchem to be smart, of good judgment, and a strategic thinker. Ultimately, he moved him into the position of deputy commissioner where he held responsibility for most day-to-day operations. "We didn't have clear delineated lines, but I traveled an awful lot and somebody had to be there to make day-to-day decisions," Beman said. "He was somebody I relied on and I had confidence in."

In recent years, Finchem had shouldered more and more of the workload. His office light burned deep into the night. Finchem coordinated Monday and Friday "Catch Up" meetings held inside the Tour's main conference room, during which the staff reported on recent developments. Ed Moorhouse, the Tour's general counsel, usually sitting to Finchem's left, lead off and everyone took turns moving clockwise around the table.

Beginning in May 1989, Finchem carried the dual title of deputy commissioner and chief operating officer. Beman long believed in the words of *The New York Times* columnist Walter Lippmann, who once wrote, "The final test of a leader is that he leaves behind him in other men the conviction and the will to carry on." Recognizing his own mortality, Beman had managed the Tour in his final decade with someone by his side that could take the reins. First it was Tim Smith. When he departed to pursue another opportunity, Finchem became his choice.

"I made sure he understood all the facets of the job so the Tour could go on without skipping much of a beat," Beman said in a Q&A with *Golfweek* in June 2006. "As commissioner, it's your responsibility. There are too many entities depending on you."

Beman kept to coy comments in dodging the question of who should replace him. He did offer this advice on what qualities the Tour should be seeking in a successor. "A caring and a love for the game, qualities and leadership for difficult decisions, and good humor to handle criticism because it's going to come," he said.

Even behind the scenes, Beman avoided campaigning for his No. 2 to be promoted, and didn't influence the Tour's selection. "Tim understood that if I stepped out and was a strong, overt advocate it might've hurt his chances because I wasn't the most beloved guy," Beman said. "I put him in that position of responsibility, and it was a clear signal that I thought he was the most qualified person to operate the Tour."

Finchem's ascent to commissioner was not a fait accompli. The search committee looked both inside and outside the organization for the right replacement. Fehr told *Golfweek* that more than 40 applications were submitted for the position, among them a half dozen players and one sportswriter. He said "a small number" were interviewed, including Jack Frazee, a former president of Sprint and CEO of Centel Corp, who emerged as Finchem's main rival.

What stuck with Haas is the memory of the independent directors saying most great corporations hire from within. Among the Tour's staff, Finchem commanded great respect. But speaking for many of the players, Haas noted that Finchem's reputation among the players was limited to serving as a point man and trouble-shooter for Beman. "He was usually the bearer of bad news," Haas said.

The list of candidates was trimmed to Finchem and Frazee. According to Fehr, Frazee proposed wholesale changes. "The Tour didn't need that," Fehr said.

Finchem's unanimous election as the third commissioner in the Tour's 25-year history was a vote for continuity over change. The tournament policy board made it official during a meeting held late in the afternoon May 9 at the Four Seasons Dallas at Las Colinas in Irving, Texas – just 10 weeks after Beman revealed his decision not to seek another contract extension: "Tim has been involved in every aspect of Tour operations and his expertise will ensure a smooth transition and a continuation of the success we have enjoyed under Deane," Ferris said in making the announcement.

Amid the crush of reporters, Finchem declared, "Deane has been a great teacher and mentor to me. My challenge is to marginally improve over what he's done. And that really is a challenge."

Back in Ponte Vedra one day later, Beman, dressed in a golf shirt and still wearing his spikes after a practice session, offered this benediction of his successor to the staff: "As a member of the PGA Tour I would like to introduce commissioner Tim Finchem."

Then the new commissioner, addressing his troops for the first time, thanked them for their support. "*The New York Times* wrote that they came down on the side of continuity versus change," Finchem said. "They would not have come down on the side of continuity unless all of you folks had done the jobs you have done...As a consequence their decision was much less me than it was the direction of the staff and the way we operate and the way we produce. I was just representative of that in a sense."

Finchem succeeded Beman on June 1, 1994. It has been a textbook transition. Jacobsen summed it up best when he told *Sports Illustrated* in 1997: "Tim Finchem's doing a great job, but it's like Deane left him a Mercedes with the tank a quarter full, and all Tim has to do is keep putting gas in it."

Finchem preserved and protected the Beman legacy with fundamentalist zeal, adhering to the principles that produced success in the first place. Finchem has played midwife to several of Beman's unfinished ideas, including the World Golf Village and The Presidents Cup.

In the years that followed, Finchem often stole a moment to glance at a framed picture, immortalizing the groundbreaking of the World Golf Village, which hung on the wall of his office. Unfolding inside the cream-colored matte is a scene of Beman standing with Finchem under a temporary tent, dressed in their blazers and ties. Beman is leaning over Finchem's left shoulder and squeezing his arms. The lighthearted words Beman has just delivered have been lost to time, but the snapshot evokes the spirit of camaraderie that long existed between the two men. Laughter fills Finchem's face.

With a touch of gallows humor, Beman inscribed the picture on a beige-colored rectangle the size of a business card with the following message: "To Tim, it's not always going to be this much fun." And as only a man speaking from experience could do, Beman underlined the last word for emphasis.

AFTERWORD

On his first day of retirement, former Tour commissioner Deane Beman spent the morning doing the type of personal chores that he never had time to handle during his work week. Then he conducted a three-hour workout at the TPC Sawgrass driving range. When Chris Smith of *The Florida Times-Union* called to ask how retirement was treating him, Beman said, "I'm laying out slumped in a chair. I'm in no shape for this type of practice session."

When Beman announced his retirement, he said he still felt the tug of competitive golf and looked forward to playing on the Senior Tour. By virtue of his four Tour victories he was exempt into the final stage of the qualifying tournament. He also could receive unlimited sponsor exemptions. The 1994 Bank One Classic in Lexington, Ky., granted Beman his first. On the eve of his Senior Tour debut, he told the media, "I'm ready for another challenge and this is it. I think I've got some more productive time to spend playing competitive golf."

Just over two decades earlier he forfeited his two-year Tour exemption to make a bigger contribution in the board room. A part of him always wanted to be between the ropes again. Now Beman was 56 and past his prime by even Senior Tour standards. Still, he had vowed to play "if the old bones were willing." Turned out they weren't. After shooting 73 in the pro-am, Beman awoke the next day with a pulled rib-cage muscle and withdrew from the tournament on Sept. 15, 1994. "I don't think it's fair to take a spot that one of the alternates could have," he said. He also suffered from a bum left shoulder that eventually required surgery. But first he played four events in late 1994.

The reaction from the players when he joined the Senior Tour was hard to qualify but easy to feel. Golf course architect Pete Dye described the situation the best he could: "He had been their policeman telling them what to do for 20 years. Once a cop, always a cop."

It was a chilly reception, made all the worse by Beman's reliance on sponsor exemptions. Some players resented him taking a spot away from "a more deserving player." Plus, hard feelings still lingered from what many players considered the commissioner's excessive punishment for their involvement in purse splitting. "I was treated with open hostility," he said.

After Beman retired, commissioner Tim Finchem called a meeting for those guilty of purse splitting and revoked the lifetime probation. Behind the scenes Jim Colbert, a fixture on the Senior Tour board, campaigned to create a special exemption that would give a former commissioner of a certain age a two-year pass to play the Senior Tour he helped spawn. But after the purse-splitting incident, the idea was quickly dropped. "I don't think he ever knew about it," Colbert said. Not one player had the courage to fight for Beman who had fought for all of them for 20 years.

But not everyone was so vengeful. Some agreed he deserved as many exemptions as he wanted, considering all he had done for the Tour. "I think it's wonderful Deane is here," Lee Trevino said. "Because of what he did for the Tour, he can come out here and walk tall and stand proud."

Beman played a total of 69 events, earning $266,480 – his best result a fifth-place finish. He said he underestimated the necessity to be in better physical shape. Beman played his last tournament in 2005 at the Constellation Energy Classic, fittingly in his native Maryland. "You know a bad day on the golf course beats a good day most other places," he said of his struggles on the Senior Tour.

"I felt sad for him because I could tell the thing he loved most was to compete," said *Golf Digest's* Jaime Diaz. "He had given so many good years to be the commissioner and now his body betrayed him and it was too late. His window had passed."

*   *   *

The gala dinner the Tour threw to commemorate Beman's tenure will long be remembered. Held at the Jacksonville Convention Center on March 21, 1995, the celebration of 1,500 of Beman's friends – including colleagues, Tour pros and industry leaders – feasted on a $500-a-plate dinner to support two of his favorite charities.

"There's a lot of irony in golf," wrote *The Atlanta Journal-Constitution* columnist Furman Bisher, "but none more than Arnold Palmer and Jack Nicklaus headlining a testimonial to Beman, disguised as his farewell…They neither soft-soaped the honored one, nor did they make him their pigeon."

Amy Grant, the "Queen of Christian rock," performed at what Tour board member Jay Haas called the largest gala he had ever attended. "It looked like you could've played the Super Bowl there," he said. Representing the players, Haas read remarks from a teleprompter, and gave Beman a 1947 Indian Chief motorcycle as a token of appreciation. "You talk about vision," Beman said of the vintage chopper. "That's my vision right there."

In his final Tour annual report to the membership in 1994, Beman wrote: "There is a temptation to reflect on how far we've come in the past two decades. But the challenge for me and the Tour is to leave the past behind and focus on the opportunities that lie ahead. The Tour has never been in better shape financially or competitively, but this is no time to rest on our laurels. The Tour must keep moving forward while maintaining its rich traditions."

When he spoke to the dinner attendees, Beman took a rare moment of reflection: "Joe Dey was the right person at the right time in 1969," Beman said. "I think I was the right person for my time." Beman had to wait for the applause to die down before adding, "I know that commissioner Tim Finchem is the right man for today.

"For all of you who love the game, I will see you on the fairways," Beman concluded. He kissed his wife, and they walked away from the podium hand-in-hand. Everyone in the room stood and applauded for a very long time.

Indeed, after retirement, Beman never ventured far from the game he loved. He followed through on his "threat" to build a course, co-designing Cannon Ridge Golf Club with architect Bobby Weed. Spread over 200 acres in Fredericksburg, Va., the course opened in 2003.

That same year, Beman developed a program for introducing and retaining prospective golfers with the stated objective of having beginners score in the 90s in 6 months. He named the program "the Deane Beman 6/90 Teaching System," and introduced the game to 400 prospects, many of them at Cannon Ridge. At the end of one year, more than 90 percent of the beginners who went through the program were playing golf. In 2005, two independent instructors reported results that surpassed those of the instructors who helped develop and refine the program. Despite the success, Beman's teaching approach met significant resistance from existing instructors. He asked more than 75 LPGA and PGA professionals to experiment with 6/90 at their own facilities. Only two facilities agreed to implement the experiment.

He also is attempting to help golfers of all ability putt better. In 2011, he introduced "Deane Beman's Aim-Check," a training aid designed to correct what he believes is the most common reason for missed putts: putter alignment. Beman continued to make Ponte Vedra his home – with summers spent in Maine – practicing and playing regularly at TPC Sawgrass. His former deputy commissioner Tim Smith likened it to having one of the founding fathers roaming the halls of the White House. "He's like George Washington walking around there," Smith said.

On Nov. 20, 2000, Beman became a permanent resident at the shrine he built to golf. He was selected for membership into the World Golf Hall of Fame via the lifetime achievement category. Beman shared the stage that night with Jackie Burke Jr., the pro who befriended him all those years ago at the 1955 U.S. Open when Beman was the youngest in the field. Four of Beman's five children sat in the front row, along with his 10 grandchildren, Bert, his 86-year-old mother, Aunt Lucy, and of course, his wife, Judy.

First as a top-flight amateur and then a touring professional, Beman developed a reputation as one of the toughest competitors in golf. He brought the same flinty, hard-charging persona to the job of commissioner. It's the third phase of his golf life that elevated him to one of golf's icons, a man who has enriched the game. Beman clutched the original black book in which he drafted his view of the position of commissioner and his vision for the Tour. He had presented it to the Tour's board in December 1973 when he applied for the job. Now he flipped through its contents and transported the audience back in time. "The game has been good to me," he read from its yellowed pages. "Serving as commissioner will provide for me the rare opportunity to put back into the game in some measure what I have gotten out of it these many years. I believe I can make a greater contribution as commissioner than as a competitor."

Beman was 35 when he wrote that. He still is the youngest man to become commissioner of a major professional sports league. Beman was the most influential golf executive of his generation, a man who by the power of his position and the sheer force of his ingenuity transformed a conservative sport into a dynamic and diverse global enterprise.

"If you stand still today, you're going backwards," Beman said. "Golf is a game shackled by tradition, both good and bad. Trying to break out of those traditions without upsetting people is a challenge."

Beman's early critics acquired a grudging respect for his cool strategic sense and tactical agility. They grew to understand that Beman changed the Tour's trajectory in a way no one ever has. "I don't think you can underestimate Deane's influence on the modern tour," said Nick Seitz, former editor-in-chief of *Golf Digest*. "He was the modern tour."

A pragmatic leader, Beman fixed his thoughts on finding the future well before others were prepared to face it. Problems were opportunities. Obstacles were challenges. Instead of worrying about hurdles, he plotted leaping over them. He treated setbacks as a test of his will and resolve to reach a goal. For 20 years, his every decision was scrutinized. Every misstep amplified. The pressure was intense. It took courage, confidence and conviction in his beliefs. Sometimes that meant accepting that his plan might not be right. Former Tour pro-turned-staff member Bob Dickson never forgot the time he and Beman were riding around Jacksonville looking for land to build the home of The Players Championship and Beman said, "Bob, I'm not a caretaker-type administrator. I'm a risk taker." Beman gambled on the notion that he could change the way people think – to make them abandon what is for what could be.

"It's really hard to do," Beman said. "You've got to believe in what you do. You've got to think longterm first and then analyze how to make the short term workable until you get to the longterm. Two things guided me: I knew how to work hard, and I knew how to think big."

In introducing Beman once at an awards ceremony, Finchem resorted to paraphrasing George Bernard Shaw, who famously said, "Some men see things as they are and ask why. Others dream things that never were and ask why not."

Ask anyone who worked with Beman to describe him and a common refrain is repeated: He was a visionary. It was that sharpened focus that allowed him to find the future for the Tour, a duty that Beman considered the highest calling of any leader of an organization. Wrote Charley Stine in a 1994 *Golfweek* commentary: "A visionary is just a dreamer unless he gets things accomplished. It takes hard work to carry an idea to fruition. It takes courage to present the new idea to people who can't see it. And it takes courage and a little bit of stubbornness to stick with it until others are convinced."

From the beginning, Beman had a clear vision of what he wanted the Tour to be. "But I never articulated the means and methods of getting there because I really didn't know at first," he confessed. "You can only formulate a truly successful plan by working in the trenches."

What he envisioned was such a radical departure from what the Tour had been as an entity. Most players saluted him for record prosperity. They pointed to more than 500 hours of scheduled television coverage of 1994 tournaments and nearly $30 million contributed to charity during his final year as commissioner as strong indicators of the game's economic strength. During his tenure he created the Senior Tour and Ben Hogan Tour adding to his dizzying number of responsibilities.

"What Deane did for the Tour is unbelievable," Colbert said. "If the Tour had been a publicly-traded company, it would have been IBM or Microsoft."

Others felt he was too powerful for the good of the game. In a business with so many moving parts, he answered to approximately 600 players, managed more than 2,000 employees, serviced more than 100 corporate sponsors, dealt with a like number of host venues, and partnered with multiple television networks and media outlets. The quality of play on the Tour improved as a result of the All-Exempt Tour (initiated in 1983) and more players were given the opportunity to prove themselves through the developmental circuit than ever before. Collectively, these achievements fueled the growth of professional golf.

"As an empire builder who was obsessed with making the U.S. men's Tour the center of the sport worldwide, he won more often than he lost and, inevitably, made enemies," wrote Jaime Diaz in *Sports Illustrated*. "But his visionary thinking and aggressive style brought title sponsorship, stadium golf and fail-safe television contracts to the Tour, constructing a foundation that is the envy of every other pro sport."

There's no denying the remarkable growth. From $400,000 in assets in 1974, when Beman succeeded Joe Dey, the Tour reported $260 million in assets in 1994 when Beman resigned. In 1986, when that figure was merely $50 million, the *Houston Post's* Mickey Herskowitz said, "This is more than growth. It's an explosion." Even Nicklaus noted in the same article: "I'm not sure he has got enough credit for that."

In the Mount Rushmore of sport's most influential executives, Beman's mug should be chiseled alongside the likes of baseball's Judge Kennesaw Mountain Landis, football's Pete Rozelle and sports broadcasting's Roone Arledge.

"So much of professional golf as it is known today...came to fruition while Beman headed the Tour that the accomplishments tend to blur like the individual successes of a straight-A student," wrote Bill Fields in *Golf World*.

Indeed, for all his accomplishments, Beman still doesn't receive his due. "I think the only time he will be appreciated is when he is planted in the ground," former PGA president Pat Reilly said. The delay is linked, fairly or not, to Beman's persona, Reilly added. "He's got those beady eyes," Reilly said.

"Don't ask a question unless you want an answer. He's not going to flower the manure. Sometimes manure doesn't taste good. But that's what it is."

Beman was accused of being cold, impersonal and utterly humorless. He could never shake the reputation of being guarded and at times unapproachable. "He was the same in bridge as he was in golf or the boardroom," Colbert said. "Hard guy to read, good at numbers and he always knew what cards were out."

His public persona disguised how he often doted on the people who helped him achieve his goals. Beman invited the entire staff to his house for a pancake breakfast on Thanksgiving morning. In what became an annual holiday tradition until the size of the staff outgrew his home, Beman flipped the pancakes himself. Nor was it disclosed that he advanced the Senior Tour's Brian Henning his salary so he could buy a home for his family, and that Beman hosted a housewarming party in which the TPC superintendent and his staff planted trees in the front yard. Nor did anyone know that he ordered Patty Cianfrocca to return the Buick she bought because Beman would personally make sure she scored a better deal.

Gary Becka, Beman's assistant, learned everything he needed to know about his boss the night his wife's water broke 10 weeks early. Beman was hosting the tournament sponsors' at his home the weekend before the 1991 Players Championship. Without a second thought, he and his wife abandoned their own party and raced to the hospital to sit with Becka until his son was born at 2:30 a.m. In those early years in Ponte Vedra, "We were like our own little colony, an outpost from the days of the English empire," the Tour's Chip Campbell said. "That's what it felt like."

To those who worked closest with him, the "Czar of golf" image was more caricature than a fair depiction of a man who epitomized integrity. "Deane was a man to me who never once told me anything that wasn't the truth," former PGA executive director Lou King said. "He never backed down on any commitment he made to me."

Former Beman staffers say he should be remembered for assembling the building blocks that are the foundation of the modern Tour. "There was a lot of heat and sparks getting it done," said Dale Antram, who after being wooed to the Tour in 1979 served stints as director of public relations, assistant to the commissioner and director of Senior Tour administration.

Dickson often recounts the time he arranged a foursome that included Beman and Jeff Sanders, who has managed Boise's Nationwide Tour event since the circuit's inception in 1990. Waiting for Beman to arrive, Sanders commented, "I don't know Deane, but I sure like his scorecard." To Dickson, that summed it up neatly. "For 20 years, Deane had a fabulous scorecard," he said. "He didn't birdie every hole, but he birdied a lot."

Beman's worldview of the job was shaped between the ropes. Improving the overall economic well-being of a tournament golfer was Job One. The Tour's Mike Bodney recalled his job interview when Beman laid out this mission to him. "He said, 'Mike, it's my job to make as many millionaires as we can out here. That's what we do here. We work for the players,'" Bodney said. "That's something that's always stuck with me. That was his whole motivation. He cared enough about the professional game to make sure it all happened."

In recognition for his 20 years of service, he received the Tour's Lifetime Achievement Award in May 2007 during The Players Championship. Just as when TPC Sawgrass opened in 1980 under a brooding sky, inclement weather forced the ceremony indoors. When he addressed the gathering, Beman celebrated the people who allowed him to transform a colony into an empire of its own. He started with his wife.

"She is the glue that has knitted together the fabric of my life for the last 20 years," Beman said at the ceremony. "She taught me to balance business, family and friends, something I never had learned before meeting her. Judy, you make every day a joy."

Beman went silent, his eyes reddening. Never before had he revealed such emotion in public. He paid tribute to former employees B.J. Tyner, Jack Tuthill and Joe Schwindemann. "They were the pioneers," he said, his voice wavering. He singled out the contributions of two of his most devoted lieutenants, Tim Smith and Vernon Kelly. He credited "The Red Coats," the name for the past chairmen of The Players Championship, for their belief in his vision. There was much to be proud of. He made his wildest dreams – for a course, for a Tour, for golf itself – come true. And he relished the fact that in the years since turning to yet another homegrown leader, the Tour had experienced even more growth under Finchem.

"The Tour's in good hands," Beman said. "I feel good about it. That's why I can play golf everyday."

ACKNOWLEDGEMENTS

This book arose from researching a profile of Deane Beman for his induction into the World Golf Hall of Fame in 2000. As a Hall of Fame staffer at the time, I was dumbfounded when I discovered a book on his tenure did not already exist. Here was a story that deserved the permanence of being told between two covers.

Five years later, after I finished earning a Master's degree in journalism, I mustered up enough courage to pitch him on this book. He turned me down. The idea never strayed far from my mind. It freshened each time he gave me the most thoughtful and insightful answers whenever I interviewed him for a magazine story. Occasionally, I'd ask if he'd changed his mind about cooperating for a book. I thought his cooperation was vital to tell the story. Still no. Then one day in 2009, an email arrived in my inbox from Deane that said simply, "I'm ready now. Do you still want to write that book?"

I gassed up my car and paid him the first of many visits that weekend. From the beginning, I made it clear that I required editorial control. All he asked for in return was the right to dedicate the book to the volunteers.

Deane devoted untold hours to answering my every question and entrusted me with the supporting documents to add depth to my reporting. He expanded my thinking every day. Many of our conversations were held Tuesdays at 8 a.m. – a convenient time for me and the same time as his old "Catch up" meetings at headquarters. My family began referring to them as "Tuesdays with Deane." Scheduled to be on the West Coast one

Tuesday and not wishing to wake at 5 a.m. after a long flight, I begged for a reprieve. Beman answered, "You know, I did that for 14 years when I started the year on the West Coast as commissioner. And you can't do it for one day." He chuckled. He gave me to 6 a.m.

My passion for writing dates to making my mother, Dianne, smile and sometimes cry when reading the birthday and Mother's Day cards I wrote her. That's how I realized the power of the written word. Buoyed by her confidence that I'd reach the finish line on this book, I made it. So did the daily concern of my grandmother, Elaine Goldin, – "Are you done yet?" – who encouraged me to finish while she was still alive.

My father, Les, who introduced me to golf at a young age, offered many wise suggestions. He read draft after draft, and only complained a little. All that education he's paid for and yet he's still circling grammatical errors as if I were a third-grader. We'll get there yet. In the meantime, he deserves a nod in the non-fiction sports-book category for best supporting actor.

Gene Yasuda, my former editor at *Golfweek*, devoted considerable energy to unlocking so many doors in telling this story. My work, as usual, is better thanks to his judgment and feel. His keen-eye and "surgical strikes" smoothed my prose. Most of all, I'd like to thank him for his friendship through it all.

I am indebted to my friends at PGA Tour Productions, where I started my career in golf (not counting the caddieshack). Charlene Landen made sure I had all-access. Mike Veneto, Tom Spence, and Rick Persons, forgoing our college hockey rivalry, gave of their time to help research a lot of the material that allowed me to describe events that I was unable to attend in vivid detail. Caryn Levy and Deb Carrillo at PGA Tour Photographic Services aided in the selection and procurement of most of the photos used in the book. Marilyn Antram used Chris Condon's beauty shot to design the book cover. Special thanks to IMG's Mark Steinberg and Tiger Woods for granting use of the image of his unforgettable birdie putt at No. 17 at TPC Sawgrass on the cover. Speaking of photos, Tracy Wilcox managed to snap a mug of me I happened to like. And a tip of the cap to Amy Ray for both her design sense and her eye for detail.

Tour players Jim Colbert, Gary McCord, Jerry Pate and

Peter Jacobsen aided me immeasurably. I reached Bob Goalby on the west coast a little too early in the morning and Charles Coody in Alaska on a cruise with his wife. Ah, the wonders of cell phones, yet they both made time to talk to me. Thirty minutes into my conversation with Coody, I asked if he needed to go yet and he answered, "Well, my wife doesn't have her bag on her shoulder yet so let's keep talking." And so it went. Everyone treated me to the boundless number of stories they could tell.

I would be remiss if I didn't mention the employees of the PGA Tour, who worked for Beman. As he said many times, he never could've accomplished what he did unless his staff performed their duties with zeal. Their stories shined a different light on an individual many of them felt was misunderstood. In particular, I owe a great debt of gratitude to Tim Smith, Vernon Kelly, Bob Dickson, and Duke Butler. Their recall of events long ago and story-telling ability furnished me with the details that gave this story color and depth. By no means were they alone; they just continued to take my calls and reply to my emails long after they surely regretted ever giving me their contact info. Commissioner Tim Finchem also took time out of his hectic schedule on multiple occasions to speak with affection of his former boss.

This project could not have been completed without the help of many people. I am grateful to the PGA Tour for arranging the occasional interview and for their help in fact-checking, particularly, media officials Doug Milne, Dave Senko, Phil Stambaugh, former director of communications of the Champions Tour, Michael McPhillips, Adam Wallace, and the "Answer Man" Dave Lancer. Steve Ethun at Augusta National provided some valuable information. Bob Denney and Una Jones confirmed details pertaining to the PGA of America. Also Robin Brendle of CBS Sports and Pete Samuels of Karsten Manufacturing Co., assisted in arranging interviews and checking details. My sincerest appreciation is extended to Cori Britt and Doc Giffin at Arnold Palmer Enterprises, Kelly Fray at Assured Management Co., Guy DeSilva at Gary Player Group, who all helped with arranging interviews with their always accessible leading men, and Scott Tolley at Jack Nicklaus Companies, for his efforts. Rand Jerris and his team at the United States Golf Association were indispensable. I would be remiss if I did not single out the efforts of Nancy Stulack, the USGA librarian, who was patient and persistent in recovering materials. She was my MVP of research. IMG's Alastair Johnston may have kept the best records this side of Beman. His diligence in checking details should not go unnoticed. Field trips to the Jacksonville public library yielded a treasure trove of historical data from *The Florida Times-Union*.

Special thanks to Eleanor and Mike Lanza, Steve and Cindy Sesnick, Craig Bowen, and Karen Smith, who hosted me during my many overnight visits to Ponte Vedra Beach, and Damian Shammas and my grandmother for keeping the light on during research trips to Far Hills, N.J., and New York City respectively.

My journalism classmate Aziza Jamgerchinova tracked down hard to find articles for me and offered a non-golfer's perspective. She and friend Angelika Huguley provided much-needed moral support, too. Scott Waxenberg was my fearless reader and offered a wealth of positive feedback. Paul Spillane is always in my corner, with the gift of lifting my spirits in one breath and keeping me humble in the next. Two people who helped me in my pursuits as a golfer and a journalist died during the writing of this book. My golf pro Gene Borek and the man who gave me my start in sports journalism, Joel Blumberg.

Nobody championed the concept of this book more than my former boss and friend, Ruffin Beckwith. He said to me this is a book that ought to be told and encouraged me to tell it.

Many other friends offered guidance along the way, none more so than my Colgate University classmates-turned-lawyers Scott Bleier and Damian, who listened to me talk of little else other than a book status update for way too long, and helped me translate the grooves legal jargon into something more digestible. The astute observations of my high school classmate, Evan Malter, surely made this a more enjoyable experience for you, the reader. And lastly to Sarah Hardimon, who endured my long days of writing and absences, and never registered a complaint.

To everyone else who deserves recognition, thanks for your unwavering support.